POLITICAL THEORY

Also by Andrew Heywood

POLITICAL IDEOLOGIES
POLITICS

Political Theory

An Introduction

Second edition

Andrew Heywood

First edition published 1994 under the title
Political Ideas and Concepts: An Introduction
Reprinted five times

Second edition 1999 published by
MACMILLAN PRESS LTD
Houndmills, Basingstoke, Hampshire RG21 2XS
and London
Companies and representatives
throughout the world

ISBN 0–333–76090–5 hardcover
ISBN 0–333–76091–3 paperback

A catalogue record for this book is available from the British Library.

Copy-edited and typeset by Povey–Edmondson
Tavistock and Rochdale, England

10   9   8   7   6   5   4   3   2
09   08   07   06   05   04   03   02   01   00

Printed and bound in Great Britain by
Creative Print & Design (Wales) Ebbw Vale

Published in the United States of America 1999 by
ST. MARTIN'S PRESS, INC.,
Scholarly and Reference Division,
175 Fifth Avenue, New York, N.Y. 10010

ISBN 0–312–22163–0 hc
ISBN 0–312–22164–9 pbk

For Kate, Roger, Elsie and Stan

. . . the slovenliness of our language makes it easier for us to have foolish thoughts.

George Orwell, 'Politics and the English Language'

If one listens one may be convinced; and a man who allows himself to be convinced by an argument is a thoroughly unreasonable person.

Oscar Wilde, *An Ideal Husband*

'*When I use a word,' Humpty Dumpty said, in rather a scornful tone, 'it means just what I choose it to mean. Neither more or less.'*

'*The question is,' said Alice, 'whether you can make words mean so many different things.'*

'*The question is,' said Humpty Dumpty, 'who is the master. That is all.'*

Lewis Carroll, *Alice in Wonderland*

Contents

Boxes   xii

Preface   xv

1 Introduction: Concepts and Theories in Politics   1

   Language and politics   1
   Understanding ideas and concepts   3
   Political science and political theory   8
   Political theory: problems and challenges   10
   Summary   15
   Further reading   15

2 Human Nature, the Individual and Society   16

   Human nature   17
   Nature versus nurture   18
   Intellect versus instinct   21
   Competition versus cooperation   24
   The individual   27
   Individualism   27
   Individual and community   32
   The individual in politics   37
   Society   40
   Collectivism   41
   Theories of society   43
   Social cleavages   45
   Summary   49
   Further reading   50

3 Politics, Government and the State   51

   Politics   52
   The art of government   52
   Public affairs   55
   Power and resources   58
   Government   64
   Why have government?   65
   Forms of government   67
   Political systems   72

The state   74
   Government and the state   74
   Theories of state   77
   Role of the state   84
Summary   87
Further reading   87

4 **Sovereignty, the Nation and Supranationalism**   89

Sovereignty   90
   Legal and political sovereignty   90
   Internal sovereignty   92
   External sovereignty   95
The nation   97
   Cultural and political nations   98
   Nationalism and cosmopolitanism   101
   A future for the nation-state?   106
Supranationalism   109
   Intergovernmentalism   110
   Federalism and federations   114
   Prospects of world government   116
Summary   120
Further reading   120

5 **Power, Authority and Legitimacy**   122

Power   123
   Decision-making   124
   Agenda-setting   126
   Thought control   128
Authority   130
   Power and authority   131
   Kinds of authority   133
   Defenders and detractors   137
Legitimacy   141
   Constitutionalism and consent   143
   Ideological hegemony   145
   Legitimation crises   147
Summary   150
Further reading   151

6 Law, Order and Justice   152

  Law   152
    The rule of law   153
    Natural and positive law   156
    Law and liberty   159
  Order   162
    Discipline and control   163
    Natural harmony   167
    Justifying punishment   171
  Justice   175
    Procedural justice   176
    Substantive justice   178
    Justifying law-breaking?   181
  Summary   185
  Further reading   186

7 Rights, Obligations and Citizenship   187

  Rights   188
    Legal and moral rights   188
    Human rights   191
    Animal and other rights?   195
  Obligations   200
    Contractual obligations   201
    Natural duty   203
    Limits of political obligation   205
  Citizenship   207
    Elements of citizenship   210
    Social citizenship   213
    Active citizenship   215
  Summary   218
  Further reading   219

8 Democracy, Representation and the Public Interest   220

  Democracy   221
    Direct and indirect democracy   224
    Liberal democracy   226
    Virtues and vices of democracy   229

Representation   233
  Representatives or delegates?   234
  Elections and mandates   236
  Characteristic representation   238
The public interest   241
  Private and public interests   241
  Is there a public interest?   244
  Dilemmas of democracy   248
Summary   252
Further reading   252

9 Freedom, Toleration and Liberation   253

Freedom   254
  Liberty and licence   255
  Negative freedom   259
  Positive freedom   261
Toleration   265
  Toleration and permissiveness   265
  The case for toleration   268
  Limits of toleration   270
Liberation   273
  National liberation   274
  Sexual liberation   276
  Politics of liberation   279
Summary   283
Further reading   284

10 Equality, Social Justice and Welfare   285

Equality   286
  Formal equality   287
  Equality of opportunity   290
  Equality of outcome   293
Social justice   295
  According to needs   296
  According to rights   300
  According to deserts   302
Welfare   304
  Welfare and poverty   305
  In praise of welfare   308
  Welfare under attack   311
Summary   316
Further reading   317

11 **Property, Planning and the Market**   **318**

Property   319
    Private property   319
    Common property   323
    State property   325
Planning   327
    The planning process   327
    Promise of planning   330
    Perils of planning   332
The market   335
    The market mechanism   336
    Miracle of the market   338
    Market failures   343
Summary   346
Further reading   346

12 **Reaction, Reform and Revolution**   **348**

Reaction   349
    Defending the status quo   349
    Reclaiming the past   351
    Change in order to conserve   354
Reform   356
    Progress and reason   357
    Reform versus revolution   359
    The march of history halted?   364
Revolution   366
    Political revolution   369
    Social revolution   372
    Cultural revolution   375
Summary   377
Further reading   378

Bibliography   379

Index   392

Boxes

Thinkers

Aquinas, Thomas	158
Arendt, Hannah	368
Aristotle	68
Augustine of Hippo	91
Gandhi, Mohandas Karamchand	182
Hegel, Georg Wilhelm Friedrich	4
Hobbes, Thomas	124
Jefferson, Thomas	192
Kant, Immanuel	117
Locke, John	269
Machiavelli, Niccolò	54
Madison, James	232
Marx, Karl	373
Mill, John Stuart	258
Nozick, Robert	320
Plato	22
Rawls, John	299
Rousseau, Jean-Jacques	243
Wollstonecroft, Mary	289

Traditions and key figures

Absolutism	164
Anticolonialism/postcolonialism	102
Communitarianism	34
Conservatism	138
Critical theory	280
Democracy	222
Ecologism	196
Feminism	60
Liberalism	29
Libertarianism	340
Marxism	81
Postmodernism	12
Rational choice theory	246

Republicanism   208
Social democracy   312
Utilitarianism   360
Utopianism   168

Preface

The first edition of this book was published under the title *Political Ideas and Concepts* and was designed, first, to provide a general introduction to politics through the analysis of political ideas and their relationship to political practice, second, to provide an accessible guide to the major concepts encountered in political analysis, and third, to serve as a primer in political theory. This edition has been retitled to reflect the fact that it is in the third of these roles that it has been mainly used and that the main changes for the second edition have been designed to enhance its suitability for this purpose.

The basic structure and general coverage of the book remain largely unchanged. The concepts discussed have been chosen because of the central role they play in political analysis. They have been grouped into sets of three interrelated terms to enable each chapter to deal with a distinctive theme, the nature of which is outlined in the introductory section. Apart from general updating, the major changes in the second edition are as follows.

Chapter 1 has been revised to extend the discussion of political theory and consider some of the problems and challenges the discipline confronts. The section on ideological perspectives has been dropped, as much of this material is now covered in boxes placed elsewhere in the book. The chapter on Human Nature, the Individual and Society has been moved from the end of the book to become Chapter 2, both to acknowledge the crucial importance to political theory of its central theme and because the issues it addresses recur at various points throughout the text. All the boxes in this edition are new and either provide an introduction to the life and ideas of key figures in the history of political thought (these being rather fuller than those that appeared in the first edition), or provide an introduction to the major traditions in political theory. These 'traditions' boxes examine the distinctive ideas and perspective of each broad school of political theory and briefly consider the contribution of their key protaganists. Books discussed in the text (but not those referred to in the boxes) appear with their date of current publication, as listed in the bibliography, and, where helpful, also with their date of first publication.

I would like to express my very warm gratitude to Andrew Gamble and Peter Jones, who each read a draft of the first edition and made extensive comments. Their advice and criticism was both constructive and insightful, and undoubtedly improved the book, deepening and sharpening discussion at a number of points. My publisher, Steven Kennedy, has, as before, been a constant source of enthusiasm, encouragement and support. In addition, I would like to thank Peter Millican for technical advice and assistance which allowed the transcript be produced speedily and efficiently. The most important person, however, has been my wife Jean. She was closely involved at every stage in the production of the book, taking sole responsibility for the preparation of the typescript and casting an editorial eye over the output. Finally, my sons, Mark and Robin, deserve a mention for allowing me to substitute publication for parenting, and for keeping me supplied with coffee in the process.

ANDREW HEYWOOD

Chapter 1

Introduction: Concepts and Theories in Politics

Introduction
Language and politics
Understanding ideas and concepts
Political science and political theory
Political theory: problems and challenges
Summary
Further reading

Introduction

It would be misleading, indeed patently foolish, to suggest that political conflict reflects nothing more than confusion in the use of language. It is certainly true that enemies often argue, fight and even go to war, both claiming to be 'defending liberty', 'upholding democracy' or that 'justice is on their side'. The intervention of some Great Lexicographer descending from the skies to demand that the parties to the dispute define their terms before they proceed, stating precisely what each means by 'liberty', 'democracy' and 'justice', would surely be to no avail. The argument, fight or war would take place anyway. Politics, in other words, can never be reduced to mere semantics. And yet there is also a sense in which sloppiness in the use of language helps to protect ignorance and preserve misunderstanding. Language is both the tool with which we think and the means by which we communicate with others. If the language we use is confused or poorly understood, it is not only difficult to express our views and opinions with any degree of accuracy but it is also impossible to know the contents of our own minds. This book sets out to clarify and examine the major concepts and theories used in political analysis and, in so doing, to provide an introduction to some of the most recurrent controversies in political thought. This introduction attempts to explain why this task is so difficult.

Language and politics

Whatever else politics might be it is a social activity. It is therefore conducted through the medium of language, whether written in books, pamphlets and manifestos, daubed on placards and walls, or spoken in

1

meetings, shouted at rallies or chanted on demonstrations and marches. At first sight, language is a simple thing: it is a system of expression which employs symbols, in this case *words*, to represent *things*, which can include physical objects, feelings, ideas and so forth. This implies that language is essentially passive, its role being to reflect reality as accurately as possible, rather as a mirror reflects the image before it. However, language is also a positive and active force, capable of firing the imagination and stirring the emotions. Words do not merely reflect the realities around us, they also help to shape what we see and structure our attitude towards it. In effect, language helps to create the world itself.

This problem is particularly acute in politics because language is so often wielded by those who have an incentive to manipulate and confuse – professional politicians. Being primarily interested in political advocacy, politicians are typically less concerned with the precision of their language than they are with its propaganda value. Language is therefore not simply a means of communication, it is a political weapon; it is shaped and honed to convey political intent. Thus, government expenditure is portrayed favourably when it is described as 'public investment', but unfavourably when we are reminded that it is 'taxpayers' money' that is being spent. Similarly, the invasion of a foreign country can be described either as a 'violation' of its sovereignty or as the 'liberation' of its people. In a still more sinister fashion, civilian casualties of war can be dismissed as 'collateral damage', and genocide can appear almost excusable when it is referred to as 'ethnic cleansing'. The language used by politicians sometimes threatens to turn euphemism into an art form, at times approaching the bizarre extremes of 'Newspeak', the language of the Ministry of Truth in George Orwell's *Nineteen Eighty-Four*, which declares that War is Peace, Freedom is Slavery and Ignorance is Strength.

Particular controversy has been raised in the late twentieth century by the movement to insist upon 'political correctness' in the use of language, often referred to simply as PC. Under pressure from feminist and civil rights movements, attempts have been made to purge language of racist, sexist and other derogatory or disparaging implications. According to this view, language invariably reflects the power structure in society at large, and so discriminates in favour of dominant groups and against subordinate ones. Obvious examples of this are the use of 'Man' or 'mankind' to refer to the human race, references to ethnic minorities as 'negroes' or 'colour-eds', and the description of third world countries as 'underdeveloped'. The goal of 'political correctness' is to develop bias-free terminology that enables political argument to be conducted in non-discriminatory language, thereby countering deeply-rooted prejudices and presuppositions. The difficulty with such a position is, however, that the hope of an unbiased and objective language of political discourse may be illusory. At best, 'negative' terms and images can be replaced by 'positive' ones; for example, the 'disabled' can be referred to as the 'differently abled', and countries can be described as 'developing' rather than as 'underdeveloped' (although even this implies that they lag behind 'developed' countries). Critics of 'political correctness' furthermore argue that it imposes an ideological straitjacket upon language that both impoverishes its descriptive power and introduces a form of censorship by denying expression to 'incorrect' views.

If the attempt to devise a neutral and scientific vocabulary for politics is hopeless, where does this leave us? The least, and possibly the most, we can do is be clear about the words we use and the meanings we assign to them. The goal is the one George Orwell outlined in his seminal essay 'Politics and the English Language' (1957): language should be 'an instrument for expressing and not for concealing or preventing thought'. When a stupid remark is uttered its stupidity should be obvious, even to the speaker. However, this requires more than just a series of definitions. A definition ties a word down to a precise meaning, something that is difficult to do with political terms because they stand for ideas, concepts and values which are themselves highly complex and often fiercely contested. Moreover, most political terms carry heavy ideological baggage, a set of assumptions and beliefs which serve to influence how the words are used and what meanings are assigned to them. Finally, there is the danger of forgetting what Samuel Johnson warned: 'that words are the daughters of earth, and that things are the sons of heaven'. In other words, language always has a limited value. However carefully words are used and however rigorously their meanings are refined, language tends to simplify and misrepresent the infinite complexity of the real world. If we mistake the 'word' for the 'thing' we are in danger, as the Zen saying puts it, of mistaking the finger pointing at the moon for the moon itself.

Understanding ideas and concepts

An idea, in its simplest form, is a mental image, an object perceived by the mind. Anything from a mere thought to a developed belief, viewpoint or theory can be described as 'an idea'. Over the centuries, philosophers have debated the nature of ideas and, more specifically, the relationship between ideas and the sensory world, that which can be seen, heard, touched, smelled and so on. The idealist tradition in philosophy, usually traced back to Plato (see p. 22) holds that mind or spirit is the most important element in reality and that the material world is in some way derived from it. In Plato's view, for instance, the material world consists of nothing more than a series of copies of a set of eternal 'Ideas' or 'Forms'. Such philosophical

Georg Wilhelm Friedrich Hegel (1770–1831)

German philosopher. Hegel was the founder of modern idealism and developed the notion that consciousness and material objects are in fact unified. In *Phenomenology of Spirit* (1807), he sought to develop a rational system that would substitute for traditional Christianity by interpreting the entire process of human history, and indeed the universe itself, in terms of the progress of absolute Mind towards self-realisation. In his view, history is, in essence, a march of the human spirit towards a determinant end-point.

Hegel's principal political work, *Philosophy of Right* (1821), advanced an organic theory of the state that portrayed it as the highest expression of human freedom. He identified three 'moments' of social existence: the family, civil society and the state. Within the family, he argued, a 'particular altruism' operates, encouraging people to set aside their own interests for the good of their relatives. He viewed civil society as a sphere of 'universal egoism' in which individuals place their own interests before those of others. However, he held that the state is an ethical community underpinned by mutual sympathy, and is thus characterised by 'universal altruism'. This stance was reflected in Hegel's admiration for the Prussian state of his day, and helped to convert liberal thinkers to the cause of state intervention. Hegel's philosophy also had considerable impact upon Marx (see p. 373) and other so-called 'young Hegelians'.

idealism was perhaps most systematically developed by G.W.F. Hegel, in the early nineteenth century. Hegel interpreted the entire process of human history, and indeed the universe itself, in terms of the progress of absolute Mind towards self-realisation. This point would be reached when Mind, operating in and through human beings, came to recognise the world as nothing more than the exteriorisation of itself, overcoming the conflict between subject and object.

The rival materialist school of philosophy has, however, roundly rejected such theories. Materialism is the belief that the world can be explained through material causes, which implies that ideas arise not from some eternal or absolute realm, but rather from our perception of sensory objects. In the seventeenth and eighteenth centuries, philosophers such as John Locke (see p. 269) and David Hume (1711–76) advanced the empiricist belief that human knowledge developed out of experience of the material world, ideas being little more than sense-impressions, mental images of material things. From a different perspective, Karl Marx (see p. 373) in the nineteenth century tried to 'turn Hegel on his head', developing what came to be called the 'materialist conception of history'. Marx dismissed the notion that ideas fall from the sky like rain and asserted instead that consciousness is conditioned by the most fundamental of human tasks: the struggle for material existence. In Marx's view, ideas, beliefs and theories are formed through interaction between human beings and the material world, suggesting that ideas themselves bear the imprint of the material or economic circumstances out of which they emerge.

Whether ideas descend from some eternal spiritual realm or arise from sensory experience, in order to be employed in the process of thinking they must first be developed into fully fledged 'concepts'. A concept is a general idea about something, usually represented by a single word or short phrase. A concept is more than a proper noun or the name of a thing. There is a difference, for example, between talking about a chair, a particular and unique chair, and holding the concept of a 'chair', the idea of a chair. The concept of a chair is an abstract notion, composed of the various features which give a chair its distinctive character – in this case, for instance, the capacity to be sat upon. In the same way, the concept of 'presidency' refers not to any specific president but rather to a set of ideas about the organisation of executive power. Concepts are therefore 'general' in the sense that they can refer to a number of objects, indeed to any object that complies with the characteristics of the general idea itself. All the terms examined in this book are concepts in this sense.

Concept formation is an essential step in the process of reasoning, in that concepts are the 'tools' with which we think, criticise, argue, explain and analyse. Merely to perceive the external world does not in itself give us knowledge about it. In order to make sense of the world we must, in a sense, impose meaning upon it, and this we do through the construction of concepts. Quite simply, to use a chair as a chair we must first have a concept of what it is and how it can be used. Precisely the same applies to the process of political reasoning: we build up our knowledge of the political world not simply by looking at it, but through developing and refining concepts which will help us make sense of it. Concepts are, in other words, the building blocks of human knowledge.

In order to go one step further and start to reason or advance arguments it is again necessary to make use of concepts. The process of reasoning is usually divided into deductive and inductive forms of argument. Deductive reasoning tries to draw conclusions from a set of assumptions or premises; it is therefore concerned with the logical development or internal coherence of a line of thought. A simple example of a deductive argument would be: (premises) my pet is a dog, and all dogs have tails; therefore (conclusion) my pet has a tail. Inductive reasoning, on the other hand, involves testing statements or premises in the light of experience or empirical evidence. For instance, evidence could be sought to establish if my pet is a dog, and if all dogs have tails. Whichever form of argument is employed, concepts are crucial to the reasoning process since all theories and every piece of understanding is constructed in terms of concepts. In this case both deductive and inductive processes depend upon concepts of dog and tail; unless we have a clear understanding of what is meant by 'dog' and what is meant by 'tail', any attempt to construct an argument will be pointless. This is why the first step towards acquiring understanding is to clarify the meaning of the concepts employed.

In politics, however, the clarification of concepts is a particularly difficult task. In the first place, the political reality upon which we seek to impose meaning is itself constantly shifting and highly complex. Concepts like 'democracy', 'capitalism' and 'socialism' are always in danger of being more rounded and more coherent than the unshapely realities which they seek to describe. Theory and practice do not always neatly coincide, however carefully concepts are drawn up and refined. This problem was, for instance, acknowledged by socialists who came to refer to the form of socialism which once existed in the Soviet Union and Eastern Europe as 'actually existing' socialism, to distinguish it from the principles and values for which they stood. The German sociologist Max Weber (1864–1920) attempted to overcome such problems by recognising particular concepts as 'ideal-types'. Weber acknowledged that social phenomena contain such a large number of interconnected elements as to be almost infinitely complex. Conceptual abstractions can therefore only be constructed by singling out certain basic or central features of the phenomenon in question, meaning that other features were downgraded or ignored altogether. The advantage of such an ideal-type is that by imposing structure upon a complex reality it enables us to make sense of it; but our knowledge always remains imperfect because the ideal-type is, at best, only an approximation of reality. For example, although it is essential to employ a concept of 'revolution' to make sense of, say, the 1789 French Revolution and the Eastern European revolutions of 1989–91, the concept itself can distort reality every bit as much as it can reveal it. In this case, the concept of 'revolution' can highlight important similarities between these two events but may also conceal vital differences. Thus it is a mistake to think of ideal types as being 'true' or 'false', but merely as being more or less 'useful'.

A further problem is that in politics concepts themselves become the subject of both intellectual and ideological controversy. It is not uncommon, as pointed out earlier, for political argument to take place between people who claim to be upholding the same principle or the same ideal. Conceptual disagreement is therefore one of the battlegrounds of politics itself. This is reflected in attempts to establish a particular conception of a concept as objectively correct, as in the case of 'true' democracy, 'true' freedom, 'true' justice and so forth. Any impartial understanding of political concepts is thus forced to recognise that most, if not all, concepts are many-faced. W.B. Gallie (1955/6) suggested that in the case of concepts such as 'power', 'justice' and 'freedom' controversy runs so deep that no neutral or settled definition can ever be developed. These concepts should be recognised, he argued, as 'essentially contested concepts'. In effect, each term encompasses a number of rival concepts, none of which can be accepted as its 'true' meaning. To acknowledge that a concept is 'essentially contested' is not, however, to abandon the attempt to understand it but rather to recognise that competing versions of the concept are equally valid.

A final problem is the difficulty in politics of distinguishing between normative and descriptive concepts. Normative concepts are often described as 'values'; they refer to moral principles or ideals, that which *should, ought* or *must* be brought about. A wide range of political concepts are 'value-loaded' in this sense – liberty, rights, justice, equality, tolerance and so on. Values or normative concepts therefore advance or prescribe certain forms of conduct rather than describe events or facts. Consequently, it is sometimes difficult to disentangle political values from the moral, philosophical and ideological beliefs of those who advance them. By contrast, descriptive or positive concepts refer to 'facts' which supposedly have an objective or demonstrable existence; they refer to what *is*. Concepts like power, authority, order and law are in this sense descriptive rather than normative. It is possible to ask whether they exist or do not exist.

The distinction between 'facts' and 'values' is often regarded as a necessary precondition for clear thinking. Whereas values may be regarded as a matter of opinion, facts can be proved to be either 'true' or 'false'. As a result, descriptive concepts are thought to be 'neutral' or 'value-free': they stand up to the rigour of scientific examination. The problem with political concepts, however, is that 'facts' and 'values' are invariably interlinked; even apparently descriptive concepts are loaded with a set of moral and ideological implications. This can be seen, for instance, in the case of 'authority'. If authority is defined as 'the right to influence the behaviour of others', it is certainly possible to use the concept descriptively to say who possesses authority and who does not, and to examine the basis upon which it is exercised. However, it is impossible completely to divorce the concept from value judgements about when, how and why authority *should* be exercised. In short, no one is neutral about the concept of authority. For example, whereas conservatives, who emphasise the need to impose order from above, tend to regard authority as rightful and healthy, anarchists, who believe government and law to be evil, invariably see authority as nakedly oppressive. All political concepts, descriptive as well as normative, must therefore be understood in the light of the ideological perspectives of those who use them. Some would, in fact, go further and cast doubt upon the very existence of objective facts. Modern scientists, after all, have abandoned the idea that they can verify hypotheses, and now accept that they only have the ability to falsify incorrect hypotheses. Indeed, what we take to be 'facts' may simply be social constructions, always possessed of an ideological character.

Political science and political theory

This book is designed to provide a guide to the major concepts and theories encountered in the academic study of politics. Political concepts are, however, treated in different ways by different political analysts. Indeed, questions about the language of political discourse go to the very heart of divisions within the academic discipline itself. Politics is usually seen to encompass two, and some would say three, distinct subdivisions. On the one hand, there is what is called political science and, on the other, political theory and political philosophy – terms that are often used interchangeably but between which distinctions are sometimes drawn.

Although political science is a child of the twentieth century, it draws upon roots which date back to the empiricism of the seventeenth century. 'Science' refers to a means of acquiring knowledge through observation, experimentation and measurement. Its central feature, 'the scientific method', involves verifying or falsifying hypotheses by testing them against empirical evidence, preferably using repeatable experiments. The almost unquestioned status which science has come to enjoy in the modern world is based upon its claim to be objective and value-free, and so to be the only reliable means of disclosing truth. Political science is therefore essentially empirical, claiming to describe, analyse and explain government and other political institutions in a rigorous and impartial manner. The high point of enthusiasm for a 'science of politics' came in the 1950s and 1960s with the emergence, most strongly in the United States, of a form of political analysis that drew heavily upon behaviouralism. Behaviouralism developed as a school of psychology which, as the name implies, studies only the observable and measurable behaviour of human beings. This encouraged political analysts such as David Easton to believe that political science could adopt the methodology of the natural sciences, leading to a proliferation of studies in areas like voting behaviour where systematic and quantifiable data was readily available.

Political theory and political philosophy may overlap, but a difference of emphasis can nevertheless be identified. Anything from a plan to a piece of abstract knowledge can be described as a 'theory'. In academic discourse, however, a theory is an explanatory proposition, an idea or set of ideas that in some way seeks to impose order or meaning upon phenomena. As such, all enquiry proceeds through the construction of theories, sometimes thought of as hypotheses, explanatory propositions waiting to be tested. Political science, no less than the natural sciences and other social sciences, therefore has an important theoretical component. For example, theories, such as that social class is the principal determinant of voting behaviour and that revolutions occur at times of rising expectations, are essential if sense is to be made of empirical evidence. This is what is called empirical political theory.

Political theory is, however, usually regarded as a distinctive approach to the subject, even though, particularly in the United States, it is seen as a subfield of political science. Political theory involves the analytical study of ideas and doctrines that have been central to political thought. Traditionally, this has taken the form of a history of political thought, focusing upon a collection of 'major' thinkers – for instance, from Plato to Marx – and a canon of 'classic' texts. As it studies the ends and means of political action, political theory is clearly concerned with ethical or normative questions, such as 'Why should I obey the state?', 'How should rewards be distributed?' and 'What should be the limits of individual liberty?'. This traditional approach has about it the character of literary analysis: it is primarily interested in examining what major thinkers said, how they developed or justified their views, and the intellectual context in which they worked. An alternative approach has been called formal political theory. This draws upon the example of economic theory in building up models based on procedural rules, usually about the rationally self-interested behaviour of the individuals involved. Most firmly established in the United States and associated in particular with the Virginia School, formal political theory has attempted to understand better the behaviour of actors like voters, politicians, lobbyists and bureaucrats, and has spawned 'rational choice,' 'public choice' and 'social choice' schools of thought. Although its proponents believe it to be strictly neutral, its individualist and egoistical assumptions have led some to suggest that it has an inbuilt conservative value-bias.

The term political philosophy can be used loosely to cover any abstract thought about politics, law or society, philosophy being, in general terms, the search for wisdom and understanding. However, philosophy has also been seen more specifically as a *second-order* discipline, in contrast to *first-order* disciplines which deal with empirical subjects. In other words, philosophy is not so much concerned with revealing truth in the manner of science, as with asking secondary questions about how knowledge is acquired and about how understanding is expressed. For instance, whereas a political scientist may examine the democratic processes at work within a particular system, a political philosopher will be interested in clarifying what is meant by 'democracy'. Political philosophy therefore addresses itself to two main tasks. First, it is concerned with the critical evaluation of political beliefs, paying attention to both inductive and deductive forms of reasoning. Secondly, it attempts to clarify and refine the concepts employed in political discourse. What this means is that, despite the best efforts of political philosophers to remain impartial and objective, they are inevitably concerned with justifying certain political viewpoints at the expense of others and with upholding a particular understanding of a concept rather than alternative ones. From this point of view, the present book can be seen primarily as a work of political theory and not political philosophy. Although the writings of political philosophers provide much of its material, its objective is to analyse and explain political ideas and concepts rather than advance any particular beliefs or interpretations.

Political theory: problems and challenges

Political theory has been in a beleaguered state through much of the twentieth century. Indeed, in his introduction to *Philosophy, Politics and Society* (1956) Peter Laslett famously declared that 'political philosophy is dead'. Its 'death' was largely a consequence of important shifts in philosophy, notably the rise of logical positivism. Logical positivism, originally advanced by a group of philosophers collectively known as the Vienna Circle, reflected a deep faith in scientific understanding and suggested that propositions that are not empirically verifiable are simply meaningless. Normative concepts such as 'liberty', 'equality', 'justice' and 'rights' were therefore discarded as nonsense, and philosophers, as a result, tended to lose interest in moral and political issues. For their part, political scientists, influenced by the 'behavioural revolution' that was one of the chief legacies of positivism, turned their backs upon the entire tradition of normative political thought. This meant, for instance, that words such as 'democracy' were redefined in terms of measurable political behaviour.

After the 1960s, however, political theory re-emerged with new vitality, and the previously sharp distinction between political science and political theory began to fade. This occurred for a number of reasons. These included a growing dissatisfaction with behaviouralism, based upon its tendency to constrain the scope of political analysis by preventing it from going beyond what is directly observable. Moreover, faith in the ability of science to uncover objective truth was undermined by advances in the philosophy of science, stemming in particular from the work of Thomas Kuhn (1962), which emphasise that scientific knowledge is not absolute but is contingent upon the principles, doctrines and theories that structure the process of enquiry. Lastly, the emergence of new social movements in the 1960s and the end of consensus politics brought normative and ideological questions back to the forefront of political analysis, as reflected in the work of a new generation of political theorists, such as John Rawls (see p. 299) and Robert Nozick (see p. 320).

However, revived political theory differs in a number of respects from its earlier manifestations. The philosophical tradition in the study of politics had previously been thought of as an analysis, through the ages, of a number of perennial problems – most obviously, the nature of justice, the grounds of political obligation, the proper balance between liberty and equality, and so on. Political philosophy therefore considered the contribution of major thinkers to our understanding of such problems and analysed how this understanding had developed from the ancient and medieval periods, through the early modern period (1500–1800 approximately) to the modern period (since 1800). One feature of modern political theory is that it has placed a greater emphasis upon the role of history and culture in shaping political understanding. What, say, Plato, Rousseau and Marx wrote perhaps tells us more about the societies and historical circumstances in which they lived than it does about any supposedly timeless moral and political issues. The extent to which contemporary understanding can be advanced through a study of past political thinkers and traditions may therefore be extremely limited. While few would conclude from this that the study of 'major' thinkers and 'classic' texts is worthless, most now accept that any interpretation of such thinkers and texts must take account of context, and recognise that, to some extent, all interpretations are entangled with our own values and understanding.

The second development is that political theory has become increasingly diffuse and diverse. In the modern period in particular, the most prominent tradition in Western political thought has been liberalism (see p. 29). Political theory therefore advanced through an on-going debate between liberalism and its major rivals, Marxist socialism (see p. 81) and conservatism (see p. 138). During the twentieth century, however, liberal theory has undergone a variety of changes as it has, for example, confronted the threat of totalitarianism, sought an accommodation with welfare and redistribution, and recoiled from growing state intervention. As a result, much of modern political theory constitutes a debate within a broad liberal tradition or between traditions that each have some kind of liberal heritage. A range of other political traditions have also emerged as critiques of, or alternatives to, liberal theory. These have included feminism (see p. 60), communitarianism (see p. 34) and ecologism (see p. 196). However, it is important to recognise that none of these traditions (which are examined in the 'traditions' boxes) is a hermetically sealed system of thought, enjoying a fixed logic and strict internal consistency. Rather, political traditions are typically fluid sets of ideas, which embrace a range of sometimes conflicting beliefs and overlap at a number of points with other traditions.

Postmodernism

Postmodernism is a controversial and confusing term that was first used to describe experimental movements in Western architecture and cultural development in general. Postmodern thought originated principally in continental Europe, especially France, and constitutes a challenge to the type of academic political theory that has come to be the norm in the Anglo-American world. Since the 1970s, however, postmodern and poststructural political theories have become increasingly fashionable. Their basis lies in a perceived social shift – from modernity to postmodernity – and a related cultural and intellectual shift – from modernism to postmodernism. Modern societies were seen to be structured by industrialisation and class solidarity, social identity being largely determined by one's position within the productive system. Postmodern societies, on the other hand, are increasingly fragmented and pluralistic 'information' societies in which individuals are transformed from producers to consumers, and individualism replaces class, religious and ethnic loyalties. Postmodernity is thus linked to postindustrialism, the development of a society no longer dependent upon manufacturing industry, but more reliant upon knowledge and communication.

Modernism, the cultural form of modernity, stemmed largely from Enlightenment ideas and theories, and was expressed politically in ideological traditions that offered rival conceptions of the good life. Liberalism (see p. 29) and Marxism (see p. 81) are its clearest examples. Modernist thought is characterised by foundationalism – the belief that it is possible to establish objective truths and universal values, usually associated with a strong faith in progress. By contrast, the central theme of postmodernism is that there is no such thing as certainty: the idea of absolute and universal truth must be discarded as an arrogant pretence. Although by its nature postmodernism does not constitute a unified body of thought, its critical attitude to truth-claims stems from the assumption that all knowledge is partial and local, a view it shares with some communitarian thinkers (see p. 34). Poststructuralism, a term sometimes used interchangeably with postmodernism, emphasises that all ideas and concepts are expressed in language which itself is enmeshed in complex relations of power. Political theory, then, does not stand above power relations and bestow dispassionate understanding; it is an intrinsic part of the power relations it claims to analyse.

Postmodernist thought has been criticised from two angles. In the first place, it has been accused of relativism, in that it holds that different modes of knowing are equally valid and thus rejects the idea that even science is able reliably to distinguish between truth and falsehood. Secondly, it has been charged with conservatism, on the grounds that a non-foundationalist political stance offers no perspective from which the existing order may be criticised and no basis for the construction of an alternative social order. Nevertheless, the attraction of postmodern theory is its remorseless questioning of apparently solid realities and accepted beliefs. Its general emphasis upon discourse, debate and democracy, reflects the fact that to reject hierarchies of ideas is also to reject any political and social hierarchies.

→

Key figures

Friedrich Nietzsche (1844–1900) A German philosopher, Nietzsche is invariably regarded as the most important precursor of postmodernism. His complex and ambitious work stresses the importance of will, especially the 'will to power', and emphasises that people create their own world and make their own values. This is most memorably expressed in the assertion that 'God is dead'. Nietzsche's nihilism, the rejection of all moral and political principles, encouraged later postmodern theorists to regard truth as a fiction and to link beliefs and values to the assertion of power. His best known writings include *Thus Spoke Zarathustra* (1883–4), *Beyond Good and Evil* (1886) and *On the Genealogy of Morals* (1887).

Martin Heidegger (1889–1976) A German philosopher, Heidegger, also a precursor of postmodernism, had a considerable impact upon the development of phenomenology and existentialism. Fundamental to his philosophical system was the question of the meaning of Being, by which he meant self-conscious existence. All previous political philosophies had made the mistake of starting out from a conception of human nature rather than recognising the 'human essence' as a 'realm of disclosure'. This had led to the dominance of technology over human existence, from which, Heidegger believed, humans could escape by developing a more receptive relationship to Being. Heidegger's most famous work is *Being and Time* (1927).

Jean-François Lyotard (1924–) A French philosopher, Lyotard was primarily responsible for popularising the term postmodern and for giving it its most succinct definition: 'An incredulity towards metanarratives.' By this he meant a scepticism about all creeds and ideologies that are based upon universal theories of history which view society as a coherent totality. This stems from science's loss of authority as it has fragmented into a number of forms of discourse and as 'performativity', or efficiency, has displaced truth as its standard of value. Lyotard's post-Marxism also reflects his belief that communism has been eliminated as an alternative to liberal capitalism. His most important work is *The Postmodern Condition* (1979).

Michel Foucault (1926–1984) A French philosopher, Foucault was primarily concerned with forms of knowledge and the construction of the human subject. His early work analysed different branches of knowledge as 'archaeologies', leading to an emphasis upon discourse, or 'discursive formation'. Central to this was his belief that knowledge is deeply enmeshed in power, truth always being a social construct, and that power can be productive as well as prohibitive. Foucault's most important works include *Madness and Civilisation* (1961), *The Archaeology of Knowledge* (1969), *Discipline and Punishment* (1975) and *History of Sexuality*, I–III (1976–84).

Jacques Derrida (1930–) A French philosopher, Derrida is the main proponent of deconstruction, although it is a term he is reluctant to use. Deconstruction (sometimes used interchangeably with poststructuralism) is the task of raising questions about the 'texts' that constitute cultural life,

→

Postmodernism continued

exposing complications and contradictions of which their 'authors' are not fully conscious and for which they are not fully responsible. Derrida's concept of 'difference' rejects the idea that there are fixed differences in language and allows for a constant sliding between meanings in that there are no polar opposites. His major works include *Writing and Difference* (1967), *Margins of Philosophy* (1972) and *Spectres of Marx* (1993).

Richard Rorty (1931–)   A US philosopher, Rorty has focused increasingly upon political issues, having established his reputation in the analysis of language and mind. His early work rejected the idea that there is an objective, transcendental standpoint from which beliefs can be judged, leading to the conclusion that philosophy itself should be understood as nothing more than a conversation. Nevertheless, he supports a pragmatic brand of liberalism that overlaps at times with social democracy (see p. 312), for which reason he has reservations about some of the relativist trends in postmodernism. Rorty's best known works include *Philosophy and the Mirror of Nature* (1979), *Consequences of Pragmatism* (1982) and *Contingency, Irony and Solidarity* (1989).

Further reading

Harvey, D. *The Condition of Postmodernity.* London: Basil Blackwell, 1989.
Hutcheon, L. *The Politics of Postmodernism.* New York: Routledge, 1989.
Lyon, D. *Postmodernity.* Milton Keynes: Open University Press, 1994.

Finally, modern political thought has lost the bold self-confidence of earlier periods, in that it has effectively abandoned the 'traditional' search for universal values acceptable to everyone. This has occurred through a growing appreciation of the role of community and local identity in shaping values, and as non-Western political traditions have been recognised as being as legitimate as Western ones. However, it is a position that has been most fully elaborated by postmodern theorists. Postmodernism has opposed 'foundationist' theorising on the grounds that it assumes that there is a moral and rational high point from which all values and claims to knowledge can be judged. The fact that fundamental disagreement persists about the location of this high point suggests that there is a plurality of legitimate ethical and political positions, and that our language and political concepts are valid only in terms of the context in which they are generated and employed. The implication of this line of thought is that political theory is not so much an accumulating body of knowledge, to which major thinkers and traditions have contributed; rather, it is a dialogue or conversation in which human beings share their differing viewpoints and understandings with one another.

Summary

1 Politics is, in part, a struggle over the legitimate meaning of terms and concepts. Language is often used as a political weapon; words are seldom neutral but carry political and ideological baggage. If a scientific vocabulary of politics is difficult to achieve, the least we can do is be clear about the words we use and the meanings we assign to them.

2 Concepts are the building blocks of knowledge. Concepts are sometimes abstract models or ideal-types, which only approximate to the reality they help to understand. They can either be descriptive, referring to 'what is', or normative, expressing views about 'what ought to be'. The meaning of political concepts is often contested; some of them may be 'essentially contested concepts', meaning that no neutral or settled definition can ever be developed.

3 When political analysis uses scientific methods of enquiry it draws a clear distinction between facts and values; seeking to disclose objective and reliable knowledge, it tends to turn away from normative theorising. While political theory involves the analytical study of ideas and concepts, both normative and descriptive, political philosophy attempts to refine our understanding of such ideas and concepts in the hope of advancing political wisdom.

4 Political theory has confronted a number of problems and challenges during the twentieth century. Most seriously, positivism suggested that the entire tradition of normative political thought is meaningless. The revival of political theory since the 1960s has nevertheless been accompanied by a growing awareness of the importance of history and culture and of the contingency of political language and concepts, as well as by greater fragmentation within the discipline.

Further reading

Bellamy, R. (ed.) *Theories and Concepts of Politics: An Introduction* Manchester and New York: Manchester University Press, 1993.

Goodin, R.E. and Pettit, P., (eds) *A Companion to Contemporary Political Philosophy*. Oxford: Basil Blackwell, 1995.

Held, D. (ed.) *Political Theory Today*. Oxford: Polity Press, 1991.

Heywood, A. *Political Ideologies: An Introduction*, 2nd edn. London: Macmillan and New York: St Martin's Press, 1997.

Kymlicka, W. *Contemporary Political Philosophy: An Introduction* Oxford and New York: Oxford University Press, 1990.

Morrow, J. *History of Political Thought: A Thematic Introduction* London: Macmillan, 1998.

Plant, R. *Modern Political Thought*. Oxford: Basil Blackwell, 1991.

Raphael, D.D. *Problems of Political Philosophy*, rev. edn. London: Macmillan, 1990.

Vincent, A. *Political Theory: Tradition and Diversity*. Cambridge: Cambridge University Press, 1997.

Chapter 2

Human Nature, the Individual and Society

Introduction
Human nature
The individual
Society
Summary
Further reading

Introduction

Throughout this book, and indeed throughout political theory, there is a recurrent theme: the relationship between the individual and society. This touches on almost all political debates and controversies – the nature of justice, the proper realm of freedom, the desirability of equality, the value of politics, and so forth. At the heart of this issue lies the idea of human nature, that which makes human beings 'human'. Almost all political doctrines and beliefs are based upon some kind of theory of human nature, sometimes explicitly formulated but in many cases simply implied. To do otherwise would be to take the complex and perhaps unpredictable human element out of politics.

However, the concept of human nature has also been a source of great difficulty for political theorists. Models of human nature have varied considerably, and each model has radically different implications for how social and political life should be organised. Are human beings, for instance, selfish or sociable, rational or irrational, essentially moral or basically corrupt? Are they, at heart, political animals or private beings? The answers to such questions bear heavily upon the relationship between the individual and society. In particular, how much of human behaviour is shaped by natural or innate forces, and how much is conditioned by the social environment? Are human beings 'individuals', independent from one another and possessed of separate and unique characters, or are they social beings, whose identity and behaviour is shaped by the groups to which they belong? Such questions have not only been enduring topics of philosophical debate – the choice between 'nurture' and 'nature' – but have also been the cornerstone of one of the deepest of ideological divisions: the conflict between individualism and collectivism.

Human nature

All too often the idea of human nature is employed in a generalised and simplistic fashion, as a kind of shorthand for 'this is what people are really like'. In practice, however, to speak of 'human nature' is to make a number of important assumptions about both human beings and the societies in which they live. Although opinions may differ about the content of human nature, the concept itself has a clear and coherent meaning. Human nature refers to the essential and immutable character of all human beings. It highlights what is innate and 'natural' about human life, as opposed to what human beings have gained from education or through social experience. This does not, however, mean that those who believe that human behaviour is shaped more by society than it is by unchanging and inborn characteristics have abandoned the idea of human nature altogether. Indeed, this very assertion is based upon clear assumptions about innate human qualities, in this case, the capacity to be shaped or moulded by external factors. A limited number of political thinkers have, nevertheless, openly rejected the idea of human nature. For instance, the French existentialist philosopher, Jean-Paul Sartre (1905–80), argued that there was no such thing as a given 'human nature', determining how people act or behave. In Sartre's view, existence comes before essence, meaning that human beings enjoy the freedom to define themselves through their own actions and deeds, in which case the assertion of any concept of human nature is an affront to that freedom.

To employ a concept of human nature is not, however, to reduce human life to a one-dimensional caricature. Most political thinkers are clearly aware that human beings are complex, multi-faceted creatures, made up of biological, physical, psychological, intellectual, social and perhaps spiritual elements. The concept of human nature does not conceal or overlook this complexity so much as attempt to impose order upon it by designating certain features as 'natural' or 'essential'. It would seem reasonable, moreover, that if any such thing as a human core exists it should be manifest in human behaviour. Human nature should therefore be reflected in behavioural patterns that are regular and distinctively human. However, this may not always be the case. Some theorists have argued that people behave in ways that deny their 'true' natures. For instance, despite abundant evidence of greedy and selfish behaviour, socialists still hold to the belief that human beings are cooperative and sociable, arguing that such behaviour is socially conditioned and not natural. In this light, it is important to remember that in no sense is human nature a descriptive or scientific concept. Even though theories of human nature may claim an empirical or scientific basis, no experiment or surgical investigation is able to uncover the human 'essence'. All models of human nature are therefore normative: they are constructed out of philosophical and moral assumptions, and are therefore in principle untestable.

Endless discussion has taken place about the nature of human beings. Certain debates have been nevertheless particularly relevant to political theory. Central amongst these is what is usually called the 'nature/nurture' debate. Are human beings the product of innate or biological factors, or are they fashioned by education and social experience? Clearly, such a question has profound implications for the relationship between the individual and society. Important questions have also been asked about the degree to which human behaviour is determined by reason, questions which bear heavily upon issues such as individual liberty and personal autonomy. Are human beings rational creatures, guided by reason, argument and calculation, or are they in some way prisoners of non-rational drives and passions? Finally, there are questions about the impulses or motivations which dominate human behaviour. In particular, are human beings naturally selfish and egoistical, or are they essentially cooperative, altruistic and sociable? Such considerations are crucial in determining the proper organisation of economic and social life, including the distribution of wealth and other resources.

Nature versus nurture

The most recurrent, and perhaps most fundamental debate about human nature relates to what factors or forces shape it. Is the essential core of human nature fixed or given, fashioned by 'nature', or is it moulded or structured by the influence of social experience or 'nurture'. 'Nature', in this case, stands for biological or genetic factors, suggesting that there is an established and unchanging human core. The political significance of such a belief is considerable. In the first place, it implies that political and social theories should be constructed on the basis of a pre-established concept of human nature. Quite simply, human beings do not reflect society, society reflects human nature. Secondly, it suggests that the roots of political understanding lie in the natural sciences in general, and in biology in particular. Political arguments shall therefore be constructed on the basis of biological theories, giving such arguments a 'scientific' character. This helps to explain why biological theories of politics have grown in popularity in the twentieth century.

Without doubt, the biological theory that has had greatest impact upon political and social thought has been the theory of natural selection, developed by Charles Darwin (1809–82) in *On the Origin of Species* ([1859] 1986). Darwin's goal was to explain the almost infinite variety of species which have existed on earth. He suggested that each species develops through a series of random genetic mutations, some of which fit the species to survive and prosper, while other less fortunate species become extinct. Although Darwin appears to have recognised that his theories had radical political implications, he chose not to develop them himself. The first attempt to advance a theory of social Darwinism was undertaken by Herbert Spencer (1820–1903) in *The Man Versus the State* ([1884] 1940). Spencer coined the term 'the survival of the fittest' to describe what he believed to be an endless struggle amongst human beings, through which those best fitted by nature to survive rise to the top, and those less favoured by nature sink to the bottom. Success and failure, wealth and poverty are, in this sense, biologically determined; and tampering with this process of natural selection will only serve to weaken the species. Such ideas deeply influenced classical liberalism (see p. 29), giving it biological grounds for opposing state intervention in economic and social life. Social Darwinism also helped to shape the fascist belief in an unending struggle amongst the various nations or races of the world.

In the twentieth century, political theories have increasingly been influenced by biological ideas. For example, ethologists such as Konrad Lorenz and Niko Timbergen, advanced theories about human behaviour on the basis of detailed studies of animal behaviour. In *On Aggression* (1966), Lorenz suggested that aggression was a natural drive found in all species, including the human species. Popularised by writers like Robert Ardrey, such ideas had considerable impact upon explanations of war and social violence by presenting such behaviour as instinctual and territorial. The 1970s saw the emergence of sociobiology, which attempts to uncover the biological basis of all social behaviour. One of the most influential works of sociobiology has been Richard Dawkins's *The Selfish Gene* (1989), which explains man as a 'gene machine'. Dawkins suggested that both selfishness and altruism have their origins in biology. Although sociobiologists accept that education and conditioning can also influence human behaviour, they nevertheless stress that biological factors are crucial in explaining political and social life.

In most cases, these biological theories embrace universalism; they hold that human beings share a common or universal character, based upon their genetic inheritance. Other theories, however, hold that there are fundamental biological differences amongst human beings, and that these are of political significance. This applies in the case of racialist theories which treat the various races as if they are distinct species. Racialists suggest that there are basic genetic differences amongst the races of the world, reflected in their unequal physical, psychological and intellectual inheritance. In its most extreme version, racialism was expressed in the Nazi doctrine of Aryanism, the belief that the Germanic peoples are a 'master race'. One school of radical feminism (see p. 60), sometimes called separatist feminism, also believes that there are biological and unchangeable differences amongst human beings, in this case between men and women. This theory is called 'essentialism' because it asserts that the difference between women and men is rooted in their 'essential' natures. Sexual inequality is not therefore based upon social conditioning but rather on the biological disposition of the male sex to dominate, exploit and oppress the female sex. For example, in *Against Our Will* (1975), Susan Brownmiller suggested that 'all men' are biologically programmed to dominate 'all women', and that they do so through rape or the fear of rape.

In marked contrast, other theories of human nature place greater emphasis upon 'nurture', the influence of the social environment or experience upon the human character. Clearly, such views play down the importance of fixed and unchanging biological factors, emphasising instead the malleable quality of human nature, or what has been called its 'plasticity'. The significance of such theories is to shift political understanding away from biology and towards sociology. Political behaviour tells us less about an immutable human essence than it does about the structure of society. Moreover, by releasing humankind from its biological chains, such theories often have optimistic, if not openly utopian, implications. When human nature is 'given', the possibility of progress and social advancement is clearly limited; however, if human nature is 'plastic', the opportunities confronting human beings immediately expand and perhaps become infinite. Evils such as poverty, social conflict, political oppression and gender inequality can be overcome precisely because their origins are social and not biological.

The idea that human nature is 'plastic', shaped by external forces, is central to many socialist theories. For instance, in *A New View of Society* ([1816] 1972), the British socialist, Robert Owen (see p. 169), advanced the simple principle that 'any general character from the best to the worst, from the ignorant to the most enlightened, may be given to any community'. In the writings of Karl Marx (see p. 373) this idea was developed through an attempt to outline why and how the social environment conditions human behaviour. Marx proclaimed that, 'It is not the consciousness of men that determines their being, but, on the contrary, their social being determines their consciousness'. Marx, and subsequent Marxists, have believed that social, political and intellectual life is conditioned by 'the mode of production of material life', the existing economic system. However, Marx did not believe human nature to be a passive reflection of its material environment. Rather, human beings are workers, *homo faber*, constantly engaged in shaping and reshaping the world in which they live. Thus, in Marx's view, human nature is formed through a dynamic or 'dialectical' relationship between humankind and the material world. The majority of feminists also subscribe to the view that human behaviour is in most cases conditioned by social factors. For example, in her seminal work, *The Second Sex* ([1949] 1968), Simone de Beauvoir (see p. 61) declared that, 'One is not born a woman: one*becomes* a woman'. In rejecting the notion of 'essential' differences between women and men, feminists have accepted a basically androgynous, or sexless, image of human nature. Because sexism has been 'bred' through a process of social conditioning, particularly in the family, it can be challenged and eventually overthrown.

The picture of human nature as essentially malleable, shaped by social factors, has also been endorsed by behavioural psychologists, such as I.V. Pavlov, John Watson and B.F. Skinner. They argue that human behaviour is explicable simply in terms of conditioned reactions or reflexes, for which reason human nature bears the imprint of its environment. Pavlov, for instance, demonstrated how animals could learn through a strict process of conditioning, by being rewarded for exhibiting 'correct' behaviour. Such ideas became the basis of psychology in the Soviet Union, where crude behaviourism was thought to provide scientific proof for Marx's social theories. The American psychologist, B.F. Skinner, discounted internal processes altogether, describing the human organism as a 'black box'. In *Beyond Freedom and Dignity* (1971), Skinner presented a highly deterministic picture of human nature, denied any form of free will, and entitled, Skinner suggested, to no more dignity or self-respect than Pavlov's dog. Such ideas have widely been used to support the idea of social engineering, the idea that we can 'make' the human beings we want simply by constructing the appropriate social environment.

Intellect versus instinct

The second debate centres upon the role of rationality in human life. This does not, however, come down to a choice between rationalism and irrationalism. The real issue is the degree to which the reasoning mind influences human conduct, suggesting a distinction between those who emphasise thinking, analysis and rational calculation, and those who highlight the role of impulse, instincts or other non-rational drives. To acknowledge the importance of the non-rational does not amount to turning one's back upon reason altogether. Indeed, many such theories are advanced in eminently rationalist, even scientific, terms.

Faith in the power of human reason reached its high point during the Enlightenment, the so-called Age of Reason, in the seventeenth and eighteenth centuries. During that period, philosophers and political thinkers turned away from religious dogmas and faith, and instead based their ideas upon rationalism, the belief that the workings of the physical and social world can be explained by the exercise of reason alone. In this view, human beings are essentially rational creatures, guided by intellect and a process of argument, analysis and debate. Such an idea was expressed with particular clarity in the dualism advanced by the French philosopher, René Descartes (1596–1650). In declaring, *Cogito ergo sum* – 'I think, therefore I am' – Descartes, in effect, portrayed human beings as thinking machines, implying that the mind is quite distinct from the body. Rationalism implies that human beings possess the capacity to fashion their own lives and their own worlds. If human beings are reason-driven creatures they clearly enjoy free will and self-determination: people are what they choose to make of themselves. Rationalist theories of human nature therefore tend to underline the importance of individual freedom and autonomy. In addition, rationalism often underpins radical or revolutionary political doctrines. To the extent that human beings possess the capacity to understand their world, they have the ability also to improve or reform it.

The earliest rationalist ideas were developed by the philosophers of Ancient Greece. Plato, for example, argued that the best possible form of government would be an enlightened despotism, rule by an intellectual elite, the philosopher-kings. Rationalist ideas were also prominent in the emergence in the nineteenth century of liberal and socialist doctrines. Liberal thinkers, such as J.S. Mill (see p. 258), largely based their theories

---

Plato (427–347 BCE)

Greek philosopher. Plato was born of an aristocratic family. He became a follower of Socrates, who is the principal figure in his ethical and philosophical dialogues. After Socrates' death in 399 BCE, Plato founded his Academy in order to train the new Athenian ruling class, which might be considered the first 'university'.

Plato taught that the material world consists of imperfect copies of abstract and eternal 'ideas'. His political philosophy, as expounded in *The Republic*, is an attempt to describe the 'ideal state' in terms of a theory of justice. Plato's just state was decidedly authoritarian and was based upon a strict division of labour that supposedly reflected different character-types and human attributes. He argued that government should be exercised exclusively by a small collection of philosopher-kings, supported by the auxiliaries (collectively termed the 'Guardians'), whose education and communistic way of life would ensure that they ruled on the basis of wisdom. In his view, knowledge and virtue are one. In *The Laws*, he advocated a system of mixed government, but continued to emphasise the subordination of the individual to the state and law. Plato's work has exerted wide influence upon Christianity and upon European culture in general.

upon the idea that human beings are rational. This, for instance, explains why Mill himself placed so much faith in individual liberty: guided by reason, individuals would be able to seek happiness and self-realisation. In the same way, he argued in favour of female suffrage, on the grounds that, like men, women are rational and so are entitled to exercise political influence. In turn, socialist theories also built upon rationalist foundations. This was most evident in the writings of Marx and Engels (see p. 82), who developed what the latter referred to as 'scientific socialism'. Rather than indulging in ethical analysis and moral assertion, the province of so-called 'utopian socialism', Marx and Engels strove to uncover the dynamics of history and society through a process of scientific analysis. When they predicted the ultimate demise of capitalism, for example, this was not because they believed it to be morally 'bad', in the sense that it deserved to be overthrown, but instead because their analysis indicated that this was what was destined to happen, this was the direction in which history was moving.

This vision of human beings as thinking machines has, however, attracted growing criticism since the late nineteenth century. The Enlightenment dream of an ordered, rational and tolerant world was badly dented by the persistence of conflict and social deprivation and the emergence of powerful and seemingly non-rational forces such as nationalism and racialism. This led to growing interest in the influence which emotion, instinct and other psychological drives exerted upon politics. In some respects, however, this development built upon an established tradition, found mainly amongst conservative thinkers, that had always disparaged the mania for rationalism. Edmund Burke (see p. 139), for example, had emphasised the intellectual imperfection of human beings, especially when they are confronted by the almost infinite complexity of social life. In short, the world is unfathomable, too intricate and too confusing for the human mind fully to unravel. Such a view has deeply conservative implications. If the rationalist theories dreamed up by liberals and socialists are unconvincing, human beings are wise to place their faith in tradition and custom, the known. Revolution and even reform are a journey into the unknown; the maps we have been given are simply unreliable.

At the same time, conservative theorists were amongst the first to acknowledge the power of the non-rational. Thomas Hobbes (see p. 124), for instance, believed in the power of human reason, but only as a means to an end. In his view, human beings are driven by non-rational appetites: aversions, fears, hopes and desires, the strongest of which is the desire to exercise power over others. This essentially pessimistic view of human nature led Hobbes to conclude that only strong, autocratic government can prevent society descending into chaos and disorder. Burke also emphasised the degree to which unreasoned sentiments and even prejudice play a role in structuring social life. While what he called 'naked reason' offers little guidance, prejudice, being born of natural instincts, provides people with security and a sense of social identity. Some modern biologists have offered a scientific explanation for such beliefs. Konrad Lorenz, in particular, argued that aggression is a form of biologically adapted behaviour which has developed through the process of evolution. Human aggression and cruelty is therefore seen as innate or 'natural', an assertion that clearly has pessimistic implications for any attempt to curb domestic violence, cure social unrest or prevent war.

One of the most influential theories to stress the impact of non-rational drives upon human behaviour was Freudian psychology, developed in the early twentieth century. Sigmund Freud (1856–1939) drew attention to the distinction between the conscious mind, which carried out rational calculations and judgements, and the unconscious mind, which contained repressed memories and a range of powerful psychological drives. In particular, Freud highlighted the importance of human sexuality, represented by the *id*, the most primitive instinct within the unconscious, and *libido*, psychic energies emanating from the *id* and usually associated with sexual desire or energy. While Freud himself emphasised the therapeutic aspect of these ideas, developing a series of techniques, popularly known as psychoanalysis, others have seized upon their political significance. Wilhelm Reich (1897–1957), one of Freud's later disciples, developed an explanation of fascism based on the idea of repressed sexuality. As discussed in greater detail in Chapter 10, New Left thinkers like Herbert Marcuse (see p. 281) and feminists such as Germaine Greer (1985) have drawn upon Freudian psychology in developing a politics of sexual liberation.

Competition versus cooperation

The third area of disagreement centres upon whether human beings are essentially self-seeking and egoistical, or naturally sociable and cooperative. This debate is of fundamental political importance because these contrasting theories of human nature support radically different forms of economic and social organisation. If human beings are naturally self-interested, competition amongst them is an inevitable feature of social life and, in certain respects, a healthy one. Such a theory of human nature is, moreover, closely linked to individualist ideas such as natural rights and private property, and has often been used as a justification for a market or capitalist economic order, within which, supposedly, individuals have the best opportunity to pursue their own interests.

Theories which portray human nature as self-interested or self seeking can be found amongst the Ancient Greeks, expressed particularly by some of the Sophists. However, they were developed most systematically in the early modern period. In political thought this was reflected in the growth of natural rights theories, which suggested that each individual has been invested by God with a set of inalienable rights. These rights belong to the individual and to the individual alone. Utilitarianism (see p. 360), developed in the late eighteenth and early nineteenth centuries, attempted to provide an objective, even scientific, explanation of human selfishness. Jeremy Bentham (see p. 361) painted a picture of human beings as essentially hedonistic and pleasure-seeking creatures. In Bentham's view, pleasure or happiness are self-evidently 'good', and pain or unhappiness self-evidently 'bad'. Individuals therefore act to maximise pleasure and minimise pain, calculating each in terms of 'utility' – in its simplest sense, use-value. This view of human nature has had considerable impact upon both economic and political theories. Economics is very largely based upon the model of 'economic man', materially self-interested 'utility maximisers'. Such philosophical assumptions are used, for example, to explain the vigour and efficiency of market capitalism. They also underpin political theories ranging from the social contract theories of the seventeenth century to 'rational choice' (see p. 246) and 'public choice' schools of modern political science.

Scientific support for human self-interestedness has usually been based upon Darwin and the idea of some kind of struggle for survival. Darwinian ideas, however, can be interpreted in very different ways. Writers such as Lorenz and Ardrey hold that each individual member of a species is biologically programmed to ensure the survival of the species itself. Such a view suggests that animals, including human beings, ultimately act 'for the good of the species', an idea reflected in the willingness of a mother to sacrifice herself in the hope of protecting her young. In other words, individuals will exhibit cooperative and sociable behaviour to the extent that they put the species before themselves. On the other hand, modern writers such as Richard Dawkins (1989) have argued that every gene, including those unique to the separate individual, has a selfish streak and seeks its own survival. Such a theory suggests that selfishness and competition amongst individuals is essentially a form of biologically programmed behaviour. This is not to say, however, that human beings are blindly selfish. Although Dawkins accepted that individuals are 'born selfish', he emphasised that such behaviour can be modified if we 'teach generosity and altruism'.

A very different image of human nature is, however, presented by the major world religions. Monotheistic religions such as Christianity, Islam and Judaism, offer a picture of humankind as the product of divine creation. The human essence is therefore conceived as spiritual rather than mental or physical, and is represented in Christianity by the idea of a 'soul'. The notion that human beings are moral creatures, bound together by divine providence, has had considerable influence upon socialist doctrines which stress the importance of compassion, natural sympathy and a common humanity. Eastern religions such as Hinduism and Buddhism lay considerable emphasis upon the oneness of all forms of life, contributing once again to the idea of a common humanity, as well as a philosophy of non-violence. It is little surprise, therefore, that religious doctrines have often underpinned the theories of ethical socialism. It would be a mistake, however, to assume that all religious theories have socialist implications. For instance, the Protestant belief in individual salvation and its stress upon the moral value of personal striving and hard work, often called the 'Protestant ethic', is more clearly linked to the ideas of self-help and the free market than it is to socialist compassion. In addition, the Christian doctrine of original sin has generated a pessimistic view of humanity which, in turn, has considerable impact upon social and political thought. This can be seen in the writings of St Augustine (see p. 91) and Martin Luther.

Secular theories have also attempted to draw attention to the 'social essence' of human nature. These have traditionally stressed the importance of social being, drawing attention to the fact that individuals both live and work collectively, as members of a community. Selfishness and competition are in no way 'natural'; rather, they have been cultivated by a capitalist society that rewards and encourages self-striving. The human essence is sociable, gregarious and cooperative, a theory which clearly lends itself to either the communist goal of collective ownership, or the more modest socialist ideal of a welfare state. One of the few attempts to develop a scientific theory of human nature along the lines of sociability and cooperativeness was undertaken by Peter Kropotkin (see p. 169). Kropotkin accepted the evolutionary ideas that had dominated biology since Darwin, but had no sympathy for the doctrine of 'the survival of the fittest'. In *Mutual Aid* ([1897] 1902, 1988), he developed an evolutionary theory that fundamentally challenged Darwinism. Instead of accepting that survival is the result of struggle or competition, Kropotkin suggested that what distinguishes the human species from less successful species is its highly developed capacity for cooperation or 'mutual aid'. Cooperation is therefore not merely an ethical or religious ideal, it is a practical necessity which the evolutionary process has made an essential part of human nature. On this basis, Kropotkin argued in favour of both a communist society, in which wealth would be owned in common by all, and a form of anarchism in which human beings could manage their own affairs cooperatively and peacefully.

The Individual

The term 'the individual' is so widely used in everyday language that its implications and political significance are often ignored. In the most obvious sense, an individual is a single human being. Nevertheless, the concept suggests rather more. First of all, it implies that the single human being is an independent and meaningful entity, possessing an identity in himself or herself. In other words, to talk of people as individuals is to suggest that they are autonomous creatures, acting according to personal choice rather than as members of a social group or collective body. Secondly, individuals are not merely independent but they are also distinct, even unique. This is what is implied, for example, by the term 'individuality', which refers to what is particular and original about each and every human being. To see society as a collection of individuals is therefore to understand human beings in personal terms and to judge them according to their particular qualities, such as character, personality, talents, skills and so on. Each individual has a personal identity. Thirdly, to understand human beings as individuals is usually to believe in universalism, to accept that human beings everywhere share certain fundamental characteristics. In that sense, individuals are not defined by social background, race, religion, gender or any other 'accident of birth', but by what they share with people everywhere: their moral worth, their personal identity and their uniqueness.

The concept of the individual is one of the cornerstones of Western political culture. Although the term itself has been used since the seventeenth century, it has now become so familiar that it is invariably taken for granted. And yet, the concept of the individual has also provoked philosophical debate and deep ideological divisions. For instance, what does it mean to believe in the individual, to be committed to individualism? Does individualism imply a clear and distinctive style of political thought, or can it be used to support a wide range of positions and policies? Moreover, no political thinker sees the individual as entirely self-reliant; all acknowledge that, to some degree, social factors sustain and influence the individual. But where does the balance between the individual and the community lie, and where should it lie? Finally, how significant are individuals in political life? Is politics, in reality, shaped by the decisions and actions of separate individuals, or do only social groups, organisations and institutions matter? In short, can the individual make a difference?

Individualism

Individualism does not simply imply a belief in the existence of individuals. Rather, it refers to a belief in the primacy of the individual over any social group or collective body, suggesting that the individual is central to any political theory or social explanation. However, individualism does not have a clear political character. Although it has often been linked to the classical liberal tradition, and ideas such as limited government and the free market, it has also been used to justify state intervention and has, at times, been embraced by socialists. For example, some thinkers see individualism and collectivism as polar opposites, representing the battle lines between capitalism and socialism; others, however, believe that the two are complementary, even inseparable: individual goals can only be fulfilled through collective action. The problem is that there is no agreement about the nature of the 'individual'. The various forms which individualism has taken therefore reflect the range of views about the content of human nature.

All individualist doctrines extol the intrinsic value of the individual, emphasising the dignity, personal worth, even sacredness, of each human being. What they disagree about, however, is how these qualities can best be realised. Early liberals expressed their individualism in the doctrine of natural rights, which held that the purpose of social organisation was to protect the inalienable rights of the individual. Social contract theory can, for instance, be seen as a form of political individualism. Government is seen to arise out of the consent of individual citizens, and its role is limited to the protection of their rights. However, if this form of individualism is pushed to its logical extreme, it can have libertarian and even anarchist implications. For example, nineteenth-century American individualists such as David Henry Thoreau (1817–62) and Benjamin Tucker (1854–1939) believed that no individual should sacrifice his or her conscience to the judgement of politicians, elected or otherwise, a position which denies that government can ever exercise rightful authority over the individual.

This anti-statist individualist tradition has also been closely linked to the defence of market capitalism. Such individualism has usually been based upon the assumption that individual human beings are self-reliant and self-interested. C.B. Macpherson (1973) termed this 'possessive individualism', which he defined as 'a conception of the individual as essentially the proprietor of his own person or capacities, owing nothing to society for them'. If individuals are essentially egoistical, placing their own interests before those of fellow human beings or society, economic individualism is clearly linked to the right of private property, the freedom to acquire, use and dispose of property however the individual may choose. As such, individualism became, in Britain and the United States in particular, an article of faith for those who revered *laissez-faire* capitalism. Laws which regulate economic and social life – by stipulating wage levels, the length of the working day, interfering with working conditions or introducing

Liberalism

Liberal ideas resulted from the breakdown of feudalism in Europe and the growth, in its place, of a market capitalist society. In its earliest form, liberalism was a political doctrine, which attacked absolutism (see p. 164) and feudal privilege, instead advocating constitutional and, later, representative government. By the nineteenth century, a distinctively liberal political creed had developed that extolled the virtues of *laissez-faire* capitalism and condemned all forms of economic and social intervention. This became the centrepiece of classical, or nineteenth-century, liberalism. From the late nineteenth century onwards, however, a form of social liberalism emerged which looked more favourably on welfare reform and economic management. This became the characteristic theme of modern, or twentieth-century, liberalism.

Liberal thought is characterised by a commitment to individualism, a belief in the supreme importance of the human individual, implying strong support for individual freedom. From the liberal viewpoint, individuals are rational creatures who are entitled to the greatest possible freedom consistent with a like freedom for fellow citizens. Classical liberalism is distinguished by a belief in a 'minimal' state, whose function is limited to the maintenance of domestic order and personal security. Classical liberals emphasise that human beings are essentially self-interested and largely self-sufficient; as far as possible, people should be responsible for their own lives and circumstances. As a result, liberals look towards the creation of a meritocratic society in which rewards are distributed according to individual talent and hard work. As an economic doctrine, classical liberalism extols the merits of a self-regulating market in which government intervention is both unnecessary and damaging. Classical liberal ideas are expressed in certain natural rights theories and utilitarianism (see p. 360), and provide a cornerstone of the libertarian political tradition (see p. 340).

Modern liberalism, however, exhibits a more sympathetic attitude towards the state. This shift was born out of the recognition that industrial capitalism had merely generated new forms of injustice and left the mass of the population subject to the vagaries of the market. This view provided the basis for social or welfare liberalism, which is characterised by the recognition that state intervention can enlarge liberty by safeguarding individuals from the social evils that blight their existence. The theoretical basis for the transition from classical to modern liberalism was provided by the development of a 'positive' view of freedom. Whereas classical liberals had understood freedom in 'negative' terms, as the absence of external constraints upon the individual, modern liberals linked freedom to personal development and self-realisation. This created clear overlaps between modern liberalism and social democracy (see p. 312).

Liberalism has undoubtedly been the most important element in Western political tradition. Indeed, some identify liberalism with Western civilisation in general. One of the implications of this is that liberalism strives not to prescribe any particular conception of the good life, but to establish

→

conditions in which individuals and groups can pursue the good life as each defines it. The great virtue of liberalism is its unrelenting commitment to individual freedom, reasoned debate and toleration. Criticisms of liberalism have nevertheless come from various directions. Marxists (see p. 81) have criticised the liberal commitment to civic rights and political equality because it ignores the reality of unequal class power; feminists (see p. 60) argue that individualism is invariably construed on the basis of a male model of self-sufficiency which ignores the reality of human interdependence; and communitarians (see p. 34) condemn liberalism for failing to provide a moral basis for social order and collective endeavour.

Key figures

John Stuart Mill (see p. 258)   Mill's importance to liberalism largely rests upon his construction of a liberal theory squarely based upon the virtues of liberty, as opposed to earlier ideas such as natural rights and utilitarianism. His conception of 'man as a progressive being' led him to recoil from interventionism, but encouraged him to develop a notion of individuality that stresses the prospects for human development and provides an important foundation for modern liberal thought.

Thomas Hill Green (1836-82)   A British philosopher and social theorist, Green highlighted the limitations of early liberal doctrines and particularly *laissez-faire*. By drawing upon Kant (see p. 117) and Hegel (see p. 4), he highlighted the limitations of the doctrine of 'negative' freedom, and developed a pioneering defence of 'positive' freedom which helped liberalism to reach an accommodation with welfarism and social justice. Green was an important influence upon the development in Britain of 'new liberalism'. His chief works include *Lectures on the Principles of Political Obligation* (1879–80) and *Prolegomena to Ethics* (1883).

Isaiah Berlin (1909–97)   A Riga-born British philosopher and historian of ideas, Berlin developed a form of pluralist liberalism that is based upon the anti-perfectionist belief that conflicts of value are an intrinsic, irremovable element in human life. As there is no standard against which values can be judged or ranked, political arrangements should attempt to secure the greatest scope to allow people to pursue their differing ends. In his influential analysis of liberty, Berlin supported 'negative' liberty over 'positive' liberty, on the grounds that the latter has monistic and authoritarian implications. Berlin's best known works include *Four Essays on Liberty* (1969), *Against the Current* (1979) and *The Crooked Timber of Humanity* (1990).

John Rawls (see p. 299)   Rawls is the most important liberal philosopher of the second half of the twentieth century. His theory of 'justice as fairness' not only condemns racial, sexual and religious discrimination, but also rejects many forms of social and economic inequality. Rawls' egalitarian form of liberalism has had a profound effect upon political philosophy generally, and has made a significant contribution to both the modern liberal and social democratic political traditions.

$\longrightarrow$

Further reading

Arblaster, A. *The Rise and Decline of Western Liberalism.* Oxford: Basil Blackwell, 1984.

Gray, J. *Liberalism*, 2nd edn. Milton Keynes: Open University Press, 1995.

Rosenblum, N. (ed.) *Liberalism and the Moral Life.* New York: Cambridge University Press, 1990.

benefits and pensions – are, from this point of view, a threat to individualism.

Very different implications, however, have sometimes been drawn from the doctrine of individualism. For example, modern liberals, such as T.H. Green (see p. 30) and L.T. Hobhouse (1864–1929), used individualism to construct arguments in favour of social welfare and state intervention. They saw the individual not as narrowly self-interested, but as socially responsible, capable of an altruistic concern for fellow human beings. Their principal goal was what J.S. Mill had termed 'individuality', the capacity of each individual to achieve fulfilment and realise whatever potential he or she may possess. Individualism was therefore transformed from a doctrine of individual greed to a philosophy of individual self-development. As a result, modern liberals have been prepared to support government action designed to promote equality of opportunity and protect individuals from the social evils that blight their lives, such as unemployment, poverty, ignorance. Some socialist thinkers have embraced the notion of individualism for the same reason. If human beings are, as socialists argue, naturally sociable and gregarious, individualism stands not for possessiveness and self-interest but for fraternal cooperation and, perhaps, communal living. This is why the French socialist Jean Jaurès (1859–1914) could proclaim, 'socialism is the logical completion of individualism'.

Individualism is not, however, only of importance as a normative principle; it has also been widely used as a methodological device. In other words, social or political theories have been constructed on the basis of a pre-established model of the human individual, taking account of whatever needs, drives, aspirations and so forth the individual is thought to possess. Such 'methodological individualism' was employed in the seventeenth century to construct social contract theories and in the twentieth century has become the basis for rational-choice models of political science. The individualist method underpinned classical and neo-classical economic theories, and has been championed in the modern period by writers such as Hayek (see p. 341). In each case, conclusions have been drawn from assumptions about a 'fixed' or 'given' human nature, usually highlighting the capacity for rationally self-interested behaviour. However, the drawback of any form of methodological individualism is that it is both asocial and ahistorical. By building political theories on the basis of a pre-established model of human nature, individualists ignore the fact that human behaviour varies from society to society, and from one historical period to the next. If historical and social factors shape the content of human nature, as advocates of 'nurture' theories suggest, the human individual should be seen as a product of society, not the other way around.

Individual and community

Support for individualism has not, however, been universal. Political thought is deeply divided about the relationship between the individual and the community: should the individual be encouraged to be independent and self-reliant, or will this make social solidarity impossible and leave individuals isolated and insecure? Advocates of the former position have normally subscribed to a particular Anglo-American tradition of individualism, described by US President Herbert Hoover as 'rugged individualism'. This tradition can be thought of as an extreme form of individualism, its roots being found in classical liberalism. It sees the individual as almost entirely separate from society, and so discounts or downgrades the importance of community. It is based upon the belief that individuals not only possess the capacity for self-reliance and hard work, but also that individual effort is the source of moral and personal development. Not only *can* individuals look after themselves, but they *should* do.

The bible of this individualist tradition is Samuel Smiles's *Self-Help* ([1859] 1986), which proclaimed that, 'The spirit of self-help is the root of all genuine growth in the individual'. Smiles (1812–1904) extolled the Victorian virtues of enterprise, application and perseverance, underpinned by the belief that 'energy accomplishes more than genius'. While self-help promotes the mental and moral development of the individual, and through promoting the entrepreneurial spirit benefits the entire nation, 'help from without', by which Smiles meant social welfare, enfeebles the individual by removing the incentive, or even need, to work. Such ideas found their highest expression in the social Darwinism of Herbert Spencer and his followers. For them, individualism had a biological basis in the form of a struggle for survival amongst all individuals. Those fitted by nature to survive should succeed; the weak and lazy should go to the wall.

Such ideas have had considerable impact upon New Right thinking. In particular, they helped to shape the social policies adopted in the United States under Reagan and Bush, and in Britain under Thatcher and Major.

In both cases, the enemy was thought to be the 'dependency culture' which over-generous welfare support had created; the poor, disadvantaged and unemployed had been turned into 'welfare junkies', robbed of the desire to work and denied dignity and self-respect. Reagan's 'frontier ideology' was very clearly based upon the merits of hard work and individual enterprise. His 'new federalism' reflected the desire to cut back on welfare programmes and reduce dependency by shifting social responsibilities from the Federal Government to the less prosperous State Governments. Individual responsibility was also the cornerstone of Thatcherism in Britain. During the 1980s and into the 1990s, levels of family allowance, unemployment and other benefits have failed to keep pace with the rate of inflation, and the social security system has been dramatically shaken up in an attempt to discourage dependency and promote a willingness to work. Critics of such policies, however, point out that so long as social inequality and deprivation continue to exist, it is difficult to see how individuals can be held entirely responsible for their own circumstances. This line of argument shifts attention away from the individual and towards the community.

A wide range of political thinkers — socialists, conservatives, nationalists and, most emphatically, fascists — have, at different times, styled themselves as anti-individualists. In most cases, anti-individualism is based upon a commitment to the importance of community and the belief that self-help and individual responsibility are a threat to social solidarity. 'Community' may refer, very loosely, to a collection of people in a given location, as when the populations of a particular town, city or nation are described as a community. However, in social and political thought the term usually has deeper implications, suggesting a social group, a neighbourhood, town, region, group of workers or whatever, within which there are strong ties and a collective identity. A genuine community is therefore distinguished by the bonds of comradeship, loyalty and duty. In that sense, community refers to the social roots of individual identity.

Amongst contemporary critics of liberal individualism have been communitarian theorists who stress the importance of common or collective interests. In that view, there is no such thing as an unencumbered self; the self is always constituted through the community. Not surprisingly, socialists have also taken up the cause of community, seeing it as a means of strengthening social responsibility and harnessing collective energies. This is why socialists have often rejected individualism, especially when it is narrowly linked to self-interest and self-reliance. Although modern social democrats acknowledge the importance of individual enterprise and market competition, they nevertheless seek to balance these against the cooperation and altruism which only a sense of community can foster. Individualism has also been regarded with suspicion by many conservative

Communitarianism

The communitarian tradition has its origins in the nineteenth-century socialist utopianism (see p. 169) of thinkers such as Robert Owen and Peter Kropotkin. Indeed, a concern with community can be seen as one of the enduring themes in modern political thought, expressed variously in the socialist stress upon fraternity and cooperation, the Marxist (see p. 81) belief in a classless communist society, the conservative (see p. 138) view of society as an organic whole, bound together by mutual obligations, and even in the fascist commitment to an indivisible national community. However, communitarianism as a school of thought articulating a particular political philosophy emerged only in the 1980s and 1990s. It developed specifically as a critique of liberalism (see p. 29), highlighting the damage done to the public culture of liberal societies by their emphasis upon individual rights and liberties over the needs of the community. So-called 'high' and 'low' forms of communitarianism are sometimes identified: the former engages primarily in philosophical debate, while the latter, whose best known figure is Amitai Etzioni, is more concerned with issues of public policy.

From the communitarian perspective, the central defect of liberalism is its view of the individual as an asocial, atomised, 'unencumbered self'. Such a view is evident in the utilitarian (see p. 360) assumption that human beings are rationally self-seeking creatures. Communitarians emphasise, by contrast, that the self is embedded in the community, in the sense that each individual is a kind of embodiment of the society that has shaped his or her desires, values and purposes. This draws attention not merely to the process of socialisation, but also to the conceptual impossibility of separating an individual's experiences and beliefs from the social context that assigns them meaning. The communitarian stance has particular implications for our understanding of justice. Liberal theories of justice tend to be based upon assumptions about personal choice and individual behaviour that, communitarians argue, make no sense because they apply to a disembodied subject. Universalist theories of justice must therefore give way to ones that are strictly local and particular, a position similar to that advanced by postmodern theories (see p. 12).

Communitarians argue that their aim is to rectify an imbalance in modern society and political thought in which individuals, unconstrained by social duty and moral responsibility, have been allowed or encouraged to take account only of their own interests and their own rights. In this moral vacuum, society, quite literally, disintegrates. The communitarian project thus attempts to restore to society its moral voice and, in a tradition that can be traced back to Aristotle (see p. 68), to construct a 'politics of the common good'. Critics of communitarianism, however, allege that it has both conservative and authoritarian implications. Communitarianism has a conservative disposition in that it amounts to a defence of *existing* social structures and moral codes. Feminists, for example, have criticised communitarianism for attempting to bolster traditional sex roles under the guise of defending the family. The authoritarian features of communitarianism stem from its tendency to emphasise the duties and responsibilities of the individual over his or her rights and entitlements.

→

Key figures

Alasdair MacIntyre (1929–) A Scottish-born moral philosopher, MacIntyre has developed a neoclassical and anti-liberal communitarian philosophy. In his view, liberalism preaches moral relativism and so is unable to provide a moral basis for social order. He argues that notions of justice and virtue are specific to particular intellectual traditions, and has developed a model of the good life that is rooted in Aristotle and the Christian tradition of Augustine (see p. 91) and Aquinas (see p. 158). MacIntyre's major works include *After Virtue* (1981), *Whose Justice? Which Rationality?* (1988) and *Three Rival Versions of Moral Enquiry* (1990).

Charles Taylor (1931–) A Canadian political philosopher and committed Roman Catholic, Taylor has been primarily concerned with the issue of the construction of the self. He portrays persons as 'embodied individuals' whose identity is largely shaped by history and the social and linguistic context in which they live; true freedom must therefore be 'situated'. However, in contrast to some other communitarians, he treats the individual, not society, as the key source of moral action. Taylor's best known writings include *Philosophical Papers* (1985), *Sources of the Self* (1989) and *Philosophical Arguments* (1995).

Michael Walzer (1935–) A US political theorist, Walzer has developed a form of communalist and pluralistic liberalism. He rejects as misguided the quest for a universal theory of justice, arguing instead for the principle of 'complex equality', according to which different rules should apply to the distribution of different social goods, thereby establishing separate 'spheres' of justice. He nevertheless evinces sympathy for a form of democratic socialism. Walzer's major works include *Spheres of Justice* (1983) and *Interpretation and Social Criticism* (1987).

Michael Sandel (1953–) A US political theorist, Sandel has fiercely criticised individualism, the notion of the 'unencumbered self'. He argues for conceptions of moral and social life that are firmly embedded in distinctive communities, and emphasises that individual choice and identity are structured by the 'moral ties' of the community. Sandel has also warned that a lack of embeddedness means that democracy may not long endure, and supports 'civic republicanism' (see p. 208), which he associates with the US political tradition. Sandel's most influential works include *Liberalism and the Limits of Justice* (1982) and *Democracy's Discontent* (1996).

Further reading

Avineri, S. and De-Shalit, A. (eds) *Communitarianism and Individualism.* Oxford: Oxford University Press, 1992.

Kamenka, E. (ed.) *Community as a Social Ideal.* London: Edward Arnold, 1982.

Tam, H. *Communitarianism: A New Agenda for Politics and Citizenship.* London: Macmillan, 1998.

theorists. From their point of view, unrestrained individualism is destructive of the social fabric. Individuals are timid and insecure creatures, who seek the rootedness and stability which only a community identity can provide. If individualism promotes a philosophy of 'each for his own' it will simply lead to 'atomism', and produce a society of vulnerable and isolated individuals. This has, for example, encouraged neo-conservatives, such as Irving Kristol (see p. 139) in the United States and Roger Scruton in Britain, to distance themselves from the free-market enthusiasms of the liberal New Right.

Socialist and conservative concepts of community have been influenced at several points by academic sociology. Sociologists have distinguished between the forms of community life which develop within traditional or rural societies, and those found in modern urban societies. The most influential such theory was that developed by the German sociologist Ferdinand Tönnies (1855–1939), who distinguished between what he called *Gemeinschaft* or 'community', and *Gesellschaft* or 'association'. Tönnies suggested that *Gemeinschaft*-relationships, typically found in rural communities, are based upon the strong bonds of natural affection and mutual respect. This traditional sense of 'community' was, however, threatened by the spread of industrialisation and urbanisation, both of which encouraged a growth of egoism and competition. The *Gesellschaft*-relationships which develop in urban societies are, by contrast, artificial and contractual; they reflect the desire for personal gain rather than any meaningful social loyalty. The French sociologist Émile Durkheim (1858–1917) also contributed to the understanding of community by developing the concept of 'anomie' to denote a condition in which the framework of social codes and norms breaks down entirely. In *Suicide* ([1897] 1951), Durkheim argued that, since human desires are unlimited, the breakdown of community, weakening social and moral norms about which forms of behaviour are acceptable and which are not, is likely to lead to greater unhappiness and, ultimately, more suicides. Once again, community rather than individualism was seen as the basis for social stability and individual happiness.

On the other hand, it is clear that a stress upon community rather than the individual may also entail dangers. In particular, it can lead to individual rights and liberties being violated in the name of the community or collective body. This was most graphically demonstrated through the experience of fascist rule. In many ways, fascism is the antithesis of individualism: in its German form it proclaimed the supreme importance of the *Völksgemeinschaft* or 'national community', and aimed to dissolve individuality, and indeed personal existence, within the social whole. This goal, distinctive to fascism, was expressed in the Nazi slogan 'Strength through Unity'. The method used to achieve this end in Nazi Germany and Fascist Italy was totalitarian terror: a police state employing repression, persecution and widespread brutality Although the fascist conception of community may be little more than a grotesque misrepresentation of the socialist idea of voluntary cooperation, extreme individualists have sometimes warned that any stress upon the collective has oppressive implications since it threatens to downgrade the importance of the individual.

The individual in politics

Questions about the role of the individual in history have engaged generations of philosophers and thinkers. Clearly, such questions are of no less importance to the study of politics. Should political analysis focus upon the aspirations, convictions and deeds of leading individuals, or should it rather examine the 'impersonal forces' that structure individual behaviour? At the outset, two fundamentally different approaches to this issue can be dismissed. The first sees politics entirely in personal terms. It holds that history is made by human individuals who, in effect, impress their own wills upon the political process. Such an approach is evident in the emphasis upon 'great men' and their deeds. From this point of view, US politics boils down to the personal contribution of presidents like Roosevelt and Kennedy, or Reagan and Clinton; while British politics should be understood through the actions of prime ministers such as Churchill, Wilson, Thatcher, Blair and so on. In its most extreme form, this approach to politics has led to the fascist *Führerprinzip*, or 'leader principle'. Fascists portray leaders such as Mussolini and Hitler as supremely gifted individuals, all-powerful and all-knowing. However, to see politics exclusively in terms of leadership and personality is to ignore the wealth of cultural, economic, social and historical factors that undoubtedly help to shape political developments. Moreover, it tends to imply that the individual comes into the world ready formed, owing nothing to society for his or her talents, qualities, attributes or whatever.

The second approach discounts the individual altogether. History is shaped by social, economic and other factors, meaning that individual actors are either irrelevant or merely act as puppets. An example of this approach to politics was found in the crude and mechanical Marxist theories that developed in the Soviet Union and other communist states. This amounted to a belief in economic determinism: political, legal, intellectual and cultural life were thought to be *determined* by the 'economic mode of production'. All of history and every aspect of individual behaviour was therefore understood in terms of the developing class struggle. Such theories are, however, based upon a highly deterministic, indeed Pavlovian, view of human nature that does not allow for the existence of a personal identity, or the exercise of any kind of free will.

Furthermore, they imply a belief in historical inevitability which even a passing knowledge of politics would bring into doubt. But where does this leave us? If individuals are neither the masters of history nor puppets controlled by it, what scope is left to the individual action? In all circumstances a balance must exist between personal and impersonal factors.

If individuals 'make politics' they do so under certain, very specific conditions, intellectual, institutional, social and historical. In the first place there is the relationship between individuals and their cultural inheritance. Political leaders are rarely major or original thinkers, examples like V.I. Lenin (see p. 82) being very much the exception. Practical politicians are therefore guided in their behaviour and decision-making, often unknowingly, by what the economist Keynes referred to as 'academic scribblers'. Margaret Thatcher did not invent Thatcherism, any more than Ronald Reagan was responsible for Reaganomics. In both cases, their ideas relied upon the classical economics of Adam Smith (see p. 340) and David Ricardo (1772–1823), as updated by twentieth-century economists such as Hayek and Friedman. Ideas, philosophies and ideologies are clearly no less important in political life than power, leadership and personality. This is not, however, to say that politics is simply shaped by those individuals who dream up the ideas in the first place. Without doubt, the ideas of thinkers such as Rousseau (see p. 243), Marx, Keynes and Hayek have 'changed history', by both inspiring and guiding political action. Nevertheless, at the same time, these individual thinkers were themselves influenced by the intellectual traditions of their time, as well as by the reigning historical and social circumstances. For example, Karl Marx, whose intellectual heritage dominated much of twentieth-century politics, constructed his theories on the basis of existing ideas, in particular, the philosophy of G.W.F. Hegel (see p. 4), the political economy of Smith and Ricardo, and the ideas of early French socialists such as Saint-Simon and Fourier.

Secondly, there is the relationship between individuals and institutions. It is often difficult to distinguish between the personal impact of a political leader and the authority or influence he or she derives from his or her office. For instance, the power of US presidents and British prime ministers is essentially derived from their office rather than their personalities. Similarly, the personality of Soviet leaders was perhaps of less significance in influencing Soviet politics than was the Communist Party's monopoly of power. The party was, after all, the source of the leader's wide-ranging authority. This is what the German sociologist Max Weber (1864–1920) meant when he suggested that in modern industrial societies legal-rational authority had largely displaced charismatic and traditional forms of authority. In this light, individual political leaders may be of less importance than the parties they lead, the government institutions they control, and the constitutions within which they operate. Nevertheless, individual leaders can and do make a difference.

There is no doubt, for example, that institutional powers are to some extent elastic, capable of being stretched or enlarged by leaders who possess particular drive, energy and conviction. This is what H.H. Asquith meant when he declared that the office of the British prime minister was whatever its holder chose to make of it. Charismatic and determined prime ministers have undoubtedly stretched the powers of the office to its very limits, as Thatcher demonstrated between 1979 and 1990. US presidents like F.D. Roosevelt and Lyndon Johnson were undoubtedly able to extend the powers of their office by the exercise of personal skills and qualities. In other cases, of course, leaders have helped to found or restructure the very institutions they lead. Lenin, for instance, founded the Bolshevik Party in 1903 and, between the 1917 Revolution and his death in 1924, was responsible for creating the institutions of Soviet government and mould- ing its constitutional structure. In the case of dictators like Hitler in Germany, Perón in Argentina and Saddam Hussein in Iraq, leaders have sought to wield absolute power by emancipating themselves from any constitutionally defined notion of leadership, attempting to rule on the basis of charismatic authority alone.

Thirdly, there is the individual's relationship with society. There is a sense in which no individual can be understood in isolation from his or her social environment: no one comes into the world ready formed. Those who, like socialists, emphasise the importance of a 'social essence' are particularly inclined to see individual behaviour as representative of social forces or interests. As pointed out earlier, in its extreme form, such a view sees the individual as nothing more than a plaything of impersonal social and historical forces. Although Marx himself did not subscribe to a narrow determinism, he certainly believed that the scope for individual action was limited, warning that 'the tradition of all the dead generations weighs like a nightmare on the brain of the living'. Politics, however, has an infinite capacity to surprise and to confound all predictions precisely because it is a personal activity. Ultimately, politics is 'made' by individuals, individuals who are clearly part of the historical process but who, nevertheless, possess some kind of capacity to shape events according to their own dreams and inclinations. It is impossible, for example, to believe that the course of Russian history would have been unaffected had V.I. Lenin never been born. Similarly, if F.D. Roosevelt had died from polio in 1920 instead of being paralysed, would America have responded as it did to the Great Depression and the outbreak of the Second World War? Would the shape of British politics in the 1980s have been the same had Margaret Thatcher decided to become a lawyer instead of going into politics? Would the

Labour Party's 'modernisation' have proceeded as it did had John Smith not died in 1994 and had Tony Blair not succeeded him?

Society

However resilient and independent individuals may be, human existence outside society is unthinkable. Human beings are not isolated Robinson Crusoes, able to live in complete and permanent isolation – even the skills and knowledge which enabled Robinson Crusoe to survive were acquired through education and social interaction before his shipwreck. However, the concept of society is often little better understood than that of the individual. In its most general sense, 'society' denotes a collection of people occupying the same territorial area. Not just any group of people, however, constitutes a society. Societies are characterised by regular patterns of social interaction, suggesting the existence of some kind of social 'structure'. Moreover, 'social' relationships involve mutual aware-ness and at least some measure of cooperation. Warring tribes, for example, do not constitute a 'society', even though they may live in close proximity to one another and interact on a regular basis. On the other hand, the internationalisation of tourism and of economic life, and the spread of transnational cultural and intellectual exchange, has created the idea of an emerging 'global society'. Nevertheless, the cooperative interaction that defines 'social' behaviour need not necessarily be reinforced by a common identity or sense of loyalty. This is what distinguishes 'society' from the stronger notion of 'community', which requires at least a measure of affinity or social solidarity, an identification with the community.

In political theory, however, society is often understood in a more specific sense, as what is called 'civil society'. In its original form, civil society referred to a political community, a community living within a framework of law and exhibiting a common allegiance to a state. Early political thinkers regarded such an ordered society as the basis of civilised life. Modern theorists, however, have tended to draw a clearer distinction between society and the state. In the tradition of Hegel and Marx, civil society takes place *outside* the state and refers to a realm of autonomous associations and groups, formed by individuals in their capacity as private citizens. Although Hegel treated civil society as separate from the family, most take the term to include the full range of economic, social, cultural, recreational and domestic institutions. The nature and significance of such institutions is, however, a matter of considerable dispute. This often revolves around the relationship between the individual and collective bodies or entities. For instance, can individualism and collectivism be reconciled, or must 'the individual' and 'society' always stand in opposition to one another? Moreover, society itself has been understood in a bewildering number of ways, each of which has important political implications. Is society, for example, a human artefact or an organic entity? Is it based upon consensus or conflict? Is society egalitarian or naturally hierarchic? Finally, attention is often drawn to the political significance of social divisions or cleavages, notably social class, gender, race, religion, nationality and language. In some cases, these are thought to hold the key to political understanding. Why are social cleavages important, and which ones have greatest impact upon politics?

Collectivism

Few political terms have caused as much confusion as collectivism, or been accorded such a broad range of meanings. For some, collectivism refers to the actions of the state and reached its highest form of development in the centrally planned economies of orthodox communist states, so-called 'state collectivism'. Others, however, use collectivism to refer to communitarianism, a preference for community action rather than self-striving, an idea that has had libertarian, even anarchist, implications, as in the 'collectivist anarchism' of Michael Bakunin (1814–76). In addition, collectivism is sometimes used as a synonym for socialism, though, to confuse matters further, this is done by critics of socialism to highlight what they see as its statist tendencies, while socialists themselves employ the term to underline their commitment to the common or collective interests of humanity. Nevertheless, it is possible to point to a common core of collectivist ideas, as well as to identify a number of competing interpretations and traditions.

At heart, collectivism stresses the capacity of human beings for collective action, stressing their willingness and ability to pursue goals by working together rather than striving for personal self interest. All forms of collectivism therefore subscribe to the notion that human beings are social animals, identifying with fellow human beings and bound together by a collective identity. The social group, whatever it might be, is meaningful, even essential, to human existence. This form of collectivism is found in a wide range of political ideologies. It is, quite clearly, fundamental to socialism. A stress upon social identity and the importance of collective action is evident in the use of the term 'comrade' to denote the common identity of those who work for social change; in the notion of 'class solidarity' to highlight the common interests of all working people; and, of course, in the idea of a 'common humanity'. Feminism also embraces collectivist ideas in stressing the importance of 'gender' and 'sisterhood', acknowledging the common identity which all women share and underlining their capacity to undertake collective political action. Similarly, nationalist and racialist doctrines draw upon a collectivist vision by interpreting humanity in terms of 'nations' or 'races'. All forms of collectivism are therefore at odds with the extreme form of individualism that portrays human beings as independent and self-striving creatures. If, however, people are thought to be naturally sociable and cooperative, collectivism may be a source of personal fulfilment rather than a denial of individuality.

The link between collectivism and the state is not, however, accidental. The state has often been seen as the agency through which collective action is organised, in which case it represents the collective interests of society rather than those of any individual. This is why New Right theorists in particular tend to portray state intervention in its various forms as evidence of collectivism. The growth of social welfare, the adoption of Keynesian techniques of economic management, and the extension of nationalisation, have thus been interpreted as 'the rise of collectivism'. From this point of view, the command economy which developed in the Soviet Union marks the highest form of collectivism. Collectivism, in this statist sense, is usually regarded as the antithesis of individualism. As the state represents sovereign, compulsory and coercive authority, it is always the enemy of individual liberty. Where the state commands, individual initiative and freedom of choice are constrained. However, this is to view the state in exclusively negative terms. If, on the other hand, the state advances the cause of individual self-development, say, by providing education or social welfare, collectivism could be regarded as entirely compatible with individualism.

Any collectivist doctrine that links it exclusively to the state must, however, be misleading. The state is, at best, only an agency through which collective action is organised. The danger of the state is that it can substitute itself for 'the collective', taking decisions and responsibilities away from ordinary citizens. In that sense, collectivism stands for collective action undertaken by free individuals out of a recognition that they possess common interests or a collective identity. This broader form of collectivism is more closely linked to the idea of self-management than it is to state control. Self-managing collectivism has been particularly attractive to anarchists and libertarian socialists. Bakunin, for instance, looked towards the creation of a stateless society in which the economy would be organised according to the principles of workers' self-management, and clearly distinguished this collectivist vision from what he saw as the authoritarianism implicit in Marxist socialism. It is also the form of collectivism found in the *kibbutz* system in Israel. Needless to say, these collectivist ideas share no similarity whatsoever with styles of individualism which emphasise personal self-reliance and individual self-interest. However, by remaining faithful to the ideals of self-management and voluntary action, this form of collectivism need not have anti-individualist implications.

Theories of society

A theory of society is of no less importance to political analysis than is a conception of human nature. Political life is intimately related to social life; politics is, after all, little more than a reflection of the tensions and conflicts which society generates. However, the interaction between politics, society and the individual is a matter of fierce disagreement and deep ideological controversy. What conflicts exist in society? Who are these conflicts between? Can these conflicts be overcome, or are they a permanent feature of political existence?

A first range of theories are based upon an individualist conception of society. These assume that society is a human artefact, constructed by individuals to serve their interests or purposes. In its extreme form this can lead to the belief, expressed by Margaret Thatcher, that 'there is no such thing as society'. In other words, all social and political behaviour can be understood in terms of the choices made by self-interested individuals, without reference to collective entities such as 'society'. The clearest example of such a theory is found in classical liberalism, which is committed to the goal of achieving the greatest possible individual freedom. Although a state is needed to guarantee a framework of order, individuals should, as far as possible, be able to pursue their own interests in their own way. This has often been described as an 'atomistic' theory of society, in that it implies that society is nothing more than a collection of individual units or atoms.

Such a view does not, however, ignore the fact that individuals pursue their interests through the formation of groups and associations, businesses, trade unions, clubs, and so forth. The cement which holds this society together, though, is self-interest, the recognition that private interests overlap, making possible the construction of contracts or voluntary agreements. Clearly, this notion of society is founded upon a strong belief in consensus, the belief that there is a natural balance or harmony amongst the competing individuals and groups in society. This was expressed in the the eighteenth century in Adam Smith's idea of an 'invisible hand' operating in the marketplace, interpreted in the twentieth century by Hayek as the 'spontaneous order' of economic life. Although workers and employers seek conflicting goals – the worker wants higher wages and the employer lower costs – they are nevertheless bound together by the fact that workers need jobs and employers need labour. Such a view of society has very clear political implications. In particular, if society can afford individuals the opportunity to pursue self-interest without generating fundamental conflict, surely Thomas Jefferson's (see p. 192) motto that 'That government is best which governs least' is correct.

A fundamentally different theory of society is based upon an organic analogy. Instead of being constructed by rational individuals to satisfy their personal interests, society may operate as an 'organic whole', exhibiting properties more normally associated with living organisms – a human being or plant. This suggests a holistic approach to society, emphasising that societies are complex networks of relationships which ultimately exist to maintain the whole: the whole is more important than its individual parts. The organic analogy was first used by Ancient Greek thinkers who referred to the 'body politic'. Some anthropologists and sociologists have subscribed to similar ideas in developing the functionalist view of society. This assumes that all social activity plays some part in maintaining the basic structures of society, and can therefore be understood in terms of its 'function'. The organic view of society has been accepted by a wide range of political thinkers, notably traditional conservatives and fascists, particularly those who have supported corporatism. There is, indeed, a sense in which organicism has clearly conservative implications. For example, it tends to legitimise the existing moral and social order, implying that it has been constructed by the forces of natural necessity. Institutions such as the family, the church and the aristocracy, as well as traditional values and culture, therefore serve to underpin social stability. Moreover, this view implies that society is naturally hierarchic. The various elements of society – social classes, sexes, economic bodies, political institutions, and the like – each have a specific role to play, a particular 'station in life'. Equality amongst them is as absurd as the idea that the heart, liver, stomach, brain and lungs are equal within the body; they may be equally important but clearly fulfil entirely different functions and purposes.

While both individualist and organic theories of society suggest the existence of an underlying social consensus, rival theories highlight the role of conflict. This can be seen, for instance, in the pluralist theory of society which draws attention to conflict between the various groups and interests in society. However, pluralists do not see such conflict as fundamental because, in the final analysis, they believe that an open and competitive political system is capable of ensuring social balance and of preventing a descent into unrest and violence. Elite theories of society, on the other hand, highlight the concentration of power in the hands of a small minority, and so underline the existence of conflict between 'the elite' and 'the masses'. Elite theorists are therefore more prepared to explain social order in terms of organisational advantage, manipulation and open coercion rather than consensus. Fascist thinkers nevertheless subscribe to a form of elitism which implies organic harmony, since they believe that the masses will willingly accept their subordination. The most influential conflict theory of society, however, has been Marxism (see p. 81). Marx believed that the roots of social conflict lie in the existence of private property, leading to fundamental and irreconcilable class conflict. Quite simply, those who produce wealth in any society, the workers, are systematically exploited and oppressed by the property owners. Marx argued that workers are not paid in accordance with their contribution to the productive process, their 'surplus value' is expropriated. In the view of orthodox Marxists, fundamental class conflict influences every aspect of social existence. Politics, for instance, is not so much a process through which rival interests are balanced against one another, as a means of perpetuating class exploitation.

Social cleavages

With the exception of extreme individualists, all political thinkers recognise the importance of social groups or collective entities. They have been concerned with the 'make-up' or composition of society. This is reflected in the attempt to explain how particular social cleavages help to structure political life. A 'social cleavage' is a split or division in society, reflecting the diversity of social formations within it. Such cleavages are born out of an unequal distribution of political influence, economic power or social status. To interpret politics in terms of social cleavages is to recognise particular social bonds, be they economic, racial, religious, cultural or sexual, as politically important, and to treat the group concerned as a major political actor. These cleavages, however, can be interpreted in a number of different ways. For some, they are fundamental and permanent divisions, rooted either in human nature or in the organic structure of society. Others, by contrast, argue that these cleavages are temporary and removable. In the same way, these divisions can be thought of as healthy and desirable, or as evidence of social injustice and oppression. The principal source of disagreement, however, is about which social cleavages are of greatest political significance.

There is little doubt that the cleavage most widely discussed in politics is social class. Class reflects economic and social divisions, based upon an unequal distribution of wealth, income or social status. A 'social class' is therefore a group of people who share a similar economic and social position, and who are thus united by a common economic interest. However, political theorists have not always agreed about the significance of social class, or about how class can be defined. Marxists, for example, regard class as the most fundamental of social cleavages and politically the most significant. Marxists understand class in terms of economic power, the ownership of the 'means of production'. The 'bourgeoisie' is the capitalist class, the owners of capital or productive wealth; while the 'proletariat', which owns no wealth, is forced to sell its labour power to survive, its members being reduced to the status of 'wage slaves'. In Marx's view, classes are major political actors, possessed of the capacity to change history. The proletariat is destined to be the 'gravedigger of capitalism', a destiny it will fulfil once it achieves 'class consciousness'. As it comes to recognise the fact of its own exploitation, the proletariat will cease to be merely a class 'in itself', an economically defined category without self-awareness, and instead will become a class 'for itself', a revolutionary force. On the other hand, Marx did not believe class divisions to be either natural or inevitable. Once wealth is owned in common by all, a classless, communist society would come into existence.

Marxist class theories have, to a large extent, been discredited by the failure of Marx's predictions and the declining evidence of class struggle, at least in advanced capitalist societies. Empirical evidence from both political scientists and sociologists suggests that the class structure of modern society has become increasingly complex and that it varies from system to system, and over time. Max Weber tried to shift the understanding of social class away from a narrow concern with property ownership to take fuller account of the 'status' enjoyed by particular occupational groups, as well as their different 'life chances'. This has led to the modern idea of occupational class, widely used by social scientists, opinion researchers and advertisers. A popular but rather crude distinction is one between the so-called 'blue collar' working class, comprising all manual workers, and the 'white collar' middle class, composed of non-manual, clerical and professional workers. Socialists themselves have been prepared to acknowledge the declining significance of the working masses, as Andres Gorz did in *Farewell to the Working Class* (1982). Nevertheless, social divisions undoubtedly persist even in the most affluent of modern societies, though these are often referred to in terms of an 'underclass', a group of people who through endemic disadvantage and deprivation are consigned to the margins of conventional society. Contemporary Western societies have thus been portrayed as 'two-thirds, one-third' societies. This was one of the implications of J.K. Galbraith's *The Culture of Contentment* (1992), which pointed to the growing political influence of a 'contented majority'. However, such an analysis also highlights the threat to social stability posed by failing to tackle problems of entrenched disadvantage, particularly as the democratic process is less likely to recognise them.

In contrast to social class, the significance of gender divisions in politics has traditionally been ignored. However, since the emergence of 'second wave' feminism in the 1960s, there has been a growing awareness of the political significance of gender. 'Gender' refers to social and cultural distinctions between males and females, in contrast to 'sex' which highlights biological and therefore ineradicable differences between men and women. Feminists have drawn attention to a sexual division of labour through which women are either confined to a domestic sphere of housework and child-rearing, or to poorly paid and low status occupations. Men, on the other hand, tend to dominate positions of power and influence in society. Radical feminists, such as Kate Millett (see p. 61) and Mary Daly, believe gender cleavages to be the deepest and most politically significant of all social divisions, and therefore practise a form of 'sexual politics'. In their view, all contemporary and historical societies have been characterised by patriarchy, the dominance of men and subordination of women, usually thought to be rooted in the rule of the husband-father within the family. In some respects, the radical feminist notion of patriarchal oppression resembles the Marxist idea of class exploitation. Patriarchy can only be overcome by a 'sexual revolution', which would fundamentally transform culture and personal relationships, as well as economic and political life.

Liberal or reformist feminists, by contrast, highlight what they see as the eradicable inequalities of public life, such as the under-representation of women in senior political, managerial and professional posts, and the inadequacy of childcare facilities and welfare support for women. They believe that such goals can be achieved through a gradual process of incremental reform, and dismiss any idea of a 'sex war' between women and men. In the 1980s it became fashionable to proclaim that gender inequality had been eradicated with the emergence of a 'post-feminist' society. However, it is difficult to see how gender will lose its political significance until a genuinely post-sexist society is created, and no society has so far emerged in which significant disparities in the treatment of men and women do not exist.

Racial and ethnic cleavages have also been significant in politics. 'Race' refers to genetic differences amongst humankind which supposedly distinguish people from one another on biological grounds like skin or hair colour, physique, physiognomy and the like. In practice, racial categories are largely based upon cultural stereotypes and have little or no foundation in genetics. The term 'ethnicity' is therefore preferred by many because it refers to cultural, linguistic and social differences, not necessarily rooted in biology. Racial or ethnic cleavages have influenced political thought in two radically different ways. The first racially based political theories emerged in the nineteenth century, against the background of European imperialism. Works such as Gobineau's *Essay on the Inequality of Human Races* ([1855] 1970) and H.S. Chamberlain's *Foundations of the Nineteenth Century* ([1899] 1913) provided a pseudo-scientific justification for the dominance of the 'white' European races over the 'black', 'brown' and 'yellow' peoples of Africa and Asia. The most grotesque twentieth-century manifestation of such racialism was, of course, found in the race theories of Nazism, which gave rise to the 'Final Solution', the attempt to exterminate European Jewry. Racialist doctrines and movements have re-emerged in various parts of Europe in the late twentieth century, stimulated in part by the insecurity and political instability which the 'collapse of communism' generated.

Very different forms of racial and ethnic politics have, however, developed out of the struggle against colonialism in particular, and against racial discrimination in general. Ethnic minorities in many Western societies are excluded from political influence and suffer from disadvantage in both the workplace and public life. This has generated new styles of political activism. The 1960s, for instance, witnessed the emergence of the civil rights movement under Martin Luther King (1929–68), and the growth of more militant organisations like the Black Power movement and the Black Muslims under Malcolm X (1926–65). In many of these cases, racial divisions are seen as eradicable, the task facing anti-racists being one of reform: the construction of a more equitable and tolerant society. Where they are seen to be fundamental, as in the case of the Black Muslims (renamed the Nation of Islam), this has generated doctrines of racial separation.

Religion also exerts immense significance upon political life, despite the advance of secularism throughout the West. This is particularly evident in societies deeply divided along religious lines, such as Northern Ireland, Sri Lanka and India. Although the origins of communal rivalry are complex, involving historical, economic and political factors, religious differences remain the obvious fault-lines within such societies. In Northern Ireland, Catholic Republicans have confronted Protestant Unionists; in Sri Lanka, Christian Tamils fight the majority Buddhist Sinhalese; and in India, Muslims in Kashmir and Sikhs in the Punjab campaign for separate homelands within an overwhelmingly Hindu country. Indeed, as the twentieth century reaches its close, religion has come to have growing importance, perhaps as a backlash against the materialism and perceived amorality of secular society. In many parts of the world, fundamentalist movements have emerged, seeking to rekindle spiritual zeal by returning to the original or most basic religious principles. Islamic fundamentalism, for example, has transformed the politics of many parts of North Africa, the Middle East and Central Asia, most obviously since the 'Islamic Revolution' in Iran in 1979. Christian fundamentalism has also been a prominent component of the political Right in the United States since the 1970s, and forms of Hindu fundamentalism have gathered strength in India during the 1990s.

Finally, language has been a very potent source of political conflict, particularly as it is so often fundamental to establishing a national identity.

Language embodies distinctive attitudes, values and forms of expression, helping to create a sense of familiarity and belonging. Although societies which contain a number of languages have been stable and successful – for instance, Switzerland where French, German and Italian are spoken – linguistic divisions have often been difficult or impossible to overcome. The example of French-speaking Quebec in Canada is an obvious case in point. In Belgium, linguistic divisions have turned the country into a loose federation, seriously impairing any unified sense of national identity. The Flemish-speaking peoples of Flanders in the north have traditionally dominated the Belgium economy and her political life; while the French-speaking Walloons in the south have striven to gain greater autonomy. Even in the United States, where the common use of English in public life has helped to overcome ethnic, religious and cultural divisions, the growing number of Spanish-speaking immigrants from Latin America has caused tension. This has led to demands from Hispanics that their language be officially recognised alongside English in public life, and campaigns by conservatives to preserve the distinctive status of the English language. It is also clear that any attempt to construct meaningful supranational institutions along the lines of the European Union must address the problem of how to foster political loyalties that transcend linguistic divisions and patriotic sentiments.

Summary

1 Human nature refers to the essential and immutable character of all human beings. Major disagreements, however, take place about the degree to which humans are shaped by biology or society, are influenced by reason or non-rational drives, or tend to be either naturally cooperative or naturally competitive.

2 Individualism is a belief in the primacy of the human individual over any social group or collective body. It is often linked to an egoistical and self-reliant view of human nature, suggesting that society is atomistic, hardly a society at all. If, however, humans are essentially social, individuals will gain fulfilment through the community.

3 Collectivism refers to a belief in the community, group or collective, stressing the importance of a common identity and the capacity for collective action. It is commonly linked to state collectivisation and central planning, but it can as easily refer to self-management and, more broadly, to social solidarity.

4 Social cleavages are divisions or splits which characterise a particular society and structure its political life. Although these differ from society to society, and from period to period, the most important social cleavages have been those of social class, race or ethnicity, gender, religion and nationality.

Further reading

Benthal, J. (ed.). *Human Nature*. London: Allen Lane, 1974.
Berry, C. *Human Nature*. London: Macmillan and Atlantic Highlands, NJ: Humanities Press, 1986.
Campbell, T. *Seven Theories of Human Society*. Oxford and New York: Oxford University Press, 1981.
Kymlicka, W. *Liberalism, Community and Culture*. Oxford: Oxford University Press, 1989.
Kingdom, J. *No Such Thing as Society? Individualism and Community*. Buckingham, UK, and Bristol, USA: Open University Press, 1992.
O'Neill, J. (ed.). *Modes of Individualism and Collectivism*. London: Gregg Revivals, 1993.
Rush, M. *Politics and Society; An Introduction to Political Sociology*. Hemel Hempstead: Harvester Wheatsheaf, 1992.
Stevenson, L. *Seven Theories of Human Nature*. Oxford and New York: Oxford University Press, 1990.

Chapter 3

Politics, Government and the State

Introduction
Politics
Government
The state
Summary
Further reading

Introduction

In the early stages of academic study students are invariably encouraged to reflect on what the subject itself is about, usually by being asked questions such as 'What is Physics?', 'What is History?' or 'What is Economics?'. Such reflections have the virtue of letting students know what they are in for: what they are about to study and what issues and topics are going to be raised. Unfortunately for the student of politics, however, the question 'What is Politics?' is more likely to generate confusion than bring comfort or reassurance. The problem with politics is that debate, controversy and disagreement lie at its very heart, and the definition of 'the political' is no exception.

The debate about 'What is Politics?' exposes some of the deepest and most intractable conflicts in political thought. The attempt to define politics raises a series of difficult questions. For example, is politics a restricted activity, confined to what goes on within government or the state, or does it occur in all areas of social life? Does politics, in other words, take place within families, schools, colleges and in the workplace? Similarly, is politics, as many believe, a corrupting and dishonest activity, or is it, rather, a healthy and ennobling one? Can politics be brought to an end? Should politics be brought to an end? A further range of arguments and debates are associated with the institution of government. Is government necessary or can societies be stable and successful in the absence of government? What form should government take, and how does government relate to broader political processes, usually called the political system? Finally, deep controversy also surrounds the nature and role of the state. For instance, since the terms 'government' and 'state' are often used interchangeably can a meaningful distinction be established between them? Is state power benevolent or oppressive: does it operate in the interests of all citizens or is it biased in favour of a narrow elite or ruling class? Moreover, what should the state do? Which responsibilities should we look to the state to fulfil and which ones should be left in the hands of private individuals?

Politics

There are almost as many definitions of politics as there are authorities willing to offer an opinion on the subject. Politics has been portrayed as the exercise of power or authority, as a process of collective decision-making, as the allocation of scarce resources, as an arena of deception or manipulation and so forth. A number of characteristic themes nevertheless crop up in most, if not all, these definitions. In the first place, politics is an activity. Although politics is also an academic subject, sometimes indicated by the use of 'Politics' with a capital letter P, it is clearly the study of the activity of 'politics'. Secondly, politics is a social activity; it arises out of interaction between or among people, and did not, for example, occur on Robinson Crusoe's island – though it certainly did once Man Friday appeared. Thirdly, politics develops out of diversity, the existence of a range of opinions, wants, needs or interests. Fourthly, this diversity is closely linked to the existence of conflict: politics involves the expression of differing opinions, competition between rival goals or a clash of irreconcilable interests. Where spontaneous agreement or natural harmony occurs, politics cannot be found. Finally, politics is about decisions, collective decisions which are in some way regarded as binding upon a group of people. It is through such decisions that conflict is resolved. However, politics is better thought of as the search for conflict-resolution rather than its achievement, since not all conflicts are, or can be, resolved.

However, this is where agreement ends. There are profound differences about when, how, where, and in relation to whom, this 'politics' takes place. For instance, which conflicts can be called 'political'? What forms of conflict-resolution can be described as 'political'? And where is this activity of 'politics' located? Three clearly distinct conceptions of politics can be identified. In the first place, politics has long been associated with the formal institutions of government and the activities which take place therein. Secondly, politics is commonly linked to public life and public activities, in contrast to what is thought of as private or personal. Thirdly, politics has been related to the distribution of power, wealth and resources, something that takes place within all institutions and at every level of social existence.

The art of government

Bismarck declared that 'politics is not a science . . . but an art'. The art he had in mind was the art of government, the exercise of control within society through the making and enforcement of collective decisions. This is perhaps the classical definition of politics, having developed from the original meaning of the term in Ancient Greece. The word 'politics' is derived from *polis*, which literally means city-state. Ancient Greek society was divided into a collection of independent city-states, each of which possessed its own system of government. The largest and most influential of these was Athens, often portrayed as the model of classical democracy. All male citizens were entitled to attend the Assembly or *Ecclesia*, very similar to a town-meeting, which met at least ten times a year, and most other public offices were filled by citizens selected on the basis of lot or rota. Nevertheless, Athenian society was based upon a rigidly hierarchical system which excluded the overwhelming majority – women, slaves and foreign residents – from political life.

In this light, politics can be understood to refer to the affairs of the*polis*; it literally means 'what concerns the *polis*'. The modern equivalent of this definition is 'what concerns the state'. This is a definition which academic political science has undoubtedly helped to perpetuate through its traditional focus upon the personnel and machinery of government. Furthermore, it is how the term 'politics' is commonly used in everyday language. For example, a person is said to be 'in politics' when they hold a public office, or to be 'entering politics' when they seek to do so. Such a definition of 'the political' links it very closely to the exercise of authority, the right of a person or institution to make decisions on behalf of the community This was made clear in the writings of the influential American political scientist, David Easton, who defined politics as the 'authoritative allocation of values'. Politics has therefore come to be associated with 'policy', formal or authoritative decisions that establish a plan of action for the community. Moreover, it takes place within a 'polity', a system of social organisation centred upon the machinery of government. It should be noted, however, that this definition is highly restrictive. Politics, in this sense, is confined to governmental institutions: it takes place in cabinet rooms, legislative chambers, government departments and the like, and it is engaged in by limited and specific groups of people, notably politicians, civil servants and lobbyists. Most people, most institutions and most social activities can thus be regarded as 'outside' politics.

For some commentators, however, politics refers not simply to the making of authoritative decisions by government but rather to the particular means by which these decisions are made. Politics has often been portrayed as 'the art of the possible', as a means of resolving conflict by compromise, conciliation and negotiation. Such a view was advanced by Bernard Crick in *In Defence of Politics* (1983), in which politics is seen as 'that solution to the problem of order which chooses conciliation rather than violence and coercion'. The conciliation of competing interests or groups requires that power is widely dispersed throughout society and apportioned according to the importance of each to the welfare and survival of the whole community. Politics is, then, no utopian solution, but only the recognition that if human beings cannot solve problems by compromise and debate they will resort to brutality. As the essence of politics is discussion, Crick asserted that the enemy of politics is 'the desire for certainty at any cost', whether this comes in the form of a closed ideology, blind faith in democracy, rabid nationalism or the promise of science to disclose objective knowledge.

Once again, such a definition of politics can clearly be found in the common usage of the term. For instance, a 'political' solution to a problem implies negotiation and rational debate, in contrast to a 'military' solution. In this light, the use of violence, force or intimidation can be seen as 'non-political', indeed as the breakdown of the political process itself. At heart, the definition of politics as compromise and conciliation has an essentially liberal character. In the first place, it reflects a deep faith in human reason and in the efficacy of debate and discussion. Secondly, it is based upon an underlying belief in consensus rather than conflict, evident in the assumption that disagreements can be settled without resort to naked power. In effect, there are no irreconcilable conflicts.

The link between politics and the affairs of the state has, however, also generated deeply negative conceptions of what politics is about. For many, politics is quite simply a 'dirty' word. It implies deception, dishonesty and even corruption. Such an image of politics stems from the association

---

Niccolò Machiavelli (1469–1527)

Italian politician and author. The son of a civil lawyer, Machiavelli's knowledge of public life was gained from a sometimes precarious existence in politically unstable Florence. He served as Second Chancellor, 1498–1512, and was despatched on missions to France, Germany and throughout Italy. After a brief period of imprisonment and the restoration of Medici rule, Machiavelli embarked on a literary career.

Machiavelli's major work, *The Prince*, written in 1513 and published in 1531, was intended to provide guidance for the ruler of a future united Italy, and drew heavily upon his first-hand observations of the statecraft of Cesare Borgia and the power politics that dominated his period. His 'scientific method' portrayed politics in strictly realistic terms and highlighted the use by the political leaders of cunning, cruelty and manipulation. This emphasis, and attacks upon him that led to his ex-communication, meant that the term 'Machiavellian' subsequently came to mean scheming and duplicitous. His *Discourses*, written in 1513–17 and published in 1531, provides a fuller account of Machiavelli's republicanism (see p. 208), but commentators have disagreed about whether it should be considered as an elaboration of or a departure from the ideas outlined in *The Prince*.

between politics and the behaviour of politicians, sometimes said to be rooted in the writings of Niccolò Machiavelli. In *The Prince* ([1531] 1961), Machiavelli attempted to develop a strictly realistic account of politics in terms of the pursuit and exercise of power, drawing upon his observations of Cesare Borgia. Because he drew attention to the use by political leaders of cunning, cruelty and manipulation, the adjective 'Machiavellian' has come to stand for underhand and deceitful behaviour.

Politicians themselves are typically held in low esteem because they are perceived to be power-seeking hypocrites who conceal personal ambition behind the rhetoric of public service and ideological conviction. A conception of politics has thus taken root which associates it with self-seeking, two-faced and unprincipled behaviour, clearly evident in the use of derogatory phrases like 'office politics' and 'politicking'. Such an image of politics also has a liberal character. Liberals have long warned that, since individuals are self-interested, the possession of political power will be corrupting in itself, encouraging those 'in power' to exploit their position for personal advantage and at the expense of others. This is clearly reflected in the British historian Lord Acton's (1834–1902) famous aphorism: 'power tends to corrupt, and absolute power corrupts absolutely.'

Public affairs

In the first conception, politics is seen as a highly restricted activity, confined to the formal exercise of authority within the machinery of government. A second and broader conception of politics moves it beyond the narrow realm of government to what is typically thought of as 'public life' or 'public affairs'. In other words, the distinction between 'the political' and 'the non-political' coincides with the division between an essentially public sphere of life and what is thought of as a private sphere. Such a view of politics is rooted in the work of the famous Greek philosopher, Aristotle (see p. 68). In *Politics*, Aristotle declared that 'Man is by nature a political animal', by which he meant that it is only within a political community that human beings can live 'the good life'. Politics is therefore the 'master science'; it is an ethical activity concerned ultimately with creating a 'just society'. According to this view, politics goes on within 'public' bodies such as government itself, political parties, trade unions, community groups and so on, but does not take place within the 'private' domain of, say, the home, family life and personal relationships. However, it is sometimes difficult in practice to establish where the line between 'public' life and 'private' life should be drawn, and to explain why it should be maintained.

The traditional distinction between the public realm and the private realm conforms to the division between the state and society. The characteristics of the state are discussed in more detail in the final section of this chapter, but for the time being the state can be defined as a political association which exercises sovereign power within a defined territorial area. In everyday language, the state is often taken to refer to a cluster of institutions, centring upon the apparatus of government but including the courts, the police, the army, nationalised industries, the social security system, and so forth. These institutions can be regarded as 'public' in the sense that they are responsible for the collective organisation of community life and are thus funded at the public's expense, out of taxation. By contrast, society consists of a collection of autonomous groups and associations, embracing family and kinship groups, private businesses, trade unions, clubs, community groups and the like. Such institutions are 'private' in the sense that they are set up and funded by individual citizens to satisfy their own interests rather than those of the larger society. On the basis of this 'public/private' dichotomy, politics is restricted to the activities of the state itself and the responsibilities which are properly exercised by public bodies. Those areas of life in which individuals can and do manage for themselves – economic, social, domestic, personal, cultural, artistic and so forth – are therefore clearly 'non-political'.

However, the 'public/private' divide is sometimes used to express a further and more subtle distinction, namely, between 'the political' and 'the personal'. Although society can be distinguished from the state, it nevertheless contains a range of institutions that may be thought of as 'public' in the wider sense that they are open institutions, operating in public and to which the public has access. This encouraged Hegel (see p. 4), for example, to use the more specific term, 'civil society', to refer to an intermediate socio-economic realm, distinct from the state on one hand and the family on the other. By comparison with domestic life, private businesses and trade unions can therefore be seen to have a public character. From this point of view, politics as a public activity stops only when it infringes upon 'personal' affairs and institutions. For this reason, while many people are prepared to accept that a form of politics takes place in the workplace, they may be offended and even threatened by the idea that politics intrudes into family, domestic and personal life.

The importance of the distinction between political and private life has been underlined by both conservative and liberal thinkers. Conservatives such as Michael Oakeshott (see p. 139) have, for instance, insisted that politics be regarded as a strictly limited activity. Politics may be necessary for the maintenance of public order and so on, but it should be restricted to its proper function: the regulation of public life. In *Rationalism in Politics*

([1962] 1991), Oakeshott advanced an essentially non-political view of human nature, emphasising that, far from being Aristotle's 'political animals', most people are security-seeking, cautious and dependent creatures. From this perspective, the inner core of human existence is a 'private' world of family, home, domesticity and personal relationships. Oakeshott therefore regarded the rough-and-tumble of political life as inhospitable, even intimidating.

From a liberal viewpoint, the maintenance of the 'public/private' distinction is vital to the preservation of individual liberty, typically understood as a form of privacy or non-interference. If politics is regarded as an essentially 'public' activity, centred upon the state, it will always have a coercive character: the state has the power to compel the obedience of its citizens. On the other hand, 'private' life is a realm of choice, freedom and individual responsibility. Liberals therefore have a clear preference for society rather than the state, for the 'private' rather than the 'public', and have thus feared the encroachment of politics upon the rights and liberties of the individual. Such a view is commonly expressed in the demand that politics be 'kept out of' private activities or institutions, matters that can, and should, be left to individuals themselves. For example, the call that politics be 'kept out of' sport implies that sport is an entirely 'private' affair over which the state and other 'public' bodies exercise no rightful responsibility. Indeed, such arguments invariably portray 'politics' in a particularly unfavourable light. In this case, for example, politics represents unwanted and unwarranted interference in an arena supposedly characterised by fair competition, personal development and the pursuit of excellence.

Not all political thinkers, however, have had such a clear preference for society over the state, or wished so dearly to keep politics at bay. There is, for instance, a tradition which portrays politics favourably precisely because it is a 'public' activity. Dating back to Aristotle, this tradition has been kept alive in the twentieth century by writers such as Hannah Arendt. In her major philosophical work, *The Human Condition* (1958), Arendt placed 'action' above both 'labour' and 'work' in what she saw as a hierarchy of worldly activities. She argued that politics is the most important form of human activity because it involves interaction amongst free and equal citizens, and so both gives meaning to life and affirms the uniqueness of each individual. Advocates of participatory democracy have also portrayed politics as a moral, healthy and even noble activity. In the view of the eighteenth-century French thinker, Jean-Jacques Rousseau (see p. 243), political participation was the very stuff of freedom itself. Only through the direct and continuous participation of all citizens in political life can the state be bound to the common good, or what Rousseau called the 'general will'. John Stuart Mill (see p. 258) took up the cause of political participation in the nineteenth century, arguing that involvement in 'public' affairs is educational in that it promotes the personal, moral and intellectual development of the individual. Rather than seeing politics as a dishonest and corrupting activity, such a view presents politics as a form of public service, benefiting practitioners and recipients alike.

A further optimistic conception of politics stems from a preference for the state rather than for civil society. Whereas liberals have regarded 'private' life as a realm of harmony and freedom, socialists have often seen it as a system of injustice and inequality. Socialists have consequently argued for an extension of the state's responsibilities in order to rectify the defects of civil society, seeing 'politics' as the solution to economic injustice. From a different perspective, Hegel portrayed the state as an ethical idea, morally superior to civil society. In *Philosophy of Right* ([1821] 1942), the state is regarded with uncritical reverence as a realm of altruism and mutual sympathy, whereas civil society is thought to be dominated by narrow self-interest. The most extreme form of such an argument is found in the fascist doctrine of the 'totalitarian state', expressed in Gentile's formula, 'Everything for the state, nothing against the state, nothing outside the state'. The fascist ideal of the absorption of the individual into the community, obliterating any trace of individual identity, could only be achieved through the 'politicisation' of every aspect of social existence, literally the abolition of 'the private'.

Power and resources

Each of the earlier two conceptions of politics view it as intrinsically related to a particular set of institutions or social sphere, in the first place the machinery of government and, secondly, the arena of public life. By contrast, the third and most radical definition of politics regards it as a distinctive form of social activity, but one that pervades every corner of human existence. As Adrian Leftwich insists in *What is Politics?* (1984): 'politics is at the heart of *all* collective social activity, formal and informal, public and private, in *all* human groups, institutions and societies'. This notion of 'the political' is linked to the production, distribution and use of resources in the course of social existence. Politics thus arises out of the existence of scarcity, out of the simple fact that while human needs and desires are infinite, the resources available to satisfy them are always limited. Politics therefore comprises any form of activity through which conflict about resource-allocation takes place. This implies, for instance, that politics is no longer confined, as Crick argued, to rational debate and peaceful conciliation, but can also encompass threats, intimidation and violence. This is summed up in Clausewitz's famous dictum, 'War is nothing more than the continuation of politics by other means'. In essence, politics is power, the ability to achieve a desired outcome, through whatever means. Harold Lasswell neatly summed up this aspect of politics in the title of his book *Politics: Who Gets What, When, How?* (1936). Such a conception of politics has been advanced by a variety of theorists, amongst the most influential of whom have been Marxists and modern feminists.

The Marxist concept of politics operates on two levels. On the first, Marx (see p. 373) used the term 'politics' in a conventional sense to refer to the apparatus of the state. This is what he meant in the *Communist Manifesto* ([1848] 1976) when he referred to political power as 'merely the organised power of one class for oppressing another'. In his view, politics, together with law and culture, was part of a 'superstructure', distinct from the economic 'base', which was the real foundation of social life. However, he did not see the economic 'base' and the political and legal 'superstructure' as discrete entities, but believed that the 'superstructure' arose out of, and reflected, the economic 'base'. At a deeper level, in other words, political power is rooted in the class system; as Lenin (see p. 82) put it, 'politics is the most concentrated expression of economics'. Far from believing that politics can be confined to the state and a narrow public sphere, Marxists can be said to hold that 'the economic is political'. Indeed, civil society, based as it is on a system of class antagonism, is the very heart of politics. However, Marx did not think that politics was an inevitable feature of social existence and he looked towards what he clearly hoped would be an end of politics. This would occur, he anticipated, once a classless, communist society came into existence, leaving no scope for class conflict, or politics. The Marxist view of politics is, nevertheless, ambivalent. On the one hand, politics is about naked power, coercion and oppression, and its 'end' is dearly to be wished for. On the other hand, politics as an expression of the class struggle is also the means through which this apolitical society is to be brought about: a proletarian revolution.

Particularly intense interest in the nature of politics has been expressed by modern feminist thinkers. Whereas nineteenth-century feminists accepted an essentially liberal conception of politics as 'public' affairs, and focused especially upon the campaign for female suffrage, radical feminists have been concerned to extend the boundaries of 'the political'. They argue that conventional definitions of politics, in effect, exclude women. Women have traditionally been confined to a 'private' existence, centred upon the family and domestic responsibilities; men, by contrast, have always dominated conventional politics and other areas of 'public' life. Radical

Feminism

Feminism is characterised primarily by its political stance: the attempt to advance the social role of women. Feminists have highlighted what they see as a political relationship between the sexes, the supremacy of men and the subjection of women in most, if not all, societies. The 'first wave' of feminism was closely associated with the women's suffrage movement, which emerged in the 1840s and 1850s. The achievement of female suffrage in most Western countries in the early twentieth century meant that the campaign for legal and civil rights assumed a lower profile and deprived the women's movement of a unifying cause. The 'second wave' of feminism arose during the 1960s and expressed, in addition to the established concern with equal rights, the more radical and sometimes revolutionary demands of the growing Women's Liberation Movement. Although feminist politics has undergone a process of de-radicalisation since the early 1970s, feminism has nevertheless gained growing respectability as a distinctive school of political theory.

Feminist political thought has primarily been concerned with two issues. First, it analyses the institutions, processes and practices through which women have been subordinated to men; and second, it explores the most appropriate and effective ways in which this subordination can be challenged. Feminist thought has rejected the conventional view that politics is confined to narrowly public activities and institutions, the most famous slogan of second-wave feminism being 'The personal is the political'. The central concept in the feminist theory of sexual politics is patriarchy, a term that draws attention to the totality of oppression and exploitation to which women are subject. This, in turn, highlights the political importance of gender, understood to refer to socially imposed rather than biological differences between men and women. Most feminists view gender as a political construct, usually based upon stereotypes of 'feminine' and 'masculine' behaviour and social roles.

Nevertheless, feminist theory and practice is highly diverse. The earliest feminist ideas derived largely from liberalism (see p. 29), and reflected a commitment to individualism and formal equality. In contrast, socialist feminism, largely derived from Marxism (see p. 81), has highlighted links between female subordination and the capitalist mode of production, drawing attention to the economic significance of women being confined to the family or domestic life. On the other hand, radical feminists moved beyond the perspectives of existing political traditions. They portray gender divisions as the most fundamental and politically significant cleavages in society, and call for the radical restructuring of personal, domestic and family life. However, the breakdown of feminism into three traditions – liberal, socialist and radical feminism – has become increasingly redundant since the 1970s as feminist thought has become yet more sophisticated and diverse. Amongst its more recent forms have been black feminism, psychoanalytic feminism, eco-feminism (see p. 196) and postmodern feminism (see p. 12).

$\longrightarrow$

The major strength of feminist political theory is that it provides a perspective on political understanding that is uncontaminated by the gender biases that pervade conventional thought. Feminism has not merely reinterpreted the contribution of major theorists and shed new light upon established concepts such as power, domination and equality, but also introduced a new sensitivity and language into political theory related to ideas such as connection, voice and difference. Feminism has nevertheless been criticised on the grounds that its internal divisions are now so sharp that feminist theory has lost all coherence and unity. Postmodern feminists, for example, even questioned whether 'woman' is a meaningful category. Others suggest that feminist theory has become disengaged from a society that is increasingly post-feminist, in that, largely thanks to feminism, the domestic, professional and public roles of women, at least in developed societies, have undergone a major transformation.

Key figures

Mary Wollstonecraft (see p. 289)   Wollstonecraft's *A Vindication of the Rights of Women* (1792) is usually regarded as the first text of modern feminism and was written against the backdrop of the French Revolution, many years before the emergence of the women's suffrage movement. In arguing that women should be entitled to the same rights and privileges as men on the grounds that they are 'human beings', she established what was to become the core principle of liberal feminism.

Simone de Beauvoir (1906–86)   A French novelist, playwright and social critic, Beauvoir helped to reopen the issue of gender politics and foreshadowed some of the themes later developed in radical feminism. She highlighted the extent to which the masculine is represented as the positive or the norm, while the feminine is portrayed as 'other'. Such 'otherness' fundamentally limits women's freedom and prevents them from expressing their full humanity. Beauvoir placed her faith in rationality and critical analysis as the means of exposing this process and giving women responsibility for their own lives. Her key feminist work is *The Second Sex* (1949).

Kate Millett (1934–)   A US writer and sculptor, Millett developed radical feminism into a systematic theory that clearly stood apart from established liberal and socialist traditions. She portrays patriarchy as a 'social constant' running through all political, social and economic structures, and grounded in a process of conditioning that operates largely through the family, 'patriarchy's chief institution'. She supports consciousness-raising as a means of challenging patriarchal oppression, and has advocated the abolition and replacement of the conventional family. Millett's major work is *Sexual Politics* (1970).

→

Feminism continued

Juliet Mitchell (1940–)   A New Zealand-born British writer, Mitchell is one of the most influential theorists of socialist feminism. She has adopted a modern Marxist perspective that allows for the interplay of economic, social, political and cultural forces in society, and has warned that, since patriarchy has cultural and ideological roots, it cannot be overthrown simply by replacing capitalism with socialism. Mitchell was also one of the first feminists to use psychoanalysis as a means of explaining sexual difference. Her major works included *Women's Estate* (1971), *Psychoanalysis and Feminism* (1974) and *Feminine Sexuality* (1985).

Shulamith Firestone (1945–)   A Canadian author and political activist, Firestone developed a theory of radical feminism that adapted Marxism to the analysis to the role of women. She argues that sexual differences stem not from conditioning but from a 'natural division of labour' within the 'biological family'. Society is thus structured not through the process of production, but through the process of reproduction. Women can, then, only achieve emancipation if they transcend their biological natures and escape from the 'curse of Eve' by the use of modern technology such as test-tube babies and artificial wombs. Firestone's best known work is *The Dialectic of Sex* (1970).

Catherine A. MacKinnon (1946–)   A US academic and political activist, MacKinnon has made a major contribution to feminist legal theory. In her view, law in a liberal state is one of the principal devices through which women's silence and subordination is maintained. In the absence of gender equality, the 'normal' status of women is inevitably defined through the application of male values and practices. She has also argued that female oppression is based in sexuality and that pornography is the root cause of that oppression. MacKinnon's major works include *Sexual Harassment and Working Women* (1979), *Towards a Feminist Theory of the State* (1989) and *Only Words* (1993).

Further reading

Bryson, V. *Feminist Political Theory: An Introduction.* London: Macmillan, 1992.
Hirsch, M. and Keller, E. F. (eds) *Conflicts in Feminism.* London: Routledge, 1990.
Pateman, C. and Gross, E. (eds) *Feminist Challenges: Social and Political Theory.* Boston: Northeastern University Press, 1986.

feminists have therefore attacked the 'public/private' dichotomy, pro-claiming instead the slogan 'the personal is the political'. Although this slogan has provoked considerable controversy and a variety of interpreta-tions, it undoubtedly encapsulates the belief that what goes on in domestic, family and personal life is intensely political. Behind this, however, stands a more radical notion of politics, defined by Kate Millett in *Sexual Politics* ([1970] 1990) as 'power-structured relationships, arrangements whereby one group of persons is controlled by another'. Politics therefore takes place whenever and wherever power and other resources are unequally distributed. From this viewpoint, it is possible to talk about 'the politics of everyday life', suggesting that relationships within the family, between husbands and wives or between parents and children, are every bit as political as relationships between employers and workers, or between government and its citizens. Such a broadening of the realm of politics has, on the other hand, deeply alarmed liberal theorists, who fear that it will encourage public authority to encroach upon the privacy and liberties of the individual.

However, if politics is conceived as the allocation of scarce resources, it takes place not so much within a particular set of institutions as on a number of levels. The lowest level of political activity is personal, family and domestic life, where it is conducted through regular or continuous face-to-face interaction. Politics, for example, occurs when two friends decide to go out for the evening but cannot agree about where they should go, or what they should do. The second level of politics is the community level, typically addressing local issues or disputes but moving away from the face-to-face interaction of personal politics to some form of representation. This will certainly include the activities of community, local or regional government, which in countries as large as the United States may well encompass two or more distinct levels of government. It also, however, includes the workplace, public institutions and business corporations, within which only a limited range of decisions are made by direct face-to-face discussions. The third level of politics is the national level, focusing upon the institutions of the nation-state and the activities of major political parties and pressure groups. This is the level to which conventional notions of politics are largely confined. Finally, there is the international or supranational level of politics. This is concerned, quite obviously, with cultural, economic and diplomatic relationships between and amongst nation-states, but also includes the activities of supranational bodies, such as the United Nations and the European Union, multinational companies and even international terrorists. One danger of expanding 'the political' to include *all* social institutions, however, is that it comes close to defining everything as politics, thus rendering the term itself almost meaningless.

Government

However politics is defined, government is undoubtedly central to it. To 'govern', in its broadest sense, is to rule or exercise control over others. The activity of government therefore involves the ability to make decisions and to ensure that they are carried out. In that sense, a form of government can be identified within most social institutions. For instance, in the family it is apparent in the control that parents exercise over children; in schools it operates through discipline and rules imposed by teachers; and in the workplace it is maintained by regulations drawn up by managers or employers. Government therefore exists whenever and wherever ordered rule occurs. However, the term 'government' is usually understood more narrowly to refer to formal and institutional processes by which rule is exercised at community, national and international levels. As such, government can be identified with a set of established and permanent institutions whose function is to maintain public order and undertake collective action.

The institutions of government are concerned with the making, implementation and interpretation of law, law being a set of enforceable rules that are binding upon society. All systems of government therefore encompass three functions: first, legislation or the making of laws; secondly, the execution or implementation of laws; and, thirdly, the interpretation of law, the adjudication of its meaning. In some systems of government these functions are carried out by separate institutions – the legislature, the executive and the judiciary – but in others they may all come under the responsibility of a single body, such as a 'ruling' party, or even a single individual, a dictator. In some cases, however, the executive branch of government alone is referred to as 'the Government', making government almost synonymous with 'the rulers' or 'the governors'. Government is thus identified more narrowly with a specific group of ministers or secretaries, operating under the leadership of a chief executive, usually a prime minister or president. This typically occurs in parliamentary systems, where it is common to refer to 'the Blair Government', 'the Schröder Government' or 'the Howard Government'.

A number of controversial issues, however, surround the concept of government. In the first place, although the need for some kind of government enjoys near-universal acceptance, there are those who argue that government of any kind is both oppressive and unnecessary. Moreover, government comes in such bewildering varieties that it is difficult to categorise or classify its different forms. Government, for instance, can be democratic or authoritarian, constitutional or dictatorial, centralised or fragmented and so forth. Finally, government cannot be understood in isolation, separate from the society over which it rules. Governments operate within political systems, networks of relationships usually involving parties, elections, pressure groups and the media, through which government can both respond to popular pressures and exercise political control.

Why have government?

People in every part of the world recognise the concept of government and would, in the overwhelming majority of cases, be able to identify institutions in their society that constitute government. Furthermore, most people accept without question that government is necessary, assuming that without it orderly and civilised existence would be impossible. Although they may disagree about the organisation of government and the role it should play, they are nevertheless convinced of the need for some kind of government. However, the widespread occurrence of government and its almost uncritical acceptance worldwide does not in itself prove that an ordered and just society can only exist through the agency of government. Indeed, one particular school of political thought is dedicated precisely to establishing that government is unnecessary, and to bringing about its abolition. This is anarchism, anarchy literally meaning 'without rule'.

The classic argument in favour of government is found in social contract theories, first proposed by seventeenth-century philosophers like Thomas Hobbes (see p. 124) and John Locke (see p. 269). Social contract theory, in fact, constitutes the basis of modern political thought. In *Leviathan* ([1651] 1968), Hobbes advanced the view that rational human beings should respect and obey their government because without it society would descend into a civil war 'of every man against every man'. Social contract theorists develop their argument with reference to an assumed or hypothetical society without government, a so-called 'state of nature'. Hobbes graphically described life in the state of nature as being 'solitary, poor, nasty, brutish and short'. In his view, human beings were essentially power-seeking and selfish creatures, who would, if unrestrained by law, seek to advance their own interests at the expense of fellow humans. Even the strongest would never be strong enough to live in security and without fear: the weak would unite against them before turning upon one another. Quite simply, without government to restrain selfish impulses, order and stability would be impossible. Hobbes suggested that, recognising this, rational individuals would seek to escape from chaos and disorder by entering into an agreement with one another, a 'social contract', through which a system of government could be established.

Social contract theorists see government as a necessary defence against evil and barbarity, based as they are upon an essentially pessimistic view of human nature. An alternative tradition however exists, which portrays government as intrinsically benign, as a means of promoting good and not just of avoiding harm. This can be seen in the writings of Aristotle, whose philosophy had a profound effect upon medieval theologians such as St Thomas Aquinas (see p. 158). In 'The Treatise of Law', part of *Summa Theologiae*, begun in 1265, Aquinas portrayed the state as 'the perfect community' and argued that the proper effect of law was to make its subjects good. He was clear, for instance, that government and law would be necessary for human beings even in the absence of original sin. This benign view of government as an instrument which enables people to cooperate for mutual benefit has been kept alive in modern politics by the social democratic tradition.

In the anarchist view, however, government and all forms of political authority are not only evil but also unnecessary. Anarchists advanced this argument by turning social contract theory on its head and offering a very different portrait of the state of nature. Social contract theorists assume, to varying degrees, that if human beings are left to their own devices rivalry, competition and open conflict will be the inevitable result. Anarchists, on the other hand, hold a more optimistic conception of human nature, stressing the capacity for rational understanding, compassion and coopera-tion. As William Godwin (see p. 341), whose *An Enquiry Concerning Political Justice* ([1793] 1976) gave the first clear statement of anarchist principles, declared: 'Man is perfectible, or in other words susceptible of perpetual improvement'. In the state of nature a 'natural' order will therefore prevail, making a 'political' order quite unnecessary. Social harmony will spontaneously develop as individuals recognise that the common interests that bind them are stronger than the selfish interests that divide them, and when disagreements do occur they can be resolved peacefully through rational debate and discussion. Indeed, anarchists see government not as a safeguard against disorder, but as the cause of conflict, unrest and violence. By imposing rule from above, government represses freedom, breeding resentment and promoting inequality.

Anarchists have often supported their arguments by the use of historical examples, such as the medieval city-states revered by Peter Kropotkin (see p. 169) or the Russian peasant commune admired by Leo Tolstoy, in which social order was supposedly maintained by rational agreement and mutual sympathy. They have also looked to traditional societies in which order and stability reign despite the absence of what would normally be recognised as government. Clearly, it is impossible to generalise about the nature of traditional societies, some of which are hierarchic and repressive, quite unappealing to anarchists. Nevertheless, sociologists have also identified highly egalitarian societies, such as that of the Bushmen of the Kalahari, where differences appear to be resolved through informal processes and personal contacts, without the need for any formal government machinery. The value of such examples, however, is that they highlight precisely why, far from dispensing with the need for organised rule, modern societies have become increasingly dependent upon government.

The difference between traditional communities like that of the Kalahari Bushmen and the urban and industrialised societies in which the world's population increasingly lives could not be more marked. Traditional societies solve the problem of maintaining order largely through the maintenance of traditions and customs, often rooted in religious belief. Social rituals, for instance, help to entrench a set of common values and pass on rules of conduct from one generation to the next. Tradition therefore serves to ensure consistent and predictable social behaviour and to maintain a clearly defined social structure. Such societies, moreover, are relatively small, enabling social intercourse to be conducted on a personal, face-to-face level. By contrast, modern societies are large, complex and highly differentiated. Industrial societies consist of sprawling urban communities containing many thousands of people and sometimes several million. As a result of the decline of religion, ritual and tradition, modern societies typically lack a unifying set of common values and cultural beliefs. Industrialisation has also made economic life more complex and generated an increasingly fragmented social structure. In short, the hallmarks of modern society are size, diversity and conflict. The informal mechanisms that underpin social order amongst the Kalahari Bushmen either do not exist or could not cope with the strains generated by modern society. It is therefore not surprising that the anarchist dream of abolishing government has been frustrated. The clear trend during most of the twentieth century has in fact been in the opposite direction: government has been seen to be increasingly necessary. Although anarcho-capitalists like Murray Rothbard (see p. 342) have tried to reverse the growth in government by demonstrating that complex economics can be entirely regulated by the market mechanism, few modern societies are not characterised by extensive government intervention in economic and social life.

Forms of government

Although all governments have the objective of ensuring orderly rule, they do so in very different ways and have assumed a wide variety of institutional and political forms. Absolute monarchies of old are, for instance, often distinguished from modern forms of constitutional and democratic government. Similarly, in the Cold War period it was common for regimes to be classified as belonging to the first world, the second world or the third world. Political thinkers have attempted to establish such classifications with one of two purposes in mind. In the case of political philosophers, they have been anxious to evaluate forms of government on normative grounds in the hope of identifying the 'ideal' constitution. Modern political scientists, however, have attempted to develop a 'science of government' in order to study the activities of government in different countries without making value judgements about them. Ideological considerations, nevertheless, tend to intrude. An example of this is the use of the term 'democratic' to describe a particular system of government, a term that indicates general approval by suggesting that in such societies government is carried out both *by* and *for* the people.

One of the earliest attempts to classify forms of government was undertaken by Aristotle. In his view, governments can be categorised on the basis of 'Who rules?' and 'Who benefits from rule?'. Government can be placed in the hands of a single individual, a small group or the many. In each case, however, government can be conducted either in the selfish interests of the rulers or for the benefit of the entire community. As a result, Aristotle identified six forms of government. Tyranny, Oligarchy and Democracy are all, he suggested, debased or perverted forms of rule in which, respectively, a single person, a small group and the masses govern in their own interests and therefore at the expense of others. By contrast, Monarchy, Aristocracy and Polity are to be preferred because the single individual, small group or the masses govern in the interests of all.

Aristotle (384–322 BCE)

Greek philosopher. Aristotle was a student of Plato and the tutor of the young Alexander the Great. He established his own school of philosophy in Athens in 335 BCE. This was called the 'peripatetic school' after his tendency to walk up and down as he talked.

Aristotle's 22 surviving treatises were compiled as lecture notes and range over logic, physics, metaphysics, astronomy, meteorology, biology, ethics and politics. His best known political work is *Politics*, a comprehensive study of the nature of political life and the forms it might take. In describing politics as the 'master science', he emphasised that it is in the public not private domain that human beings strive for justice and live the 'good life'. Aristotle's taxomony of forms of government led him to prefer those that aim at the common good over those that benefit sectional interests, and to recommend a mixture of democracy and oligarchy, in the form of what he called polity. The communitarianism (see p. 34) of *Politics*, in which the citizen is portrayed as strictly part of the political community, is qualified by an insistence upon choice and autonomy in works such as *Nicomachean Ethics*. In the middle ages, Aristotle's work became the foundation of Islamic philosophy, and it was later incorporated into Christian theology.

Aristotle declared that Tyranny is clearly the worst of all possible constitutions since it reduces all citizens to the status of slaves. Monarchy and Aristocracy are, on the other hand, impractical because they are based upon a god-like willingness to place the good of the community before one's own interests. Aristotle accepted that Polity, rule by the many in the interests of all, is the most practicable of constitutions, but feared that the masses might resent the wealth of the few and too easily come under the sway of a demagogue. He therefore advocated a 'mixed' constitution which would leave government in the hands of the 'middle classes', those who are neither rich nor poor.

Modern government, however, is far too complex to be classified simply on an Aristotelian basis. Moreover, the simplistic classification of regimes as first world, second world and third world has become impossible to sustain in the light of the political and economic changes that have occurred in the former communist bloc since the revolutions of 1989-91. What used to be called first world regimes are better categorised as 'liberal democracies'. They are found throughout the industrialised West – North America, Europe and Australasia – have developed in parts of Eastern Europe and in some developing countries, such as the world's largest liberal democracy, India.

Such systems of government are 'liberal' in the sense that they respect the principle of limited government; individual rights and liberties enjoy some form of protection from government. Limited government is typically upheld in three ways. In the first place, liberal democratic government is constitutional. A constitution defines the duties, responsibilities and functions of the various institutions of government and establishes the relationship between government and the individual. Put most simply, it is the rules which govern the government. In most liberal democracies – Britain and Israel are exceptions – constitutional rules are codified and entrenched in a single authoritative document, a 'written' constitution, which constitutes the highest law of the land. Secondly, government is limited by the fact that power is fragmented and dispersed throughout a number of institutions, creating internal tensions or 'checks and balances'. Thirdly, government is limited by the existence of a vigorous and independent civil society, consisting of autonomous groups such as businesses, trade unions, pressure groups and so forth, meaning that in practice there is a strong correlation between liberal democratic political structures and capitalist economic ones.

Liberal democracies are 'democratic' in the sense that government rests upon the consent of the governed. This implies a form of representative democracy in which the right to exercise government power is gained by success in regular and competitive elections. Typically, such systems possess universal adult suffrage, secret ballot elections and respect a range of democratic rights such as freedom of expression, freedom of assembly and freedom of movement. The cornerstone of liberal democratic government is political pluralism, the existence of a variety of political creeds, ideologies or philosophies and of open competition for power amongst a number of parties. The democratic credentials of such a system are examined in greater depth in Chapter 8.

There are, however, a number of differences amongst liberal democratic systems of government. Some of them, like the United States and France, are republics, whose head of state is elected, while countries such as Britain and the Netherlands are constitutional monarchies. Most liberal democracies have a parliamentary system of government in which legislative and executive power is fused. In countries such as Britain, Germany, Canada and Australia, the government is both drawn from the legislature and accountable to it, in the sense that it can be removed by an adverse vote. The United States, on the other hand, is the classic example of a presidential system of government, based as it is upon a strict separation of powers between the legislature and the executive. President and Congress are separately elected and each possesses a range of constitutional powers, enabling it to check the other. France, however, possesses a hybrid system in which a separately elected president presides over a prime minister and government which is nevertheless drawn from and accountable to the legislature.

Some liberal democracies, however, possess majoritarian governments. These occur when a single party, either because of its electoral support or the nature of the electoral system, is able to form a government on its own. Typically, majoritarian democracies possess two-party systems in which power alternates between two major parties, as has traditionally occurred in Britain and New Zealand. Presidential systems of government are sometimes seen as a bulwark against majoritarianism in that they foster institutional tension between the legislature and the executive, which in the United States has led at times to the phenomenon of 'government gridlock'. In continental Europe, on the other hand, coalition government is the norm, the focal point of which is a continual process of bargaining amongst the parties that share government power and the interests they represent. In countries such as Austria, Belgium and the Netherlands in which linguistic or religious differences are acute, so-called consociational forms of democracy have developed based upon a permanent form of power-sharing within a divided society.

In the aftermath of the collapse of communism, and with the steady emergence of competitive and electoral processes at least in the newly industrialised states of the developing world, 'end of ideology' theorists such as Francis Fukuyama (1992) proclaimed that government throughout the world was being irresistibly remodelled on liberal democratic lines.

However, despite the advance of democratisation in the 1980s and 1990s, a number of alternatives to the Western liberal model of government can be identified. These include postcommunist government, East Asian government, Islamic government and military government. Postcommunist government has generally assumed an outwardly liberal democratic form, with the adoption of multi-party elections and the introduction of market-based economic reforms. Nevertheless, to varying degrees, government in postcommunist states is distinguished by three factors. First, the need to deal with the politico–cultural consequences of communist rule, especially the absence or weakness of a civic culture that emphasises participation, bargaining and consensus; second, instabilities arising from the difficult transition from central planning to some form of market capitalism; and third, the general weakness of state power, particularly when the state is confronted by the re-emergence of ethnic and nationalist tensions or the rise of organised crime.

Government forms in East Asia, notably in Japan and the so-called 'tiger' economies of South Korea, Taiwan, Hong Kong, Singapore and Malaysia, have tended to be characterised by the priority given to boosting growth and delivering prosperity, over considerations such as individual freedom in the Western sense of civil liberty. They often exhibit broad support for 'strong' government, sometimes exercised through powerful leaders or 'ruling' parties, underpinned by widely respected Confucian principles such as loyalty, discipline and duty. However, the future of such regimes is likely to be shaped by how they respond to the economic downturn of the late 1990s. Islamic government contains both fundamentalist and pluralist forms. The fundamentalist version of political Islam is most commonly associated with Iran and states such as Sudan, Pakistan and Afghanistan that have, in different ways, followed the Iranian example. Militant political Islam, as inspired by Ayatollah Khomeini (see p. 103) involves the construction of a theocracy in which political and other affairs are structured according to 'higher' religious principles and political office is closely linked to religious status. By contrast, in states such as Malaysia, Islam has the status of an official state religion but operates alongside a form of 'guided' democracy which allows at least the semblance of political competition. Despite a general trend towards civilian government and some form of electoral democracy, military government continues to be important in Africa, the Middle East and parts of South-East Asia and Latin America. The classical form of military government is the junta, a clique of senior officers that seizes power through a revolution or *coup d'état*. Other forms of military government include military-backed personalised dictatorships and regimes in which military leaders content themselves with 'pulling the strings' behind the scenes, creating a facade of civilian rule and constitutionality.

Political systems

Classifications of government are clearly linked to what are called 'political systems'. However, the notion that politics is a 'system' is relatively new, only emerging in the 1950s, influenced by the development of systems theory and its application in works like Talcott Parsons's *The Social System* (1951). It has, nevertheless, brought about a significant shift in the understanding of governmental processes. Traditional approaches to government focused upon the machinery of the state and examined the constitutional rules and institutional structure of a particular system of government. Systems analysis has, however, broadened the understanding of government by highlighting the complex interaction between it and the larger society. A 'system' is an organised or complex whole, a set of interrelated and interdependent parts that form a collective entity. Systems analysis therefore rejects a piecemeal approach to politics in favour of an overall approach: the whole is more important than its individual parts. Moreover, it emphasises the importance of relationships, implying that each part only has meaning in terms of its function within the whole. A political system therefore extends far beyond the institutions of government themselves and encompasses all those processes, relationships and institutions through which government is linked to the governed.

The seminal work in this area was David Easton's *The Political System* ([1953] 1981). In defining politics as 'the authoritative allocation of values', Easton drew attention to all those processes which shape the making of binding decisions. A political system consists of a linkage between what Easton called 'inputs' and 'outputs'. Inputs into the political system consist of both demands and supports. Demands can take the form of the desire for higher living standards, improved employment prospects or welfare benefits, greater participation in politics, protection for minority and individual rights and so forth. Supports, on the other hand, are the ways in which the public contributes to the political system by paying taxes, offering compliance and being willing to participate in public life. Outputs consist of the decisions and actions of government, including the making of policy, the passing of laws, the imposition of taxes and the allocation of public funds. Clearly, these outputs generate 'feedback' which in turn will shape further demands and supports. As Easton conceived it, the political system is thus a dynamic process, within which stability is only achieved if outputs bear some relationship to inputs. In other words, if policy outputs do not satisfy popular demands these will progressively increase until the point when 'systemic breakdown' will occur. The capacity to achieve such stability is based upon how the flow of inputs into the political system is regulated by 'gate keepers', such as interest groups and political parties, and the success of government itself in converting inputs into outputs.

Some political systems will be far more successful in achieving stability than others. It is sometimes argued that this explains the survival and spread of liberal-democratic forms of government. Liberal democracies contain a number of institutional mechanisms which force government to pay heed to popular demands, creating channels of communication between government and the governed. For instance, the existence of competitive party systems means that government power is gained by that set of politicians whose policies most closely correspond to the preferences of the general public. Even if politicians are self-seeking careerists, they must respond to electoral pressures to have any chance of winning office. Demands that are not expressed by parties or articulated at election time can be championed by interest groups or other lobbyists. Further, the institutional fragmentation typically found in liberal democracies offers competing interests a number of points of access to government.

On the other hand, stress can also build up within liberal democratic systems. Electoral democracy, for example, may degenerate into a tyranny of the majority, depriving economic, ethnic or religious minorities of an effective voice. Similarly, parties and interest groups may be far more successful in advancing the demands of the wealthy, the educated and the articulate than they are in representing the poor and disadvantaged. Nevertheless, by comparison with liberal democracies, second world regimes operated within political systems that were clearly less stable. In the absence of party competition and independent pressure groups, the dominant party-state apparatus simply lacked mechanisms through which demands could be articulated, so preventing policy outputs from coming into line with inputs. Tensions built up in these systems, first expressed in dissent and later in open protest, fuelled by the emergence of better educated and more sophisticated urban populations and by the material affluence and political liberty apparently enjoyed in Western liberal democracies.

The analysis of government as a systemic process is, however, not without its critics. Although systems analysis is portrayed as a neutral and scientific approach to government, normative and ideological biases undoubtedly operate within it. Easton's work, for example, reflects an essential liberal conception of politics. In the first place, it is based upon a consensus model of society that suggests that any conflicts or tensions that occur can be reconciled through the political process. This implies that an underlying social harmony exists within liberal capitalist societies. Furthermore, Easton's model assumes that a fundamental bias operates within the political system in favour of stability and balance. Systems are self-regulating mechanisms which seek to perpetuate their own existence, and the political system is no exception. Once again, this reflects the liberal theory that government institutions are neutral in the sense that they are willing and able to respond to all interests and groups in society. Such beliefs are linked not only to a particular conception of society but also to a distinctive view of the nature of state power.

The state

The term 'state' can be used to refer to a bewildering range of things: a collection of institutions, a territorial unit, a historical entity, a philosophical idea and so on. In everyday language, the state is often confused with the government, the two terms being used interchangeably. However, although some form of government has probably always existed, at least within large communities, the state in its modern form did not emerge until about the fifteenth century. The precise relationship between state and government is, nevertheless, highly complex. Government is part of the state, and in some respects is its most important part, but it is only an element within a much larger and more powerful entity. So powerful and extensive is the modern state that its nature has become the centrepiece of political argument and ideological debate. This is reflected, in the first place, in disagreement about the nature of state power and the interests it represents, that is, competing theories of the state. Secondly, there are profound differences about the proper function or role of the state: what should be done by the state and what should be left to private individuals.

Government and the state

The state is often defined narrowly as a separate institution or set of institutions, as what is commonly thought of as *'the* state'. For example when Louis XIV declared, 'L'état c'est moi', he was referring to the absolute power that was vested in himself as monarch. The state therefore stands for the apparatus of government in its broadest sense, for those institutions that are recognisably 'public' in that they are responsible for the collective organisation of communal life and are funded at the public's expense. Thus the state is usually distinguished from civil society. The state comprises the various institutions of government, the bureaucracy, the military, police, courts, social security system and so forth; it can be identified with the entire 'body politic'. It is in this sense, for instance, that it is possible to talk about 'rolling forward' or 'rolling back' the state, by which is meant expanding or contracting the responsibilities of state institutions and, in the process, enlarging or reducing the machinery of the state. However, such an institutional definition fails to take account of the fact that, in their capacity as citizens, individuals are also part of the political community, members of the state. Moreover, the state has a vital territorial component, its authority being confined to a precise geographical area. This is why the state is best thought of not just as a set of institutions but as a particular kind of political association, specifically one that establishes sovereign jurisdiction within defined territorial borders. In that sense, its institutional apparatus merely gives expression to state authority.

The defining feature of the state is sovereignty, its absolute and unrestricted power, discussed at greater length in Chapter 4. The state commands supreme power in that it stands above all other associations and groups in society; its laws demand the compliance of all those who live within the territory. Thomas Hobbes conveyed this image of the state as the supreme power by portraying it as a 'Leviathan', a gigantic monster, usually represented as a sea creature. It is precisely its sovereignty which distinguishes the modern state from earlier forms of political association. In medieval times, for instance, rulers exercised power but only alongside a range of other bodies, notably the church, the nobility, and the feudal guilds. Indeed, it was widely accepted that religious authority, centring upon the Pope, stood above the temporal authority of any earthly ruler. The modern state, however, which first emerged in fifteenth- and sixteenth-century Europe, took the form of a system of centralised rule that succeeded in subordinating all other institutions and groups, spiritual and temporal. Although such a state is now the most common form of political community worldwide, usually taking the form of the nation-state, there are still examples of stateless societies. Traditional societies, for instance, found amongst semi-nomadic peoples and sometimes settled tribes, can be said to be stateless in that they lack a central and sovereign authority, even though they may possess mechanisms of social control that can be described as government. Furthermore, a state can break down when its claim to exercise sovereign power is successfully challenged by another group or body, as occurs at times of civil war. In this way, Lebanon in the 1980s, racked by war amongst rival militias and invaded by Israeli and Syrian armies, and the former Yugoslavia in the early 1990s, can both be described as stateless societies.

In addition to sovereignty, states can be distinguished by the particular form of authority that they exercise. In the first place, state authority is territorially limited: states claim sovereignty only within their own borders and thus regulate the flow of persons and goods across these borders. In most cases these are land borders, but they may also extend several miles into the sea. Secondly, the jurisdiction of the state within its borders is universal, that is, everyone living within a state is subject to its authority. This is usually expressed through citizenship, literally membership of the state, which entails both rights and duties. Non-citizens resident in a state may not be entitled to certain rights, like the right to vote or hold public office, and may be exempt from particular obligations, such as jury service or military service, but they are nevertheless still subject to the law of the land.

Thirdly, states exercise compulsory jurisdiction. Those living within a state rarely exercise choice about whether or not to accept its authority. Most people become subject to the authority of a state by virtue of being born within its borders; in other cases this may be a result of conquest. Immigrants and naturalised citizens are here exceptions since they alone can be said to have voluntarily accepted the authority of a state. Finally, state authority is backed up by coercion: the state must have the capacity to ensure that its laws are obeyed, which in practice means that it must possess the ability to punish transgressors. Max Weber (1864–1920) suggested in 'Politics as a Vocation' (1948) that 'the state is a human community that (successfully) claims the monopoly of the legitimate use of physical force within a given territory'. By this he meant not only that the state had the ability to ensure the obedience of its citizens but also the acknowledged *right* to do so. A monopoly of 'legitimate violence' is therefore the practical expression of state sovereignty.

Nevertheless, the relationship between the state and government remains complex. The state is an inclusive association, which in a sense embraces the entire community and encompasses those institutions that constitute the public sphere. Government can thus be seen as merely part of the state. Moreover, the state is a continuing, even permanent, entity. By contrast, government is temporary: governments come and go and systems of government are remodelled. On the other hand, although government may be possible without a state, the state is inconceivable in the absence of government. As a mechanism through which collective decisions are enacted, government is responsible for making and implementing state policy. Government is, in effect, 'the brains' of the state, it gives authoritative expression to the state. In this way, government is usually thought to dictate to and control other state bodies, the police and military, educational and welfare systems and the like. By implementing the various state functions, government serves to maintain the state itself in existence.

The distinction between state and government is not, however, simply an academic refinement; it goes to the very heart of constitutional rule. Government power can only be held in check when the government of the day is prevented from encroaching upon the absolute and unlimited authority of the state. This is particularly important given the conflicting interests which the state and the government represent. The state supposedly reflects the permanent interests of society – the maintenance of public order, social stability, long-term prosperity and national security – while government is inevitably influenced by the partisan sympathies and ideological preferences of the politicians who happen to be in power. If government succeeds in harnessing the sovereign power of the state to its own partisan goals, dictatorship is the likely result. Liberal democratic regimes have sought to counter this possibility by creating a clear divide between the personnel and machinery of government on the one hand, and the personnel and machinery of the state on the other. Thus the personnel of state institutions, like the civil service, the courts and the military, are recruited and trained in a bureaucratic manner, and are expected to observe strict political neutrality, enabling them to resist the ideological enthusiasms of the government of the day. However, such are the powers of patronage possessed by modern chief executives like the US president and the British prime minister, that this apparently clear division is often blurred in practice.

Theories of the state

In most Western industrialised countries the state possesses clear liberal democratic features. Liberal democratic states are, for instance, characterised by constitutional government, a system of checks and balances amongst major institutions, fair and regular elections, a democratic franchise, a competitive party system, the protection of individual rights and civil liberties and so forth. Although there is broad agreement about the characteristic features of the liberal democratic state, there is far less agreement about the nature of state power and the interests that it represents. Controversy about the nature of the state has, in fact, increasingly dominated modern political analysis and goes to the very heart of ideological and theoretical disagreements. In this sense, the state is an 'essentially contested' concept: there are a number of rival theories of the state, each offering a different account of its origins, development and impact.

Mainstream political analysis is dominated by the liberal theory of the state. This dates back to the emergence of modern political theory in the writings of social contract theorists such as Hobbes and Locke. These thinkers argued that the state had risen out of a voluntary agreement, or social contract, made by individuals who recognised that only the establishment of a sovereign power could safeguard them from the insecurity, disorder and brutality of the 'state of nature'. In liberal theory, the state is thus a neutral arbiter amongst competing groups and individuals in society; it is an 'umpire' or 'referee', capable of protecting each citizen from the encroachment of his or her fellow citizens. The state is therefore a neutral entity, acting in the interests of all and representing what can be called the 'common good' or 'public interest'.

This basic theory has been elaborated by modern writers into a pluralist theory of the state. Pluralism is, at heart, the theory that political power is dispersed amongst a wide variety of social groups rather than an elite or ruling class. It is related to what Robert Dahl (see p. 223) termed 'polyarchy', rule by the many. Although distinct from the classical conception of democracy as popular self-government, this nevertheless accepts that democratic processes are at work within the modern state: electoral choice ensures that government must respond to public opinion, and organised interests offer all citizens a voice in political life. Above all, pluralists believe that a rough equality exists amongst organised groups and interests in that each enjoys some measure of access to government and government is prepared to listen impartially to all. At the hub of the liberal democratic state stand elected politicians who are publicly accountable because they operate within an open and competitive system. Non-elected state bodies like the civil service, judiciary, police, army and so on, carry out their responsibilities with strict impartiality, and are anyway subordinate to their elected political masters.

An alternative, neo-pluralist theory of the state has been developed by writers such as J.K. Galbraith and Charles Lindblom. They argue that the modern industrialised state is both more complex and less responsive to popular pressures than the classical pluralist model suggests. While not dispensing altogether with the notion of the state as an umpire acting in the public interest or common good, they insist that this picture needs qualifying. It is commonly argued by neo-pluralists, for instance, that it is impossible to portray all organised interests as equally powerful since in a capitalist economy business enjoys advantages which other groups clearly cannot rival. In *The Affluent Society* ([1962] 1985), Galbraith emphasised the ability of business to shape public tastes and wants through the power of advertising, and drew attention to the domination of major corporations over small firms and, in some cases, government bodies. Lindblom, in *Politics and Markets* (1977), pointed out that, as the major investor and largest employer in society, business is bound to exercise considerable sway over any government, whatever its ideological leanings or manifesto promises. Although neo-pluralists do not describe business as an 'elite group', capable of dictating to government in all areas, still less as a 'ruling class', they nevertheless accept that a liberal democracy is a 'deformed polyarchy' in which business usually exerts pre-eminent influence, especially over the economic agenda.

New Right ideas and theories became increasingly influential from the 1970s onwards. Like neo-pluralism, they built upon traditional liberal foundations but now constitute a major rival to classical pluralism. The New Right, or at least its neo-liberal or libertarian wing, is distinguished by strong antipathy towards government intervention in economic and social life, born of the belief that the state is a parasitic growth which threatens both individual liberty and economic security. The state is no longer an impartial referee but has become a self-serving monster, a 'nanny' or 'leviathan' state, interfering in every aspect of life. New Right thinkers have tried, in particular, to highlight the forces that have led to the growth of state intervention and which, in their view, must be countered. Criticism has, for instance, focused upon the process of party competition, or what Samuel Britten (1977) called 'the economic consequences of democracy'. New Right theorists believe that the democratic process encourages politicians to outbid one another by making vote-winning promises to the electorate, and encourages electors to vote according to short-term self-interest rather than long-term well-being. Equally, closer links between government and major economic interests, business and trade unions in particular, has greatly increased pressure for subsidies, grants, public investment, higher wages, welfare benefits and so forth, so leading to what Anthony King (1975) called the problem of government 'overload'. Public choice theorists such as William Niskanen (1971) have also suggested that 'big' government has been generated from within the machinery of the state itself by the problem of 'bureaucratic over-supply'. Pressure for the expansion of the state comes from civil servants and other public employees, who recognise that it will bring them job security, higher pay and improved promotion prospects.

Pluralism has been more radically rejected by elitist thinkers who believe that behind the facade of liberal democracy there lies the permanent power of a 'ruling elite'. Classical elitists such as Gaetano Mosca (1857–1941), Vilfredo Pareto (1848–1923) and Robert Michels (1876–1936) were concerned to demonstrate that political power *always* lies in the hands of a small elite and that egalitarian ideas, such as socialism and democracy, are a myth. Modern elitists, by contrast, have put forward strictly empirical theories about the distribution of power in particular societies, but have nevertheless drawn the conclusion that political power is concentrated in the hands of the few. An example of this was Joseph Schumpeter (see p. 223), whose *Capitalism, Socialism and Democracy* ([1944] 1976) suggested the theory of democratic elitism. Schumpeter described democracy as 'that institutional arrangement for arriving at political decisions in which individuals acquire the power to decide by means of a competitive struggle for the people's vote'. The electorate can decide which elite rules, but cannot change the fact that the power is always exercised by an elite. Radical elite theorists have gone further and decried the importance of elections altogether. In *The Managerial Revolution* (1941), James Burnham suggested that a 'managerial class' dominated all industrial societies, both capitalist and communist, by virtue of its technical and scientific knowledge and its administrative skills. Perhaps the most influential of modern elite theorists, C. Wright Mills, argued in *The Power Elite* (1956) that American politics was dominated by big business and the military, commonly referred to as the 'military-industrial complex', which dictated government policy, largely immune from electoral pressure.

Marxism offers an analysis of state power that fundamentally challenges the liberal image of the state as a neutral arbiter or umpire. Marxists argue that the state cannot be understood separate from the economic structure of society: the state emerges out of the class system, its function being to maintain and defend class domination and exploitation. The classical Marxist view is expressed in Marx's often-quoted dictum from *The Communist Manifesto* ([1848] 1976): 'the executive of the modern state is but a committee for managing the common affairs of the whole bourgeoisie'. This view was stated still more starkly by Lenin (see p. 82) in *The State and Revolution* ([1917] 1973), who referred to the state simply as 'an instrument for the oppression of the exploited class'. Whereas classical Marxists stressed the coercive role of the state, modern Marxists have been forced to take account of the apparent legitimacy of the 'bourgeois' state, particularly in the light of the achievement of universal suffrage and the development of the welfare state. For example, Antonio Gramsci (see p. 83) emphasised the degree to which the domination of the ruling class is achieved not only by open coercion but is also elicited by consent. He believed that the bourgeoisie had established 'hegemony', ideological leadership or domination, over the proletariat, and insisted that the state played an important role in this process. Other Marxists have found in Marx himself the more sophisticated notion that the state can enjoy 'relative autonomy' from the ruling class and so can respond at times to the interests of other classes. In *Political Power and Social Class* (1973), Nicos Poulantzas portrayed the state as a 'unifying social formation', capable of diluting class tensions through, for example, the spread of political rights and welfare benefits. However, although this neo-Marxist theory echoes liberalism in seeing the state as an arbiter, it nevertheless emphasises the class character of the modern state by pointing out that it operates in the long-term interests of capitalism and therefore perpetuates a system of unequal class power.

The most radical condemnation of state power is, however, found in the writings of anarchists. Anarchists believe that the state and indeed all forms of political authority are both evil and unnecessary. They view the state as a concentrated form of oppression: it reflects nothing more than the desire of those in power, often loosely referred to as a 'ruling class', to subordinate others for their own benefit. In the words of the nineteenth-century Russian anarchist, Michael Bakhunin (1914–76), the state is 'the most flagrant, the most cynical and the most complete negation of humanity'. Even modern anarcho-capitalists such as Murray Rothbard

Marxism

Marxism as a theoretical system developed out of, and drew inspiration from, the writings of Karl Marx. However, 'Marxism' as a codified body of thought came into existence only after Marx's death. It was the product of the attempt by later Marxists to condense Marx's ideas and theories into a systematic and comprehensive world view that suited the needs of the growing socialist movement. However, a variety of Marxist traditions can be identified, including 'classical' Marxism (the Marxism of Marx), 'orthodox' Marxism or 'dialectical materialism', the mechanistic form of Marxism that served as the basis for Soviet communism, and 'Western', 'modern' or 'neo' Marxism, which tend to view Marxism as a humanist philosophy and are sceptical about its scientistic and determinist pretensions.

The cornerstone of Marxist philosophy is what Engels called the 'materialist conception of history'. This highlights the importance of economic life and the conditions under which people produce and reproduce their means of subsistence, reflected, simplistically, in the belief that the economic 'base', consisting essentially of the 'mode of production', or economic system, conditions or determines the ideological and political 'superstructure'. Marxist theory therefore explains social, historical and cultural development in terms of material and class factors. The basis of the Marxist tradition is Marx's teleological theory of history, which suggests that history is driven forward through a dialectical process in which internal contradictions within each mode of production are reflected in class antagonism. Capitalism, then, is only the most technologically advanced of class societies, and is itself destined to be overthrown in a proletarian revolution which will culminate in the establishment of a classless, communist society.

Marxism has constituted for most of the modern period the principal alternative to liberalism (see p. 29) as the basis for political thought. Its critique of liberalism amounts to an attack on individualism and the narrow concern with civic and political rights, on the grounds that it ignores wider social and historical developments and thereby conceals the reality of unequal class power. Liberalism is thus the classic example of bourgeois ideology, in that it serves to legitimise capitalist class relations. Nevertheless, modern Marxists, repelled by the Bolshevik model of orthodox communism, have sometimes sought to blend Marxism with aspects of liberal democracy, notably political pluralism and electoral democracy. Marxist theories have influenced feminism (see p. 60) and provide the basis of socialist feminism, which highlights links between capitalism and patriarchy. Marxism, further, provided the basis for critical theory (see p. 280), which attempted to blend Marxist political economy with Hegelian philosophy and Freudian psychology. Attempts have also been made to fuse Marxism with certain rational choice theories (see p. 246), notably in the form of so-called analytical Marxism.

$\longrightarrow$

Marxism continued

The intellectual attraction of Marxism has been that it embodies a remarkable breadth of vision, offering to understand and explain virtually all aspects of social and political existence and uncovering the significance of processes that conventional theory ignores. Politically, it has attacked exploitation and oppression, and had a particularly strong appeal to disadvantaged groups and peoples. However, Marxism's star has dimmed markedly in the late twentieth century. To some extent, this occurred as the tyrannical and dictatorial features of communist regimes themselves were traced back to Marx's ideas and assumptions. Marxist theories were, for instances, seen as implicitly monistic in that rival belief systems are dismissed as ideological. The crisis of Marxism, however, intensified as a result of the collapse of communism in the revolutions of 1989–91. This suggested that if the social and political forms which Marxism had inspired (however unfaithful they may have been to Marx's original ideas) no longer exist, Marxism as a world-historical force is effectively dead.

Key figures

Karl Marx (see p. 373)   The breadth and complexity of Marx's own writings has made it difficult to establish the 'Marxism of Marx'. A distinction is sometimes drawn between the 'young Marx' and the 'mature Marx'. Marx's early writings portray him to be a humanist socialist, concerned about alienation, the commodification and depersonalisation of labour under capitalism, and interested in human self-realisation under communism. However, in his later writings, Marx undertook a highly detailed examination of the economic conditions of capitalism, leading some to describe him as an economic determinist and the progenitor of later orthodox Marxism.

Friedrich Engels (1820–95)   A German industrialist and life-long friend and collaborator of Marx, Engels elaborated Marx's ideas and theories for the benefit of the growing socialist movement in the late nineteenth century. He emphasised the role of the dialectic as a force operating in both social life and nature, helping to give rise to dialectical materialism as a distinct brand of Marxism, and portraying Marxism in terms of a specific set of historical laws. Engels also extended materialist analysis to the family, arguing that monogamous marriage involves the subjection of women by men and has its origins in the institution of private property. Engels' major works include *Anti-Dühring* (1877–8), *The Origins of the Family, Private Property and the State* (1884) and *Dialectics of Nature* (1925).

Vladimir Illich Lenin (1870–1924)   A Russian revolutionary and leader of the Soviet Union, 1917–24, Lenin was the most influential Marxist theorist of the twentieth century. He was primarily concerned with the issues of organisation and revolution, emphasising the central importance of a tightly-organised 'vanguard' party to lead and guide the proletarian class. Lenin analysed colonialism as an economic phenomenon and highlighted the possibility of

→

turning world war into class war. He was also firmly committed to the 'insurrectionary road' to socialism and rejected electoral democracy as 'parliamentary cretinism'. Lenin's best known works include *What is to be Done?* (1902), *Imperialism, the Highest Stage of Capitalism* (1916) and *The State and Revolution* (1917).

Rosa Luxemburg (1871–1919) A Polish-born German communist, Luxemburg established her reputation as a Marxist theorist in her fierce denunciation of revisionism. Her strong belief in revolutionary spontaneity led her to criticise her friend, Lenin, for emphasising hierarchic organisation and the leadership of a vanguard party. Luxemburg interpreted imperialism as a competitive struggle between capitalist nations which would lead, she predicted, to an inevitable capitalist breakdown. Her major works include *Social Reform or Revolution* (1899), *Mass Strike, Party and Trade Unions* (1906) and *The Accumulation of Capital* (1913).

Leon Trotsky (1879–1940) A Russian revolutionary and political thinker, Trotsky was an early critic of Lenin's theory of the party, but joined the Bolsheviks in 1917. His theoretical contribution to Marxism centres on the theory of permanent revolution, which suggested that socialism could be established in Russia without the need for the bourgeois stage of development. Trotskyism is usually associated with an unwavering commitment to internationalism and with a denunciation of Stalinism that portrays it as a form of bureaucratic degeneration. Trotsky's major writings include *Results and Prospects* (1906), *History of the Russian Revolution* (1931) and *The Revolution Betrayed* (1936).

Antonio Gramsci (1891–1937) An Italian Marxist and social theorist, Gramsci tried to redress the emphasis within orthodox Marxism upon economic and material factors. He rejected any form of 'scientific' determinism by stressing, through the theory of hegemony (the dominance of bourgeois ideas and beliefs), the importance of the political and intellectual struggle. Gramsci highlighted the degree to which ideology is embedded at every level in society and called for the establishment of a rival 'proletarian hegemony', based upon socialist principles, values and theories. Gramsci's major work is *Prison Notebooks* (1929–35).

Mao Zedong (1893–1976) A Chinese Marxist theorist and leader of the People's Republic of China, 1949–76, Mao adapted Marxism–Leninism to the needs of an overwhelmingly agricultural and still traditional society. His ideological legacy is often associated with the Cultural Revolution, 1966–70, a radical egalitarian movement that denounced elitism and 'capitalist roaders'. Maoism emphasises the importance of politics in the form of the radical zeal of the masses, acknowledges the necessity of opposition and conflict, and stresses community rather than hierarchic state organisation. Mao's main works include *On the People's Democratic Dictatorship* (1949), *On the Ten Major Relationships* (1956) and *On the Correct Handling of Contradictions Among People* (1957).

→

Marxism continued

Further reading

Avineri, S. *The Social and Political Thought of Karl Marx.* Cambridge: Cambridge University Press, 1968.
Kolakowski, L. *Main Currents of Marxism,* 3 vols. Oxford: Oxford University Press, 1978.
McLellan, D. *Marxism After Marx.* London: Macmillan, 1980.

---

simply dismiss the state as a 'criminal band' or 'protection racket', which has no legitimate claim to exercise authority over the individual. Modern anarchists, however, are less willing than the classic anarchist thinkers to denounce the state as nothing more than an instrument of organised violence. In *The Ecology of Freedom* (1982), for instance, Murray Bookchin (see p. 197) described the state as 'an instilled mentality for ordering reality', emphasising that in addition to its bureaucratic and coercive institutions the state is also a state of mind.

Role of the state

With the exception of anarchists, all political thinkers have regarded the state as, in some sense, a worthwhile or necessary association. Even revolutionary socialists have accepted the need for a proletarian state to preside over the transition from capitalism to communism, in the form of the 'dictatorship of the proletariat'. Thinkers have, however, profoundly disagreed about the exact role that the state should play in society. This has often been portrayed as the balance between the state and civil society. The state, as explained earlier, necessarily reflects sovereign, compulsory and coercive authority. Civil society, on the other hand, embraces those areas of life in which individuals are free to exercise choice and make their own decisions; in other words, it is a realm of voluntary and autonomous associations.

At one extreme in this debate, classical liberals have argued that individuals should enjoy the widest possible liberty and have therefore insisted that the state be confined to a minimal role. This minimal role is simply to provide a framework of peace and social order within which private citizens can conduct their lives as they think best. The state therefore acts rather like a nightwatchman, whose services are only called upon when orderly existence is threatened. This nevertheless leaves the state with three important functions. The central function of the 'minimal' or 'nightwatchman' state is the maintenance of domestic order, in effect, protecting individual citizens from one another. All states thus possess some kind of machinery for upholding law and order. Secondly, it is necessary to ensure that the voluntary agreements or contracts which private individuals enter into are respected, which requires that they can be enforced through a court system. Thirdly, there is the need to provide protection against the possibility of external attack, necessitating some form of armed service. Such minimal states, with institutional apparatus restricted to little more than a police force, court system and army, commonly existed in the nineteenth century. In the twentieth century, however, they have become rare. Newly industrialised countries such as Hong Kong, South Korea and Taiwan are perhaps the best examples, though even in these cases the state has played an important economic role. The minimal state is nevertheless the ideal of the liberal New Right, which argues that economic and social matters should be left entirely in the hands of individuals or private businesses. In their view, an economy free from state interference will be competitive, efficient and productive; and individuals freed from the dead hand of government will be able to rise and fall according to their talents and willingness to work.

Despite efforts since the 1970s to roll back the frontiers of the state, the dominant trend in the twentieth century has been for the state's role progressively to expand. This has occurred in response to electoral pressures for economic and social security, supported by a broad ideological coalition including social democrats, modern liberals and paternalistic conservatives. The principal field of government activism has been the provision of welfare designed to reduce poverty and social inequality. The form which social welfare has taken has, however, varied considerably. In some cases, the social security system operates as little more than a 'safety net' intended to alleviate the worst incidents of hardship. In the United States, for example, welfare provision has usually emphasised self-reliance, and targeted benefits on those in demonstrable need. On the other hand, developed welfare states have been established in many Western European countries. These have attempted to bring about a wholesale redistribution of wealth through a comprehensive system of public services and state benefits, financed though progressive taxation. *The Beveridge Report* (1942), the model upon which the British welfare state was constructed in the 1940s, envisaged a system of social security that would operate 'from the cradle to the grave'. The concept of welfare and controversies about it are examined in greater depth in Chapter 10.

The second major form state intervention has taken is economic management. As industrialised economies develop they require some kind of management by a central authority. In most Western societies this has led to the emergence of 'managed capitalism'. From the viewpoint of the New Right, however, government's economic responsibilities should be restricted to creating conditions within which market forces can most effectively operate. In practice, this means that the state should only promote competition and ensure stable prices by regulating the supply of money. Others, however, have accepted the need for more far-reaching economic management. Keynesian economic policies have, for instance, been endorsed by social democrats and modern liberals in the hope that they will reduce unemployment and promote growth. Under their influence, public expenditure grew and the state became the most influential of economic actors. Nationalisation, widely adopted in the early postwar period, led to the development of so-called 'mixed economies', allowing the state to control certain industries directly and to have an indirect influence over the entire economy. Although there is now widespread recognition of the need for a balance between the state and the market in economic life, party politics in much of the industrialised West boils down to a debate about where that balance should be struck. Ideological battles often focus upon precisely how far the state should intervene in economic and social life as opposed to leaving matters to the impersonal pressures of the market. These issues are more fully discussed in Chapter 11.

A more extensive form of state intervention, however, developed in orthodox communist countries such as the Soviet Union. These sought to abolish private enterprise altogether and set up centrally planned economies, administered by a network of economic ministries and planning committees. The economy was thus transferred entirely from civil society to the state, creating collectivised states. The justification for collectivising economic life lies in the Marxist belief that capitalism is a system of class exploitation, suggesting that central planning is both morally superior and economically more efficient. The experience of communist regimes in the second half of the twentieth century, however, suggests that state collectivisation struggled to produce the levels of economic growth and general prosperity that were achieved in Western capitalist countries. Without doubt, the failure of central planning contributed to the collapse of orthodox communism in the Eastern European revolutions of 1989–91.

The most extreme form of state control is found in totalitarian states. The essence of totalitarianism is the construction of an all-embracing state, whose influence penetrates every aspect of human existence, the economy, education, culture, religion, family life and so forth. Totalitarian states are characterised by a pervasive system of ideological manipulation and a comprehensive process of surveillance and terroristic policing. Clearly, all the mechanisms through which opposition can be expressed – competitive elections, political parties, pressure groups and free media – have to be weakened or removed. The best examples of such regimes were Nazi Germany and the Soviet Union under Stalin. In effect, totalitarianism amounts to the outright abolition of civil society, the abolition of 'the private', a goal which only fascists, who wish to dissolve individual identity within the social whole, are prepared openly to endorse. In one sense, totalitarianism sets out to politicise every aspect of human existence: it seeks to establish comprehensive state control. However, in another sense, it can be regarded as the death of politics, in that its goal is a monolithic society in which individuality, diversity and conflict are abolished.

Summary

1   Politics involves diversity, conflict and attempts to resolve conflict. While some have seen politics as narrowly related to the affairs of government or to a public sphere of life, others believe that it reflects the distribution of power or resources and so can be found in every social institution.

2   Government refers to ordered rule, a characteristic of all organised societies. First world liberal-democratic forms of government can be distinguished from state socialist second world and various forms of third world government, though such distinctions have been blurred by developments such as the fall of communism.

3   The state is a sovereign political association operating in a defined territorial area. In the view of pluralists, the liberal democratic state acts impartially and responds to popular pressures. However, others suggest that the state is characterised by biases which either systematically favour the bureaucracy or state elite or benefit major economic interests.

4   The role of the state is perhaps the dominant theme of party political disagreement, reflecting different views about the proper relationship between the state and the individual. While some wish to roll back the state and leave matters in the hands of individuals and the market, others want to roll it forward in the cause of social justice and widespread prosperity.

Further reading

Crick, B. *In Defence of Politics*. Harmondsworth and New York: Penguin, 1983.

Dunleavy, P. and O'Leary, B. *Theories of the State: The Politics of Liberal Democracy*. London: Macmillan and New York: New Amsterdam, 1987.

Easton, D. *A Systems Analysis of Political Life*. 2nd edn, Chicago: University of Chicago Press, 1979.

Hague, R., Harrop, M. and Breslin, S. *Comparative Government and Politics: an Introduction*. London: Macmillan, 1998. US edition: 4th edn, *Political Science: A Comparative Introduction*. New York: St Martin's Press, 1998.

Held, D. *Political Theory and the Modern State*. Oxford: Polity and Stanford: Stanford University Press, 1990.

Laver, M. *Invitation to Politics.* Oxford and New York: Basil Blackwell, 1983.

Leftwich, A. (ed.). *What is Politics? The Activity and its Study.* Oxford and New York: Basil Blackwell, 1984.

McLennon, G., Held, D. and Hall, S. (eds). *The Idea of the Modern State.* Milton Keynes and Philadelphia: Open University Press, 1984.

Chapter 4

Sovereignty, the Nation and Supranationalism

Introduction
Sovereignty
The nation
Supranationalism
Summary
Futher reading

Introduction

In virtually all communities political rule is exercised through the institutions of government or the state. However, it is less clear what the proper or appropriate unit of political rule might be. In other words, over what population group and within what territorial boundaries should state power operate? For the last two hundred years the dominant answer to that question has been 'the nation'. It has almost been taken for granted that the nation is the only legitimate political community, and therefore that the nation-state is the highest form of political organisation. Indeed, national sovereignty is usually understood to be the corner-stone of international law, giving each nation the right of self-defence and to determine its own destiny. Nevertheless, the twentieth century has been marked by growing internationalism, reflected in the growth of economic independence as national economies have been incorporated into a global one, and in the emergence of supranational bodies like the League of Nations, the United Nations and the European Union (EU).

While some have applauded this development, arguing that international federations and even world government now constitute the only viable units of political rule, others have protested vehemently about the loss of national independence and self-determination. This debate has usually focused upon the question of sovereignty and, in particular, the merits or otherwise of national sovereignty. Is the exercise of sovereign power essential for the existence of a stable political community, and where should that sovereignty be located? More-over, considerable controversy surrounds the idea of the nation: what factors define a nation, and what makes the nation a viable, perhaps the only viable, unit of political rule? Finally, in an increasingly global society, forms of internationalism and supranationalism have proliferated. What forms has supranational govern-ment taken, and do supranational bodies have the potential eventually to replace the nation-state?

Sovereignty

The concept of sovereignty was born in the seventeenth century, as a result of the emergence in Europe of the modern state. In the medieval period, princes, kings and emperors had acknowledged a higher authority than themselves in the form of God – the 'King of Kings' – and the Papacy. Moreover, authority was divided, in particular between spiritual and temporal sources of authority. However, as feudalism faded in the fifteenth and sixteenth centuries, the authority of transnational institutions, such as the Catholic Church and the Holy Roman Empire, was replaced by that of centralising monarchies. In England this was achieved under the Tudor dynasty, in France under the Bourbons, in Spain under the Habsburgs and so on. For the first time, secular rulers were able to claim to exercise supreme power, and this they did in a new language of sovereignty.

Sovereignty means absolute and unlimited power. However, this apparently simple principle conceals a wealth of confusion, misunderstanding and disagreement. In the first place, it is unclear what this absolute power consists of. Sovereignty can either refer to supreme legal authority or to unchallengeable political power. This controversy relates to the distinction between two kinds of sovereignty, termed by the nineteenth-century constitutional theorist, A.V. Dicey ([1885] 1939), legal sovereignty and political sovereignty. The concept of sovereignty has also been used in two contrasting ways. In the form of internal sovereignty it refers to the distribution of power within the state, and leads to questions about the need for supreme power and its location within the political system. In the form of external sovereignty it is related to the state's role within the international order and to whether or not it is able to operate as an independent and autonomous actor.

Legal and political sovereignty

The distinction between legal sovereignty and political sovereignty is often traced back to a difference of emphasis found in the writings of the classical exponents of the principle, Jean Bodin (see p. 165) and Thomas Hobbes (see p. 124). In *The Six Books of the Commonweal* ([1576] 1962), Bodin argued for a sovereign who made laws but was not himself bound by those laws. Law, according to this view, amounted to little more than the command of the sovereign, and subjects were required simply to obey. Bodin did not, however, advocate or justify despotic rule, but claimed, rather, that the sovereign monarch was constrained by the existence of a higher law, in the form of the will of God or natural law. The sovereignty of temporal rulers was therefore underpinned by divine authority. Hobbes, on the other hand, described sovereignty in terms of power rather than

---

Augustine of Hippo (354–430)

Theologian and political philosopher. Born in North Africa, Augustine
moved to Rome where he became professor of rhetoric. He converted to
Christianity in 386 and returned to North Africa as the Bishop of Hippo. He
wrote against the backdrop of the sacking of Rome by the Goths in 410.

Augustine's defence of Christianity drew upon neo-Platonic philosophy,
Christian doctrine and biblical history. His major work, *City of God*
(413–25), considers the relationship between church and state and examines
the characteristics of two symbolic cities, the earthly city and the heavenly
city, Jerusalem and Babylon. The heavenly city is based upon spiritual grace
and a love of God, and binds both rulers and subjects to the 'common good';
its members will be saved and will go to Heaven hereafter. By contrast, the
earthly city is shaped by a love of self and is characterised by absolute power
or sovereignty; its members are reprobates and will suffer eternal
damnation. Augustine believed that fallen humanity is tainted by original sin
and that without sin there would be no need for government. Government
can curb sinful conduct by the threat or use of punishment, but it cannot
cure original sin. Although Augustine insisted that the church should obey
the laws of the state, his emphasis upon the moral superiority of Christian
principles over political society, and his belief that the church should imbue
society with these principles, has been interpreted as a justification for
theocracy.

---

authority. He built upon a tradition dating back to Augustine which
explained the need for a sovereign in terms of the moral evil that resides
within humankind. In *Leviathan* ([1651] 1968), Hobbes defined sovereignty
as a monopoly of coercive power and advocated that it be vested in the
hands of a single ruler. Although Hobbes's preferred form of government
was a monarchy, he was prepared to accept that, so long as it was
unchallengeable, the sovereign could be an oligarchic group or even
democratic assembly.

This distinction therefore reflects the one between authority and power.
Legal sovereignty is based upon the belief that ultimate and final authority
resides in the laws of the state. This is *de jure* sovereignty, supreme power
defined in terms of legal authority. In other words, it is based upon the
right to require somebody to comply, as defined by law. By contrast,
political sovereignty is not in any way based upon a claim to legal
authority but is concerned simply about the actual distribution of power,
that is, *de facto* sovereignty. Political sovereignty therefore refers to the
existence of a supreme political power, possessed of the *ability* to
command obedience because it monopolises coercive force. However,
although these two concepts can be distinguished analytically, they are

closely related in practice. There are reasons to believe that on their own neither constitutes a viable form of sovereignty.

In a sense, sovereignty always involves a claim to exercise legal authority, a claim to exercise power by right and not merely by virtue of force. All substantial claims to sovereignty therefore have a crucial legal dimension. The sovereignty of modern states, for example, is reflected in the supremacy of law: families, clubs, trade unions, businesses and so on, can establish rules which command authority, but only within limits defined by law. Nevertheless, law on its own does not secure compliance. No society has yet been constructed in which law is universally obeyed and crime entirely unheard of. This is evident in the simple fact that systems of law are everywhere backed up by a machinery of punishment, involving the police, courts, prisons and even the gallows. Legal authority, in other words, is underpinned by the exercise of power. Lacking the ability to enforce a command, a claim to legal sovereignty will carry only moral weight, as the peoples of the Baltic States – Latvia, Estonia and Lithuania – recognised between their invasion by the Soviet Union in 1940 and their eventual achievement of independence in 1991.

A very similar lesson applies to the political conception of sovereignty. Although all states seek a monopoly of coercive power and prevent, or at least limit, their citizens' access to it, very few rule through the use of force alone. Constitutional and democratic government has, in part, come into existence in an attempt to persuade citizens that the state has the right to rule, to exercise authority and not merely power. Perhaps the most obvious exceptions to this are brutally repressive states, such as those in Nazi Germany, Stalinist Russia or Pol Pot's Cambodia, which came close to establishing an exclusively political form of sovereignty because they ruled largely through their ability to repress, manipulate and coerce. However, even in these cases it is doubtful that such states were ever sovereign in the sense of being supreme and unchallengeable; none of them, for instance, was enduringly successful, and their very use of open terror bears witness to the survival of opposition and resistance. Moreover, in building up vast ideological apparatuses, totalitarian leaders like Hitler, Stalin and Pol Pot clearly recognised the need to give their regimes at least the mantle of legal authority.

Internal sovereignty

Internal sovereignty refers to the internal affairs of the state and the location of supreme power within it. An internal sovereign is therefore a political body that possesses ultimate, final and independent authority; one whose decisions are binding upon all citizens, groups and institutions in society. Much of political theory has been an attempt to decide precisely where such sovereignty should be located. Early thinkers, as already noted, were inclined to the belief that sovereignty should be vested in the hands of a single person, a monarch. Absolute monarchs described themselves as 'Sovereigns', and could declare, as did Louis XIV of France in the eighteenth century, that they *were* the state. The overriding merit of vesting sovereignty in a single individual was that sovereignty would then be indivisible; it would be expressed in a single voice that could claim final authority. The most radical departure from this absolutist notion of sovereignty came in the eighteenth century with Jean-Jacques Rousseau (see p. 243). Rousseau rejected monarchical rule in favour of the notion of popular sovereignty, the belief that ultimate authority is vested in the people themselves, expressed in the idea of the 'general will'. The doctrine of popular sovereignty has often been seen as the basis of modern democratic theory. However, sovereignty has also been located in legislative bodies. For example, John Austin (1790–1859) argued that British sovereignty was vested neither in the Crown nor in the people but in the 'Monarch in Parliament'. This was the origin of the doctrine of parliamentary sovereignty, usually seen as the fundamental principle of the British constitution.

What all such thinkers, however, had in common is that they believed that sovereignty could be, and should be, located in a determinant body. They believed that political rule required the existence of an ultimate authority, and only disagreed about who or what this ultimate authority should be. This has come to be known as the 'traditional' doctrine of sovereignty. In an age of pluralistic and democratic government, however, the traditional doctrine has come in for growing criticism. Its opponents argue either that it is intrinsically linked to its absolutist past and so is frankly undesirable, or that it is no longer applicable to modern systems of government which operate according to a network of checks and balances. It has been suggested, for instance, that liberal-democratic principles are the very antithesis of sovereignty in that they argue for a distribution of power amongst a number of institutions, none of which can meaningfully claim to be sovereign. This applies even in the case of popular sovereignty. Although Rousseau never wavered from the belief that sovereignty resides with the people, he acknowledged that the 'general will' was an indivisible whole which could only be articulated by a single individual, who he called 'the legislator'. This has encouraged commentators such as J. L. Talmon (1952) to suggest that Rousseau is the principal intellectual forebear of twentieth-century totalitarianism. Similar claims have been made regarding the British principle of parliamentary sovereignty. Governments that achieve majority control of the House of Commons gain access to unlimited constitutional authority, creating what has been called an 'elective dictatorship' or 'modern autocracy'.

The task of locating an internal sovereign in modern government is particularly difficult. This is clearest in the case of federal states, such as the United States, Canada, Australia and India, where government is divided into two levels, each of which exercises a range of autonomous powers. Federalism is often said to involve a sharing of sovereignty between these two levels, between the centre and the periphery. However, in developing the notion of a shared or divided sovereignty, federalism moves the concept away from the classical belief in a single and indivisible sovereign power. It may, furthermore, suggest that neither level of government can finally be described as sovereign because sovereignty rests with the document which apportions power to each level: the constitution. The government of the United States offers a particularly good example of such complexities.

It can certainly be argued that in the United States legal sovereignty resides in the Constitution because it defines the powers of federal government by allocating duties, powers and functions to Congress, the Presidency and the Supreme Court, and so defines the nature of the federal system. Nevertheless, by possessing the power to interpret the Constitution it can be suggested that sovereignty resides with the Supreme Court. In effect, the Constitution means what a majority of the nine Supreme Court Justices say it means. The Supreme Court, however, cannot properly be portrayed as the supreme constitutional arbiter since its interpretation of the Constitution can be overturned by amendments to the original document. In this sense, sovereignty can be said to reside with the institution empowered to amend the Constitution: two-thirds majorities in both Houses of Congress and three-quarters of America's state legislatures, or in a convention specifically called for the purpose. On the other hand, one clause of the Constitution – the state's representation in the Senate – specifically forbids amendment. To complicate matters further, it can be argued that sovereignty in the United States is ultimately vested in the American people themselves. This is expressed in the Constitution of the United States of America, 1787, which opens with the words 'We the people . . .' and in its Tenth Amendment which stipulates that powers not otherwise allocated belong 'to the states respectively, or to the people'. In view of these complexities, a polycentric concept of sovereignty has taken root in the United States that is clearly distinct from its European counterpart.

By contrast, it has long been argued that in Britain a single, unchallengeable legal authority exists in the form of the Westminster Parliament. In the words of John Stuart Mill (see p. 258), 'Parliament can do anything except turn a man into a woman'. The British Parliament appears to enjoy unlimited legal power; it can make, amend and repeal any law it wishes. It possesses this power because Britain, unlike the vast majority of states, does not possess a 'written' or codified constitution that defines the powers of government institutions, Parliament included. Moreover, since Britain possesses a unitary rather than federal system of government, no rival legislatures exist to challenge the authority of Parliament; all legislation derives from a single source. Parliament-made law, statute law, is also the highest law of the land, and will therefore prevail over other kinds of law, common law, case law, judge-made law and so forth. Finally, no Parliament is able to bind its successors, since to do so would restrict the laws which any future Parliament could introduce and curtail its sovereign power.

It can be argued, however, that in reality the British Parliament enjoys neither legal nor political sovereignty. Its legal sovereignty has been compromised by membership of the European Union. As an EU member, Britain is obliged to conform to European law and is thus subject to the jurisdiction of the European Court of Justice in Luxemburg. This was underlined in the Factortame case of 1991 when for the first time the European Court of Justice declared British legislation to be unlawful, in this case the Merchant Shipping Act (1988), because it contravened European laws guaranteeing a free movement of goods and persons within the European Community (as it then was). If Parliament can any longer be described as legally sovereign it is only by virtue of the fact that it retains the legal right to withdraw from the EU. In political terms, it is unlikely that Parliament has ever enjoyed sovereignty; it cannot simply act as it pleases. In practice, a wide range of institutions constrain its behaviour, including the electorate, organised interests, particularly those which possess financial or economic muscle, major trading partners, supranational organisations, international treaties and so forth. Parliament's right to withdraw Britain from the EU is, for instance, only notional. As most British trade is now with other EU states, revoking Britain's membership would involve such heavy economic costs as to be, for all practical purposes, unthinkable.

External sovereignty

External sovereignty refers to the state's place in the international order and therefore to its sovereign independence in relation to other states. A state can be considered sovereign over its people and territory despite the fact that no sovereign figures in its internal structure of government. External sovereignty can thus be respected even though internal sovereignty may be a matter of dispute or confusion. Moreover, while questions about internal sovereignty have in a democratic age appeared increasingly outdated, the issue of external sovereignty has become absolutely vital. Indeed, some of the deepest divisions in modern politics involve disputed claims to such sovereignty. The Arab–Israeli conflict, for example, turns on the question of sovereignty. The Palestinians have long sought to establish a homeland and ultimately a sovereign state in territory still claimed by Israel; in turn, Israel has traditionally seen such demands as a challenge to its own sovereignty. The continuing importance of external sovereignty was also underlined by the disintegration of multinational states such as the Soviet Union and Yugoslavia. Following the collapse of the soviet military coup in August 1991, each of the USSR's fifteen republics asserted its independence by proclaiming itself to be a sovereign state. Similarly, in 1992 Yugoslav republics, led by Croatia, Slovenia and Bosnia, broke away from the federation by declaring their sovereignty. This was, however, fiercely resisted by the most powerful republic, Serbia, which, initially at least, presented itself as the defender of Yugoslav sovereignty.

Historically, this notion of sovereignty has been closely linked to the struggle for popular government, the two ideas fusing to create the modern notion of 'national sovereignty'. External sovereignty has thus come to embody the principles of national independence and self-government. Only if a nation is sovereign are its people capable of fashioning their own destiny in accordance with their particular needs and interests. To ask a nation to surrender its sovereignty is tantamount to asking its people to give up their freedom. This is why external or national sovereignty is so keenly felt and, when it is threatened, so fiercely defended. The potent appeal of political nationalism is the best evidence of this.

Although the principle of external sovereignty is widely recognised, and indeed enshrined as a basic principle of international law, it is not without its critics. Some have pointed out, for instance, the sinister implications of granting each state exclusive jurisdiction over its own territory and the capacity to treat its citizens in whatever way it may choose. The twentieth century has, unfortunately, provided abundant evidence of the capacity of states to abuse, terrorise and even exterminate their own citizens. As a result, it is now widely accepted that states should conform to a higher set of moral principles, usually expressed in the doctrine of human rights. Attempts have been made to embody such principles in international law, notably in the United Nations Declaration of Human Rights (1948). Moreover, it is sometimes suggested that the classical argument for sovereignty points beyond national sovereignty. Thinkers such as Bodin and Hobbes emphasised that sovereignty was the only alternative to disorder, chaos and anarchy. Yet this is precisely what a rigorous application of the principle of national sovereignty would turn international politics into. In the absence of some supreme international authority, disputes between rival states will surely lead to armed conflict and war, just as without an internal sovereign conflict among individuals leads to brutality and injustice. In this way, the classical doctrine of sovereignty can be turned into an argument for world government.

Finally, many have questioned whether the notion of an independent or sovereign state is any longer meaningful in an increasingly interdependent world. Modern economic life, for example, is so dominated by multinational companies and international trade that for any nation-state to regard itself as sovereign is a wilful delusion. In addition, if sovereignty is understood in political terms, it is difficult to see how many, or perhaps any, states can be said to be externally sovereign. Coercive power is clearly distributed unequally amongst the states of the world. For much of the post-Second World War period the world was dominated by two mighty 'superpowers', the United States and the Soviet Union, which not only possessed the bulk of the world's nuclear weaponry but also developed a network of alliances to bolster their power. It could therefore be argued that only these two states were sovereign in that only they possessed the economic and military might to enjoy genuine independence. On the other hand, the mere existence of the other superpower served to deny either of them sovereignty, forcing both the United States and the Soviet Union, for example, to press ahead with more costly military programmes than would otherwise have been the case. Nor is it possible to argue that the collapse of the Soviet Union finally made a reality of political sovereignty by creating a world dominated by a single all-powerful state, the United States. This fact was clearly demonstrated by the Gulf War of 1991. Although the war itself provided dramatic proof of US military power, it also underlined the dependence of the United States, in this case upon the coalition of Arab states and Western powers which had made military action diplomatically possible. The fragility of this anti-Iraq coalition was, for instance, one of the factors which pursuaded the Bush administration to end the war once Iraq had been expelled from Kuwait but before the overthrow of Saddam Hussein.

The nation

For over two hundred years the nation has been regarded as the proper, indeed only legitimate, unit of political rule. This belief has been reflected in the remarkable appeal of nationalism, without doubt the most influential of the world's political creeds during much of the nineteenth and twentieth centuries. Nationalism is, at heart, the doctrine that each nation is entitled to self-determination, reflected in the belief that, as far as possible, the boundaries of the nation and those of the state should coincide. Thus the idea of a 'nation' has been used as a way of establishing a non-arbitrary basis for the boundaries of the state. This implies that the highest form of political organisation is the nation-state; in effect, the nation, each nation, is a sovereign entity.

Nationalism has redrawn the map of the world and continues to do so, from the process of European nation-building in the nineteenth century, through the national liberation struggles of the post-Second World War period, to the collapse of the last of the major multinational states, the Soviet Union and Yugoslavia, at the end of the twentieth century. However, it is often far from clear what constitutes a 'nation', or why nations should be regarded as the only legitimate unit of political rule. It is still more difficult to identify the political character of nationalism, a force that has at times been linked to racialism and aggression, but at other times has been associated with international stability and harmony. Finally, it has been suggested that the days of the nation-state are numbered, that the idea of the nation is a hangover from the disintegration of the European empires of the nineteenth century and has no place in a world of ever-closer international cooperation.

Cultural and political nations

All too frequently, the term 'nation' is confused with 'country' or 'state'. This is evident, for example, when 'nationality' is used to indicated membership of a particular state, more properly called 'citizenship'. The confusion is also found in the title of the 'United Nations', an organisation that is clearly one of states rather than nations or peoples. A nation is a cultural entity, a body of people bound together by a shared cultural heritage. It is not, therefore, a political association, nor is it necessarily linked to a particular territorial area. Nations may lack statehood either because, like all African and many Asian nations in the early years of the twentieth century, they are the subjects of a foreign imperial power, or because they are incorporated into multinational states such as the United Kingdom and the Soviet Union of old. Nations may also be landless, as the Jews were until the creation of the state of Israel in 1948, and as the Palestinians have been since.

The cultural factors that define a nation are usually a common language, religion, traditions, historical consciousness and so on. These are*objective* characteristics but they do not in any sense provide a blueprint for deciding when a nation exists, and when one does not. There are, in other words, many examples of enduring and successful nations which contain, like Switzerland, several languages, or, like Indonesia, more than one religion, or, as in the case of the United States, a diverse range of historical traditions and ethnic backgrounds. Ultimately, nations can only be defined *subjectively*, that is by a people's awareness of its nationality or what can be called their national consciousness. This consciousness clearly encompasses a sense of belonging or loyalty to a particular community, usually referred to as 'patriotism', literally a love of one's country. Commentators such as Ernest Gellner in *Nations and Nationalism* (1983) have, however, insisted that the defining feature of national consciousness is not merely the sentiment of loyalty towards or affection for one's nation but the aspiration for self-government and independence. In effect, a nation defines itself by its quest for independent statehood; if it is contained within an existing larger state it seeks to separate from it and redraw state boundaries. An alternative school of thought, however, sees the quest for statehood as merely one expression of nationalist sentiment, the defining feature of nationalism being its capacity to represent the material or economic interests of a national group. This view would accept, for example, that the desire of the French Basques to preserve their language and culture is every bit as 'nationalist' as the openly separatist struggle waged by Basques in Spain.

Because the assertion of nationhood often carries with it significant political demands, the definition of 'nation' tends to be fiercely contested. Many of the most enduring political conflicts turn on whether a particular group is, or should be regarded as, a nation. This is evident in the Sikh struggle for an independent homeland, 'Khalistan', in the Indian state of Punjab, the campaign in Quebec to break away from Canada, and demands by the Scottish National Party (SNP) for independence within Europe. Not infrequently, national identities overlap and are difficult to disentangle from one another. This is particularly clear in the United Kingdom, which could either be regarded as a single British nation or as four separate nations, the English, the Scots, the Welsh and the Northern Irish, or indeed as five nations if divisions between Catholics and Protestants in Northern Ireland are taken into account. Such complications occur because the balance between the political and cultural components of nationhood are almost infinitely variable. The German historian, Friedrich Meinecke, tried to resolve this issue in *Cosmopolitanism and the Nation State* ([1907] 1970) by distinguishing between what he called 'cultural nations' and 'political nations', but when cultural and political considerations are so closely interlinked this task is notoriously difficult.

There are strong reasons for believing that to some degree all nations have been shaped by historical, cultural or ethnic factors. In *The Ethnic Origins of Nations* (1986), Anthony Smith stressed the extent to which modern nations emerged by drawing upon the symbolism and mythology of pre-modern ethnic communities, which he calls 'ethnies'. The nation is therefore historically embedded: it is rooted in a common cultural heritage and language that may long predate the achievement of statehood or even the quest for national independence. Modern nations thus came into existence when these established ethnies were linked to the emerging doctrine of popular sovereignty and associated with a historic homeland. This explains why national identity is so often expressed in the traditions and customs of past generations, as clearly occurs in the case of the Greeks, the Germans, the Russians, the English, the Irish, and so on. From this perspective, nations can be regarded as 'organic', in that they have been fashioned by natural or historical forces rather than by political ones. This may, in turn, mean that 'cultural' nations are stable and cohesive, bound together by a powerful and historical sense of national unity.

Some forms of nationalism are very clearly cultural rather than political in character. For instance, despite the demands of Plaid Cymru for a separate Welsh state, nationalism in Wales largely consists of the desire to defend Welsh culture and, in particular, preserve the Welsh language. Equally, the nationalist pride of the Breton peoples of Brittany is expressed as a cultural movement rather than in any attempt to secede from France. Cultural nationalism is perhaps best thought of as a form of ethnocentrism, an attachment to a particular culture as a source of identity and explanatory frame of reference. Like nations, ethnic groups such as the Afro-Caribbean communities of the United States and Britain share a distinct, and often highly developed, cultural identity. However, unlike nations, ethnic groups are usually content to preserve their cultural identity without demanding political independence. In practice, however, the distinction between an 'ethnic minority' and a fully fledged 'nation' may be blurred; cultural nationalism can in certain circumstances take on a clearly political character. Although black nationalism in the United States places heavy stress upon ethnicity, for example in the desire to reclaim African cultural traditions and identities, in the Black Power movement of the 1960s it assumed a political and revolutionary form, expressed in demands by leaders such as Malcolm X (1926–65) for strict racial segregation. Indeed, the enduring vitality of ethnic identity, often by contrast with the more abstract claims of nationhood, has fuelled centrifugal forces within modern states, creating demands for local or regional power as opposed to international integration.

In other cases, national identity has been forged by circumstances that are more clearly political. Britain, the United States and France have often been seen as the classic examples of this. In Britain's case, the nation or United Kingdom was founded upon the union of what, in effect, were four 'cultural' nations: England, Scotland, Wales and Northern Ireland. The United States is, in a sense, a 'land of immigrants' and so contains peoples from literally all round the world. In such circumstances, a sense of American nationhood has developed more out of a common allegiance to the liberal democratic principles expressed by the Declaration of Independence and the US Constitution than out of a recognition of cultural or historical ties. French national identity is largely based upon traditions linked to the 1789 Revolution and the principles of liberty, equality and fraternity which underlay it. Such nations have, in theory, been founded upon a voluntary acceptance of a common set of principles or goals as opposed to an already-existing cultural identity. It is sometimes argued that the style of nationalism which develops in such societies is typically tolerant and democratic. The United States has, for example, sustained a remarkable degree of social harmony and political unity against a background of profound religious, linguistic, cultural and racial diversity. On the other hand, 'political' nations can at times fail to generate the social solidarity and sense of historical unity which is found in 'cultural' nations. This can be seen in the growth of Scottish and Welsh nationalism in Britain since the 1960s.

Particular problems have been encountered by developing world states struggling to achieve a national identity. Developing world nations can be seen as 'political' in one of two senses. In the first place, in many cases they have achieved statehood only after a struggle against colonial rule, for which reason their national identity is deeply influenced by the unifying quest for national liberation. Nationalism in the devloping world therefore took the form of anticolonialism, and in the period since liberation has assumed a distinctively postcolonial character (see p. 102). Secondly, these nations have often been shaped by territorial boundaries inherited from their former colonial rulers. This is particularly evident in Africa, whose 'nations' often encompass a wide range of ethnic, religious and regional groups, bound together by little more than a common colonial past. African states have, as a result, sometimes experienced deep factional divisions and civil unrest. Nigeria, for example, which contains over 250 tribal groups, experienced a three-year civil war in the 1960s when the Ibo in the east of the country attempted to break away and found an independent state of Biafra. In East Africa, Sudan has been bedevilled by a prolonged civil war in the south, in which mainly Christian Sudanese have risen against the predominantly Muslim north, a conflict deepened by attempts to establish Sudan as an Islamic state.

Nationalism and cosmopolitanism

At the heart of nationalism lies a particular conception of human nature. If the nation is regarded as the only legitimate political community, this is because human beings are thought naturally to gravitate towards people with whom they share cultural similarities. In that sense, nations are organic communities which develop spontaneously. Conservative thinkers have usually been prepared to advance this argument in the belief that humans are dependent creatures, irresistibly drawn together by the prospect of security and social identity which nationhood offers. Socio-

Anticolonialism/postcolonialism

Anticolonialism is a form of nationalism that emerged as the experience of colonial rule, in Africa and Asia in particular, helped to forge a sense of nationhood and a desire for 'national liberation'. Its origins lay in the inter-war period, but it reached its high point in the early post-Second World War period, as the British, French, Dutch and other European empires collapsed in the face of the growing strength of independence movements. In a sense, the colonising Europeans had taken with them the seed of their own destruction, the doctrine of nationalism. Anticolonialism was thus founded upon the same principle of national self-determination that had inspired European nation-building in the nineteenth century, and which had provided the basis for the reorganisation of Europe after the First World War. However, anti-colonialism did not simply replicate classical European nationalism but was also shaped by the distinctive political, cultural and economic circumstances that prevailed in the developing world. In many ways, the desire to pursue a distinctively developing-world political course strengthened rather than weakened once independence had been achieved. Postcolonialism has therefore been drawn towards non-Western and sometimes anti-Western political philosophies.

Most African and Asian anticolonial movements were attracted to some form of socialism. This occurred for two reasons. First, the quest for political independence was closely related to an awareness of economic under-development and subordination to the industrialised states of Europe and North America. Socialism was attractive because it articulated a philosophy of social justice and economic emancipation. Second, socialism provided an analysis of inequality and exploitation through which the colonial experience could be understood and colonial rule challenged. Marxism (see p. 81) was particularly influential in this respect. Its strength was both that its theory of class struggle provided an explanation of imperialism in terms of the capitalist quest for profit, and that its commitment to revolution provided colonised peoples with a means of emancipation in the form of the armed struggle. However, since the 1970s, the influence of Marxism has steadily declined, its place being taken mainly by forms of religious fundamentalism, most significantly Islamic fundamentalism. The fundamentalist impulse in religion is sometimes based upon a belief in the literal truth of sacred texts, but is expressed politically in the assertion that religion provides the basis for social order and political conduct, as well as private morality. Islamic fundamentalists, for instance, call for the founding of an 'Islamic state', a theocracy ruled by spiritual rather than temporal authority.

Anticolonial and postcolonial political theory has the virtue that it challenges a predominantly Eurocentric world view. Whether expressed in revolutionary Marxism or in non-Western religions or philosophies, it attempts to give the developing world a distinctive political voice separate from the universalist pretensions of liberalism (see p. 29). This has encouraged a broader reassessment within political thought, in that, for instance, Islamic

→

and liberal ideas are increasingly considered to be equally legitimate in articulating the traditions and and values of their own communities. Critics, nevertheless, have portrayed postcolonialism in particular as a political dead-end and warned against its authoritarian tendencies. In this view, religious fundamentalism is not a viable political project, but merely a symptom of the difficult adjustments that the process of modernisation brings about. Its further danger is that it is implicitly totalitarian, laying down principles for political organisation that are by definition absolute and unquestionable.

Key figures

Mohandas Karamchand Gandhi (see p. 182)   Gandhi advanced a political philosophy based upon a religious ethic of non-violence and self-sacrifice, ultimately rooted in Hinduism. In his view, violence, 'the doctrine of the sword', was a Western imposition upon India. His notion of non-violent non-cooperation, *satyagarha*, was intended both to manifest national strength and to constitute a new form of spiritual freedom.

Marcus Garvey (1887–1940)   A Jamaican political thinker and activist, Garvey was a pioneer of black nationalism. His political message mixed a call for black pride with an insistence upon economic self-sufficiency. A leader of the 'back to Africa' movement, Garvey developed a philosophy based upon racial segregation and the re-establishment of black consciousness through an emphasis upon African culture and identity. Garvey's ideas helped to shape the Black Power movement of the 1960s and have influenced groups such as the Nation of Islam.

Ayatollah Ruhollah Khomeini (1900–89)   An Iranian cleric and political leader, Khomeini was the foremost exponent of militant political Islam. His world view was rooted in a clear division between the oppressed, understood largely as the poor and excluded of the developing world, and the oppressors, seen as the twin Satans: the United States and the Soviet Union. He called for the establishment of an 'Islamic republic' as a system of institutionalised clerical rule, recognising that this was based upon a novel interpretation of Islamic doctrine. Under his influence, Islam became a theo-political project aimed at regenerating the Islamic world by ridding it of occupation and corruption from outside.

Franz Fanon (1926–61)   A Martinique-born French revolutionary theorist, Fanon is best known for his emphasis upon violence as a feature of the anticolonial struggle. His theory of imperialism emphasised the psychological dimension of colonial subjugation. Decolonialisation is therefore not merely a political process, but one through which a new 'species' of man is created. Fanon argued that only the cathartic experience of violence is powerful enough to bring about this psycho–political regeneration. Fanon's major works include *Black Skin, White Masks* (1952), *The Wretched of the Earth* (1962) and *Towards the African Revolution* (1964).

→

Anticolonialism/postcolonialism continued

Ernesto 'Che' Guevara (1928–67) An Argentinian revolutionary, Che Guevara was a leading exponent of the Marxist version of national liberation. He linked the idea of building a new society with a socialist economic base to the notion of the 'new man', a morally regenerated human being. Guevara's Marxism thus had a strong humanist emphasis in that it stressed the fight against alienation and reflected little interest in 'dry economic socialism'. As a theorist of guerrilla warfare, he proclaimed the possibility of mobilising the peasantry through the activities of a revolutionary nucleus, or *foco*.

Further reading

Essien-Udom, E. V. *Black Nationalism: A Search for Identity in America* Chicago: Chicago University Press, 1972.
Williams, P. (ed.) *Colonial Discourse/Postcolonial Theory.* New York: Colombia University Press, 1994.
Zubaida, Sami *Islam, the People and the State.* London: Routledge, 1989.

biologists such as Ronald Dawkins (1989) have even suggested that the tendency to form kinship groups is rooted in human genes, a notion that can clearly be extended to explain the emergence of ethnic and national groupings. On the other hand, nations have also been thought to be 'constructed' by political and ideological forces. In *Imagined Communities* (1991), Benedict Anderson stressed the degree to which nations exist as mental images rather than genuine communities. Not even in the smallest nation will a person ever meet most of those with whom he or she supposedly shares a cultural identity. Whether they are natural or ideological entities, the belief in the nation undoubtedly has far-reaching political significance. Its precise nature is, however, a matter of considerable debate. In particular, are nations exclusive groups, un-welcoming and intolerant of minorities, and naturally suspicious, even aggressive, towards other nations? Or can nations live in peace and harmony with one another and also accept a high degree of cultural and ethnic pluralism within their borders?

Certain forms of nationalism are without doubt illiberal and intolerant. This applies when nationhood is defined in narrow or exclusive terms, creating a sharp divide between those who are members of a nation and those who are alien to it. Exclusive nationalism is usually a response to the perception that the nation is under threat from within or without, a perception that provokes a heightened sense of unity and is often expressed in hostility or resentment. The integrity of the nation can be challenged by a broad variety of factors, including rapid socio-economic change, political instability, communal rivalry, an upsurge in immigration and the growing power of neighbouring states. In such cases, nationalism offers a vision of an ordered, secure and cohesive community. However, this form of nationalism invariably rejects liberal democratic principles and is more commonly associated with authoritarian creeds. This can most graphically be seen in the case of fascism, which preaches a militant form of nationalism called ultra-nationalism. Termed by Charles Maurras (1862–1952), leader of the right-wing Action Française, 'integral nationalism', this demands the absolute subordination of the individual to the nation. Typically, integral nationalism breeds a sharp distinction between 'us' and 'them', between an in-group and an out-group. Not surprisingly, its clearest manifestation has been found in the pseudo-scientific doctrines of Aryan superiority and anti-Semitism preached by the German Nazis.

Exclusive nationalism also has clear implications for international relations. If immigrants and minorities within the nation are regarded as 'alien', foreigners outside are likely to be regarded with the same distrust and hostility. National exclusivity is thus often reflected in the form of xenophobia, a fear or hatred of foreigners. In such cases, nationalism becomes chauvinistic, aggressive and expansionist. There can be little doubt, for example, that both war and imperialism have at times had their origin in nationalism. The First World War was closely linked to a mood of popular nationalism affecting most of the major European powers, which found expression in demands for colonial expansion and finally war. The Second World War resulted from a programme of conquest and military expansion undertaken by Nazi Germany, fuelled by a heightened sense of nationalist zeal and legitimised by Nazi doctrines of racial superiority.

Such forms of nationalism are, however, very different from those proclaimed by liberal democratic theorists. Liberals have traditionally argued that nationalism is a tolerant and democratic creed which is perfectly reconcilable with international peace and cosmopolitanism. In origin, cosmopolitanism suggests the establishment of a *cosmo polis* or 'world state' that would embrace all humanity. Liberal thinkers have, however, seldom gone this far, and indeed have traditionally accepted the nation as the only legitimate political community. Cosmopolitanism has therefore come to stand for peace and harmony amongst nations, founded upon understanding, tolerance and interdependence. Since the early nineteenth century, thinkers such as the Manchester liberals, Richard Cobden (1804–65) and John Bright (1811–89), have advocated free trade on the grounds that it will promote international understanding and economic interdependence, ultimately making war impossible. The hope is that a stable and peaceful world order will emerge as sovereign nations come to cooperate for mutual benefit. Indeed, liberals believe that if the central goal of nationalism is achieved – each nation becoming a self-governing entity – the principal cause of international conflict will have been removed: nations will have no incentive to go to war against one another. Just as liberals reject the idea that nationalism breeds war they also deny that it necessarily leads to intolerance and racial bigotry. Far from threatening national cohesion, cultural and ethnic diversity is thought to enrich society and promote human understanding.

Such ideas, however, look beyond the nation and nationalism. As embraced by both liberal and socialist theorists, cosmopolitanism challenges the idea that nations are organic or natural entities. Liberals and socialists subscribe to forms of internationalism which hold that political activity should ultimately be organised in the interests of humankind rather than for the benefit of any particular nation. Such a belief is based upon the notion of a 'universal' human nature, which transcends linguistic, religious, territorial, ethnic and national boundaries. It would be wrong, however, to think, that internationalism is necessarily an enemy of the nation. The nation may, for example, still constitute a viable unit of self-government and can perhaps offer a sense of cultural identity and level of social cohesiveness which a global state would be incapable of doing. Nevertheless, if human beings can, and should, identify themselves with humanity as a whole, rather than simply with their nation, this suggests that supranational forms of political association will increasingly play a meaningful and legitimate role. In other words, the days of the sovereign nation-state may be numbered.

A future for the nation-state?

Nationalists have proclaimed the nation-state to be the highest form of political organisation, reflecting as it does the principle that the nation is the sole legitimate unit of political rule. Since 1789 the world has been remodelled according to this principle. In 1810, for instance, only 15 of the 159 states recognised in 1989 as full members of the United Nations were in existence. Well into the twentieth century, most of the world's population were still colonial subjects of one of the European empires. Only three of the 65 states now found in the Middle East and Africa were in existence before 1910, and no fewer than 74 states have come into being since 1959. In large part, these changes have been fuelled by the quest for national independence, expressed in the desire to found a nation-state. In practice, however, the nation-state is an ideal type and has probably never existed in perfect form anywhere in the world. No state is culturally homogeneous; all contain some kind of cultural or ethnic mix. Only an outright ban upon immigration and the forcible expulsion of 'alien' minorities could forge the 'true' nation-state – as Hitler and the Nazis recognised. As a principle to move towards, however, the nation state represents independence and self-government; it has elicited support from peoples in all parts of the world, almost regardless of the political creed they may espouse.

The attraction of the nation-state is that it offers the prospect of both cultural cohesion and political unity. When a group of people who share a common cultural identity gain the right to self-government, community and citizenship coincide. This is why nationalists believe that the forces that have created a world of independent nation-states are natural and irresistible: no other social group could constitute a meaningful political community. This is also why nationalists have been prepared to accord the nation rights similar to those that are usually thought to belong to the individual, treating national self-determination, for instance, with the same respect as individual liberty. Nevertheless, even though the nation-state principle achieved its widest support in the twentieth century, other, very powerful, forces have threatened to make it redundant. Chief amongst these have been advances in the technology of warfare, the progressive internationalisation of economic life, and the growing realisation that the survival of humankind requires the maintenance of a global ecological balance.

The first and most potent factor suggesting that political life should be organised not on a national but on an international level is the devastation wreaked by modern warfare. The strict application of national sovereignty implies that each nation should be entirely independent, in which case the international order is characterised by anarchy. Classical sovereignty theorists showed little anxiety about the dangers inherent in international anarchy, perhaps because warfare at the time was limited to relatively small armies and did not directly affect civilian populations. The carnage of the First World War changed all this. Conscript armies of several million and increasingly mechanised weaponry – tanks, poison gas and aeroplanes were used for the first time – led to the deaths of over 10 million people and brought havoc to much of continental Europe. The First World War was, as a result, followed by attempts to establish a new international order, within which the independence of individual states, and particularly their ability to wage war, was constrained.

The centrepiece of this new order was the ill-fated League of Nations, which aimed to control the spread of arms and prevent war by providing a forum for settling international disputes through negotiation, backed up, at least in theory, by the power to apply both economic and military sanctions. A further series of initiatives followed, leading in 1928 to the signing by 65 nations of the Kellogg–Briand Pact which, in effect, outlawed war except in the case of self-defence. The Second World War underlined this message, particularly as it culminated in 1945 with the first use of nuclear weapons, against the Japanese cities of Hiroshima and Nagasaki. Plans to set up the United Nations Organisation emerged during the war itself and were formally approved by 50 nations at the San Francisco Conference in June 1945. Although the UN recognises each nation as a sovereign legal entity and respects the right to self-determination, measures approved by its Security Council or resolutions passed by its General Assembly constitute the most authoritative source of international law in the modern world. In a nuclear age, in which an ever-larger number of nations possess the means of mass extermination, the anarchy of sovereign and independent nationhood may simply no longer be acceptable. If the desire for a sovereign arose, in the first place, out of the danger posed by disputes between individuals, the prospect of conflict between nation-states in an era of 'total war' surely underlines the need for a sovereign body in the realm of international affairs.

The nation-state may also have little future in an economic order increasingly dominated by multinational companies and international patterns of trade. Just as, in the nineteenth century, the quest for nationhood was fuelled by the desire for larger, national markets, the twentieth century has witnessed the pursuit of economic advantage by the progressive internationalisation of trade. International trade offers the prospect of mutual benefit because it allows nations to specialise in the manufacture of those goods which they are best suited to produce and can thus produce most efficiently. Since the Second World War, strenuous efforts have been made to promote international trade through the influence of supranational bodies such as the International Monetary Fund (IMF), the World Bank and the World Trade Organisation (WTO). The process of economic integration has been taken furthest in Europe through the creation, first, of the European Coal and Steel Community in 1952, and then the European Economic Community and European Community which came into existence in 1958 and 1967 respectively. The history of the European Union (EU), set up in 1993 under the Maastricht treaty, indicates how closely economic integration is tied up with political change. The goal of economic development brought about by the free movement of economic resources within a genuinely 'common market' set off a chain of events which has progressively eroded national sovereignty. As economic circumstances within the EU converge, especially with the introduction of a single currency, the control of economic life has inevitably passed from national governments to EU institutions. If politics necessarily follows economics, the independent nation-state may soon become an anachronism.

Finally, the nation-state may be the enemy of natural environment and could even pose a threat to the survival to the human species itself. Since the 1960s ecologism (see p. 196) has highlighted how close human beings have come to bringing about environmental catastrophe. The central principle of ecology is that all forms of life are interdependent; each species, including humankind, is sustained by a complex network of interrelationships, usually called an ecosystem. The human ecosystem, for instance, comprises myriad other species, vital natural resources, climatic conditions and so forth. However, this fragile ecosystem has increasingly been threatened as a result of the growing size of the human population, the depletion of reserves of fossil fuels like oil and gas, and a dramatic increase in the production of pollution and waste. Although it would be foolish to suggest that the nation-state is the underlying cause of this crisis, it may nevertheless be true that national sovereignty offends against the central principles of ecology.

National sovereignty enables states to make decisions in the short-term interests of their own people without taking the ecological implications of these decisions into account. This can clearly be seen in the case of acid rain: forests can be destroyed and lakes rendered lifeless in one country as a result of the emission of nitrate and sulphuric gases from power stations in another country hundreds of miles away. The Chernobyl nuclear accident in the Ukraine in 1986 released a wave of nuclear radiation across northern Europe which, over 50 years, will cause an estimated 2000 cancer deaths in Europe. If nations are to be protected environmentally from one another, and if the global ecosystem is to be preserved, national sovereignty will have to be curtailed by the creation of international bodies capable of articulating the long-term interests of humanity rather than the immediate interests of particular nations. Progress in this direction, however, requires that international and supranational institutions be constructed that are able both to command allegiance and to exercise authority.

Supranationalism

Even as nationalism completed its task of constructing a world of independent nation-states, supranational bodies emerged in growing number to challenge their authority. A supranational body is one which exercises jurisdiction not over any single state but within an international area comprising several states. While the twentieth century has seen national sovereignty treated as an almost sacred principle, as well as the virtually universal acceptance that political life should be organised around the nation, the twenty-first century may see government operating on an increasingly supranational level. There is, however, nothing new about supranational political systems, indeed these long predate the modern nation-state and could be regarded historically as the most traditional form of political organisation.

The most common supranational bodies have been empires, ranging from the ancient empires of Eygpt, China, Persia and Imperial Rome to the modern European empires of Britain, France, Portugal and Holland. Empires are structures of political domination, comprising a diverse collection of cultures, ethnic groups and nationalities, held together by force or the threat of force. Although colonies continue to exist – for example, Tibet's subordination to China – the collapse of the Soviet Union in 1991 brought to an end the last of the major empires, the Russian empire. Modern supranational bodies, by contrast, have a very different character. They have developed by voluntary agreement amongst states, either out of a recognition of the advantages which international cooperation will bring or in the hope of gaining security in the face of a common threat or danger. In that sense, the advance of supranationalism reflects the growing impact of what is called globalisation. This does not mean that national boundaries have become irrelevant but simply that our lives are increasingly shaped by decisions made at a great distance from us, often by decisions made in countries far away. This global interdependence has spread from strategic and economic matters into political, social and cultural spheres of life, creating the impression of a shrinking world. The supranational bodies that this process has generated have, however, varied considerably. In most cases, they merely serve to facilitate intergovernmental cooperation, allowing states to work together and perhaps undertake concerted action but without sacrificing national independence. In a growing number of cases, however, they have developed collective institutions and bureaucratic apparatuses, and acquired the ability to impose their will upon member states. Such bodies are best thought of as international federations. The emergence of more powerful international institutions and the progressive globalisation of modern life have led some to suggest that we are now on the verge of realising the highest form of supranationalism: a global state or some kind of world government.

Intergovernmentalism

Intergovernmentalism is the weakest form of supranational cooperation; it encompasses any form of state interaction which preserves the independence and sovereignty of each nation. The most common form of intergovernmentalism is treaties or alliances, the simplest of which involve bilateral agreements between states. In some cases, these have resulted from a desire to achieve economic development, as in the series of treaties in mid-nineteenth-century Europe through which free trade was spread by mutual reductions in tariff levels. Since 1948, GATT has provided a forum within which tariffs and other forms of protectionism can be reduced or removed by negotiation amongst signatory states. The goal of establishing a tariff free trading zone was the inspiration behind the founding of the European Economic Community and the creation of the North American Free Trade Area (NAFTA), the world's largest trading block, encompassing the United States, Canada and Mexico. However, alliances have more commonly been formed in a search for mutual security against a perceived aggressor. The years leading up to 1914, for example, saw Europe divided into two rival alliances: the Triple Alliance of Germany, Austria and Italy, confronting the Triple Entente, composed of Britain, France and Russia. During the inter-war period, Nazi Germany and Fascist Italy entered into the Rome–Berlin Axis (1936) which expanded to incorporate Japan in the Anti-Comintern Pact of 1937. In the aftermath of the Second World War rival alliance systems developed in the form of NATO (North Atlantic Treaty Organisation) and the Warsaw Pact, formed in 1949 and 1955 respectively, and in other regional defence alliances such as SEATO (South-East Asian Treaty Organisation), covering South-East Asia. The terms of such alliances have, of course, varied considerably. They have ranged from little more than an expression of common principles, as in the case of the Axis between Germany and Italy, to an agreement in specified circumstances to undertake concerted and coordinated military action, which is provided for by the joint NATO Command Organisation.

Such treaties and alliances are highly specific: they involve agreement on a particular area of policy-making, whether economic or military, and rarely address general or broader issues. Moreover, in signing such treaties states do not formally surrender national sovereignty. Treaties are signed and alliances are made in pursuit of national interests; states are therefore only likely to fulfil their obligations if they perceive that the treaty continues to reflect these interests, there being no institutional means of treaty enforcement. This was evident in the case of Italy in 1914, which, despite being a member of the Triple Alliance, did not go to war alongside Germany and Austria, but instead entered the war in 1915 on the side of the Entente powers. Similarly, in 1958 France withdrew her troops from NATO, not wanting them to be subject to the joint command structure.

The central weakness of this form of supranationalism is that progress towards international cooperation is restricted to those areas where mutual trust exists and where national interests clearly coincide. This can be seen in the faltering progress made by arms control in the four decades following the Second World War. During that period the United States and the Soviet Union each developed nuclear armouries capable of destroying the world many times over. In the 1970s, SALT I and II (Strategic Arms Limitation Talks) were designed to limit the escalation in nuclear weapons, and START (Strategic Arms Reduction Talks) talks were commenced in 1982 with the intention of reducing nuclear stockpiles. However, the ideological distrust and the rivalry inherent in a bipolar world order, and reflected in the Cold War, rendered such intergovernmental solutions ineffective and allowed the arms race to reach new heights in the 1980s. By the signing of the INF Treaty (Intermediate Nuclear Forces) in 1987, the first treaty to reduce nuclear arsenals rather than control their expansion, relations between the United States and the Soviet Union had changed significantly, particularly in the light of Gorbachev's attempt to reform the ailing Soviet economy by cutting military spending. Although further deep cuts have subsequently been negotiated between the US and the successor Soviet states, intergovernmentalism has nevertheless failed to halt the worldwide spread of nuclear weapons, which by 1998 were known to be in the hands of at least nine powers.

Other forms of intergovernmentalism have involved not just bilateral treaties and alliances but broader agreements amongst a number of states to construct leagues or confederations. Leagues existed in ancient times, for example, the Achaean and Aetolian Leagues in Greece; in modern times the most famous has been the League of Nations, formed in 1919. In 1991, upon the disintegration of the Soviet Union, twelve of its former republics moved to found the Confederation of Independent States (CIS). Leagues or confederations encompass a collection of states which agree to abide by a founding treaty or charter, usually in the hope of gaining strategic or economic advantages. The League of Nations was the first great experiment in supranational government in the twentieth century. In the hope of its leading proponent, US President Woodrow Wilson, the League would replace the 'power politics' of international rivalry, aggression and expansion, by a process of negotiation and arbitration which would make possible the peaceful settlement of international disputes. The League of Nations, nevertheless, proved to be quite incapable of checking the rampant and aggressive nationalism of the period.

In the first place, the League was weakened by the fact that it was never genuinely a 'league of nations'. Despite Wilson's efforts, the USA did not become a member; Germany, defeated in the First World War, was admitted to the League only in 1926 and resigned from it once Hitler took power in 1933; Japan walked out of the League in 1932 after criticism of its invasion of Manchuria. The Soviet Union, on the other hand, did not join until 1934, after Germany and Japan had departed. Furthermore, the League found it difficult to take decisive action: decisions taken in its Council had to receive unanimous support and, without a military force of its own to enforce its will, the League was forced to rely upon economic sanctions, which were widely flouted. The successes of the League of Nations were therefore confined to resolving minor disputes between small states; the League was little more than a powerless spectator as Japan, Italy and Germany embarked upon the programmes of rearmament and military expansionism that eventually led to war in 1939.

International confederations have proved to be more common. These have often been regional organisations designed to promote common political, social and economic ends, for instance, the Organisation of African Unity, the Organisation of American States and OPEC (the Organisation of Petroleum Exporting Countries). In other cases, such organisations have had no distinct geographical character at all, as in the case of the OECD (Organisation for Economic Cooperation and Development), which represents the world's industrially most advanced states. The Commonwealth of Nations, an organisation of former British colonies and successor to the British Empire, is also geographically diffuse, covering the Caribbean, Asia, Australasia, Europe and Africa. Confederations are voluntary associations whose members continue to enjoy sovereign power. Although confederations may develop permanent headquarters and bureaucratic staffs, they rarely possess an effective executive authority. In effect, confederations offer nothing more than a forum for consultation, deliberation and negotiation. Their value is that they enable states to undertake coordinated action, very clearly exemplified by OPEC's ability since the 1970s to regulate the price of oil.

However, as member states retain their independence, continue to retain control over defence and diplomacy, and are very reluctant to be bound by majority decisions, confederations have rarely been able to undertake united and effective action. This was evident in the inability of the Organisation of African Unity and the Commonwealth of Nations to exert concerted pressure upon South Africa for the removal of apartheid, which therefore amounted to little more than diplomatic condemnation and faltering attempts to establish economic sanctions. Such weaknesses have encouraged some confederations to transform themselves into federal states, possessed of a stronger central authority. Precisely this happened in the case of the 13 former British colonies in North America, which declared independence in 1776 and joined together in a loose commonwealth under the Articles of Confederation, adopted in 1777. The newly independent states, however, soon became aware of the need for joint diplomatic recognition and the advantages of closer economic ties. Consequently, they founded a federal republic, the United States of America, through the framing of the US Constitution in 1787. Similarly, the federal states which developed in Germany and Switzerland both started life as confederations of independent states. In the case of the CIS, conflicts between the newly independent states, and a common desire to avoid creating a successor to the Soviet Union, soon meant that it fell into abeyance.

Federalism and federations

Federalism involves the division of law-making power between a central body and a number of territorial units. Each level of government is allocated a range of duties, powers and functions, specified by some kind of constitutional document. Sovereignty is therefore divided between the centre and the periphery as, at least in theory, neither level of government can encroach upon the powers of the other. Traditionally, federalism has been applied to the organisation of state power: central or federal government is in effect the national government, as occurs, for instance, in the United States, Canada, Australia, Germany, Switzerland and India; peripheral government therefore constitutes some form of state, provincial or regional government. As a result, federal states may be regarded as sovereign and independent entities in international affairs even though sovereign power is divided within their borders; they possess external sovereignty though lack an internally sovereign body or level of government. However, during the twentieth century federalism has developed from being a principle exclusively applied to the internal organisation of the state into one that has increasingly been applied to supranational bodies.

The most advanced example of an international federation is the European Union, the core of which is the European Community (EC), created in 1967 through the fusion of three existing European organisations: the European Coal and Steel Community, which had come into being in 1952, and the Atomic Energy Community and European Economic Community (EEC), which were established by the Treaty of Rome (1957). In the aftermath of the Second World War, powerful political, economic and strategic considerations pointed in the direction of European integration, and this goal was often understood in clearly federal terms, Winston Churchill envisaging as early as 1946 'a kind of United States of Europe'. Politically, European countries wished to ensure that there would be no repeat of 1914 and 1939, when European conflicts had devastated the continent and spilled over into world war. Economically, there was a strong desire for international cooperation and trade to rebuild a Europe ravaged by war. Strategically, many in Europe felt threatened by the expansion of Soviet power into Eastern Europe in the late 1940s, and by the prospect that Europe would become irrelevant in the emerging bipolar world order.

Early federalist dreams, however, came to nothing. For example, plans for a European parliament in 1948 led only to the creation of the Council of Europe, which developed into nothing more than a debating society with no power to promote legislation, and is composed of members not properly elected but appointed by national governments. Instead, a 'functionalist' road to unity was followed which allowed for incremental steps towards European integration, but only within specific areas of policy-making, usually economic, and at a pace controlled by member states. Although the functionalist approach was cautious and gradual, it nevertheless had far-reaching implications: progressive moves towards economic integration had unavoidable, if sometimes unintended, implications.

This became particularly clear after the signing of the Single European Act in 1986, which envisaged an unrestricted flow of goods, services and people throughout Europe, literally a 'common market', to be introduced by 1993. If the EC was to become a single economic entity, a single market, economic performance within the Community and the policies of member states had to converge. Increasingly, EC decisions were made by a process of qualified majority voting, a practice that was significantly extended once the Community agreed in the Treaty of European Union (the Maastricht treaty) of 1993 to push ahead with the European monetary union (EMU). The acceptance of majority voting, even on a specified range of issues, implied that member states could be bound against their will by Community decisions. In effect, by the 1990s the EC had ceased to be a confederation of independent states but had developed into a federal supranational body, in the words of the Maastricht treaty, a European Union. Within the EU a significant range of powers are still exercised by national governments, but others lie in the hands of European institutions. This balance, however, will inevitably be affected by the EU's boldest economic initiatives, the introduction of a single European currency. EMU, involving eleven of the fifteen member states, started in 1999; however, euro notes and coins will not be available until 2002.

Moves towards European integration have, however, stimulated deep divisions and wide-ranging debate. On the one hand, some have remained fiercely loyal to the principle of national sovereignty, believing that it embodies the best opportunity for achieving democratic self-government. This was best reflected in the 1960s in the vision of French president, Charles de Gaulle, of a *'Europe des patries'*, a Europe within which member states would continue to retain the right to veto decisions they considered a threat to vital national interests. In the 1980s Margaret Thatcher took up the same theme, dismissing as folly in her famous Bruges speech in 1988 moves towards the creation of a 'United States of Europe'. De Gaulle's and Thatcher's vision of Europe is therefore one of independent nation-states, a confederal not a federal Europe. From this point of view a centralised European state will never enjoy broad public support, and the attempt to establish what Thatcher called an 'identikit European personality' will only serve to undermine national cultures and identities.

On the other hand, the goal of a federal Europe has been openly embraced by many politicians within the EU on both economic and political grounds. The economic benefits of closer integration and increased trade have been borne out by the high growth rates enjoyed particularly by the original member states. Moreover, the planned single European market creates the prospect of a trading zone larger than either the United States or Japan. In political terms, European integration offers the advantages of cosmopolitanism, reflected in either growing understanding and tolerance amongst the peoples of Europe who nevertheless retain their distinctive national identities, or in the emergence of a supranational, European political culture which somehow incorporates the various national traditions. What is clear, however, is that the momentum towards European unity can only be sustained if Europe, or at least the EU, is regarded by its peoples as a meaningful political entity.

The genius of the nation-state was that political rule was underpinned by social cohesion: government was legitimate because it was exercised within what was thought to be a natural or organic community. Nations have a number of clear advantages in this respect, being, in most cases, bound together by a common culture, language, traditions and so forth. Supranational entities, like regions or continents, must seek to develop political solidarity amongst peoples who speak different languages, practise different religions, and are bound to very different traditions and cultures. In short, nationalism must give way to some form of supranationalism or internationalism. The difficulty of achieving this was underlined by the sometimes tortuous process of ratifying the Maastricht treaty. This was only achieved in France, previously thought to be one of the strongest supporters of European unity, by the slimmest possible referendum result; and in Denmark it took a second referendum to demonstrate public support for the treaty. In Britain where no referendum was held, in part because it was likely to produce the 'wrong' result, Parliament only ratified Maastricht after the government declared the issue to be a matter of confidence and threatened to call a general election if defeated. What is clear is that if further integration takes place without broad popular support this is likely to provoke a nationalist backlash against institutions that are not perceived to exercise legitimate authority; and this form of nationalism is likely to be resentful, insular and possibly aggressive.

Prospects of world government

World government would be the highest form of supranational organisation. It looks to the construction of a global state which would stand above all other states, national and supranational. Indeed, strictly speaking, it would render both the nation-state and the supranational state meaningless, in that neither would any longer enjoy sovereign power. Two, sharply contrasting, models of such a body have been envisaged. The first is embodied in the notion of world domination by a single, all-powerful state. In some respects, Imperial Rome established such an empire in ancient times, at least within what for them was the known world. In the twentieth century, Germany under Adolf Hitler embarked upon a programme of expansion which, if Hitler's writings are to be taken seriously, ultimately aimed to establish Aryan world domination. Such a world empire, like all earlier empires, could only be held together by military domination, and from what is known of the potency of nationalism it is doubtful that this form of world government could ever establish a stable and enduring existence.

The second model of world government would, in effect, be a 'state of states'. Immanuel Kant developed what amounted to an early version of world government in his proposal for a 'league of nations'. Formed through voluntary agreement, by some form of international social contract, such a global state could develop the kind of federal structure which the United States and the European Union already possess. Existing

Immanuel Kant (1724–1804)

German philosopher. Kant spent his entire life in Königsberg (which was then in East Prussia), becoming professor of logic and metaphysics at the University of Königsberg in 1770. Apart from his philosophical work, Kant's life was distinguished by its uneventfulness.

Kant's 'critical' philosophy holds that knowledge is not merely an aggregate of sense impressions; it depends upon the conceptual apparatus of human understanding. His political thought was shaped by the central importance of morality. He believed that the 'law of reason' dictates certain categorical imperatives, the most important of which is the obligation to treat others as 'ends', and never only as 'means'. Freedom, for Kant, thus meant more than simply the absence of external constraints upon the individual; it is a moral and rational freedom, the capacity to make moral choices. Kant's ethical individualism has had considerable impact upon liberal thought. It also helped to inspire the idealistic tradition in international politics, in suggesting that reason and morality combine to dictate that there should be no war and that the future of humankind should be based upon 'universal and lasting peace'. Kant's most important works include *Critique of Pure Reason* (1781), *Critique of Practical Reason* (1788) and *Critique of Judgement* (1790).

nation-states would, in other words, become peripheral institutions, enabling nations to retain their separate identities and to control their own internal affairs. However, central government in the form of the global state would be responsible for international affairs, coordinating economic interaction, arbitrating in cases of disputes amongst nations and providing collective security for all peoples of the world. For a global state of this kind to be viable it must, as all states do, monopolise the means of legitimate violence within its territorial jurisdiction, or at least have access to greater military power than is possessed by any individual state. This vision of ordered rule extending throughout the world provided the inspiration for both the League of Nations and the United Nations Organisation.

The argument for world government is clear and familiar. In the seventeenth and eighteenth centuries, political thinkers argued the case for government by envisaging what life would be like in a 'state of nature', a stateless society. They suggested that if individuals were not constrained by enforceable laws, social life would quickly descend into chaos, disorder and, ultimately, civil war. They concluded, therefore, that rational individuals would willingly enter into a social contract to establish a system of law and government which alone could guarantee orderly existence. During this period, human societies were relatively small and it made sense to invest power in the hands of national governments. However, in the nineteenth and twentieth centuries a genuinely international society has come into existence through an increase in travel and tourism, the internationalisation of economic life and, facilitated by modern technology, widespread media, cultural and intellectual exchanges amongst nations. In such circumstances, social contract theory can be re-cast. Without some form of global state, the world order will degenerate into what G.L. Dickinson (1926), in the light of the First World War, called 'international anarchy', each individual state being bent on pursuing its selfish national interests. The absence of a sovereign international power is a recipe for chaos, disorder and, as the twentieth century has twice demonstrated, world war. Individual states will therefore realise, just as did individuals in the state of nature, that their interests are best served by the establishment of a supreme authority, which in this case would take the form of a global state.

Clearly, however, major obstacles stand in the way of such a development. Perhaps the most crucial of these is the irony that the power politics which makes some form of world government so desirable also threatens to make it impossible to achieve. Economically powerful and militarily strong states undoubtedly reap benefits within an anarchic international order and may be very reluctant to concede power to a higher, supranational authority. This can be seen in the case of the United Nations, the most advanced experiment in world government so far attempted. The UN is a difficult organisation to characterise. Like the League of Nations which it replaced, the UN is dedicated to the maintenance of international peace and security, and to fostering international cooperation in solving political, economic, social and humanitarian problems. It has, however, been far more successful than the League in establishing itself as a genuinely world body, comprising almost all the world's independent states. The UN has undoubtedly achieved a number of successes, for example, in negotiating a cease-fire between India and Pakistan in 1959 and mediating between the Dutch and the Indonesians over West Irian (New Guinea) in 1962. However, for much of its history it has been virtually paralysed by superpower rivalry.

The UN Security Council, which has prime responsibility for maintaining peace and security, contains five permanent members – USA, Russia, Britain, France and China – each of which possesses a veto, and a further ten non-permanent members, elected by the General Assembly for two-year periods. The Cold War ensured that on most issues the United States and the Soviet Union took opposing positions, thus preventing the Security Council from taking decisive action. Consequently, the UN stood by powerless as the world came close to nuclear war during the Cuban Missile Crisis (1962), it was unable to prevent the Soviet invasions of Hungary (1956), Czechoslovakia (1968) and Afghanistan (1979); and it had only very limited influence upon a succession of Arab–Israeli wars in 1948, 1956, 1967 and 1973. The ending of the Cold War in the late 1980s may, however, have opened up a new chapter in the UN's history. It offered the prospect of the UN fulfilling its obligation to maintain peace and deter aggression by undertaking more decisive military action, as it did in the Gulf war of 1991, albeit with troops under US rather than UN control. However, the continuing difficulty of taking concerted international action under the auspices of the UN was underlined in the 1990s by the ineffectiveness of UN-negotiated ceasefires and UN-backed sanctions against Serbia, and by the UN's failure to act during the genocidal slaughter in Rwanda.

The possibility that the UN could develop into some form of global state is clearly dependent upon the development of a very high level of international trust and cooperation. This must, moreover, apply not only at the state level, amongst national politicians, but also at the level of ordinary people, amongst national populations. Just as the success of supranational federations ultimately requires that they are perceived to be legitimate political associations, so world government will be impossible to establish unless the concept of world citizenship becomes meaningful and attractive. This vision is one which supporters of 'universalist' creeds such as liberalism (see p. 29) and socialism are drawn to because they have traditionally looked beyond the nation and proclaimed the importance of human rights or a common humanity. However, so long as nationalism continues to exert a potent appeal, the prospect of a global state, underpinned by the idea of world citizenship, will remain a utopian dream.

Summary

1   Sovereignty means absolute and unlimited power. This may, however, take the form of legal sovereignty, ultimate legal authority, or political sovereignty, unchallengeable coercive power. Internal sovereignty refers to the location of a final authority within the state. Although much of political theory involves a debate about where such sovereignty should be located, the idea may be inapplicable to fragmented and pluralistic modern societies.

2   External sovereignty refers to a state's autonomy in international affairs. Fused with the idea of democratic government, this has developed into the principle of national sovereignty, embodying the ideals of independence and self-government. Critics nevertheless argue that in view of the internationalisation of many areas of modern life, the idea may now be redundant or, since it gives a state exclusive jurisdiction over its people, dangerous.

3   The nation is a cultural entity, reflecting a sense of linguistic, religious, ethnic or historical unity: the nation-state therefore offers the prospect of both cultural cohesion and political unity. Although the nation has traditionally been viewed as the only legitimate unit of political rule, offering the virtues of stability, security and a sense of identity, it may also be the enemy of cosmopolitanism and breed insularity and conflict.

4   Supranational forms of rule have developed to enable states to take concerted action and to cooperate for mutual benefit. In the form of intergovernmentalism – treaties, alliances and confederations – national security can be preserved; however, in emerging federal bodies sovereignty is divided between supranational institutions and member states. The success of such bodies depends on their ability to establish legitimacy and command popular allegiance, ultimately their ability to transcend political nationalism.

Further reading

Burgess, M. and Gagnon, A. G. (eds) *Comparative Federalism and Federation.* Hemel Hempstead: Harvester Wheatsheaf, 1993.

Canovan, M. *Nationhood and Political Theory.* Cheltenham: Edward Elgar, 1996.

Gellner, E. *Nations and Nationalism.* Oxford: Basil Blackwell and Ithaca, NY: Cornell University Press, 1983.

Hindley, F.H. *Sovereignty*, 2nd edn. New York: Basic Books, 1986.
King, P. *Federalism and Federation.* London: Croom Helm, 1982.
Smith, A.D. *Theories of Nationalism.* London: Duckworth, 1991.
Taylor, P. 'Elements of Supranationalism' in *International Organisations: a Conceptual Approach*, ed. P. Taylor and A.J.R. Groom. London: Pinter, 1978, pp. 216–35.
Tivey, L. (ed.). *The Nation-State.* Oxford: Martin Robertson, 1980.

Chapter 5

Power, Authority and Legitimacy

Introduction
Power
Authority
Legitimacy
Summary
Further reading

Introduction

All politics is about power. The practice of politics is often portrayed as little more than the exercise of power, and the academic subject as, in essence, the study of power. Without doubt, students of politics are students of power: they seek to know who has it, how it is used and on what basis it is exercised. Such concerns are particularly apparent in deep and recurrent disagreements about the distribution of power within modern society. Is power distributed widely and evenly dispersed, or is it concentrated in the hands of the few, a 'power elite' or 'ruling class'? Is power essentially benign, enabling people to achieve their collective goals, or is it a form of oppression or domination? Such questions are, however, bedevilled by the difficult task of defining power. Perhaps because power is so central to the understanding of politics, fierce controversy has surrounded its meaning. Some have gone as far as to suggest that there is no single, agreed concept of power but rather a number of competing concepts or theories.

Moreover, the notion that power is a form of domination or control that *forces* one person to obey another, runs into the problem that in political life power is very commonly exercised through the acceptance and willing obedience of the public. Those 'in power' do not merely possess the *ability* to enforce compliance, but are usually thought to have the *right* to do so as well. This highlights the distinction between power and authority. What is it, however, that transforms power into authority, and on what basis can authority be rightfully exercised? This leads, finally, to questions about legitimacy, the perception that power is exercised in a manner that is rightful, justified or acceptable. Legitimacy is usually seen as the basis of stable government, being linked to the capacity of a regime to command the allegiance and support of its citizens. All governments seek legitimacy, but on what basis do they gain it, and what happens when their legitimacy is called into question?

Power

Concepts of power abound. In the natural sciences, power is usually understood as 'force' or 'energy'. In the social sciences, the most general concept of power links it to the ability to achieve a desired outcome, sometimes referred to as power *to*. This could include the accomplishment of actions as simple as walking across a room or buying a newspaper. In most cases, however, power is thought of as a relationship, as the exercise of control by one person over another, or as power *over*. A distinction is, nevertheless, sometimes drawn between forms of such control, between what is termed 'power' and what is thought of as 'influence'. Power is here seen as the capacity to make formal decisions which are in some way binding upon others, whether these are made by teachers in the classroom, parents in the family or by government ministers in relation to the whole of society. Influence, by contrast, is the ability to affect the content of these decisions through some form of external pressure, highlighting the fact that formal and binding decisions are not made in a vacuum. Influence may therefore involve anything from organised lobbying and rational persuasion, through to open intimidation. This, further, raises questions about whether the exercise of power must always be deliberate or intentional. Can advertising be said to exert power by promoting the spread of materialistic values, even though advertisers themselves may only be concerned about selling their products? In the same way, there is a controversy between the 'intentionalist' and 'structuralist' understandings of power. The former holds that power is always an attribute of an identifiable agent, be it an interest group, political party, major corporation or whatever. The latter sees power as a feature of a social system, a view held both by conservative sociologists like Talcott Parsons and neo-Marxists such as Louis Althusser.

One attempt to resolve these controversies is to accept that power is an 'essentially contested' concept and to highlight its various concepts or conception, acknowledging that no settled or agreed definition can ever be developed. This is the approach adopted by Steven Lukes in *Power: A Radical View* (1974), which distinguishes between three 'faces' or 'dimensions' of power. In practice, a perfectly acceptable, if broad, definition of power can encompass all its various manifestations: if A gets B to do something A wants but which B would not have chosen to do, power is being exercised. In other words, power is the ability to get someone to do what they would not otherwise have done. Lukes's distinctions are nevertheless of value in drawing attention to how power is exercised in the real world, to the various ways in which A can influence B's behaviour. In this light, power can be said to have three faces. First, it can involve the ability to influence the making of decisions; second, it may be reflected in the capacity to shape the political agenda and thus prevent decisions being made; and third, it may take the form of controlling people's thoughts by the manipulation of their needs and preferences.

Decision-making

The first 'face' of power dates back to Thomas Hobbes's suggestion that power is the ability of an 'agent' to affect the behaviour of a 'patient'. This notion is in fact analogous to the idea of physical or mechanical power, in that it implies that power involves being 'pulled' or 'pushed' against one's will. Such a notion of power has been central to conventional political science, its classic statement being found in Robert Dahl's 'A Critique of the Ruling Elite Model' (1958). Dahl (see p. 223) was deeply critical of suggestions that in the United States power was concentrated in the hands of a 'ruling elite', arguing that such theories had largely been developed on the basis of reputation: asking where power was believed or reputed to be located. He wished, instead, to base the understanding of power upon systematic and testable hypotheses. To this end, Dahl proposed three criteria that had to be fulfilled before the 'ruling elite' thesis could be

Thomas Hobbes (1588–1679)

English political philosopher. Hobbes was the son of a minor clergyman who subsequently abandoned his family. He became tutor to the exiled Prince of Wales, Charles Stewart, and lived under the patronage of the Cavendish family. Writing at a time of uncertainty and civil strife, precipitated by the English Revolution, Hobbes developed the first comprehensive theory of nature and human behaviour since Aristotle.

Hobbes' major work *Leviathan* (1651), defended absolutist government as the only alternative to anarchy and disorder. He portrayed life in a stateless society, the state of nature, as 'solitary, poor, nasty, brutish and short', based upon the belief that human beings are essentially power-seeking and self-interested creatures. He argued that citizens have an unqualified obligation towards the state, on the grounds that to limit the power of government is to risk a descent into the state of nature. Any system of political rule, however tyrannical, is preferable to no rule at all. Hobbes thus provided a rationalist defence for absolutism (see p. 164); however, because he based authority upon consent and allowed that sovereign authority may take forms other than monarchy, he upset supporters of the divine right of kings. Hobbes pessimistic view of human nature and his emphasis upon the vital importance of authority had considerable impact upon conservative thought (see p. 138); but his individualist methodology and the use he made of social contract theory, prefigured early liberalism (see p. 29).

validated. First, the ruling elite, if it existed at all, must be a well-defined group. Secondly, a number of 'key political decisions' must be identified over which the preferences of the ruling elite run counter to those of any other group. Thirdly, there must be evidence that the preferences of the elite regularly prevail over those of other groups. In effect, Dahl treated power as the ability to influence the decision-making process, an approach he believed to be both objective and quantifiable.

According to this view, power is a question of who gets their way, how often they get their way, and over what issues they get their way. The attraction of this treatment of power is that it corresponds to the commonsense belief that power is somehow about getting things done, and is therefore most clearly reflected in decisions and how they are made. It also has the advantage, as Dahl pointed out, that it makes possible an empirical, even scientific, study of the distribution of power within any group, community or society. The method of study was clear: select a number of 'key' decision-making areas; identify the actors involved and discover their preferences; and, finally, analyse the decisions made and compare these with the known preferences of the actors. This procedure was enthusiastically adopted by political scientists and sociologists, especially in America, in the late 1950s and 1960s, and spawned a large number of community power studies. The most famous such study was Dahl's own analysis of the distribution of power in New Haven, Connecticut, described in *Who Governs?* (1963). These studies focused upon local communities, usually cities, on the grounds that they provided more manageable units for empirical study than did national politics, but also on the assumption that conclusions about the distribution of power at the national level could reasonably be drawn from knowledge of its local distribution.

In New Haven, Dahl selected three 'key' policy areas to study: urban renewal, public education and the nomination of political candidates. In each area, he acknowledged that there was a wide disparity between the influence exerted, on the one hand, by the politically privileged and the economically powerful, and, on the other hand, by ordinary citizens. However, he nevertheless claimed to find evidence that different elite groups determined policy in different issue areas, dismissing any idea of a ruling or permanent elite. His conclusion was that 'New Haven is an example of a democratic system, warts and all'. Indeed, so commonly have community power studies reached the conclusion that power is widely dispersed throughout society, that the face of power they recognise – the ability to influence decisions – is often referred to as the 'pluralist' view of power, suggesting the existence of plural or many centres of power. This is, however, misleading: pluralist conclusions are not built into this understanding of power, nor into its methodology for identifying power.

There is no reason, for example, why elitist conclusions could not be drawn if the preferences of a single cohesive group are seen to prevail over those of other groups on a regular basis. However, a more telling criticism is that by focusing exclusively upon decisions, this approach recognises only one face of power and, in particular, ignores those circumstances in which decisions are prevented from happening, the area of non-decision-making.

Agenda-setting

To define power simply as the ability to influence the content of decisions raises a number of difficulties. First of all, there are obviously problems about how hypotheses about the distribution of power can be reliably tested. For example, on what basis can 'key' decisions, which are studied, be distinguished from 'routine' ones, which are ignored; and is it reasonable to assume that the distribution of power at the national level will reflect that found at community level? Furthermore, this view of power focuses exclusively upon behaviour, the *exercise* of power by A over B. In so doing, it ignores the extent to which power is a possession, reflected perhaps in wealth, political position, social status and so forth; power may exist but not be exercised. Groups may, for example, have the capacity to influence decision-making but choose not to involve themselves for the simple reason that they do not anticipate that the decisions made will adversely affect them. In this way, private businesses may show little interest in issues like health, housing and education – unless, of course, increased welfare spending threatens to push up taxes. In the same way, there are circumstances in which people defer to a superior by anticipating his or her wishes without the need for explicit instructions, the so-called 'law of anticipated reactions'. A further problem, however, is that this first approach disregards an entirely different face of power.

In their seminal essay 'The Two Faces of Power' ([1962] 1981), P. Bachrach and M. Baratz described non-decision-making as the 'second face of power'. Although Bachrach and Baratz accepted that power is reflected in the decision-making process, they insisted that 'to the extent that a person or group – consciously or unconsciously – creates or reinforces barriers to the public airing of policy conflicts, that person or group has power'. As E.E. Schattschneider succinctly put it, 'Some issues are organised into politics while others are organised out'; power, quite simply, is the ability to set the political agenda. This form of power may be more difficult but not impossible to identify, requiring as it does an understanding of the dynamics of non-decision-making. Whereas the decision-making approach to power encourages attention to focus upon the active participation of groups in the process, non-decisions highlight the importance of political organisation in blocking the participation of certain groups and the expression of particular opinions. Schattschneider summed this up in his famous assertion that 'organisation is the mobilisation of bias'. In the view of Bachrach and Baratz, any adequate understanding of power must take full account of 'the dominant values and the political myths, rituals and institutions which tend to favour the vested interests of one or more groups, relative to others'.

A process of non-decision-making can be seen to operate within liberal-democratic systems in a number of respects. For example, although political parties are normally seen as vehicles through which interests are expressed or demands articulated, they can just as easily block particular views and opinions. This can happen either when all major parties disregard an issue or policy option, or when parties fundamentally agree, in which case the issue is never raised. This applies to problems such as debt in the developing world, divisions between North and South and the environmental crisis, which have seldom been regarded as priority issues by mainstream political parties. A process of non-decision-making also helped to sustain the arms race during the Cold War. During much of the period, Western political parties agreed on the need for a military deterrent against a potentially aggressive Soviet Union, and therefore seldom examined options such as unilateral disarmament. Similar biases also operate within interest-group politics, favouring the articulation of certain views and interests while restricting the expression of others. For example, there are groups that clearly have interests they want to advance or protect but are unable to do so either because they are geographically dispersed and difficult to organise, or because they lack vital resources like education, knowledge, finance and economic muscle. Interest groups that represent the well-informed, the prosperous and the articulate will therefore stand a better chance of shaping the political agenda than groups such as the unemployed, the homeless, the poor and the elderly.

The analysis of power as non-decision-making has often generated elitist rather than pluralist conclusions. Bachrach and Baratz, for instance pointed out that the 'mobilisation of bias' in conventional politics normally operates in the interests of what they call 'status quo defenders', privileged or elite groups. Elitists have, indeed, sometimes portrayed liberal democratic politics as a series of filters through which radical proposals are weeded out and kept off the political agenda. However, it is, once again, a mistake to believe that a particular approach to the study of power predetermines its empirical conclusions. Even if a 'mobilisation of bias' can be seen to operate within a political system, there are times when popular pressures can, and do, prevail over 'vested interests', as is demonstrated by the success of campaigns for welfare rights and improved consumer and environmental protection. A further problem nevertheless exists. Even though agenda-setting may be recognised with decision-making as an important face of power, neither takes account of the fact that power can also be wielded through the manipulation of what people think.

Thought control

The two previous approaches to power – as decision-making and non-decision-making – share the basic assumption that what individuals and groups want is what they say they want. This applies even though they may lack the capacity to achieve their goals or, perhaps, get their objectives on to the political agenda. Indeed, both perspectives agree that it is only when groups have clearly stated preferences that it is possible to say who has power and who does not. The problem with such a position, however, is that it treats individuals and groups as rational and autonomous actors, capable of knowing their own interests and of articulating them clearly. In reality, no human being possesses an entirely independent mind; the ideas, opinions and preferences of all are structured and shaped by social experience, through the influence of family, peer groups, school, the workplace, the mass media, political parties and so forth. Vance Packard (1914–96), for instance, described this ability to manipulate human behaviour by the creation of needs in his classic study of the power of advertising, *The Hidden Persuaders* (1960).

This suggests a third, and most insidious, 'face' of power: the ability of A to exercise power over B, not by getting B to do what he would not otherwise do, but, in Steven Lukes's words, by 'influencing, shaping or determining his very wants'. In *One-Dimensional Man* (1964), Herbert Marcuse (see p. 281), the New Left theorist, took this analysis further and suggested that advanced industrial societies could be regarded as 'totalitarian'. Unlike earlier totalitarian societies, such as Nazi Germany and Stalinist Russia, which repressed their citizens through terror and open brutality, advanced industrial societies control them through the pervasive manipulation of needs, made possible by modern technology. This created what Marcuse called 'a comfortable, smooth, reasonable, democratic unfreedom'. In such circumstances, the absence of conflict in society may not attest to general contentment and a wide dispersal of power. Rather, a 'society without opposition' may be evidence of the success of an insidious process of indoctrination and psychological control. This is what Lukes termed the 'radical view' of power.

A central theme in the radical view of power is the distinction between wants and needs, between subjective or 'felt' interests, and objective or 'real' interests. People, quite simply, do not always know their own minds. This is a conception of power that has been particularly attractive to

Marxists, for whom the distinction between wants and needs is both meaningful and necessary. Capitalism, Marxists argue, is a system of class exploitation and oppression, within which power is concentrated in the hands of a 'ruling class', the bourgeoisie. The power of the bourgeoisie is economic, political and ideological. The root of bourgeois domination lies in economic power, its ownership of productive wealth or the 'means of production', which gives it control over both labour and its product. Political power is exercised through the agency of the state – which is thought to favour the interests of private property and the long-term survival of the capitalist system. However, Marx (see p. 373) did not believe that the class system rested upon exploitation and oppression alone. The dominant ideas, values and beliefs of any society are, he argued, the ideas of its ruling class. Thus the exploited class, the proletariat, is deluded by the weight of bourgeois ideas and theories and comes to suffer from what Engels (see p. 82) termed 'false consciousness'. In effect, it is prevented from recognising the fact of its own exploitation. In this way, the objective or 'real' interests of the proletariat, which would be served only by the abolition of capitalism, differ from their subjective or 'felt' interests. Lenin (see p. 82) argued that the power of 'bourgeois ideology' was such that, left to its own devices, the proletariat would only be able to achieve 'trade union consciousness', the desire to improve their material conditions but within the capitalist system. Such theories are discussed at greater length in relation to legitimacy in the final section of this chapter.

This view of power, however, also has its critics. Clearly, it is impossible to argue that what a person says he or she wants is simply a delusion unless we know what their 'real' needs might be, what would genuinely benefit them. Liberal thinkers, who regard human beings as rationally self-interested creatures, have usually stressed that the individual, and the individual alone, can identify what is in his or her own interests. In effect, the expressed preferences of each person are the only reliable guide to their genuine interests; 'felt' interests *are* 'real' interests. To impose any other conception of 'real' interests is elitist, indeed authoritarian, since it denies that ordinary people know what is best for themselves. Critics, moreover, claim that the radical view does now allow theories about the distribution of power in society to be tested empirically or challenged. If people's stated preferences are not to be relied upon, how is it possible to prove what their 'real' interests might be? For example, if class antagonisms are submerged under the influence of bourgeois ideology, how can the Marxist notion of a 'ruling class' ever be tested? Lukes's solution to this problem is to suggest that people's real interests are 'what they would want and prefer were they able to make the choice'. In other words, only rational and autonomous individuals are capable of identifying their own 'real' interests. The problem with such a position, however, is that it begs the question: how are we to decide when individuals are capable of making rational and autonomous judgements?

Authority

Although politics is traditionally concerned with the exercise of power, it is often more narrowly interested in the phenomenon called 'authority', and especially 'political authority'. In its broadest sense, authority is a form of power; it is a means through which one person can influence the behaviour of another. However, more usually, power and authority are distinguished from one another as contrasting means through which compliance or obedience is achieved. Whereas power can be defined as the *ability* to influence the behaviour of another, authority can be understood as the *right* to do so. Power brings about compliance through persuasion, pressure, threats, coercion or violence. Authority, on the other hand, is based upon a perceived 'right to rule' and brings about compliance through a moral obligation on the part of the ruled to obey. Although political philosophers have disputed the basis upon which authority rests, they have nevertheless agreed that it always has a moral character. This implies that it is less important that authority *is* obeyed than that it *should be* obeyed. In this sense, the Stuart kings of England could go on claiming the authority to rule after their expulsion in 1688, even though the majority of the population did not recognise that right. Likewise, a teacher can be said to have the authority to demand homework from students even if they persistently disobey.

A very different notion of authority has, however, been employed by modern sociologists. This is largely derived from the writings of the German sociologist, Max Weber (1864–1920). Weber was concerned to explain why, and under what circumstances, people were prepared to accept the exercise of power as rightful or legitimate. In other words, he defined authority simply as a matter of people's belief about its rightfulness, regardless of where that belief came from and whether or not it is morally justified. Weber's approach treats authority as a form of power; authority is 'legitimate power', power cloaked in legitimacy. According to this view, a government that is obeyed can be said to exercise authority, even though that obedience may have been brought about by systematic indoctrination and propaganda.

The relationship between authority and an acknowledged 'right to rule' explains why the concept is so central to the practice of government: in the absence of willing compliance, governments are only able to maintain order by the use of fear, intimidation and violence. Nevertheless, the concept of authority is both complex and controversial. For example, although power and authority can be distinguished analytically, in practice the two tend to overlap and be confused with one another. Furthermore, since authority is obeyed for a variety of reasons and in contrasting circumstances, it is important to distinguish between the different forms it can take. Finally, authority is by no means the subject of universal approval. While many have regarded authority as an essential guarantee of order and stability, lamenting what they see as the 'decline of authority' in modern society, others have warned that authority is closely linked to authoritarianism and can easily become the enemy of liberty and democracy.

Power and authority

Power and authority are mutually exclusive notions, but ones that are often difficult in practice to disentangle. Authority can best be understood as a means of gaining compliance which avoids both persuasion and rational argument, on the one hand, and any form of pressure or coercion on the other. Persuasion is an effective and widely used means of influencing the behaviour of another, but, strictly speaking, it does not involve the exercise of authority. Much of electoral politics amounts to an exercise in persuasion: political parties campaign, advertise, organise meetings and rallies, all in the hope of influencing voters on election day. Persuasion invariably involves one of two forms of influence: it either takes the form of rational argument and attempts to show that a particular set of policies 'make sense', or it appeals to self-interest and tries to demonstrate that voters will be 'better off' under one party rather than another. In both cases, the elector's decision about how to vote is contingent upon the issues that competing parties address, the arguments they put forward and the way they are able to put them across. Quite simply, parties at election time are not exercising authority since voters need to be persuaded. Because it is based upon the acknowledgement of a 'duty to obey', the exercise of authority should be reflected in automatic and unquestioning obedience. In this case, political parties can only be said to exercise authority over their most loyal and obedient supporters – those who need no persuasion.

Similarly, in its Weberian sense, authority can be distinguished from the various manifestations of power. If authority involves the right to influence others, while power refers to the ability to do so, the exercise of power always draws upon some kind of resources. In other words, power involves the ability to either reward or punish another. This applies whether power takes the form of pressure, intimidation, coercion or violence. Unlike rational argument or persuasion, pressure is reflected in the use of rewards and punishments, but ones that stop short of open coercion. This can be seen, for instance, in the activities of so-called pressure groups. Although pressure groups may seek to influence the political process through persuasion and argument, they also exercise power by, for example, making financial contributions to political parties or candidates, threatening strike action, holding marches and demonstrations and so on. Intimidation, coercion and violence contrast still more starkly with authority. Since it is based upon the threat or exercise of force, coercion can be regarded as the antithesis of authority. When government exercises authority, its citizens obey the law peacefully and willingly; when obedience is not willingly offered, government is forced to compel it.

Nevertheless, although the concepts of power and authority can be distinguished analytically, the exercise of power and the exercise of authority often overlap. Authority is seldom exercised in the absence of power; and power usually involves the operation of at least a limited form of authority. For example, political leadership almost always calls for a blend of authority and power. A prime minister or president may, for instance, enjoy support from cabinet colleagues out of a sense of party loyalty, because of respect for the office held, or in recognition of the leader's personal achievements or qualities. In such cases, the prime minister or president concerned is exercising authority rather than power. However, political leadership never rests upon authority alone. The support which a prime minister or president receives also reflects the power they command, exercised, for example, in their ability to reward colleagues by promoting them or to punish colleagues by sacking them. Similarly, as discussed in Chapter 6, the authority of law rests, in part, upon the power to enforce it. The obligation to live peacefully and within the law would perhaps be meaningless if law was not backed up by the machinery of coercion, a police force, court system, prison service and so forth.

It is clear that authority is very rarely exercised in the absence of power. The British monarchy is sometimes presented as an example of authority without power. Its remaining powers are either, like the ability to veto legislation, never used, or they are exercised by others, as in the case of the appointment of ministers and the signing of treaties. Nevertheless, the British monarchy is perhaps best thought of not as an example of authority without power but rather as an institution that no longer possesses any significant authority. The royal prerogative, the monarchy's right to rule, has largely been transferred to ministers accountable to Parliament. In the absence of both power and significant authority, the monarchy has become a mere figurehead, little more than a symbol of constitutional authority. Examples of power being exercised without authority are no more easy to identify. Power without authority suggests the maintenance of political rule entirely through a system of intimidation, coercion and violence. Even in the case of totalitarian dictatorships like those of Hitler, Pol Pot or Saddam Hussein, some measure of authority was exerted, at least over those citizens who are ideologically committed to the regime or who were under the spell of their charismatic leaders. The clearest case of power without authority is perhaps a military coup – although even here the successful exercise of power depends upon a structure of authority persisting within the military itself.

A final difficulty in clarifying the meaning of authority arises from the contrasting uses of the term. For example, people can be described as being either 'in authority' or 'an authority'. To describe a person as being *in* authority is to refer to his or her position within an institutional hierarchy. A teacher, policeman, civil servant, judge or minister exercises authority in precisely this sense. They are office-holders whose authority is based upon the formal 'powers' of their post or position. By contrast, to be described as *an* authority is to be recognised as possessing superior knowledge or expertise, and to have one's views treated with special respect as a result. People as varied as scientists, doctors, teachers, lawyers and academics may be thought of, in this sense, as 'authorities' and their pronouncements may be regarded as 'authoratative'. This is what is usually described as 'expert authority'.

Some commentators have argued that this distinction highlights two contrasting types of authority. To be *in* authority implies the right to command obedience in the sense that a police officer controlling traffic can require drivers to obey his or her instructions. To be *an* authority, on the other hand, undoubtedly implies that a person's views will be respected and treated with special consideration, but by no means suggests that they will be automatically obeyed. In this way, a noted historian's account of the origins of the Second World War will elicit a different response from academic colleagues than will his or her instruction to students to hand in their essays on time. In the first instance the historian is respected as *an* authority; in the second he or she is obeyed by virtue of being *in* authority. In the same way, a person who is respected as *an* authority is regarded as being in some sense 'superior' to others, whereas those who are merely *in* authority are not in themselves superior to those they command; it is only their office or post that sets them apart.

Kinds of authority

Without doubt, the most influential attempt to categorise types of authority was undertaken by Max Weber. Weber was concerned to categorise particular 'systems of domination', and to highlight in each case the grounds upon which obedience was established. He did this by constructing three 'ideal-types', which he accepted were only conceptual models but which, he hoped, would help to make sense of the highly complex nature of political rule. These ideal-types were traditional authority, charismatic authority and legal-rational authority, each of which laid the claim to exercise power legitimately on a very different basis. In identifying the different forms which political authority could take, Weber also sought to understand the transformation of society itself, contrasting the system of domination found in relatively simple, 'traditional' societies with those typically found in industrialised and highly bureaucratic modern ones.

Weber suggested that in traditional societies authority is based upon respect for long-established customs and traditions. In effect, traditional authority is regarded as legitimate because it has 'always existed' and was accepted by earlier generations. This form of authority is therefore sanctified by history and is based upon 'immemorial custom'. In practice, it tends to operate through a hierarchical system which allocates to each person within the society a particular status. However, the 'status' of a person, unlike modern posts or offices, is not precisely defined and so grants those in authority what Weber referred to as a sphere of 'free grace'. Such authority is nevertheless constrained by a body of concrete rules, fixed and unquestioned customs, that do not need to be justified because they reflect the way things always have been. The most obvious examples of traditional authority are found amongst tribes or small groups, in the form of 'patriarchalism' – the domination of the father within the family or the 'master' over his servants – and 'gerontocracy' – the rule of the aged, normally reflected in the authority of village 'elders'. Traditional authority is thus closely tied up with hereditary systems of power and privilege. Few examples of traditional authority have survived in modern industrial societies, both because the impact of tradition has diminished with the enormous increase in the pace of social change, and because it is difficult to square the idea of hereditary status with modern principles like democratic government and equal opportunities. Nevertheless, vestiges of traditional authority can be found in the survival of the institution of monarchy, even in advanced industrial societies such as Britain, Belgium, the Netherlands and Spain, and in institutions such as the British House of Lords, which still respect the hereditary principle.

Weber's second form of legitimate domination was charismatic authority. This form of authority is based entirely upon the power of an individual's personality, his or her 'charisma'. The word itself is derived from Christianity and refers to divinely bestowed power, a 'gift of grace', reflected in the power which Jesus exerted over his disciples. Charismatic authority owes nothing to a person's status, social position or office, and everything to his or her personal qualities and, in particular, the ability to make a direct and personal appeal to others. This form of authority must always have operated in political life because all forms of leadership require the ability to communicate and the capacity to inspire loyalty. In some cases, political leadership is constructed almost entirely on the basis of charismatic authority, as in the case of fascist leaders such as Mussolini and Hitler, who, in portraying themselves as 'The Leader', deliberately sought to achieve unrestricted power by emancipating themselves from any constitutionally defined notion of leadership. It would be a mistake, nevertheless, to think of charismatic authority simply as a gift or natural propensity. Political leaders often try to 'manufacture' charisma, either by cultivating their media image and sharpening their oratorical skills or, in cases such as Mussolini, Stalin, Hitler and Mao Zedong (see p. 83), by orchestrating an elaborate 'cult of personality' through the control of a propaganda machine.

Whether natural or manufactured, charismatic authority is often looked upon with suspicion. This reflects the belief that it is invariably linked to authoritarianism, the demand for unquestioning obedience, the imposi-tions of authority regardless of consent. Since it is based upon personality rather than status or office, charismatic authority is not confined by any rules or procedures and may thus create the spectre of 'total power'. Furthermore, charismatic authority demands from its followers not only willing obedience but also discipleship, even devotion. Ultimately, the charismatic leader is obeyed because submission carries with it the prospect that one's life can be transformed. Charismatic authority has frequently therefore had an intense, messianic quality; leaders such as Napoleon, Hitler and Stalin each presented themselves as a 'messiah' come to save, liberate or otherwise transform his country. This form of authority may be less crucial in liberal democratic regimes where the limits of leadership are constitutionally defined, but is nevertheless still significant. It is important to remember, moreover, that charismatic qualities are not only evident in the impassioned leadership of Margaret Thatcher or Charles de Gaulle, but also in the more modest, but no less effective, 'fireside chats' of F.D. Roosevelt and the practised televisual skills of almost all modern leaders.

The third form of domination Weber identified was what he called legal-rational authority. This was the most important kind of authority since, in Weber's view, it had almost entirely displaced traditional authority and become the dominant mode of organisation within modern industrial societies. In particular, Weber suggested that legal-rational authority was characteristic of the large-scale, bureaucratic organisations that had come to dominate modern society. Legal-rational authority operates through the existence of a body of clearly defined rules; in effect, legal-rational authority attaches entirely to the office and its formal 'powers', and not to the office-holder. As such, legal-rational authority is clearly distinct from any form of charismatic authority; but it is also very different from traditional authority, based as it is upon a clearly defined bureaucratic role rather than the broader notion of status.

Legal-rational authority arises out of respect for the 'rule of law', in that power is always clearly and legally defined, ensuring that those who exercise power do so within a framework of law. Modern government, for instance, can be said to operate very largely on the basis of legal-rational authority. The power which a president, prime minister or other government officer is able to exercise is determined in almost all circumstances by formal, constitutional rules, which constrain or limit what an office-holder is able to do. From Weber's point of view, this form of authority is certainly to be preferred to either traditional or charismatic authority. In the first place, in clearly defining the realm of authority and attaching it to an office rather than a person, bureaucratic authority is less likely to be abused or give rise to injustice. In addition, bureaucratic order is shaped, Weber believed, by the need for efficiency and a rational division of labour. In his view, the bureaucratic order that dominates modern society is supremely efficient. Yet he also recognised a darker side to the onward march of bureaucratic authority. The price of greater efficiency, he feared, was a more de-personalised and inhuman social environment, typified by the relentless spread of bureaucratic forms of organisation.

An alternative means of identifying kinds of authority is the distinction between *de jure* authority (authority in law), and *de facto* authority (authority in practice). *De jure* authority operates according to a set of procedures or rules which designate who possesses authority, and over what issues. For example, anyone described as being 'in authority' can be said to possess *de jure* authority: their 'powers' can be traced back to a particular office. In that sense, both traditional and legal-rational authority, as defined by Weber, are forms of *de jure* authority. There are occasions, however, when authority is undoubtedly exercised but cannot be traced back to a set of procedural rules; this type of authority can be called *de facto* authority. Being 'an authority', for example, may be based upon expertise in a definable area but it cannot be said to be based upon a set of authorising rules. This would also apply, for instance, in the case of a passer-by who spontaneously takes charge at the scene of a road accident, directing traffic and issuing instructions, but without having any official authorisation to do so. The person concerned would be exercising *de facto* authority without possessing any legal right or *de jure* authority. All forms of charismatic authority are of this kind. They amount to *de facto* authority in that they are based entirely upon an individual's personality and do not in any sense refer to a set of external rules.

Defenders and detractors

The concept of authority is not only highly complex, but also deeply controversial. Questions about the need for authority and whether it should be regarded as an unqualified blessing, go to the very heart of political theory and correspond closely to the debate about the need for government, discussed in Chapter 3. In the late twentieth century, however, the issue of authority has become particularly contentious. On the one hand, the progressive expansion of individual rights and liberties in modern society, and the advance of a tolerant or permissive social ethic, has encouraged some to view authority in largely negative terms, seeing it either as outdated and unnecessary or as implicitly oppressive. On the other hand, this process has stimulated a backlash encouraging defenders of authority to reassert its importance. In their view, the erosion of authority in the home, the workplace, and in schools, colleges and universities, brings with it the danger of disorder, instability and social breakdown.

The social contract theories of the seventeenth and eighteenth centuries provide a classic justification for authority. These proceed by constructing the image of a society without an established system of authority, a so-called 'state of nature', and emphasise that the result would be barbarity and injustice as individuals struggle against one another to achieve their various ends. This implies, however, an ambivalent attitude towards authority, an ambivalence that has been inherited by many liberal theorists (see p. 29). It suggests, in the first place, that the need for authority will be recognised by all rational individuals, who respect authority both because it establishes order and stability and because authority defends individual liberty from the encroachments of fellow citizens. In that sense, liberals always emphasise that authority arises 'from below': it is based upon the consent of the governed. At the same time, however, authority necessarily constrains liberty and has the capacity to become a tyranny against the individual. As a result, liberals insist that authority be constrained, preferring legal-rational forms of authority that operate within clearly defined legal or constitutional boundaries.

Conservative thinkers have traditionally adopted a rather different attitude to authority. In their view, authority is seldom based upon consent but arises out of what Roger Scruton (1984) has called 'natural necessity'. Authority is thus regarded as an essential feature of all social institutions; it reflects a basic need for leadership, guidance and support. Conservatives point out, for example, that the authority of parents within the family is in no meaningful sense based upon the consent of children. Parental authority arises instead from the desire of parents to nurture, care for and love their children. In this sense, it is exercised 'from above' for the benefit of those

Conservatism

Conservative ideas and doctrines first emerged in the late eighteenth and early nineteenth centuries as a reaction against the growing pace of economic and political change, which was in many ways symbolised by the French Revolution. However, from the outset, divisions in conservative thought were apparent. In continental Europe, an authoritarian and reactionary form of conservatism developed that rejected out of hand any idea of reform. A more cautious, more flexible, and ultimately more successful form of conservatism nevertheless emerged in Britain and the United States that prudently accepted 'natural' change, or 'change in order to conserve'. This stance enabled conservatives from the late nineteenth century onwards to embrace the cause of social reform under the banner of paternalism and social duty. Nevertheless, such ideas came under increasing pressure from the 1970s onwards as a result of the development of the New Right.

Conservatives have typically distrusted the developed theories and abstract principles which characterise other political traditions, preferring instead to trust in tradition, history and experience. An enduring theme in conservative thought is the perception of society as a moral community, held together by shared values and beliefs, and functioning as an organic whole. This inclines conservatives to advocate strong government and the strict enforcement of law and order but, mindful of the danger of despotism, they have usually insisted upon a balanced constitution. Although traditional conservatives have been firm supporters of private property, they have typically advocated a non-ideological and pragmatic attitude to the relationship between the state and the individual. Whereas conservatism in the United States carries with it the implication of limited government, the paternalistic tradition, evident in 'One Nation conservatism' in Britain and Christian Democracy in continental Europe, overlaps with the welfarist and interventionist beliefs found in modern liberalism (see p. 29) and social democracy (see p. 312).

The New Right encompasses two distinct and, some would argue, conflicting traditions: economic liberalism and social conservatism. Economic liberalism or neo-liberalism, often seen as the dominant theme within the New Right, draws heavily upon classical liberalism and advocates rolling back the frontiers of the state in the name of private enterprise, the free market and individual responsibility. As a backlash against the steady growth of state power perpetrated through much of the twentieth century by liberal, socialist and conservative governments, neo-liberalism can be seen as a manifestation of the libertarian tradition (see p. 340). Social conservatives, or neo-conservatives, draw attention to the perceived breakdown of order and social stability that has resulted from the spread of liberal and permissive values. They highlight the dangers implicit in moral and cultural diversity, propose that traditional values be strengthened, and argue for a restoration of authority and social discipline.

Conservative political thought has always been open to the charge that it amounts to ruling-class ideology. In proclaiming the need to resist change, it legitimises the status quo and defends the interests of dominant or elite groups. Other critics allege that divisions between traditional conservatism and the New Right runs so deep that the conservative tradition has become entirely incoherent. However, in their defence, conservatives argue that they are merely advancing certain enduring, if unpalatable, truths about human nature and the societies we live in. That human beings are morally and intellectually imperfect, and seek the security that only tradition, authority and a shared culture can offer, merely underlines the wisdom of 'travelling light' in theoretical terms. Experience and history will always provide a sounder basis for political theory than will abstract principles such as liberty, equality and justice.

Key figures

Edmund Burke (1729–97) A Dublin-born British statesman and political theorist, Burke was the father of the Anglo-American conservative political tradition. A supporter of the American Revolution of 1776, he was deeply opposed to the French Revolution on the grounds that wisdom resides not in abstract principles but in experience, tradition and history. In Burke's view, society is a partnership between 'those who are living, those who are dead and those who are to be born'. Burke had a gloomy view of government, recognising that, although it can prevent evil, it rarely promotes good. He also supported the classical economics of Adam Smith (see p. 340) and regarded market forces as 'natural law'. Burke's major works include *Reflections on the Revolution in France* (1790) and *Appeal from the New to the Old Whigs* (1791).

Michael Oakeshott (1901–90) A British political philosopher, Oakeshott made a major contribution to conservative traditionalism. By highlighting the importance of civil association and insisting upon the limited province of politics, he developed themes closely associated with liberal thought. Oakeshott outlined a powerful defence of a non-ideological style of politics, arguing in favour of traditional values and established customs on the grounds that the conservative disposition is 'to prefer the familiar to the unknown, to prefer the tried to the untried, fact to misery, the actual to the possible'. Oakeshott's best known works include *Rationalism in Politics and Other Essays* (1962) and *On Human Conduct* (1975).

Irving Kristol (1920–) A US journalist and social critic, Kristol has been one of the leading exponents of American neo-conservatism. He was a member of a group of intellectuals and academics, centred around journals such as *Commentary* and *The Public Interest*, who in the 1970s abandoned liberalism and became increasingly critical of the spread of welfarism and the 'counterculture'. Whilst accepting the need for a predominantly market economy and fiercely rejecting socialism, Kristol criticises libertarianism in the marketplace as well as in morality. In particular, he defends the family and religion as the indispensable pillars of a decent society. Kristol's best known writings include *Two Cheers for Capitalism* (1978) and *Reflections of a Neo-Conservative* (1983).

→

Conservatism continued

Further reading

Honderich, T. *Conservatism*. London: Hamish Hamilton, 1990.
Kirk, R. *The Conservative Mind*, 7th edn. London: Faber, 1986.
Scruton, R. *The Meaning of Conservatism*, 2nd edn. London: Macmillan, 1984.

---

below. From the conservative perspective, authority promotes social cohesion and serves to strengthen the fabric of society; it is the basis of any genuine community. This is why neo-conservatives have been so fiercely critical of the spread of permissiveness, believing that by undermining the authority of, say, parents, teachers and the police, it has created a 'pathless desert' leading to a rise in crime, delinquency and general discourtesy.

It has, further, been suggested that the erosion of authority can pave the way for totalitarian rule. Hannah Arendt (see p. 368), who was herself forced to flee Germany by the rise of Nazism, argued that society is, in effect, held together by respect for traditional authority. Strong traditional norms, reflected in standards of moral and social behaviour, act as a form of cement binding society together. The virtue of authority is that it provides individuals with a sense of social identity, stability and reassurance; the 'collapse of authority' leaves them lonely and disorientated, prey to the entreaties of demagogues and would-be dictators. In *The Origins of Totalitarianism* (1951), Arendt suggested that the decline of traditional values and hierarchies was one of the factors which explained the advent of Nazism and Stalinism. In her view, a clear distinction exists between authoritarian and totalitarian societies. In the former, political opposition and civil liberty may routinely be suppressed but a considerable degree of individual freedom is nevertheless permitted, at least in the realm of economic, social and cultural life. By comparison, totalitarian regimes stamp out individual freedom altogether by controlling every aspect of human existence, thereby establishing 'total power'.

Authority has also, however, been regarded with deep suspicion and sometimes open hostility. The central theme of this argument is that authority is the enemy of liberty. All forms of authority can be regarded as a threat to the individual, in that authority, by definition, calls for unquestioning obedience. In that sense, there is always a trade-off between liberty and authority: as the sphere of authority expands, liberty is necessarily constrained. Thus there may be every reason to celebrate the decline of authority. If parents, teachers and the state no longer command unquestionable authority, surely this is reflected in the growing responsibilities and freedom of, respectively, children, students and individual citizens. From this point of view, there is particular cause to fear forms of authority that have an unlimited character. Charismatic authority, and indeed any notion that authority is exercised 'from above', create the spectre of unchecked power. What, for instance, restricts the authority which parents can rightfully exercise over their children if that authority is not based upon consent?

Authority can, furthermore, be seen as a threat to reason and critical understanding. Authority demands unconditional, unquestioning obedience, and can therefore engender a climate of deference, an abdication of responsibility, and an uncritical trust in the judgement of others. Such tendencies have been highlighted by psychological studies that have linked the exercise of authority to the development of authoritarian character traits: the inclination towards either domination or submission. In *The Mass Psychology of Fascism* ([1933] 1975), Wilhelm Reich (1897–1957) presented an account of the origins of fascism which drew attention to the damaging repression brought about by the domination of fathers within traditionally authoritarian families. This analysis was taken further by Theodore Adorno (see p. 281) and others in *The Authoritarian Personality* (1950). They claimed to find evidence that individuals who ranked high on the 'F-scale', indicating fascist tendencies, included those who had a strong propensity to defer to authority. The psychologist Stanley Milgram (1974) claimed to find experimental evidence to support this theory. This shows that people with a strong inclination to obey authority can more easily be induced to behave in a barbaric fashion, for example, by inflicting what they believe to be considerable amounts of pain upon others. Milgram argued that his evidence helps to explain the inhuman behaviour of guards in Nazi death camps, as well as atrocities that were carried out by the US military during the Vietnam War.

Legitimacy

Legitimacy is usually defined simply as 'rightfulness'. As such, it is crucial to the distinction between power and authority. Legitimacy is the quality that transforms naked power into rightful authority; it confers upon an order or command an authoritative or binding character, ensuring that it is obeyed out of duty rather than because of fear. Clearly, there is a close relationship between legitimacy and authority, the two terms sometimes being used synonymously. As they are most commonly used, however, people are said to have authority whereas it is political systems that are described as legitimate. Indeed, much of political theory amounts to a discussion about when, and on what grounds, government can command legitimacy. This question is of vital importance because, as noted earlier, in the absence of legitimacy, government can only be sustained by fear, intimidation and violence. As Rousseau (see p. 243) put it in *The Social Contract* ([1762] 1969), 'The strongest is never strong enough to be always the master unless he transforms strength into right and obedience into duty'.

Deep disagreement nevertheless surrounds the concept of legitimacy. The most widely used meaning of the term is drawn, once again, from Weber. Weber took legitimacy to refer to nothing more or less than a belief in the 'right to rule', a *belief* in legitimacy. In other words, providing its peoples are prepared to comply, a system of rule can be described as legitimate. This contrasts sharply with the inclination of most political philosophers, which is to try to identify a moral or rational basis for legitimacy, thereby suggesting a clear and objective difference between legitimate and illegitimate forms of rule. For instance, Aristotle (see p. 68) argued that rule was legitimate only when it operated to the benefit of the whole society rather than in the selfish interests of the rulers, while Rousseau argued that government was legitimate if it was based upon the 'general will'. In *The Legitimation of Power* (1991), David Beetham attempted to develop a social-scientific concept of legitimacy but one that departs significantly from Weber's. In Beetham's view, to define legitimacy as nothing more than a 'belief in legitimacy' is to ignore how it is brought about. This leaves the matter largely in the hands of the powerful, who may be able to manufacture rightfulness by public relations campaigns and the like. He therefore proposed that power can only be said to be legitimate if three conditions are fulfilled. First, power must be exercised according to established rules, whether embodied in formal legal codes or informal conventions. Secondly, these rules must be justified in terms of the shared beliefs of the government and the governed. Thirdly, legitimacy must be demonstrated by the expression of consent on the part of the governed.

In addition to disagreement about the meaning of the term, there is also debate about the *means* through which power is legitimised, or what is referred to as the 'legitimation process'. Following Beetham, it can be argued that legitimacy is only conferred upon regimes that exercise power according to established and accepted principles, notably regimes that rule on the basis of popular consent. Others, however, have suggested that most, and perhaps all, regimes attempt to manufacture legitimacy by manipulating what their citizens know, think or believe. In effect, legitimacy may simply be a form of ideological hegemony or dominance. Moreover, there are also questions about when, how and why political systems lose their legitimacy and suffer what are called 'legitimation crises'. A legitimation crisis is particularly serious since it casts doubt upon the very survival of the regime or political system: no regime has so far endured permanently through the exercise of coercion alone.

Constitutionalism and consent

Liberal democracy is often portrayed as the only stable and enduringly successful form of government. Its virtue, its supporters argue, is that it contains the means of its own preservation: it is able to guarantee continued legitimacy by ensuring that government power is not unchecked or arbitrary but is, rather, exercised in accordance with the wishes, preferences and interests of the general public. This is achieved through two principal devices. In the first place, such regimes operate within certain 'rules of power', taking the form of some kind of constitution. These supposedly ensure that individual liberty is protected and government power is constrained. Secondly, liberal democracies provide a basis for popular consent in the form of regular, open and competitive elections. From this point of view, legitimacy is founded upon the willing and rational obedience of the governed; government is rightful only so long as it responds to popular pressure.

A constitution can be understood, in its simplest sense, as the rules which govern the government. Constitutions are thus sets of rules which allocate duties, powers and functions to the various institutions of government and define the relationship between individuals and the state. In so doing, constitutions define and limit government power, preventing government acting simply as it chooses. However, constitutions can take a variety of different forms. In most countries, and virtually all liberal democracies, so-called 'written' or codified constitutions exist. These draw together major constitutional rules in a single authoratative document, 'the Constitution'. The first example of such a document was the US Constitution, drawn up at the Philadelphia Convention of 1787. The 'written' constitution itself is a form of higher or supreme law, which stands above statute laws made by the legislature. In this way, codified constitutions both entrench major constitutional rules and invest the courts with the power of judicial review, making them the 'guardians of the constitution'. In a small number of liberal democracies – Britain and Israel are now the only examples – no such codified document exists. In these so-called 'unwritten' constitutions, supreme constitutional authority rests, in theory, with the legislature, in Britain's case Parliament. Other constitutional rules may be found in sources as diverse as conventions, common law and works of constitutional authority.

Constitutions confer legitimacy upon a regime by making government a rule-bound activity. Constitutional governments therefore exercise legal-rational authority; their powers are authorised by constitutional law. Historically, the demand for constitutional government arose when the earlier claim that legitimacy was based upon the will of God – the Divine Right of Kings – was called into question. However, the mere existence of a constitution does not in itself ensure that government power is rightfully exercised. In other words, constitutions do not merely confer legitimacy, they are themselves bodies of rules which are subject to questions of legitimacy. In reality, as Beetham insists, a constitution only confers legitimacy when its principles reflect values and beliefs which are widely held in society. Government power is therefore legitimate if it is exercised in accordance with rules that are reasonable and acceptable in the eyes of the governed. For instance, despite the enactment of four successive constitutions – in 1918, 1924, 1936 and 1977 – the Soviet Union strove with limited success to achieve legitimacy. This occurred both because many of the provisions of the constitution, notably those stipulating individual rights, were never respected, and because major principles like the Communist Party's monopoly of power simply did not correspond with the values and aspirations of the mass of the Soviet people.

Conformity to accepted rules may be a necessary condition for legitimacy, but it is not a sufficient one. Constitutional governments may nevertheless fail to establish legitimacy if they do not, in some way, ensure that government rests upon the consent or agreement of the people. The idea of consent arose out of social contract theory and the belief that government had somehow arisen out of a voluntary agreement undertaken by free individuals. John Locke (see p. 269), for instance, was perfectly aware that government had not in practice developed out of a social contract, but argued, rather, that citizens ought to behave as if it had. He therefore developed the notion of 'tacit consent', an implied agreement amongst citizens to obey the law and respect government. However, for consent to confer legitimacy upon a regime it must take the form not of an implied agreement but of voluntary and active participation in the political life of the community. Political participation is thus the active expression of consent.

Many forms of political rule have sought legitimacy through encouraging expressions of popular consent. This applies even in the case of fascist dictatorships like Mussolini's Italy and Hitler's Germany, where considerable effort was put into mobilising mass support for the regime by plebiscites, rallies, marches, demonstrations and so on. The most common way in which popular consent can be demonstrated, however, is through elections. Even one-party states, such as orthodox communist regimes, have found it desirable to maintain elections in the hope of generating legitimacy. As these were single-party and single-candidate elections, however, their significance was limited to their propaganda value. Quite simply, voters rarely regard non-competitive elections as a meaningful form of political participation or as an opportunity to express willing consent. By contrast, open and competitive electoral systems, typically found in liberal democracies, offer citizens a meaningful choice, and so give them the power to remove politicians and parties that are thought to have failed. In such circumstances, the act of voting is a genuine expression of active consent. From this perspective, liberal-democratic regimes can be said to maintain legitimacy through their willingness to share power with the general public.

Ideological hegemony

The conventional image of liberal democracies is that they enjoy legitimacy because, on the one hand, they respect individual liberty and, on the other, they are responsive to public opinion. Critics, however, suggest that constitutionalism and democracy are little more than a facade concealing the domination of a 'power elite' or 'ruling class'. Neo-Marxists such as Ralph Miliband (1982) have, for example, portrayed liberal democracy as a 'capitalist democracy', suggesting that within it there are biases which serve the interests of private property and ensure the long-term stability of capitalism. Since the capitalist system is based upon unequal class power, Marxists have been reluctant to accept that the legitimacy of such regimes is genuinely based upon willing obedience and rational consent. Radicals and Marxists have, as a result, adopted a more critical approach to the legitimation process, one which emphasises the degree to which legitimacy is produced by ideological manipulation and indoctrination.

It is widely accepted that ideological control can be used to maintain stability and build legitimacy. This is reflected, for example, in the 'radical view' of power, discussed earlier, which highlights the capacity to manipulate human needs. The clearest examples of ideological manipulation are found in totalitarian regimes which propagate an 'official ideology' and ruthlessly suppress all rival creeds, doctrines and beliefs. The means through which this is achieved are also clear: education is reduced to a process of ideological indoctrination; the mass media is turned into a propaganda machine; 'unreliable' beliefs are strictly censored; political opposition is brutally stamped out, and so on. In this way, National Socialism became a state religion in Nazi Germany, as did Marxism-Leninism in the Soviet Union.

Marxists, however, claim to identify a similar process at work within liberal democracies. Despite the existence of competitive party systems, autonomous pressure groups, a free press and constitutionally guaranteed civil liberties, Marxists argue that liberal democracies are nevertheless dominated by what they call 'bourgeois ideology'. The concept of 'ideology' has had a chequered history, not least because it has been ascribed such very different meanings. The term itself was coined by Destutt de Tracy in 1796 to describe a new 'science of ideas'. This meaning did not, however, long survive the French Revolution, and the term was taken up in the nineteenth century in the writings of Karl Marx (see p. 373). For Marx, 'ideology' denotes sets of ideas which tend to conceal the contradictions upon which all class societies were based. Ideologies therefore propagate falsehood, delusion and mystification. They nevertheless serve a powerful social function: they stabilise and consolidate the class system by reconciling the exploited to their exploitation. Ideology thus operates in the interests of a 'ruling class', which controls the process of intellectual production as completely as it controls the process of material production. In a capitalist society, for example, the bourgeoisie dominates the educational, cultural, intellectual and artistic life. As Marx put it in *The German Ideology* ([1844)] 1970), 'The ideas of the ruling class are in every epoch the ruling ideas'.

This is not, however, to suggest that these 'ruling ideas' monopolise intellectual life and exclude all rival views. Indeed, modern Marxists have clearly acknowledged that cultural, ideological and political competition does exist, but stress that this competition is unequal, in that the ideas and views which uphold the capitalist order enjoy a crushing advantage over the ideas and theories which question or challenge it. Such indoctrination may, in fact, be far more successful precisely because it operates behind the illusion of free speech, open competition and political pluralism. The most influential twentieth-century exponent of such a view was Antonio Gramsci (see p. 83), who drew attention to the degree to which the class system was upheld not simply by unequal economic and political power but also by what he termed bourgeois 'hegemony', the ascendancy or domination of bourgeois ideas in every sphere of life. The implications of ideological domination were clear: deluded by bourgeois theories and philosophies, the proletariat would be incapable of achieving class consciousness and would never realise its revolutionary potential. It would remain a 'class in itself' and never become what Marx called a 'class for itself'. Gramsci's ideas have been particularly influential amongst modern Marxists because they help to explain why, despite class oppression, the capitalist system has survived: the bourgeoisie has succeeded in manufacturing legitimacy. Nevertheless, the theory also has radical implications for Marxist politics. In particular, Gramsci suggested that 'bourgeois hegemony' could only be challenged by a rival 'proletarian hegemony'. In other words, the establishment of socialism requires, first, a cultural revolution through which socialist principles, values and theories displace, or at least challenge, capitalist ones. This general concern with the role of ideology has also been expressed by thinkers who subscribe to critical theory (see p. 280).

A similar line of thought has been pursued by what is called the 'sociology of knowledge'. This has sometimes been seen as an alternative to the Marxist belief in a 'dominant' or ruling ideology. One of the founding fathers of this school of sociology, Karl Mannheim (1893–1947), described its goal as uncovering 'the social roots of our knowledge'. Mannheim (1960) held that 'how men actually think' can be traced back to their position in society and the social groups to which they belong, each of which has its own distinctive way of looking at the world. Ideologies, therefore, are 'socially determined' and reflect the social circumstances and aspirations of the groups which develop them. In their influential book, *The Social Construction of Reality* (1971), Berger and Luckman broadened this analysis by suggesting that not only organised creeds and ideologies but everything that passes for 'knowledge' in society is socially constructed. The political significance of such an analysis is to highlight the extent to which human beings see the world not as it is, but as they*think* it is, or as society tells them it is. The sociology of knowledge has radical implications for any notion of legitimacy since it implies that individuals cannot be regarded simply as independent and rational actors, capable of distinguishing legitimate forms of rule from non-legitimate ones. In short, legitimacy is always a 'social construction'.

Legitimation crises

Whether legitimacy is conferred by willing consent or is manufactured by ideological indoctrination, it is, as already emphasised, essential for the maintenance of any system of political rule. Attention has therefore focused not only on the machinery through which legitimacy is maintained but also upon the circumstances in which the legitimacy of a regime is called into question and, ultimately, collapses. In *Legitimation Crisis* (1973), the neo-Marxist Jurgen Habermas (see p. 281) argued that within liberal democracies there were 'crisis tendencies' which challenged the stability of such regimes by undermining legitimacy. The core of this argument was the tension between a private-enterprise or capitalist economy, on one hand, and a democratic political system, on the other; in effect, the system of capitalist democracy may be inherently unstable.

The democratic process forces government to respond to popular pressures, either because political parties outbid each other in attempting to get into power or because pressure groups make unrelenting demands upon politicians once in power. This is reflected in the inexorable rise of public spending and the progressive expansion of the state's responsibilities, especially in economic and social life. Anthony King (1975) described this problem as one of government 'overload'. Government was overloaded quite simply because in attempting to meet the demands made of them, democratic politicians came to pursue policies which threatened the health and long-term survival of the capitalist economic order. For instance, growing public spending created a fiscal crisis in which high taxes became a disincentive to enterprise, and ever-rising government borrowing led to permanently high inflation. Habermas's analysis suggested that liberal democracies could not permanently satisfy both popular demands for social security and welfare rights, and the requirements of a market economy based upon private profit. Forced either to resist democratic pressures or to risk economic collapse, capitalist democracies would, in his view, find it increasingly difficult to maintain legitimacy.

To some extent, fears of a legitimation crisis painted an over-gloomy picture of liberal democratic politics in the 1970s. Habermas claimed to identify 'crisis tendencies' which are beyond the capacity of liberal democracies to control. In practice, however, the electoral mechanism allows liberal democracies to adjust policy in response to competing demands, thus enabling the system as a whole to retain a high degree of legitimacy, even though particular policies may attract criticism and provoke unpopularity. Much of liberal democratic politics therefore amounts to shifts from interventionist policies to free market ones and then back again, as power alternates between left-wing and right-wing governments. There is a sense, however, in which the rise of the New Right in the 1970s and 1980s can be seen as a response to a legitimation crisis. In the first place, the New Right recognised that the problem of 'overload' arose, in part, out of the perception that government could, and would, solve all problems, economic and social problems as well as political ones. As a consequence, New Right politicians such as Reagan in the United States and Thatcher in Britain sought to lower popular expectations of government. This they did by trying to shift responsibility from the state to the individual. Thus welfare was portrayed as largely a matter of individual responsibility, individuals being encouraged to provide for themselves by hard work, savings, medical insurance, private pensions and so forth. Moreover, unemployment was no longer seen as a responsibility of government: there was a 'natural rate' of unemployment which could only be pushed up by workers 'pricing themselves out of jobs'.

More radically, the New Right attempted to challenge and finally displace the theories and values which had previously legitimised the progressive expansion of the state's responsibilities. In this sense, the New Right amounted to a 'hegemonic project' that tried to establish the ascendancy of a rival set of pro-market values and theories. This amounted to a public philosophy which extolled rugged individualism and denigrated the 'nanny' state. This project had two themes, a neo-liberal and neo-conservative one. Neo-liberal theories attempt to reassert the autonomy of the market by proclaiming, in essence, that 'the economy works best when left alone by government'. In this way, economic and social life is portrayed as a private sphere over which the state exercises no rightful influence. Neo-conservatives, on the other hand, call for the restoration of authority, order and discipline. In particular, this reflects a desire to strengthen the authority of government, at least in relation to what the New Right regard as its proper role: law and order, public morality and defence.

While liberal democratic regimes in the industrialised West have remained relatively immune from legitimation crises, the same cannot be said of liberal democratic government in the developing world. Few developing world countries have been able to sustain political systems based upon an open and competitive struggle for power and respect for a significant range of civil liberties. Although a growing number have developed liberal democratic features, enduringly successful ones like those in India and Venezuela are still rare. Liberal democratic experiments have often culminated in military coups or the emergence of single-party rule. Such developments have about them some of the characteristics of a legitimation crisis. For example, structural problems, such as chronic underdevelopment, an over-reliance upon cash crops, indebtedness to Western banks and so on, make it difficult, and perhaps impossible, for third world regimes to satisfy the expectations which democratic government creates. Furthermore, multi-party democracy often appears inappropriate, and may even be regarded as an obstacle, when society is confronted by the single, overriding goal: the need for social development. From another point of view, however, it is questionable that such regimes ever enjoyed legitimacy, in which case their fall can hardly be described as a legitimation crisis. Liberal democratic regimes were often bequeathed to newly independent states by former colonial rulers and reflect values like individualism and competition which are foreign to many parts of the third world.

The collapse of orthodox communist regimes in Eastern Europe and the Soviet Union, 1989–91, appears to provide a particularly good example of a legitimation crisis or a series of legitimation crises. These crises had a political, economic and social dimension. Politically, orthodox communist regimes were one-party states dominated by a 'ruling' communist party whose influence extended over virtually all groups in society. Economically, the centrally planned economies that operated within such regimes proved to be highly inefficient and incapable of generating the widespread, if unequal, prosperity found in the capitalist West. Socially, orthodox communist regimes were undermined by their very achievements: industrialisation and the expansion of mass education created a better informed and increasingly sophisticated body of citizens whose demands for the civil liberties and consumer goods thought to be available in the West simply outstripped the capacity of the regime to respond. Such factors progressively undermined the rightfulness or legitimacy of orthodox communism, eventually precipitating mass demonstrations, in 1989 throughout Eastern Europe, and in the Soviet Union in 1991.

An alternative explanation of the collapse of communism is, however, that these regimes never enjoyed legitimacy but only survived as long as they did out of a combination of systematic repression and the habits of inertia and apathy which a lack of political participation engenders. Certainly, it is difficult to say that the Marxist-Leninist principles upon which these regimes were based ever enjoyed broad support amongst the general public. This can be seen most clearly in Eastern Europe where, with the exception of Yugoslavia, communist rule was in effect imposed after 1945 by the Soviet Red Army. By comparison, where domestic revolutions occurred, as in the Soviet Union, China and Cuba, communism can be said to have enjoyed at least a measure of legitimacy. In such regimes, legitimacy was constructed on the basis of traditional and charismatic authority. The 'right to rule' was based upon a combination of the revolutionary heritage, kept alive by rituals and celebrations, and the cults of personality which were built up around leaders such as Stalin, Mao, Tito and Castro.

Summary

1   Power is central to the understanding and practice of politics. It can be exercised on three levels: through the ability to make or influence decisions; through the ability to set the agenda and prevent decisions being made; and through the ability to manipulate what people think and want.

2   Power is the *ability* to influence the behaviour of others, based upon the capacity to reward or punish. By contrast, authority is the *right* to influence others, based upon their acknowledged duty to obey. Weber distinguished between three kinds of authority: traditional authority based upon custom and history; charismatic authority, the power of personality; and legal-rational authority derived from the formal powers of an office or post.

3   Authority provokes deep political and ideological disagreements. Some regard it as essential to the maintenance of an ordered, stable and healthy society, providing individuals with clear guidance and support. Others warn that authority tends to be the enemy of liberty and to undermine reason and moral responsibility; authority tends to lead to authoritarianism.

4   Legitimacy refers to the 'rightfulness' of a political system. It is crucial to the stability and long-term survival of a system of rule because it is regarded as justified or acceptable. Legitimacy may require conformity to widely accepted constitutional rules and broad public support; but it may also be 'manufactured' through a process of ideological manipulation and control for the benefit of political or social elites.

Further reading

Almond, G. and Verba, S. *The Civic Culture Revisited.* Princeton, NJ: Princeton University Press, 1980.

Barnes, B. *The Nature of Power.* Cambridge: Polity Press, 1988.

Beetham, D. *The Legitimation of Power.* London: Macmillan and Atlantic Highlands, NJ: Humanities Press, 1991.

Bocock, R. *Hegemony.* London and New York: Tavistock, 1986.

Flathman, R. *The Practice of Political Authority: Authority and the Authoritative* Chicago: University of Chicago Press, 1980.

Lukes, S. (ed.) *Power.* Oxford: Basil Blackwell, 1986.

Raz, J. *The Authority of Law.* Oxford and New York: Oxford University Press, 1979.

Wolff, R.P. *In Defence of Anarchism.* New York: Harper & Row, 1970.

Chapter 6

Law, Order and Justice

Introduction
Law
Order
Justice
Summary
Further reading

Introduction

Law is found in all modern societies, and is usually regarded as the bedrock of civilised existence. Law commands citizens, telling them what they *must* do; it lays down prohibitions indicating what citizens *cannot* do; and it allocates entitlements defining what citizens have the *right* to do. Although it is widely accepted that law is a necessary feature of any healthy and stable society, there is considerable debate about the nature and role of law. Opinions, for instance, conflict about the origins and purpose of law. Does it liberate or oppress? Do laws exist to safeguard all individuals and promote the common good, or do they merely serve the interests of the propertied and privileged few? Moreover, there is controversy about the relationship between law and morality. Does law enforce moral standards; should it try to? How much freedom should the law allow the individual, and over what issues?

Such questions also relate to the need for personal security and social order. Indeed, in the mouths of politicians, the concepts of order and law often appear to be fused into the composite notion of 'law-and-order'. Rolling these two ideas together sees law as the principal device through which order is maintained, but raises a series of further problems. In particular, is order only secured through a system of rule-enforcement and punishment, or can it emerge naturally through the influence of social solidarity and rational good sense? Finally, there is the complex problem of the relationship between law and justice. Is the purpose of law to see that justice is done, and, anyway, what would that entail? Furthermore, how is it possible to distinguish between just and unjust laws, and, in particular, does the distinction suggest that in certain circumstances it may be justifiable to break the law?

Law

The term 'law' has been used in a wide variety of ways. In the first place, there are scientific laws or what are called descriptive laws. These describe regular or necessary patterns of behaviour found in either natural or social life. The most obvious examples are found in the natural sciences; for instance, in the laws of motion and thermodynamics advanced by physicists. But this notion of law has also been employed by social theorists, in an attempt to highlight predictable, even inevitable, patterns of social behaviour. This can be seen in Engels's assertion that Marx (see p. 373) uncovered the 'laws' of historical and social development, and in the so-called 'laws' of demand and supply which underlie economic theory. An alternative use, however, treats law generally as a means of enforcing norms or standards of social behaviour. Sociologists have thus seen forms of law at work in all organised societies, ranging from informal processes usually found in traditional societies to the formal legal systems typical of modern societies. By contrast, political theorists have tended to understand law more specifically, seeing it as a distinctive social institution clearly separate from other social rules or norms and only found in modern societies.

In a general sense, law constitutes a set of rules, including, as said earlier, commands, prohibitions and entitlements. However, what is it that distinguishes law from other social rules? First, law is made by the government and so applies throughout society. In that way, law reflects the 'will of the state' and therefore takes precedence over all other norms and social rules. For instance, conformity to the rules of a sports club, church or trade union does not provide citizens with immunity if they have broken the 'law of the land'. Secondly, law is compulsory; citizens are not allowed to choose which laws to obey and which to ignore, because law is backed up by a system of coercion and punishment. Thirdly, law has a 'public' quality in that it consists of published and recognised rules. This is, in part, achieved by enacting law through a formal, and usually public, legislative process. Moreover, the punishments handed down for law-breaking are predictable and can be anticipated, whereas arbitrary arrest or imprisonment has a random and dictatorial character. Fourthly, law is usually recognised as binding upon those to whom it applies, even if particular laws may be regarded as 'unjust' or 'unfair'. Law is therefore more than simply a set of enforced commands; it also embodies moral claims, implying that legal rules *should* be obeyed.

The rule of law

The rule of law is a constitutional principle respected with almost devotional intensity in liberal democratic states. At heart, it is quite simply the principle that the law should 'rule', that it should provide a framework within which all citizens act and beyond which no one, neither private citizen nor government official, should go. The principle of the rule of law developed out of a long-established liberal theory of law. From John Locke (see p. 269) onwards, liberals have regarded law not as a constraint upon the individual but as an essential guarantee of this liberty. Without the protection of law, each person is constantly under threat from every other member of society, as indeed they are from him. The danger of unrestrained individual conduct was graphically represented by the barbarism of the 'state of nature'. The fundamental purpose of law is therefore to protect individual rights, which in Locke's view meant the right to life, liberty and property.

The supreme virtue of the rule of law is therefore that it serves to protect the individual citizen from the state; it ensures a 'government of laws and not of men'. Such an idea was enshrined in the German concept of the *Rechtsstaat*, a state based on law, which came to be widely adopted throughout continental Europe and encouraged the development of codified and professional legal systems. The rule of law, however, has a distinctively Anglo-American character. In the United States, the supremacy of law is emphasised by the status of the US Constitution, by the checks and balances it establishes and the individual rights outlined in the Bill of Rights. This is made clear in the Fifth and Fourteenth Amendments, which specifically forbid federal or state government from denying any person life, liberty and property without 'due process of law'. The doctrine of 'due process' not only restricts the discretionary power of public officials but also enshrines a number of individual rights, notably the right to a fair trial and to equal treatment under the law. Nevertheless, it also vests considerable power in the hands of judges who, by interpreting the law, effectively determine the proper realm of government action.

By contrast, the British conception of the rule of law has seen it as typical of uncodified constitutional systems, within which rights and duties are rooted in common law, laws derived from long-established customs and traditions. The classic account of such a view is found in A.V. Dicey's *Introduction to the Study of the Law of the Constitution* ([1885] 1939). In Dicey's view, the rule of law embraces four separate features. First, no one should be punished except for breaches of law. This is the most fundamental feature of the rule of law because it distinguishes between rule-bound government and arbitrary government, suggesting that where the rule of law exists government cannot simply act as it pleases; for instance, it cannot punish citizens merely because it objects to their opinions or disapproves of their behaviour. Secondly, the rule of law requires what Dicey called 'equal subjection' to the law, more commonly understood as equality before the law. Quite simply, the law should be no respecter of persons, it should not discriminate against people on grounds of race, gender, religious creed, social background and so forth, and it should apply equally to ordinary citizens and to government officials. Thirdly, when law is broken there must be a certainty of punishment. The law can only 'rule' if it is applied at all times and in all circumstances; the law rules only selectively when some law-breakers are prosecuted and punished, while others are not. Finally, the rule of law requires that the rights and liberties of the individual are embodied in the 'ordinary law' of the land. This would ensure, Dicey hoped, that when individual rights are violated citizens can seek redress through the courts.

Although Dicey believed that the rule of law was typical of the British system of government and those modelled upon it, in a number of respects Britain offers a particularly poor example of the rule of law. For instance, though Dicey strove to reconcile the two, it can be argued that parliamentary sovereignty, the central principle of Britain's uncodified constitution, violates the very idea of a rule of law. It is difficult to suggest that the law 'rules' if the legislature itself is not bound by any external constraints. This problem has been exacerbated by the growth of executive power and the effective control which the government of the day exercises over Parliament, made possible by party discipline. This encouraged Lord Hailsham (1976) to describe the British system of government as an 'elective dictatorship'. Moreover, in the absence of a Bill of Rights, individual rights and liberties often enjoy little protection, meaning that grievances cannot be redressed through the courts. The establishment of a meaningful rule of law in Britain may therefore require far-reaching constitutional reform, including the codification of the constitution, the introduction of a Bill of Rights and the construction of a clear separation of powers between legislature and executive.

In its broad sense, the rule of law is a core liberal-democratic principle, embodying ideas such as constitutionalism and limited government to which most modern states aspire. In particular, the rule of law imposes significant constraints upon how law is made and how it is adjudicated. For example, it suggests that all laws should be 'general' in the sense that they apply to all citizens and do not select particular individuals or groups for special treatment, good or bad. It is, further, vital that citizens know 'where they stand'; laws should therefore be precisely framed and accessible to the public. Retrospective legislation, for example, is clearly unacceptable on such grounds, since it allows citizens to be punished for actions that were legal at the time they occurred. In the same way, the rule of law is usually thought to be irreconcilable with cruel and inhuman forms of punishment. Above all, the principle implies that the courts should be impartial and accessible to all. This can only be achieved if the judiciary, whose role it is to interpret law and adjudicate between the parties to a dispute, enjoys independence from government. The independence of the judiciary is designed to ensure that judges are 'above' or 'outside' the machinery of government. Law, in other words, must be kept strictly separate from politics.

Nevertheless, the rule of law also has its critics. Some have, for instance, suggested that it is a truism: to say that the law 'rules' may acknowledge nothing more than that citizens are compelled to obey it. In this narrow sense, the rule of law is reduced to the statement that 'everybody must obey the law'. Others have argued that the principle pays little attention to the content of law. Some have therefore argued that the rule of law was observed in the Third Reich and in the Soviet Union simply because oppression wore the cloak of legality. Even its keenest defenders will acknowledge that although the rule of law may be a necessary condition for just government, it is not in itself a sufficient one. Marxist critics go further, however. Marxists (see p. 81) have traditionally regarded law not as a safeguard for individual liberty but as a means for securing property rights and protecting the capitalist system. For Marx, law, like politics and ideology, was part of a 'superstructure' conditioned by the economic 'base', in this case the capitalist mode of production. Law thus protects private property, social inequality and class domination. The formal equality which the rule of law proclaims contrasts, Marxists argue, with social and economic inequalities that, for instance, restrict access to law and to effective legal advice. Furthermore, class biases operate within a judiciary that is drawn disproportionately from the ranks of the propertied and the privileged, whose interpretation of law is conditioned by their class origins.

Natural and positive law

The relationship between law and morality is one of the thorniest problems in political theory. Philosophers have long been taxed by questions related to the nature of law, its origins and purpose. Does law, for instance, merely give effect to a set of higher moral principles, or is there a clear distinction between law and morality? How far does, or should, the law of the community seek to enforce standards of ethical behaviour? Such questions go to the heart of the distinction between two contrasting theories of law: natural law and positive law.

On the surface, law and morality are very different things. Law refers to a distinctive form of social control backed up by the means of enforcement; it therefore defines what *can* and what *cannot* be done. Morality, on the other hand, is concerned with ethical questions and the difference between 'right' and 'wrong'; it thus prescribes what *should* and what *should not* be done. In one important respect, however, law is an easier concept to grasp than morality. Law can be understood as a social fact, it has an objective character that can be studied and analysed. In contrast, morality is by its very nature a subjective entity, a matter of opinion or personal judgement. For this reason, it is often unclear what the term 'morality' refers to. Are morals simply the customs and conventions which reign within a particular community, its mores? Need morality be based upon clearly defined and well-established principles, rational or religious, which sanction certain forms of behaviour while condemning others? Are moral ideals those that each individual is entitled to impose on himself or herself; is morality, in short, of concern only to the individual?

Those thinkers who insist that law is, or should be, rooted in a moral system subscribe to some kind of theory of 'natural law'. Theories of natural law date back to Plato (see p. 22) and Aristotle (see p. 68). Plato believed that behind the ever-changing forms of social and political life lay unchanging archetypal forms, the Ideas, of which only an enlightened elite, the philosopher-kings, had knowledge. A 'just' society was therefore one in which human laws conformed as far as possible to this transcendental wisdom. This line of thought was continued by Aristotle, who believed that the purpose of law and organised social life was to encourage humankind to live in accordance with virtue. In his view, there was a perfect law, fixed for all time, which would provide the basis for citizenship and all other forms of social behaviour. Medieval thinkers such as Thomas Aquinas (see p. 158) also took it for granted that human laws had a moral basis. Natural law, he argued, could be penetrated through our God-given natural reason and guides us towards the attainment of the good life on earth.

The demands of natural law came to be expressed through the idea of natural rights. Natural rights were thought to have been invested in humankind either by God or by nature. Thinkers such as Locke and Thomas Jefferson (see p. 192) proposed that the purpose of human-made law was to protect these God-given and inalienable rights. However, the rise of rationalism and scientific thought served by the nineteenth century to make natural law theories distinctly unfashionable. Nevertheless, the twentieth century has witnessed a revival of such ideas, precipitated, in part, by the cloak of legality behind which Nazi and Stalinist terror took place. The desire to establish a higher set of moral values against which national law could be judged was, for example, one of the problems which the Nuremberg Trials (1945–6) had to address. Under the auspices of the newly created United Nations, major Nazi figures were prosecuted for war crimes, even though in many cases they had acted legally in the eyes of the Nazi regime itself. This was made possible by reference to the notion of natural law, albeit dressed up in the modern language of human rights. Indeed, it is now widely accepted that both national and international law should conform to the higher moral principles set out in the doctrine of human rights. Such ideas are discussed at greater length in Chapter 7.

Thomas Aquinas (1224-74)

Italian Dominican monk, theologian and philosopher. Born near Naples, the son of a noble family, Aquinas joined the Dominican order against his family's wishes. He was canonised in 1324, and in the nineteenth century, Pope Leo III recognised Aquinas' writings as the basis of Catholic theology.

Aquinas took part in the theological debates of the day, arguing that reason and faith are compatible, and defending the admission of Aristotle (see p. 68) into the university curriculum. His vast but unfinished *Summa Theologiae*, begun in 1265, deals with the nature of God, morality and law – eternal, divine, natural and human. He viewed 'natural law' as the basic moral rules on which political society depends, believing that these can be elaborated by rational reflection on human nature. As, in Aquinas' view, human law should be framed in accordance with natural law, its purpose is ultimately to 'lead men to virtue', reflecting his belief that law, government and the state are natural featues of the human condition rather than (as Augustine (see p. 91) had argued) consequences of original sin. Aquinas nevertheless recognised that human law is an imperfect instrument, in that some moral faults cannot be legally prohibited and attempts to prohibit others may cause more harm than good. The political tradition that Aquinas founded has come to be known as Thomism, with neo-Thomism, since the late nineteenth century, attempting to keep alive the spirit of the 'angelic doctor'.

The central theme of all conceptions of natural law is the idea that law should conform to some prior moral standards, that the purpose of law is to enforce morality. This notion, however, came under attack in the nineteenth century from what John Osbourne called 'the science of positive law'. The idea of positive law sought to free the understanding of law from moral, religious and mystical assumptions. Many have seen its roots in Thomas Hobbes's (see p. 124) command theory of law: 'law is the word of him that by right hath command over others'. In effect, law is nothing more than the will of the sovereign. By the nineteenth century, John Austin (1790–1859) had developed this into the theory of 'legal positivism', which saw the defining feature of law not as its conformity to higher moral or religious principles, but in the fact that it is established and enforced by a political superior, a 'sovereign person or body'. This boils down to the belief that law is law because it is obeyed. One of its implications is, for instance, that the notion of international law is highly questionable. If the treaties and UN resolutions that constitute what is called 'international law' cannot be enforced, they should be regarded as a collection of moral principles and ideals, and not a law. A modern attempt to refine legal positivism was undertaken in H.L.A. Hart's *The Concept of Law* (1961). Hart was concerned to explain law not in terms of moral principles but by reference to its purpose within human society. Law, he suggested, stems from the 'union of primary and secondary rules', each of which serves a particular function. The role of primary rules is to regulate social behaviour; these can be thought of as the 'content' of the legal system, for instance, criminal law. Secondary rules, on the other hand, are rules which confer powers upon the institutions of government; they lay down how primary rules are made, enforced and adjudicated, and so determine their validity.

While natural law theories are criticised as being hopelessly philosophical, positive law theories threaten to divorce law entirely from morality. The most extreme case of this was Hobbes, who insisted that citizens had an obligation to obey all laws, however oppressive, since to do otherwise would risk a descent into the chaos of the state of nature. However, other legal positivists allow that law can, and should, be subject to moral scrutiny, and perhaps that it should be changed if it is morally faulty. Their position, however, is simply that moral questions do not affect whether law is law. In other words, whereas natural law theorists seek to run together the issues 'what the law is' and 'what the law ought to be', legal positivists treat these matters as strictly separate. An alternative view of law, however, emerged in the early part of the century, associated with the ideas of the famous American jurist, Oliver Wendell Holmes (1809–94). This is legal realism, the theory that it is really judges who make law because it is they who decide how cases are to be resolved. In this sense, all laws can be thought to be judge-made. However, as judges are non-elected, this view has disturbing implications for the prospect of democratic government.

Law and liberty

While political philosophers have been concerned about broad questions such as the nature of law itself, everyday debates about the relationship between law and morality have tended to focus upon the moral content of specific laws. Which laws are morally justified, and which ones are not? How far, if at all, should the law seek to 'teach morals'? Such questions often arise out of the moral controversies of the day, and seek to know whether the law should permit or prohibit practices such as abortion, prostitution, pornography, television violence, surrogate motherhood, genetic engineering and so forth. At the heart of these questions is the issue of individual liberty and the balance between those moral choices that should properly be made by the individual and those that should be decided by society and enforced through law.

In many ways the classic contribution to this debate was made in the nineteenth century by John Stuart Mill (see p. 258), who, in *On Liberty* ([1859] 1972), asserted that, 'The only purpose for which power can rightfully be exercised over any member of a civilised community against his will is to prevent harm to others'. Mill's position on law was libertarian: he wanted the individual to enjoy the broadest possible realm of freedom. 'Over himself', Mill proclaimed, 'over his own body and mind the individual is sovereign'. However, such a principle, often referred to as the 'harm principle', implies a very clear distinction between actions that are 'self-regarding', whose impact is largely or entirely confined to the person in question, and those that can be thought of as 'other-regarding'. In Mill's view, the law has no right to interfere with 'self-regarding' actions; in this realm individuals are entitled to exercise unrestrained liberty. Law should therefore only restrict the individual in the realm of 'other-regarding' actions, and then only in the event of harm being done to others. The strict application of this principle would clearly challenge a wide range of laws currently in existence, notably those that are paternalistic. For instance, laws prohibiting suicide and prostitution are clearly unacceptable, since their primary intent is to prevent people damaging or harming themselves. The same could be said of laws prohibiting drug-taking or enforcing the use of seat-belts or crash-helmets, to the extent that these reflect a concern about the individuals concerned as opposed to the costs (harm) imposed on society.

Mill's ideas reflect a fierce commitment to individual liberty, born out of a faith in human reason and the conviction that only through the exercise of personal choice would human beings develop and achieve 'individuality'. His ideas, however, raise a number of difficulties. In the first place, what is meant by 'harm'? Mill clearly understood harm to mean physical harm, but there are at least grounds for extending the notion of harm to include psychological, mental, moral and even spiritual harm. For example, although blasphemy clearly does not cause physical harm it may, nevertheless, cause 'offence'; it may challenge the most sacred principles of a religious group and so threaten its security. Just such an argument was used by Muslim fundamentalists in their campaign against the publication of Salman Rushdie's *The Satanic Verses*. In the same way, it could be argued that in economic life price agreements between firms should be illegal because they both harm the interests of consumers, who end up paying higher prices, as well as those of competitor firms. Secondly, who counts as the 'others' who should not be harmed? This question is most obviously raised by issues like abortion and embryo research where it is the status of the unborn which is in question. As will be discussed more fully in Chapter 7, if a human embryo is treated as an 'other', interfering with it or harming it in any way is morally reprehensible. However, if the embryo remains part of the mother until it is born she has a perfect right to do with it what she pleases.

A third problem relates to individual autonomy. Mill undoubtedly wanted people to exercise the greatest possible degree of control over their own destinies, but even he recognised that this could not always be achieved, as, for instance, in the case of children. Children, he accepted, possessed neither the experience nor the understanding to make wise decisions on their own behalf; as a result, he regarded the exercise of parental authority as perfectly acceptable. However, this principle can also be applied on grounds other than age, for example, in relation to alcohol consumption and drug-taking. On the face of it, these are 'self-regarding' actions, unless, of course, the principle of 'harm' is extended to include the distress caused to the family involved or the healthcare costs incurred by society. Nevertheless, the use of addictive substances raises the additional problem that they rob the user of free will and so deprive him or her of the capacity to make rational decisions. Paternalistic legislation may well be justifiable on precisely these grounds. Indeed, the principle could be extended almost indefinitely. For example, it could perhaps be argued that smoking should be banned on the grounds that nicotine is physically and psychologically addictive, and that those who endanger their health through smoking must either be poorly informed or be incapable of making wise judgements on their own behalf. In short, they must be saved from themselves.

An alternative basis for establishing the relationship between law and morality is by considering not the claims of individual liberty but the damage which unrestrained liberty can do to the fabric of society. A classic statement of this position was advanced in *The Enforcement of Morals* (1968) by Patrick Devlin, which argues that there is a 'public morality' which society had a right to enforce through the instrument of law. Devlin's concern with this issue was raised by the legalisation of homo-sexuality and other pieces of so-called 'permissive' legislation in the 1960s. Underlying his position is the belief that society is held together by a 'shared' morality, a fundamental agreement about what is 'good' and what is 'evil'. Law therefore has the right to 'enforce morals' when changes in lifestyle and moral behaviour threaten the social fabric and the security of all citizens living within it. Such a view, however, differs from paternalism in that the latter is more narrowly concerned with making people do what is in their interests, though in cases like banning pornography it can be argued that paternalism and the enforcement of morals coincide. Devlin can be said to have extended Mill's notion of harm to include 'offence', at least when actions provoke what Devlin called 'real feelings of revulsion' rather than simply dislike. Such a position has also been adopted by the conservative New Right since the 1970s in relation to what it regards as 'moral pollution'. This is reflected in anxiety about the portrayal of sex and violence on television and the spread of gay and lesbian rights. Against the twin threats of permissiveness and multi-culturalism, conservative thinkers (see p. 138) have usually extolled the virtues of 'traditional morality' and 'family values'.

The central theme of such arguments is that morality is simply too important to be left to the individual. Where the interests of 'society' and those of the 'individual' conflict, law must always take the side of the former. Such a position, however, raises some serious questions. First, is there any such thing as a 'public morality'? Is there a set of 'majority' values which can be distinguished from 'minority' ones? Apart from acts like murder, physical violence, rape and theft, moral views in fact diverge considerably from generation to generation, from social group to social group, and indeed from individual to individual. This ethical pluralism is particularly evident in those areas of personal and sexual morality – homosexuality, abortion, violence on television and so on – with which the moral New Right is especially concerned. Secondly, there is a danger that under the banner of traditional morality, law is doing little more than enforcing social prejudice. If acts are banned simply because they cause offence to the majority, this comes close to saying that morality comes down to a show of hands. Surely, moral judgements must always be critical, at least in the sense that they are based upon clear and rational principles rather than just widely held beliefs. Do laws persecuting the Jews, for instance, become morally acceptable simply because anti-Semitic ideas are widely held in society? Finally, it is by no means clear that a healthy and stable society can only exist where a shared morality prevails. This belief, for example, calls the very idea of a multi-cultural and multi-faith society into question. This issue, however, is best pursued by an analysis of social order and the conditions that maintain it.

Order

Fear of disorder and social instability has been perhaps the most fundamental and abiding concern of Western political philosophy. Dating back to the social contract theories of the seventeenth century, political thinkers have grappled with the problem of order and sought ways of preventing human existence degenerating into chaos and confusion. Without order and stability, human life would, in Hobbes's words, be 'solitary, poor, nasty, brutish and short'. Such fears are also evident in the everyday use of the word 'anarchy' to imply disorder, chaos and violence. For these reasons, order has attracted almost unqualified approval from political theorists, at least in so far as none of them are prepared to defend 'disorder'. At the same time, however, the term order conjures up very different images for different political thinkers. At one extreme, traditional conservatives believe that order is inseparable from notions like control, discipline and obedience; at the other, anarchists have suggested that order is related to natural harmony, equilibrium and balance. Such ideological divisions reflect profound disagreement not only about the concept of order but also about how it can be established and how it should be maintained.

Whilst there may be competing conceptions of order, certain common characteristics can nevertheless be identified. Order, in everyday language, refers to regular and tidy patterns, as when soldiers are said to stand 'in order' or the universe is described as being 'ordered'. In social life, order describes regular, stable and predictable forms of behaviour, for which reason social order suggests continuity, even permanence. Social disorder, by contrast, implies chaotic, random and violent behaviour, that is by its very nature unstable and constantly changing. Above all, the virtue that is associated with order is personal security, both physical security, freedom from intimidation and violence and the fear of such, and psychological security, the comfort and stability which only regular and familiar circumstances engender.

Discipline and control

Order is often linked to the ideas of discipline, regulation and authority. In this sense, order comes to stand for a form of social control which has, in some way, to be imposed 'from above'. Social order has to be imposed because, quite simply, it does not occur naturally. All notions of order are based upon a conception of disorder and of the forces that cause it. What causes delinquency, vandalism, crime and social unrest? Those who believe that order is impossible without the exercise of control or discipline usually locate the roots of disorder in the individual human being. In other words, human beings are naturally corrupt, and if not restrained or controlled they will behave in an anti-social and uncivilised fashion. Such ideas are sometimes religious in origin, as in the case of the Christian doctrine of 'original sin'. In other cases, they are explained by the belief that human beings are essentially self-seeking or egoistical. If left to their own devices, individuals act to further their own interests or ends, and will do so at the expense of fellow human beings. One of the most pessimistic such accounts of human nature is found in the writings of absolutist thinkers such as Thomas Hobbes, who in *Leviathan* ([1655] 1968) described the principal human inclination as 'a perpetual and restless desire for power after power, that ceaseth only in death'. This explains why his description of the state of nature is so graphic. In his view, its

Absolutism

Absolutism is the theory or practice of absolute government. Government is 'absolute' in the sense that it possesses unfettered power: government cannot be constrained by a body external to itself. Absolute government is usually associated with the political forms that dominated Europe in the seventeenth and eighteenth centuries, its most prominent manifestation being the absolute monarchy. However, there is no necessary connection between monarchy and absolute government. Although unfettered power can be placed in the hands of the monarch, it can also be vested in a collective body such as a supreme legislature. Absolutism, nevertheless, differs from modern versions of dictatorship, notably totalitarianism. Whereas absolutist regimes aspired to a monopoly of political power, usually achieved by excluding the masses from politics, totalitarianism involves the establishment of 'total power' through the politicisation of every aspect of social and personal existence. Absolutist theory thus differs significantly from, for instance, fascist doctrines.

Absolute government and absolute power are not the same thing, however. The absolutist principle resides in the claim to an unlimited right to rule, rather than in the exercise of unchallengeable power. This why absolutist theories are closely linked to the concept of sovereignty, representing an unchallengeable and indivisible source of legal authority. There are both rationalist and theological versions of absolutist theory. Rationalist theories of absolutism generally advance the belief that only absolute government can guarantee order and social stability. Divided sovereignty or challengeable power is therefore a recipe for chaos and disorder. Theological theories of absolutism are based upon the doctrine of divine right, according to which the absolute control a monarch exercises over his subjects derives from, and is analogous to, the power of God over his creation. Monarchical power is therefore unchallengeable because it is the temporal expression of God's authority.

Absolutist theories have the virtue that they articulate some enduring political truths. In particular, they emphasise the central importance to politics of order, and remind us that the primary objective of political society is to maintain stability and security. Absolutist theories can nevertheless be criticised as being both politically redundant and ideologically objectionable. Absolutist government collapsed in the face of the advance of constitutionalism and representation, and where dictatorship has survived it has assumed a quite different political character. Indeed, by the time that the term absolutism was coined in the nineteenth century, the phenomenon itself had largely disappeared. The objectionable feature of absolutism is that it is now widely seen as merely a cloak for tyranny and arbitrary government. Modern

→

political thought, linked to ideas such as individual rights and democratic accountability, is largely an attempt to protect against the dangers of absolutism.

Key figures

Jean Bodin (1530-96)   A French political philosopher, Bodin was the first important theorist of sovereignty, which he defined as 'the absolute and perpetual power of a commonwealth'. In his view, the only guarantee of political and social stability is the existence of a sovereign with final law-making power; in that sense, law reflects the 'will' of the sovereign. Although the sovereign is above the law, in that he cannot be bound by an expression of its will, Bodin recognised the limitation imposed by natural law and what he termed 'fundamental laws', and so did not take sovereignty to imply arbitrary power. Bodin's most important work is *The Six Books of the Commonweal* (1576).

Thomas Hobbes (see p. 124)   Hobbes followed Bodin in seeing the maintenance of order as the primary goal of politics, and in accepting that this can be achieved only by the establishment of an absolute sovereign. However, his strictly rationalist account of absolutism, advanced in the form of social contract theory, did not rely upon conventional notions of natural law and allowed the sovereign's actions to be arbitrary as well as absolute.

Joseph de Maistre (1753-1821)   A French aristocrat and political thinker, Maistre was a fierce critic of the French Revolution and a supporter of hereditary monarchy. His political philosophy was based upon willing and complete subordination to 'the master'. Maistre believed that society is organic, and would fragment or collapse if it were not bound together by the twin principles of 'throne and altar'. In his view, earthly monarchies are ultimately subject to the supreme spiritual power of the Pope. Maistre's chief political works include *Considérations sur la France* (1796) and *Du pape* (1817).

Further reading

Anderson, P. *Lineages of the Absolutist State.* London: New Left Books, 1974.

Shennan, J. H. *Liberty and Order in Early Modern Europe: The Subject and the State 1650–1800.* London: Longman, 1986.

Skinner, Q. *The Foundations of Modern Political Thought,* 2 vols. Cambridge: Cambridge University Press, 1978.

dominant feature would be war, a barbaric and unending war of 'every man against every man'.

The traditional conservative conception of order has been deeply influenced by this pessimistic view of human nature. Conservatives have, for example, typically shown very little patience for attempts to explain crime by reference to poverty or social deprivation. Crime, and for that matter most other forms of anti-social behaviour – hooliganism, vandalism, delinquency and even plain rudeness – is nothing more than an individual phenomenon reflecting the moral corruption that lies within each human being. The criminal is therefore a morally 'bad' person, and deserves to be treated as such. This is why conservatives tend to see an intrinsic link between the notions of order and law, and are inclined to refer to the fused concept of law-and-order. In effect, public order is quite unthinkable without clearly enforced laws. Conservatives are therefore often in the forefront of campaigns to strengthen the powers of the police and calls for stiffer penalties against criminals and vandals. This was evident in the case of the British Conservative Party, especially during the Thatcher period. In the United States, a succession of Republican presidents – Nixon, Reagan and Bush – placed heavy stress upon the need to fight crime by imposing stiffer punishments, in particular by the reintroduction of the death penalty. Nevertheless, the link between order and law is one which many liberals and some social democrats would also subscribe to. Although liberals tend to place a heavier emphasis upon human rationality, and to give greater credence to social explanations of crime and disorder, in believing that human beings are essentially self-seeking they accept that they are prone to abuse and exploit one another. It is notable that supposedly centre-left politicians such as Clinton in the United States and Blair in Britain have adopted the stance that they should be 'tough' on crime and not merely on the causes of crime.

The conservative analysis, nevertheless, goes further. Conservatives hold not only that human beings are morally corrupt but also emphasise the degree to which social order, and indeed human civilisation itself, is fragile. In accordance with the eighteenth-century writings of Edmund Burke (see p. 139), conservatives have traditionally portrayed society as 'organic', as a living entity within which each element is linked in a delicate balance to every other element. The 'social whole' is therefore more than simply a collection of its individual parts, and if any part is damaged the whole is threatened. In particular, conservatives have emphasised that society is held together by the maintenance of traditional institutions such as the family and by respect for an established culture, based upon religion, tradition and custom. The defence of the 'fabric' of society has become one of the central themes of neo-conservatism, advanced in the United States by social theorists such as Irving Kristol (see p. 139) and Daniel Bell, who have warned against the destruction of spiritual values brought about by both market pressures and the permissive ethic. From this point of view, law can be seen not only as a way of maintaining order by threatening the wrong-doer with punishment but also as a means of upholding traditional values and established beliefs. This is why conservatives have usually agreed with Patrick Devlin in believing that the proper function of law is to 'teach morality'.

Order has, finally, been defended on psychological grounds. This view emphasises that human beings are limited and psychologically insecure creatures. Above all, people seek safety and security; they are drawn naturally towards the familiar, the known, the traditional. Order is therefore a vital, perhaps the most vital, of human needs. This implies that human beings will recoil from the unfamiliar, the new, the alien. In this way, for example, Edmund Burke was able to portray prejudice against people different from ourselves as both natural and beneficial, arguing that it gives individuals a sense of security and a social identity. Such a view, however, has very radical implications for the maintenance of order. It may, for instance, be entirely at odds with the multi-cultural and multi-faith nature of contemporary societies, suggesting that disorder and insecurity must always lie close to the surface in such societies. As a result, some conservatives have objected to unchecked immigration, or demanded that immigrants be encouraged to assimilate into the culture of their 'host' country. This was evident in Britain in the 1960s in the predictions by Enoch Powell that continued African and Asian immigration into the country brought with it the danger of racial violence and civil unrest. The British National Party, the French National Front and the New Democratic Party in Germany have each advocated the repatriation of immigrants on precisely the same grounds.

Natural harmony

A very different conception of order emerges from the writings of socialists and anarchists. Anarchists, for instance, advocate the abolition of the state and all forms of political authority, including, of course, the machinery of law and order. Marxist socialists have also sympathised with this utopian vision. Marx himself believed that the state, and with it law and other forms of social control, would gradually 'wither away' once social inequality was abolished. Parliamentary socialists and modern liberals have made more modest proposals, but they have nevertheless been critical of the belief that order can only be maintained by strict laws and stiff penalties. Although such views are critical of the conventional notion of 'law and order', they do not amount to an outright rejection of 'order' itself. Rather, they are based upon the alternative belief that social order

Utopianism

A utopia (from the Greek *utopia*, meaning 'no place', or the Greek *eutopia*, meaning 'good place') is literally an ideal or perfect society. The term was coined by the English humanist and author Thomas More (1478–1535), and was first used in his *Utopia* (1516). More's work purported to describe a perfect society supposedly set on a South Pacific island; however, commentators have disagreed about whether his purpose was advocacy or satire.

Utopianism is a style of social theorising that develops a critique of the existing order by constructing a model of an ideal or perfect alternative. As such, it usually exhibits three features. First, it embodies a radical and comprehensive rejection of the status quo; present social and political arrangements are deemed to be fundamentally defective and in need of root-and-branch change. Second, utopian thought highlights the potential for human self-development, either based upon highly optimistic assumptions about human nature or optimistic assumptions about the capacity of economic, social or political institutions to ameliorate baser human drives and instincts. Third, utopianism usually transcends the public/private divide in that it suggests the possibility of complete or near-complete personal fulfilment. For the alternative society to be ideal, it must offer the prospect of emancipation in the personal realm as well as in the political or public realm.

However, utopianism is not a political philosophy nor an ideological tradition. Substantive utopias differ from one another, and utopian thinkers have not advanced a common conception of the good life. Nevertheless, most utopias are characterised by the abolition of want, the absence of conflict, and the avoidance of violence and oppression. Socialism in general, and anarchism and Marxism (see p. 81) in particular, have a marked disposition towards utopianism, reflecting their belief in the human potential for sociable, cooperative and gregarious behaviour. Socialist utopias, as a result, are strongly egalitarian and typically characterised by collective property ownership and a reduction in, or eradication of, political authority. Feminism (see p. 60) and ecologism (see p. 196) have also spawned utopian theories. Liberalism's (see p. 29) capacity to generate utopian thought is restricted by its stress upon human self-interestedness and competition; however, an extreme belief in free-market capitalism can be viewed as a form of market utopianism. Other utopias have been based upon faith in the benign influence of government and political authority. Plato's (see p. 22)*Republic*, the earliest example of political utopianism, advocated enlightened despotism, while More's society was hierarchical, authoritarian and patriarchal, albeit within a context of economic equality.

Criticisms of utopian thought fall into two categories. The first (in line with the pejorative, everyday use of the term utopian) suggests that utopianism is deluded or fanciful thinking, a belief in an unrealistic and unachievable goal. Marx (see p. 373), for instance, denounced 'utopian socialism' on the grounds that it advances a moral vision that is in no way

→

grounded in historical and social realities. By contrast, 'scientific socialism' sought to explain how and why a socialist society would come into being (Marxism's utopian character is nevertheless evident in the nature of its ultimate goal: the construction of a classless, communist society). The second category of criticisms holds that utopianism is implicitly totalitarian, in that it promotes a single set of indisputable values and so is intolerant of free debate and diversity. The strength of utopianism is that it enables political theory to think beyond the present and to challenge the 'boundaries of the possible'. The establishment of 'concrete' utopias is a way of uncovering the potential for growth and development within existing circumstances. Without a vision of what could be, political theory may simply be overwhelmed by what is, and thereby lose its critical edge.

Key figures

Robert Owen (1771–1858) A British socialist, industrialist and pioneer of the cooperative movement, Owen's thought was based upon the belief that human character is formed by the social environment, and he therefore asserted that progress requires the construction of a 'rational system of society'. He particularly opposed organised religion, the conventional institution of marriage and private property. Owen advocated the construction of small-scale cooperative communities in which property would be communally owned and essential goods freely distributed. Owen's principal work is *A New View of Society* (1816).

Pierre-Joseph Proudhon (1809–65) A French anarchist, Proudhon attacked both traditional property rights and communism, arguing instead for mutualism, a cooperative productive system geared towards need rather than profit and organised within self-governing communities. His famous dictum, 'property is theft', rejected the accumulation of wealth but allowed for small-scale property ownership in the form of 'possessions', a vital source of independence and initiative. Proudhon's major works include *What is Property?* (1840), *Philosophy of Poverty* (an attack on Marx) (1846), *The Idea of the Revolution in the Nineteenth Century* (1851) and *The Federal Principle* (1863).

Peter Kropotkin (1842–1921) A Russian anarchist and geographer, Kropotkin's work was imbued with a scientific spirit and was based upon a theory of evolution that provided an alternative to Darwin's. By seeing 'mutual aid' as the principal means of human and animal development, he claimed to provide an empirical basis for both anarchism and communism. He looked to the construction of a society consisting of a collection of largely self-managing communes within which life would be regulated by 'liberty and fraternal care'. Kropotkin's best known works include *Mutual Aid* (1897), *Fields, Factories and Workshops* (1901) and *The Conquest of Bread* (1906).

Utopianism continued

Paul Goodman (1911–72) A US writer and social critic, Goodman's anarchist and anti-authoritarian ideas had a considerable impact upon the New Left of the 1960s. His enduring concern with personal growth and human well-being, reflected, in part, in his interest in Gestalt therapy, led him to support a communitarian brand of anarchism, progressive education, pacifism, an ethic of sexual liberation, and the reconstruction of communities to facilitate local autonomy and face-to-face interaction. Goodman's major works include *Growing Up Absurd* (1960), *Communitas* (1960) and *Utopian Essays and Practical Proposals* (1962).

Further reading

Goodwin, B. and Taylor, K. *The Politics of Utopia*. London: Hutchinson, 1982.

Kumar, K. *Utopianism*. Milton Keynes: Open University Press and Minneapolis: University of Minneapolis Press, 1991.

Levitas, R. *The Concept of Utopia*. Hemel Hempstead: Philip Allen, 1990.

---

can take the form of spontaneous harmony, regulated only by the natural good sense of individuals themselves.

Such a concept of order is based upon the assumption that disorder is rooted not in the individual himself or herself but in the structure of society. Human beings are not born corrupt, tainted by 'original sin'; rather, they are corrupted by society. This image is portrayed in the famous opening words of Rousseau's *Social Contract* ([1762] 1969), 'Man is born free but is everywhere in chains'. This is the most basic assumption of utopian political thought. Society can corrupt individuals in a number of ways. Socialists and many liberals point to a link between crime and social deprivation, arguing that laws which protect property are bound to be broken so long as poverty and social inequality persist. Such a view suggests that order can best be promoted not by a fear of punishment but through a programme of social reform designed, for example, to improve housing, counter urban decay, reduce unemployment and so forth. Marxists and classical anarchists have taken such arguments further and called for a social revolution. In their view, crime and disorder are rooted in the institution of private property and in the economic inequality which it gives rise to.

In addition, socialists have suggested that the selfish and acquisitive behaviour that is so often blamed for social disorder is, in reality, bred by society itself. Capitalism encourages human beings to be self-seeking and competitive, and indeed rewards them for putting their own interests before those of fellow human beings. Socialists therefore argue that social order can more easily be maintained in a society which encourages and rewards social solidarity and cooperative behaviour, one based upon collective principles rather than selfishness. Anarchists, for their part, have pointed the finger at law itself, accusing it of being the principal cause of disorder and crime. The Russian anarchist Peter Kropotkin argued in 'Law and Authority' ([1886] 1977), for instance, that, 'the main supports of crime are idleness, law and authority'. For anarchists, law is not simply a means of protecting property from the propertyless but it is also a form of 'organised violence', to use Tolstoy's words. Law is the naked exercise of power over others; all laws are oppressive. This is why law can only be maintained through a system of coercion and punishment, in Tolstoy's view, 'by blows, by deprivation of liberty and by murder'. The solution to the problem of social disorder is therefore simple: abolish all laws and allow people to act freely.

Such beliefs are rooted in very clear assumptions about human behaviour. Rather than needing to be disciplined or controlled, people are thought to be capable of living together in peace and natural harmony. Order is thus 'natural' in the sense that it arises spontaneously out of the actions of free individuals. The belief in 'natural order' is based upon one of two theories of human nature. In the first, human beings are portrayed as rational beings, capable of solving whatever disagreements may arise between them through debate, negotiation and compromise rather than violence. It was, for instance, his deep faith in reason which encouraged J.S. Mill to advocate that law be restricted to the limited task of preventing us from harming each other. Anarchist thinkers such as William Godwin (see p. 341), went further, declaring that 'sound reason and truth' would in all circumstances prevent conflict from leading to disorder. The alternative theory of human nature is the essentially socialist belief that people are naturally sociable, cooperative and gregarious. No dominant culture or traditional morality, nor any form of social control exercised from above, is needed to secure order and stability. Rather, this will emerge naturally and irresistibly out of the sympathy, compassion and concern which each person feels for all fellow human beings. In short, harmony and social order are simply a recognition of our common humanity.

Justifying punishment

Discussions about order invariably address the question of punishment. For example, politicians who use the phrase 'law and order' often employ it as a euphemism for strict punishment and harsh penalties. In the same way, when politicians are described as being 'firm' on law and order, this means that they are likely to support capital punishment, longer gaol sentences, harsh prison regimes and the like. Very frequently, however, punishment is advocated without a clear idea of its aim or purpose.

'Punishment' refers to a penalty inflicted on a person for a crime or offence. Unlike revenge, which can be random and arbitrary, punishment is formal in the sense that specific punishments are linked to particular kinds of offence. Moreover, punishment has a moral character that distinguishes it, for instance, from simple vindictiveness. Punishment is not motivated by spite or the desire to inflict pain, discomfort or inconvenience for its own sake, but rather because a 'wrong' has been done. This is why what are thought of as cruel or inhuman punishments, such as torture and perhaps the death penalty, are often prohibited. However, if punishment has a moral character it must be justified in moral terms. Three such justifications have normally been proposed, based respectively upon the ideas of retribution, deterrence and rehabilitation. Each of these is founded on very different moral and philosophical principles, and each serves to endorse very different forms of punishment. Though the tensions between them are clear, it is nevertheless possible in practice to develop a philosophy of punishment that draws from two or more of them.

In many ways, the most ancient justification for punishment is based upon the idea of retribution. Retribution means to take vengeance against a wrong-doer. The idea is rooted in the religious notion of sin, the belief that there is a discernible quality of 'evil' about particular actions and, possibly, certain thoughts. In this case, punishment for wrong-doing is a moral judgement, which demarcates firmly between 'good' and 'evil'. Wrong-doers *deserve* to be punished; punishment is their 'just desert'. Modern attempts to present the retribution argument often point out, in addition, that its benefits extend to society at large. To punish wrong-doers is not merely to treat them as they deserve to be treated, but also expresses the revulsion of society towards their crime. In so doing, punishment strengthens the 'moral fabric' of society by underlining for all the difference between right and wrong.

The retribution theory suggests some very specific forms of punishment. Precisely because punishment is vengeance it should be proportional to the wrong done. In short, 'the punishment should fit the crime'. The most famous expression of this principle is found in the Old Testament of the Bible which declares, 'an eye for an eye, a tooth for a tooth'. Retribution theory therefore provides a clear justification for the death penalty in the case of murder. Someone who has killed thereby forfeits their own right to life; death is their 'just desert'. Indeed, retribution suggests that, in a sense, society has a moral obligation to kill a murderer in an attempt to give expression to society's abhorrence of the crime. Such principles, however, rely upon an established and rigid moral framework within which 'right' is clearly distinguishable from 'wrong'. The retribution theory is, therefore, of greatest value in societies where traditional moral principles, usually based upon religious belief, are still widely respected; but it is less applicable in the secularised and pluralist societies of the industrialised West. Moreover, in locating responsibility for wrong-doing entirely in the human individual, indeed in the phenomenon of 'personal evil', the retribution theory is unable to take account of social and other external influences upon the individual, and is thus incapable of understanding the complexity of crime in the modern world.

The second major theory of punishment is the deterrence theory. This is less concerned with punishment as a just reward for wrong-doing than with using punishment to shape the future conduct of others. As Jeremy Bentham (see p. 361) put it, 'General prevention ought to be the chief end of punishment as it is its real justification'. Punishment is thus a device which aims to deter people from crime or anti-social behaviour by making them aware of the consequences of their actions. Fear of punishment is therefore the key to order and social stability. Whereas retribution was based upon clear and fixed moral principles, deterrence may be thought of as simply a form of social engineering. Crime, in other words, may not be an expression of personal evil which deserves to be punished, so much as a kind of anti-social behaviour which it is prudent to discourage.

Unlike retribution theory, deterrence does not point to specific forms of punishment. In practice, it suggests that the punishment selected should have the capacity to deter other potential wrong-doers. For this reason, deterrence theory may at times justify far stricter and even crueller punishments than retribution ever can. To punish the wrong-doer is to 'set an example' to others; the more dramatic that example, the more effective its deterrence value. This may, for example, justify cutting off the hand of a petty thief, as is recommended in Islamic *Shari'a* law, in the hope of preventing future thieving. The severity of the penalty imposed upon one individual must be balanced against the benefit of preventing similar crimes occurring in future. The problem, however, is that the idea of deterrence comes dangerously close to divorcing the wrong that has been done from the punishment meted out, and so runs the risk of victimising the initial wrong-doer. Indeed, deterrence theory sets no limits to the form of punishment that may be applied, even for the most trivial offence.

A further difficulty is that deterrence is based upon the assumption that criminals and wrong-doers act rationally, at least in so far as they weigh up the likely consequences of their actions. When this is not the case, deterrence theory collapses. There is reason to believe, for example, that many murderers will not be deterred by the threat of punishment, even capital punishment. This is because murder is often a domestic affair in the sense that it takes place within the family unit, and its perpetrators usually act under the most severe psychological and emotional strain. In such circumstances, the people concerned are not capable of reaching balanced judgements, still less of examining the likely consequences of their actions. If such people acted in a rational and calculating fashion, crimes of passion like these would simply never occur in the first place.

The final justification for punishment is based upon the idea of reform or rehabilitation. This theory shifts responsibility for wrong-doing away from the individual and towards society. The criminal is not thought of as somebody who is morally evil or who should be made an example of; rather, the criminal should be helped, supported and, indeed, educated. Such an idea contrasts sharply with that of retribution because it is based upon an essentially optimistic conception of human nature that makes little or no allowance for the notion of 'personal evil'. Hooliganism, vandalism and crime highlight the failings of society and not the defects of the individual. In effect, crime and disorder are 'bred' by social problems like unemployment, poverty, poor housing and inequality. The only exception to this which deterrence theory would recognise is people who are traditionally mad. However, even in this case people cannot be held personally responsible for their actions.

Quite clearly, rehabilitation suggests very different forms of punishment from either retribution or deterrence. In fact, if the goal is to 'reform' the wrong-doer, punishment moves some way from the popular image of it as a penalty involving the infliction of pain, deprivation or, at the very least, inconvenience. Certainly, no justification can be found in rehabilitation theory for capital punishment – in any circumstances. Moreover, if the purpose of punishment is to educate rather than penalise, non-custodial sentences should be preferred to custodial ones; community service will be preferred to prison; and prison regimes should be designed to promote self-esteem and personal development, and should give transgressors the opportunity to acquire the skills and qualifications which will help them re-integrate into society after their release. A modern and increasingly fashionable version of rehabilitation theory can be found in the notion of restorative justice. This sets out to give wrong-doers an insight into the nature and impact of their crimes by forcing them to 'make good' any damage or harm caused, and possibly to meet with the victims of their crimes.

One difficulty with general rehabilitation theory, however, is that it views punishment as a form of personal engineering, designed to produce 'better people' through a process of re-education. In so doing, it seeks to mould and re-mould human nature itself. Furthermore, by dismissing the notion of personal evil, rehabilitation theories come close to absolving the individual from any moral responsibility whatsoever. To say 'hate the crime but love the criminal' is to run the risk of blaming society for all forms of unpleasantness and wrong-doing. This is to confuse explanation and justification. There is little doubt, for instance, that human beings act under a wide range of social pressures, but to 'blame' society for everything they do is to suggest that they are nothing more than robots, incapable of exercising any form of free will. To decide precisely when the individual is acting as an independent agent, morally responsible for his or her own actions, is, however, one of the most difficult questions not just in relation to punishment, but in political theory itself.

Justice

Justice has been of central importance to political philosophy for over two thousand years. Through the ages, political thinkers have portrayed the 'good society' as a 'just' society. However, there has been far less agreement about what justice stands for. In everyday language, in fact, justice is used so imprecisely that it is taken to mean 'fairness', 'rightness' or, simply, that which is 'morally correct'. Without doubt, justice is a moral or normative concept: that which is 'just' is certainly morally 'good', and to call something 'unjust' is to condemn it as morally 'bad'. But justice does not simply mean 'moral'. Rather, it denotes a particular kind of moral judgement, in particular one about the distribution of rewards and punishments. Justice, in short, is about giving each person what he or she is 'due'. However, it is much more difficult to define what that 'due' might be. Justice is perhaps the archetypal example of an 'essentially contested' concept. No settled or objective concept of justice exists, only a set of competing concepts.

Moreover, although justice is a distributive concept, it is less clear what it is trying to distribute. What rewards and penalties does the concept of justice address? Justice could concern itself with the distribution of almost anything: wealth, income, leisure, liberty, friendship, sexual love and so forth. The concept of justice could be applied to the distribution of any of these 'goods', but there is no reason why the same principle of distribution should be considered 'just' in each case. For example, those who may advocate an equal distribution of material wealth may nevertheless regard the idea of an equal distribution of sexual love as quite bizarre, if not as frankly unjust. In that sense, it is quite impossible to construct an overriding principle of justice applicable to all areas of life. As Walzer (see p. 35) argued, different principles of justice may therefore be appropriate in different spheres of life. During the twentieth century, for instance, justice has usually been discussed in relation to social life in general, and the distribution of material rewards in particular. This is what is usually termed 'social justice', and is discussed in greater length in Chapter 10.

In this chapter, however, justice is examined primarily in relation to law, and therefore through the concept of 'legal justice'. Legal justice is concerned with the way in which law distributes penalties for wrongdoing, or allocates compensation in the case of injury or damage. Justice in this sense clearly involves the creation and enforcement of a public set of rules, but to be 'just' these rules must themselves have a moral underpinning. Two forms of justice can be identified at work in the legal process. First, there is procedural justice, which relates to how the rules are made and applied. Secondly, there is substantive justice, which is concerned with the rules themselves and whether they are 'just' or 'unjust'. Questions about justice in either of these senses are crucial because they bear on the issue of legitimacy. People recognise law as binding, and so acknowledge an obligation to obey it, precisely because they believe it to be just. If, however, law is not administered in accordance with justice, or law itself is seen to be unjust, citizens may possess a moral justification for breaking the law.

Procedural justice

Procedural or 'formal' justice refers to the manner in which decisions or outcomes are achieved, as opposed to the content of the decisions themselves. There are those, for instance, who suggest that legal justice is not so much concerned with the outcomes of law – judgements, verdicts, sentences and so forth – as with how these outcomes are arrived at. There is no doubt that on certain occasions justice is entirely a procedural matter: a just and acceptable outcome is guaranteed by the application of particular procedural rules. This clearly applies, for example, in the case of sporting competition. The object of a running race is to establish, quite simply, who is the fastest runner. Justice in this respect is achieved if procedural rules are applied which ensure that all factors other than running talent are irrelevant to the outcome of the race. Thus justice demands that every competitor runs the same distance, that they start at the same time, that none enjoys an unfair advantage gained through performance-enhancing drugs, that officials adjudicating the race are impartial, and so on.

Legal systems can claim to be just in precisely the same way: they operate according to an established set of rules designed to ensure a just outcome. In short, justice is 'seen to be done'. These procedural rules can, however, take one of two forms. In the case of what John Rawls (see p. 299) called 'pure procedural justice' the question of justice is solely determined by the application of just procedures, as with the example of a running race or a lottery. In a court of law, on the other hand, there is prior knowledge of what would constitute a just outcome, in which case the justice of the procedures consists of their tendency to produce that outcome. For example, in a criminal trial the procedural rules are designed to ensure that the guilty are punished, that punishment fits the crime, and so forth.

Many of these procedural rules are, however, not exclusive to the legal system but also apply to other areas of life, ranging from formal debate in legislative chambers or committees to informal discussions amongst friends or family. Indeed, it is often suggested that these rules reflect a widely held and perhaps innate sense of what is fair or reasonable, what is usually called 'natural' justice. This can be seen, for instance, in the widespread belief that it is fair in argument and debate for all parties to have the opportunity to express their views, or when decisions are taken for those affected by them to be consulted beforehand. Because the fairness of such rules is considered by many to be self-evident, there is often considerable agreement about what makes the administration of law procedurally just.

At the heart of procedural justice stands the principle of formal equality. The law should be applied in a manner that does not discriminate between individuals on grounds like gender, race, religion or social background. This, in turn, requires that law be impartially applied, which can only be achieved if judges are strictly independent and unbiased. Where the judiciary has clear political sympathies, as in the case of the US Supreme Court, or when judges are thought to be biased because they are predominantly male, white and wealthy, this may be seen as a cause of injustice. The widespread use of the jury system, at least in criminal cases, may also be justified in terms of procedural justice. The virtue of trial by jury is that juries are randomly selected and so are likely to be impartial and to be capable of applying a standard of justice commonly held in society. The defendant is judged by his or her 'peers'.

Moreover, the legal system must acknowledge the possibility that mistakes can be made and provide some machinery through which these can be rectified. This is achieved in practice through a hierarchy of courts, higher courts being able to consider appeals from lower courts. However, miscarriages of justice may be more difficult to rectify when the process of appeal is placed entirely in the hands of the judges, who may fear bringing the court system, and the judiciary itself, into disrepute. This was highlighted in Britain by the cases of the Guildford Four and the Birmingham Six, whose convictions for terrorism were overturned in 1989 and 1991, but only after they had served 14 and 16 years in gaol respectively. Procedural justice is also said to require the presumption that the accused is 'innocent until proved guilty'. This has been described as the 'golden thread' running through the English legal system and those derived from it. The presumption of innocence ensures that the mere fact of an accusation does not in itself constitute proof; the onus is on the prosecution to offer evidence which can prove guilt beyond 'reasonable doubt'. This is also why certain evidence, for instance about the accused's previous criminal record, may be inadmissible in court, since it could taint the jury's views and prevent a verdict being reached on the 'facts of the case'. In the same way, an accused person has traditionally been accorded a right to silence, on the grounds that it is the prosecution's job to establish guilt. In the United States, for example, this is enshrined in the Fifth Amendment of the Constitution which guarantees the right to avoid self-incrimination.

The principle of equal treatment has applications at every point in the legal process. For example, it suggests that ordinary citizens should not be disadvantaged by their ignorance when dealing with the police, the prosecution or the judiciary. It is normally accepted therefore that an accused person should be clearly informed about the charges made, and that he or she should be informed at the outset about their rights, notably their right to legal advice. Such rules of procedural justice have been most clearly defined in the United States. For example, in *Miranda* v. *Arizona* (1966), the Supreme Court laid down very strict procedures which the police have to follow when questioning suspects; and in *Gideon* v. *Wainwright* (1963) it guaranteed defendants the right to a lawyer, regardless of their financial circumstances. In other cases, however, governments have ignored such principles in the belief that they unnecessarily hamper the pursuit of criminals. In Britain, the Prevention of Terrorism Act (1976) gave the police the power to arrest and question suspects without legal representation and to detain them for up to seven days without charge or appearance in court. The Act, however, was condemned by the European Court of Human Rights precisely because it violated the rights of defendants and so breached the principles of procedural justice.

Substantive justice

As pointed out earlier, the requirements of legal justice cannot be entirely met by the application of procedural rules, however fair these rules may be and however scrupulously they may be applied. This is the sense in which law is different from competitive sport; its outcomes, and not merely its procedures, are claimed to be just. The legal process may thus generate injustice not because law is unfairly applied but because law itself is unjust. For instance, laws which prohibit women from voting, or which ban ethnic minorities from owning property, are not made 'just' by the fact that they are applied by courts whose procedures are fair and impartial. The content of law must therefore be judged in the light of a principle of substantive or 'concrete' justice.

Whereas there is considerable agreement about the rules of procedural justice, the same cannot be said of substantive justice. Legal justice has traditionally been linked to the idea that law aims to treat people according to their 'just deserts', or, in the words of the Roman Emperor Justinian, justice means 'giving each man his due'. The difficulty of doing this was illustrated by the earlier discussion of competing theories of punishment. Supporters of retribution argue that in principle justice demands that the murderer's life be forfeit in punishment for his crime; those who advocate deterrence will accept capital punishment but only when empirical evidence indicates that it will reduce the number of murders; rehabilitation theorists reject capital punishment in all circumstances, regarding it as little more than a form of legalised murder. No amount of debate and analysis is likely to shift any of these positions because they are based upon fundamentally different moral principles. The same applies to the attempt to distribute material rewards justly. While some argue that social justice requires a high level of material equality on the grounds that wealth should be distributed according to individual needs, others are happy to accept a high level of material inequality so long as this is based upon the unequal talents of the people involved.

Like all normative principles, the idea of substantive justice is subjective; at heart, it is a matter of opinion. Notions of justice therefore vary from individual to individual, from group to group, from society to society, and from period to period. Indeed, the decline of religion and traditional values, and the growth of both social and geographical mobility, has encouraged the development of moral pluralism. Ethical and cultural diversity make it impossible to make any firm or authoritative judgements about the moral content of law, or to establish reliable criteria for distinguishing just laws from unjust ones. Justice is, in this sense, a relative concept. It perhaps only has meaning for particular individuals or groups, and cannot be applied to society at large.

One way round this problem is to try to relate justice to a set of dominant or commonly held values in society. This is precisely what Patrick Devlin (1965) meant when he proposed that law should 'enforce morality'. In Devlin's view, law is based upon the moral values of the average citizen or, in his words, 'the man on the Clapham omnibus'. Thus he proposed a distinction between what he called 'consensus laws' and 'non-consensus laws'. Consensus laws are ones which conform to commonly held standards of fairness or justice; they are laws which, in Devlin's view, people are 'prepared to put up with'. On the other hand, non-consensus laws are ones widely regarded as unacceptable or unjust, normally reflected in the fact of widespread disobedience. Devlin did not go as far as to suggest that breaking non-consensus laws was justified, but he nevertheless warned that their enforcement would only bring the judiciary and the legal process into disrepute. An example of non-consensus law might be the 'poll tax' in Britain, which, when introduced in England and Wales in 1990, gave rise to a widespread campaign of protest and non-payment, based upon the belief that the tax violated generally held views of social justice.

Devlin believed that judges, who are strictly impartial and stand apart from the political process, are in the best position to apply the distinction between consensus and non-consensus law. After all, judges have had years of experience adjudicating disputes and arbitrating between conflicting interpretations of law. However, this form of judicial activism has proved to be highly controversial, allowing as it does non-elected judges to make decisions that have a clear moral and political content. The issue has been particularly relevant in the United States in view of the widely acknowledged role of the Supreme Court in making public policy. During the New Deal period of the 1930s, for instance, the Court struck down important social welfare programmes. In the 1950s and 1960s, however, the Warren Court was responsible for advancing civil rights on a number of fronts. The danger of such 'activism', however, is that there is no way of knowing whether judges' interpretations of law reflect widely held views about what is right or acceptable, or simply their own personal beliefs. It is clear that, since they are not elected, their definition of consensus morality enjoys no electoral mandate. Moreover, in the light of the socially unrepresentative nature of the judiciary, it is questionable that the judges know much about what Devlon called 'the man on the Clapham omnibus'.

Regardless of who is empowered to define consensus morality, there are reasons to believe that the idea itself may not stand up to serious scrutiny. In the first place, it implies that a reliable distinction can be made between consensus and non-consensus laws. In practice, few, if any, issues provoke widespread agreement, still less unanimity. All governments pass legislation that is politically controversial in that it provokes protest or at least a significant measure of criticism. This could be applied to almost every area of government policy, economic management, taxation, industrial relations, education, health, housing, law and order, race relations and so on. The danger of Devlin's argument is that it threatens to classify most laws as non-consensus on the grounds that somebody or other is not 'prepared to put up with' them. This leads to difficult questions about how many people need to object, and what form their objections need to take, before a law can be regarded as non-consensus. Such difficulties, however, merely reflect a deeper problem. In many respects, the idea of a consensus morality is simply a hangover from the days of traditional and homogeneous communities. In modern societies, characterised by ethnic, religious, racial, cultural and moral pluralism, any attempt to identify consensus beliefs is doomed to failure.

Justifying law-breaking?

The question 'Why should I obey the law?' elicits from many people the simple response: 'Because it is the law'. The law, in other words, is usually acknowledged to be legitimate, in the sense that most citizens accept an obligation to obey it. Law is therefore recognised as binding upon those to whom it applies. In a formal sense, the law is the law only because it is obeyed – at least by the vast majority of the population. There is thus a sense in which laws remaining on the statute book but which are no longer obeyed or enforced, cease to be law. This applies, perhaps, in the case of copyright laws which prohibit the taping of audio or video cassettes and, in some countries, laws which ban the use of so-called 'soft' drugs like cannabis. Indeed, in countries such as the Netherlands an attempt has been made to formalise this anomaly by 'de-criminalising' the use of 'soft' drugs. Nevertheless, despite the general acknowledgement that law is legitimate, it is clear that all laws are broken to some degree – otherwise the machinery of law enforcement would simply be redundant. It is important to acknowledge, however, that incidents of law-breaking fall into two separate categories.

In most cases, laws are broken by people described, rather quaintly, as 'common criminals'. Common criminals seldom put forward a moral justification for their actions, and rarely portray their behaviour as other than nakedly self-seeking. Criminal behaviour of this kind undoubtedly raises some interesting questions, for example, about the psychological or social factors which help to explain law-breaking, and the possible means through which others can be deterred from pursuing the same course. However, these are descriptive questions about why the law *is* obeyed, or why it *is not* obeyed. However reluctant they may be to be caught or prosecuted, so-called common criminals usually acknowledge that they *should* have obeyed the law, and so recognise the law as binding. On the other hand, there are incidents of law-breaking which are principled and, maybe, justifiable in moral or political terms. Some legal systems, indeed, acknowledge this fact by categorising certain law-breakers as 'political prisoners' and treating them differently from everyday criminals. The distinction between the two may, however, be both unclear and politically controversial. This is clearly evident in the case of terrorist groups, such as the IRA in Britain and ETA, the Basque separatist movement in Spain, which have at different times aspired to be granted 'political status' on the grounds that they are not criminals but 'freedom fighters'. Some go further and extend the notion of 'political' crimes to include criminal acts which result from social circumstances like deprivation, poverty or inequality, even though their perpetrators may not claim any conscious political motivation. Anarchists, in fact, are not prepared to recognise any distinction between criminal and political offences, in that they regard all laws as immoral and therefore see moral justification in each and every case of law-breaking.

The moral justification for law-breaking can be examined in two ways. One is to ask the question: 'Why should I obey the law?' This raises the issue of political obligation and is addressed more fully in Chapter 7. The alternative is to stand the question on its head and ask: 'What justification is there for breaking the law?' This raises the issue of what is called civil disobedience, law-breaking that is justified by reference to religious, moral or political principles. Civil disobedience has a long and respectable heritage, drawing as it does upon the ideas of writers such as Henry David Thoreau (1817–62) and the example of political leaders such as Mahatma Gandhi and Martin Luther King (1929–68). Under Gandhi's

Mohandas Karamchand Gandhi (1869–1948)

Indian spiritual and political leader, called Mahatma ('Great Soul'). A lawyer trained in Britain, Gandhi developed his political philosophy whilst working in South Africa where he organised protests against discrimination. After returning to India in 1915, he became the leader of the nationalist movement, campaigning tirelessly for independence, finally achieved in 1947. Gandhi was assassinated in 1948 by a fanatical Hindu, becoming a victim of the ferocious Hindu–Moslem violence which followed independence.

Gandhi's ethic of non-violent resistance, *satyagraha*, reinforced by his ascetic lifestyle, gave the movement for Indian independence enormous moral authority and provided a model for later civil rights activists. First outlined in *Hind Swaraj* (Home Rule) (1909), it was based upon a philosophy ultimately derived from Hinduism in which the universe is regulated by the primacy of truth, or *satya*. As humankind is 'ultimately one', love, care and a concern for others is the natural basis for human relations; indeed, he described love as 'the law of our being'. For Gandhi, non-violence not only expressed the proper moral relationship amongst people, but also, when linked to self-sacrifice, or *tapasya*, constituted a powerful social and political programme. He condemned Western civilisation for its materialism and moral weakness, and regarded it as the source of violence and injustice. Gandhi favoured small, self-governing and largely self-sufficient rural communities, and gave support to the redistribution of land and the promotion of social justice.

influence, non-violent civil disobedience became a powerful weapon in the campaign for Indian independence, finally granted in 1947. In the early 1960s, Martin Luther King adopted similar political tactics in the struggle for black civil rights in the American South.

Civil disobedience is an overt and public act: it aims to break a law in order to 'make a point' rather than in an attempt to get away with it. Civil disobedience is thus distinguished from other criminal acts by its motives, which are conscientious or principled in the sense that they aim to bring about some kind of legal or political change; it does not merely serve the interests of the law-breaker himself or herself. Indeed, in many cases it is precisely the willing acceptance of the penalties which law-breaking involves that gives civil disobedience its moral authority and emotional power. Finally, at least in the tradition of Thoreau, Gandhi and King, civil disobedience is non-violent, a fact which helps to underline the moral character of the act itself. Gandhi was particularly insistent upon this, calling his form of non-violent non cooperation *satyagraha*, literally meaning defence of, and by, the truth. Civil disobedience thus stands apart from a very different tradition of political law-breaking, which takes the form of popular revolt, terrorism and revolution.

In some cases, civil disobedience may involve the breaking of laws which are themselves considered to be wicked or unjust, its aim being to protest against the law in question and achieve its removal. In other cases, however, it involves breaking the law in order to protest against a wider injustice, even though the law being broken may not itself be objection-able. An example of the former would be the burning of draft cards or the refusal to pay that proportion of taxation which is devoted to military purposes, forms of protest adopted by opponents of the Vietnam War in the United States. Similarly, Sikhs in Britain openly flouted the law compelling motorcyclists to wear crash-helmets because it threatened their religious duty to wear turbans. On the other hand, Thoreau, who refused all payment of tax in an act of protest against the Mexican–American War of the 1840s and the continuation of slavery in the South, is an example of the latter. On some occasions Gandhi combined the two goals. In his famous 'march to the sea' in 1930, for instance, he sought to protest against the law banning Indians from making salt by making a symbolic amount of salt from sea water and thus courting arrest, but only as part of a larger campaign for national independence.

Whether it is designed to attack a particular law or advance a wider cause, all acts of civil disobedience are justified by asserting a distinction between law and justice. At the heart of civil disobedience stands the belief that the individual rather than government is the ultimate moral authority; to believe otherwise would be to imply that all laws are just and to reduce justice to mere legality. In the twentieth century, the distinction between law and justice has usually been based upon the doctrine of human rights, asserting as it does that there is a set of higher moral principles against which human law can be judged and to which it should conform. Individuals are therefore justified in breaking the law to highlight violations of human rights or to challenge laws which themselves threaten human rights. Arguments about the existence of such rights, and about how they can be defined, are examined in the next chapter.

Other justifications for civil disobedience focus upon the nature of the political process and the lack of alternative – legal – opportunities for expressing views and exerting pressure. For example, few would fail to sympathise with the actions of those who in Nazi Germany broke the law by sheltering Jews or assisting their passage out of the country. This applies not only because of the morally repulsive nature of the laws concerned but also because in a fascist dictatorship no form of legal or constitutional protest was possible. Similarly, the use of civil disobedience to gain votes for women in the nineteenth and early twentieth centuries can be justified by the simple fact that, deprived of the right to vote, women had no other way of making their voices heard. Civil disobedience campaigns were also used to achieve black suffrage in the American South and in South Africa. Even when universal suffrage exists it can perhaps be argued that the ballot box alone does not ensure that individual and minority rights are respected. A permanent minority, like the Catholic community in Northern Ireland, may therefore turn to civil disobedience, and at times support political violence, even though they may possess formal political rights. Finally, it is sometimes argued that democratic and electoral politics may simply be too slow or time-consuming to provide an adequate means of exerting political pressure when human life itself is under imminent threat. This is, for example, the case made out by anti-nuclear campaigners and by environmental activists, both of whom believe that the urgency of their cause overrides what by comparison appears to be the almost trivial obligation to obey the law.

Since the 1960s civil disobedience has become more widespread and politically acceptable. In some respects, it is now regarded as a constitutional act which aims to correct a specific wrong and is prepared to conform to a set of established rules, notably about peaceful non-violence. Civil disobedience is, for example, now accepted by many as a legitimate weapon available to cause groups and interest groups. Sit-ins or sit-down protests help to attract publicity and demonstrate the strength of protesters' convictions, and may, in turn, help to promote public sympathy. Of course, such acts may also be counter-productive, making the individuals or group concerned appear irresponsible or extremist. In these cases, the question of civil disobedience becomes a tactical matter rather than a moral one. Critics of the principle nevertheless argue that it brings with it a number of insidious dangers. The first of these is that as civil disobedience becomes fashionable it threatens to undermine respect for alternative, legal and democratic means of exerting influence. At a deeper level, however, the spread of civil disobedience may ultimately threaten both social order and political stability by eroding the fear of illegality. When people cease obeying the law automatically and only do so out of personal choice, the authority of law itself is brought into question. As a result, acts of civil disobedience may gradually weaken the principles upon which a regime is based and so be linked to rebellion and even revolution. This was evident in 1989 when a mounting wave of illegal but usually peaceful demonstrations in countries such as East Germany and what was then Czechoslavakia led eventually to the collapse of their political regimes.

Summary

1 Law consists of a set of general, public and enforceable rules, usually regarded as binding in the society to which it applies. It is valued as the principal means through which liberty and order are maintained. This is usually achieved through the rule of law, the belief that all behaviour should conform to a framework of law, a doctrine closely linked to constitutionalism and limited government.

2 Whereas law is a distinctive form of social control, morality addresses normative or ethical questions: what *should* be. Although they are analytically separate, some believe that law and morality do, and should, coincide. This is advanced by natural law theorists who hold that human law reflects higher moral principles. The alternative idea of positive law suggests that its defining feature is that it is obeyed, moral questions being set aside.

3 Order may universally be regarded as a good thing, bringing with it the promise of stability and personal security, but attitudes diverge about how it can best be secured. Some argue that since human beings are imperfect, order has to be imposed; it can only be achieved through discipline and control. Others place their faith in reason and social solidarity, believing that the natural relationship amongst people is one of harmony.

4 Justice is about giving each person what he or she is 'due'. It can be understood in a procedural sense to refer to the rules which guide the legal process, and in a substantive sense to refer to the outcomes or content of law. The issue of justice lies at the heart of questions about legitimacy and orderly existence, determining whether citizens are willing to accept the law as binding.

Further reading

Campbell, T. *Justice.* London: Macmillan and Atlantic Highlands, NJ: Humanities Press, 1988.

Fine, B. *Democracy and the Rule of Law: Liberal Ideals and Marxist Critiques* London: Pluto, 1984.

Harden, I. and Lewis, N. *The Noble Lie: The British Constitution and the Rule of Law.* London: Hutchinson, 1986.

Honderich, T. *Punishment: The Supposed Justifications.* Harmondsworth: Penguin, 1990.

Lee, S. *Law and Morals.* Oxford and New York: Oxford University Press, 1986.

Oakeshott, M. *On Human Conduct.* London and New York: Oxford University Press, 1975.

Perry, M. *Morality, Politics and Law.* Oxford and New York: Oxford Univerity Press, 1988.

Walzer, M. *Spheres of Justice.* New York: Basic Books, and Oxford: Martin Robertson, 1983.

Chapter 7

Rights, Obligations and Citizenship

Introduction
Rights
Obligations
Citizenship
Summary
Further reading

Introduction

Since antiquity, political thinkers have debated the proper relationship between the individual and the state. In Ancient Greece, this relationship was embodied in the notion of the 'citizen', literally a member of the state. Within Greek city-states, citizenship was reflected in the right to participate in the political life of the community and the obligation, if selected, to shoulder the burden of public office. This was, however, restricted to a small minority living in such states, in effect, free-born propertied males. The modern concept of citizenship is, by contrast, founded upon the principle of universal rights and obligations. Its roots lie in seventeenth-century ideas about natural rights, elaborated in the twentieth century into the doctrine of human rights. Although such ideas are now commonplace, cropping up in everyday discussions as regularly as in political argument, it is less than clear what the term 'rights' refers to and how it should be used. For instance, what does it mean to say that somebody has a 'right'? On what basis can they be said to enjoy it? And how far does this doctrine of rights stretch: to what rights are we entitled?

Citizens are not, however, merely bearers of rights, able to make claims against their state, they also have duties and obligations towards the state that has protected, nurtured and cared for them. These obligations may indeed include compulsory military service, entailing the duty to fight, kill and possibly die in defence of one's state. Once again, however, this raises difficult questions. In particular, what are the origins of such obligations, and what kind of claim do they make upon the citizen? Moreover, are these claims absolute, or can citizens, in certain circumstances, be released from them? All such questions are linked to the idea of citizenship, the notion of a proper balance between the rights and obligations of the citizen. However, while politicians and political theorists are eager to extol the virtues of citizenship, the concept itself invariably carries heavy ideological baggage. Is the 'good citizen', for example, a self-reliant and hard-working individual who makes few demands upon his or her community, or is it a person who is able to participate fully in its public and political life? Most importantly, what does citizenship demand of the individual, and what does it demand of the state?

Rights

Political debate is littered with references to rights – the right to work, the right to education, the right to abortion, the right to life, the right to free speech, the right to own property and so forth. The idea is no less important in everyday language: children may claim the 'right' to stay up late or choose their own clothes; parents, for their part, may insist upon their 'right' to control what their children eat or watch on television. In its original meaning, the term 'right' stood for a power or privilege as in the right of the nobility, the right of the clergy, and, of course, the divine right of kings. However, in its modern sense, it refers to an entitlement to act or be treated in a particular way. Although it would be wrong to suggest that the doctrine of rights is universally accepted, most modern political thinkers have nevertheless been prepared to express their ideas in terms of rights or entitlements. The concept of rights is, in that sense, politically less contentious than, say, equality or social justice. However, there is far less agreement about the grounds upon which these rights are based, who should possess them, and which ones they should have.

There is, in the first place, a distinction between legal and moral rights. Some rights are laid down in law or in a system of formal rules and so are enforceable; others, however, only exist as moral or philosophical claims. Furthermore, particular problems surround the notion of human rights. Who, for instance, is to be regarded as 'human'? Does this extend to children and embryos as well as to adults? Are particular groups of people, perhaps women and ethnic minorities, entitled to special rights by virtue either of their biological needs or social position? Finally, the conventional understanding of rights has been challenged by the emergence of the environmental and animal liberation movements, which have raised questions about the rights of non-humans, the rights of animals and other species. Are there rational grounds for refusing to extend rights to all species, or is this merely an irrational prejudice akin to sexism or racism?

Legal and moral rights

Legal rights are rights which are enshrined in law and are therefore enforceable through the courts. They have been described as 'positive' rights in that they are enjoyed or upheld regardless of their moral content, in keeping with the idea of 'positive law' discussed in the last chapter. Indeed, some legal rights remain in force for many years even though they are widely regarded as immoral. This can be said, for instance, about the legal right enjoyed by British husbands until 1992 to rape their wives. Legal rights extend over a broad range of legal relationships. A classic attempt to categorise such rights was undertaken by Wesley Hohfeld in *Fundamental*

Legal Conceptions (1923). Hohfeld identified four types of legal right. First, there are privileges or liberty-rights. These allow a person to do something in the simple sense that they have no obligation *not* to do it; they are 'at liberty' to do it – for instance, to use the public highway. Secondly, there are claim-rights, on the basis of which another person owes another a corresponding duty – for example, the right of one person not to be assaulted by another. Thirdly, there are legal powers. These are best thought of as legal abilities, empowering someone to do something – for example, the right to get married or the right to vote. Fourthly, there are immunities, according to which one person can avoid being subject to the power of another – for instance, the right of young, elderly and disabled people not to be drafted into the army.

The status which these legal rights enjoy within a political system varies considerably from country to country. In Britain, the content of legal rights has traditionally been vague and their status questionable. Until the incorporation of the European Convention of Human Rights in 1998, most individual rights, such as the right to free speech, freedom of movement and freedom of religious worship, were not embodied in statute law. Indeed, British statute law largely consisted of prohibitions which constrained what the individual could do or say. For example, although there was no statutory right to free speech in Britain, there were a host of laws which restricted what British citizens could say on grounds of slander, libel, defamation, blasphemy, incitement to riot, incitement to racial hatred, and so forth. Legal rights in Britain were often therefore described as 'residual', in that they were based upon the common law assumption that 'everything is permitted that is not prohibited'. The danger of this situation is that, lacking clear legal definition, it may be difficult or impossible to uphold individual rights in court. This was evident in the ease with which in the late 1980s the British government gained court injunctions preventing newspapers publishing extracts from Peter Wright's *Spy Catcher*. The book had made a series of serious allegations, including that in the 1970s the security services had attempted to destabilise the Wilson Labour government.

In marked contrast, in *New York Times* v. *United States* (1971) the US Supreme Court upheld the publication of the so-called 'Pentagon Papers', classified and highly sensitive documents relating to American involvement in the Vietnam War. The American case was based upon the existence of a Bill of Rights and specifically upon the First Amendment of the US Constitution which guarantees, amongst other things, freedom of speech and freedom of the press. A Bill of Rights is a codified set of individual rights and liberties, enshrined in constitutional or 'higher' law. It is usually said to 'entrench' individual rights because such documents are complicated or difficult to amend. As such, a Bill of Rights can be seen to offer a number of clear advantages. In the first place, unlike the 'residual' rights existing in Britain, a Bill of Rights provides a clear legal definition of individual rights. Moreover, it can be said to have an educational value: by making people more aware of the rights they have it can promote within government, in the courts and amongst the general public what has been called a 'human rights culture'. Most significantly, however, a Bill of Rights establishes a mechanism through which rights can be legally defended and thus protects the individual from over-mighty government. This it achieves by investing in the courts the power of 'judicial review', enabling them to check the power of other public bodies if they should infringe upon individual rights.

A Bill of Rights, nevertheless, may also bring disadvantages. British Conservatives, for instance, have traditionally argued that individual rights are best protected by common law because rights are then rooted in customs and traditions that lie at the very heart of the legal system. By comparison, a Bill of Rights may appear both inflexible and artificial. On the other hand, socialists have often objected to Bills of Rights on the grounds that they serve to protect class interests and so preserve social inequality. This can occur through the entrenchment of property rights, making nationalisation impossible and blocking radical social reform. One of the most serious drawbacks of a Bill of Rights is, however, that it dramatically enlarges the authority of the judiciary. Given the typically vague or broad formulation of rights, judges end up deciding the proper scope of these, which, in effect, means that political decisions are taken by judges rather than by democratically elected politicians. Finally, it is clear that the mere existence of a Bill of Rights does not in itself guarantee that individual liberty will be respected. The Soviet Constitutions of 1936 and 1977, for example, established a truly impressive array of individual rights; but the subordination of the Soviet judiciary to the Communist Party ensured that few of these rights were upheld in practice. Similarly, despite the enactment in 1870 of the Fifth Amendment of the US Constitution granting the right to vote regardless of race, colour or previous condition of servitude, blacks in many Southern states were not able to vote until the 1960s.

A different range of rights, however, may have no legal substance but only exist as moral claims. The simplest example of this is a promise. A promise, freely and rationally made, invests one person with a moral obligation to fulfil its terms, and so grants the other party the right that it *should* be fulfilled. Unless the promise takes the form of a legally binding contract, it is enforced by moral considerations alone. It is, quite simply, the fact that it is freely made that creates the expectation that a promise will be, and should be, fulfilled. In most cases, however, moral rights are based, rather, upon their content. In other words, moral rights are more commonly 'ideal' rights, which bestow upon a person a benefit that they need or deserve. Moral rights therefore reflect what a person *should* have, from the perspective of a particular moral or religious system.

The danger with moral rights is, however, that they may become impossibly vague and degenerate into little more than an expression of what is morally desirable. This was precisely the view taken by Jeremy Bentham (see p. 361), the British utilitarian philosopher, who rejected the very idea of moral rights, believing them to be nothing more than a mistaken way of describing legal rights that *ought* to exist. Nevertheless, despite Bentham's scepticism, most systems of legal rights are under-pinned, at least in theory, by some kind of moral considerations. For example, legal documents like the United States' Bill of Rights, the UN Universal Declaration of Human Rights (1948) and the European Convention for the Protection of Human Rights and Fundamental Freedoms (1953), have all developed out of attempts by philosophers to define 'the Rights of Man'. In order to investigate moral rights further it is necessary to examine the most influential form of moral rights – human rights.

Human rights

The idea of human rights developed out of the 'natural rights' theories of the early modern period. Such theories arose, primarily, out of the desire to establish some limits upon how individuals may be treated by others, especially by those who wield political power. However, if rights are to act as a check upon political authority, they must in a sense be 'pre-legal', law being merely the creation of political authority. In the seventeenth century, John Locke (see p. 269) identified as natural rights the right to 'life, liberty and property'; a century later, Thomas Jefferson defined them as the right to 'life, liberty and the pursuit of happiness'. Such rights were described as 'natural' in that they were thought to be God-given and therefore to be part of the very core of human nature. Natural rights did not exist simply as moral claims but were, rather, considered to reflect the most fundamental inner human drives; they were the basic conditions for leading a truly human existence. As such, natural rights theories were psychological models every bit as much as they were ethical systems.

By the twentieth century, the decline of religious belief had led to the secularisation of natural rights theories, which were reborn in the form of 'human' rights. Human rights are rights to which people are entitled by virtue of being human. They are therefore 'universal' rights in the sense that they belong to all human beings rather than to members of any particular nation, race, religion, gender, social class or whatever. Human rights are also 'fundamental' rights in that they are inalienable; they cannot be traded away or revoked. This was clearly expressed in the words of the American Declaration of Independence (1776), written by Jefferson, which

Thomas Jefferson (1743–1826)

US political philosopher and statesman. A wealthy Virginian planter who was governor of Virginia, 1779–81, Jefferson served as the first US secretary of state, 1789–94. He was the third president of the United States, 1801–9. Jefferson was the principal author of the Declaration of Independence (1776), and wrote a vast number of addresses and letters.

Jefferson articulated a strong Enlightenment faith in the perfectibility of humankind and the capacity to solve political problems through the application of scientific method. He used the natural rights ideas of Locke (see p. 269) to develop a classic defence of national independence and government by consent. Jeffersonianism is usually viewed as a democratic form of agrarianism that sought to blend a belief in rule by a natural aristocracy with a commitment to limited government and *laissez-faire*, reflecting the belief that, 'That government is best which governs least'. He nevertheless demonstrated sympathy for social reform, favouring the extension of public education, the abolition of slavery, and greater economic equality. Although Jefferson is regarded as one of the founders of the Democratic coalition, he was fiercely critical of parties and factions, believing that they would promote conflict and destroy the underlying unity of society.

proclaimed, 'We hold these truths to be self-evident, that all men are created equal; that they are endowed by their Creator with certain unalienable rights'. Many have further suggested that human rights are 'absolute' rights in that they must be upheld at all times and in all circumstances. However, this view is more difficult to sustain since in practice rights are often balanced against one another. For example, does the assertion of a right to life rule out capital punishment and all forms of warfare, whatever the provocation? The right to life cannot be absolute if a right to self-defence is also acknowledged.

The concept of human rights raises a number of very different questions, about both who can be regarded as 'human' and the rights to which human beings are entitled. There is, for example, fierce controversy about the point at which 'human' life begins and so the point at which individuals acquire entitlements or rights. In particular, does human life begin at the moment of conception or does it begin at birth? Those who hold the former view uphold what they see as the rights of the unborn and reject absolutely practices like abortion and embryo research. On the other hand, however, if human life is thought to start at birth, abortion is quite acceptable since it reflects a woman's right to control her own body. Such contrasting positions do not only reflect different conceptions of life but also allocate rights to human beings on very different grounds. Those who regard embryos as 'human' in the same sense as adults, draw upon the belief that life is sacred. According to this view, all living things are entitled to rights, regardless of the form or quality of life with which they may be blessed. However, if life itself is regarded as the basis for rights it becomes difficult to see why rights should be restricted to humans and not extended to animals and other forms of life. To argue, by contrast, that 'human' life only begins at birth is to establish a narrower basis for allocating rights, such as the ability to live independently, to enjoy a measure of self-consciousness, or the ability to make rational or moral choices. If such criteria are employed, however, it is difficult to see how human rights can be granted to groups of people who do not themselves fulfil such requirements, for example, children and people with mental or physical disabilities.

A further problem arises from the fact that while human rights are universal, human beings are not identical. This can clearly be seen in the notion that women in some sense enjoy rights that are different from men's. To advance the cause of 'women's rights' may simply be to argue that human rights, initially developed with men in mind, should also be extended to women. This would apply in the case of women's right to education, their right to enter particular professions, their right to equal pay and so forth. However, the idea of women's rights may also be based upon the fact that women have specific needs and capacities which entitle them to rights which in relation to men would be unnecessary or simply meaningless. Such rights would include those related to childbirth or childcare, such as the right to perinatal maternity leave. More controversial, however, is the notion that women are entitled to a set of rights in addition to men's in an attempt to compensate them for their unequal treatment by society. For example, social conventions that link child-bearing and child-rearing and so channel women into a domestic realm of motherhood and housework undermine their capacity to gain an education and pursue a career. In such circumstances, women's rights could extend to a form of reverse discrimination which seeks to rectify past injustices by, say, establishing quotas for the number of women in higher education and in certain professions. In so far as such rights are based upon a commitment to equal treatment it can be argued that they draw upon the notion of human rights. However, it is difficult to regard women's rights in this sense as fundamental human rights since they are not allocated to all human beings. Rights that arise out of unequal or unjust treatment will only be meaningful so long as the inequality or injustice that justifies their existence persists.

Even when such controversies are set aside, there are very deep divisions about what rights human beings should enjoy. The idea that rights-based theories in some way stand above ideological and political differences is clearly misguided. From the outset, the idea of natural rights was closely linked to the liberal notion of limited government. The traditional formulation that human beings are entitled to the right to life, liberty and property, or the pursuit of happiness, regarded rights as a private sphere within which the individual could enjoy independence from the encroachments of other individuals and, more particularly, from the interference of the state. These rights are therefore 'negative' rights or 'forbearance' rights; they can only be enjoyed if constraints are placed upon others. For instance, the right to property requires that limits be set to the government's ability to tax, an idea clearly reflected in the principle of 'no taxation without representation'.

During the twentieth century, however, another range of rights have been added to these traditional liberal ones, an acknowledgement of government's growing responsibility for economic and social life. These are welfare rights, social and economic rights, and they are 'positive' in the sense that they demand not forbearance but active government intervention. The right to health care, for example, requires some form of health insurance, if not a publicly funded system of health provision. The UN Universal Declaration of Human Rights includes not only classical 'negative' rights, like the right to 'freedom of thought, conscience and religion' (Article 18), but also 'positive' rights such as the 'right to work' (Article 23) and the 'right to education' (Article 26). Such welfare rights have, however, provoked fierce disagreement between socialists and conservatives, leading to the development of two contrasting models of citizenship. This controversy is examined in the final section of the chapter in relation to social citizenship.

Finally, the very idea of natural or human rights has been attacked, notably by utilitarians (see p. 360) and classical Marxists (see p. 81). As pointed out earlier, Jeremy Bentham was only prepared to acknowledge the existence of 'positive' or legal rights. Natural rights were subjective or metaphysical entities, which Bentham dismissed as 'nonsense on stilts'. Marx (see p. 373), on the other hand, regarded the doctrine of 'the Rights of Man' as little more than a means of advancing the interests of private property. In his view, every right was a 'right of inequality' since it applied an equal standard to unequal individuals. For instance, the right to property can be regarded as a 'bourgeois' right because it has very different implications for the rich and the poor. The theory of universal entitlements thus embodies powerful class interests. Modern Marxists have nevertheless softened their attitude towards human rights. To some extent, this resulted from the extension of the concept to include welfare or social rights, creating the prospect that it could advance the interests of the working masses. In other cases, Marxists have acknowledged the contribution of human rights to advancing the boundaries of political liberty In his struggle to reform the Soviet Union, for instance, Mikhail Gorbachev suggested that human rights were equally applicable in capitalist and communist countries, and proposed that the doctrine transcends the traditional left-right ideological divide.

Animal and other rights?

The late twentieth century has witnessed the emergence of the animal welfare and animal liberation movements as part of the broader growth of ecologism. These have campaigned, for instance, in favour of vegetarianism and improved treatment of farm animals, and against the fur trade and animal experiments. Such campaigns have typically been carried out under the banner of 'animal rights'. This amounts to the assertion that animals have rights in the same sense that human beings do; indeed, it implies that once human beings are invested with rights it is impossible not to extend these same rights to animals. In effect, the doctrine of human rights leads irresistibly in the direction of animal rights. However, on what basis can animals be said to have rights, and is the notion of animal rights at all meaningful or coherent?

Animal rights theories have developed in popularity since the 1960s as a result of the growth of ecological theories that have tried to redefine the relationship between humans and the natural world. Traditional attitudes towards animals and nature in general in the West were shaped by the Christian belief that human beings enjoyed a God-given dominion over the world, reflected in their stewardship over all other species. In medieval Europe, it was not uncommon for animals to be tried before ecclesiastical courts for alleged wrong-doing, on the grounds that as God's creatures they, like humans, were subject to 'natural law'. At the same time, however, Christianity taught that humankind was the centrepiece of creation and that animals had been placed on the earth for the sole purpose of providing for human needs. Since they do not possess immortal souls, animals can in no sense be regarded as equal to humans. Environmentalist theories, by contrast, hold that human beings are neither above nor beyond the natural world but are, rather, an inseparable part of it. This belief is much closer to the pre-Christian notion of an Earth Mother and to the emphasis found in Eastern religions like Hinduism and Buddhism upon the oneness of all forms of life. In the process, the clear distinction once thought to exist between humans and animals has come under increasing pressure.

It is important, however, to distinguish between the notion of 'animal welfare' and the more radical idea of 'animal rights'. Animal welfare reflects an altruistic concern for the well-being of other species, but not one which necessarily places them on the same level as humans. Such an

Ecologism

The term ecology was coined by the German zoologist Ernst Haeckel in 1866 to refer to 'the investigations of the total relations of the animal both to its organic and its inorganic environment'. Ecological or green political ideas can be traced back to the nineteenth-century backlash against the spread of industrialisation and urbanisation. Modern ecologism emerged during the 1960s along with renewed concern about the damage done to the environment by pollution, resource depletion, over-population and so on. Such concerns have been articulated politically by a growing number of Green parties which now operate in most developed societies and, at least in the case of the German Greens, have shared government power, and through the influence of a powerful environmentalist lobby whose philosophy is 'think globally, act locally'.

The central feature of ecologism is that it regards nature as an interconnected whole, embracing humans and non-humans as well as the inanimate world. This view is expressed in the adoption of an ecocentric or biocentric perspective that accords priority to nature or the planet and thus differs from the anthropocentric or human-centred perspective of conventional political thought. Nevertheless, two strains of ecologism are normally identified. 'Deep ecology' completely rejects any lingering belief that the human species is in some way superior to, or more important than, any other species – or, indeed, nature itself. 'Shallow ecology', by contrast, accepts the lessons of ecology but harnesses them to human needs and ends. In other words, it preaches that if we can serve and cherish the natural world, it will, in turn, continue to sustain human life.

Shallow or humanist ecologism is compatible with a number of other creeds, creating hybrid political traditions. Ecosocialism, usually influenced by modern Marxism (see p. 81), explains environmental destruction in terms of capitalism's rapacious quest for profit; eco-anarchism draws parallels between natural equilibrium in nature and in human communities, using the idea of social ecology; and ecofeminism has portrayed patriarchy as the source of the ecological crisis. On the other hand, deep ecology goes beyond the perspective of conventional political creeds. It tends to regard both capitalism and socialism as examples of the 'super-ideology' of industrialism, characterised by large-scale production, the accumulation of capital and relentless growth. It supports biocentric equality, holding that the rights of animals have the same moral status as those of humans, and portraying nature as an ethical community within which human beings are merely 'plain citizens'.

However, the spread of ecological thought has been hampered by a number of factors. These include the limited attraction of its anti-growth, or at least sustainable growth, economic model, and that its critique of industrial society is sometimes advanced from a pastoral and anti-technology perspective that is quite out of step with the modern world. Some, as a result, dismiss ecologism as simply an urban fad, a form of post-industrial romanticism. Ecologism,

$\longrightarrow$

nevertheless, has at least two major strengths. First, it draws attention to an imbalance in the relationship between humans and the natural world that is manifest in a growing catalogue of threats to the well-being of both. Second, ecologism has gone further than any other tradition in questioning and transcending the limited focus of Western political thought. In keeping with globalisation, it is the nearest thing political theory has to a world philosophy and it has allowed political thought to be fertilised by the insights of pagan religions and native cultures, and Eastern religions such as Buddhism, Hinduism and Taoism.

Key figures

Ernst Friedrich Schumacher (1911–77) A German-born British economist and environmental theorist, 'Fritz' Schumacher championed the cause of human-scale production and helped to develop an ecological philosophy. His notion of 'Buddhist' economics ('economics as if people mattered') stressed the importance of morality and 'right livelihood', and warned against the depletion of finite energy sources. Though an opponent of industrial giantism, Schumacher believed in 'appropriate' scale production, and was a keen advocate of 'intermediate' technology. His seminal work is *Small is Beautiful* (1973).

James Lovelock (1919–) A Canadian atmospheric chemist, inventor and environmental theorist, Lovelock is best known for having developed the Gaia hypothesis. This portrays the Earth's biosphere as a complex, self-regulating, living 'being', called Gaia after the Greek goddess of the earth. Although the Gaia hypothesis extends the ecological idea by applying it to the planet as an ecosystem and offers a holistic approach to nature, Lovelock supports technology and industrialisation and is an opponent of 'back to nature' mysticism and ideas such as Earth worship. His major writings include *Gaia* (1979) and *The Ages of Gaia* (1989).

Murray Bookchin (1921–) A US anarchist social philosopher and environmentalist, Bookchin is the leading proponent of 'social ecology'. As an anarchist he has emphasised the potential for non-hierarchic cooperation within conditions of post-scarcity and promoted decentralisation and community within modern societies. His principle of social ecology propounds the view that ecological principles can be applied to social organisation and argues that the environmental crisis is a result of the breakdown of the organic fabric of both society and nature. Bookchin's major works include *Post-Scarcity Anarchism* (1971), *The Ecology of Freedom* (1982) and *Remaking Society* (1989).

Rudolph Bahro (1936–98) A German writer and Green activist, Bahro attempted to reconcile socialism with ecological theories. His argument that capitalism is the root cause of environmental problems led him to assert that those concerned with human survival should convert to socialism, and that people who support social justice must take account of ecological

→

Ecologism continued

sustainability. Bahro subsequently moved beyond conventional ecosocialism, concluding that the ecological crisis is so pressing that it must take precedence over the class struggle. Bahro's chief works include *Socialism and Survival* (1982), *From Red to Green* (1984) and *Building the Green Movement* (1986).

Carolyn Merchant (1936–)   A US academic and feminist, Merchant's work has highlighted links between gender oppression and the 'death of nature'. She developed a socialist feminist critique of the scientific revolution that ultimately explains environmental destruction in terms the application by men of a mechanistic view of nature. According to this view, a global ecological revolution would reconstruct gender relations as well as the relationship between humans and nature. Her ideas have had a considerable impact on environmental history and philosophy as well as on ecofeminism. Merchant's chief works include *The Death of Nature* (1980) and *Radical Ecology* (1991).

Further reading

Bramwell, A. *Ecology in the 20th Century: A History.* New Haven & London: Yale University Press, 1989.
Dobson, A. *Green Political Thought.* London: HarperCollins, 1990.
Eckersley, R. *Environmentalism and Political Theory: Towards an Ecocentric Approach.* London: UCL Press, 1992.

argument was, for example, advanced by the philosopher Peter Singer (see p. 361) in *Animal Liberation* (1975). Singer argued that concern for the welfare of animals is based upon the fact that as sentient beings they are capable of suffering. Like humans, animals clearly have an interest in avoiding physical pain. For Singer, the interests of animals and humans in this respect are equal, and he condemns any attempt to place the interests of humans above those of animals as 'speciesism', an arbitrary and irrational prejudice not unlike sexism or racism. The animal welfare argument emphasises the need to treat animals with respect and to try, whenever possible, to minimise their suffering. It may, nevertheless, acknowledge that it is natural or inevitable for humans, like all species, to prefer their own kind and to place human interests before those of other species. The animal welfare movement may therefore oppose factory farming because it is cruel to animals, but not go as far as to insist upon vegetarianism. Altruistic concern does not imply equal treatment. The animal rights argument, on the other hand, has more radical implications precisely because it is derived directly from human rights theories.

Animal rights theories commence by examining the grounds upon which rights are allocated to humans. One possibility is that rights spring out of the existence of life itself: human beings have rights because they are living individuals. If this is true, however, it naturally follows that the same rights should be granted to other living creatures. For instance, the US philosopher Tom Regan argued in *The Case for Animal Rights* (1983) that all creatures that are 'the subject of a life' qualify for rights. He therefore suggested that as the right to life is the most fundamental of all rights, the killing of an animal, however painless, is as morally indefensible as the killing of a human being. Regan acknowledges, however, that in some cases rights are invested in human beings on very different grounds, notably that they, unlike animals, are capable of rational thought and moral autonomy. The right to free speech, freedom of worship and to gain an education may seem absurd if invested in animals. Regan nevertheless points out that such an argument fails to draw a clear distinction between the animal and human worlds. There are, for instance, what Regan calls 'marginal cases', human beings who because of mental disability have very little capacity to exercise reason or enjoy autonomy. If rights are invested on the grounds of rational and moral capacity rather than life itself, surely such humans can be treated as animals traditionally have been: they can be used for food, clothing, scientific experimentation and so forth. At the same time, there are clearly animals that possess mental capacities more normally associated with humans; for instance, research has shown dolphin communication systems to be every bit as sophisticated as human language. Logically pursued, therefore, this argument may justify the allocation to some animals of rights which are nevertheless denied to 'marginal' humans.

It is difficult, however, to see how these ideas can be confined to animals alone. If the distinction between humans and animals is called into question, how adequate are distinctions between mammals and fish, or between animals and plants? Evidence from biologists such as Lyall Watson (1973) suggests that, in contrast to conventional assumptions, plant life may possess the capacity to experience physical pain. What is clear is that if rights belong to humans and animals it is absurd to deny them to fish on the grounds that they live in water, or to deny them to plants simply because they do not run around on two legs or four. Although such ideas seem bizarre from the conventional Western standpoint, they merely restate a belief in the interconnectedness of all forms of life long expressed by Eastern religions and acknowledged by pre-Christian 'pagan' creeds. On the other hand, it is reasonable to remember that the material and social progress that the human species has made has been achieved, in part, because of a willingness to treat other species, and indeed the natural world, as a resource available for human use. To alter this relationship by acknowledging the rights of other species has profound implications not only for moral conduct but also for the material and social organisation of human life.

Obligations

An obligation is a requirement or duty to act in a particular way. H.L.A. Hart (1961) distinguished between 'being obliged' to do something, which implies an element of coercion, and 'having an obligation' to do something, which suggests only a moral duty. Though a cashier in a bank may feel obliged to hand over money to a gunman, he is under no obligation, in the second sense, to do so. This can be seen in the distinction between legal and moral obligations. Legal obligations, such as the requirement to pay taxes and observe other laws, are enforceable through the courts and backed up by a system of penalties. Such obligations may be upheld on grounds of simple prudence: whether laws are right or wrong they are obeyed out of a fear of punishment. Moral obligations, with which this chapter is concerned, are fulfilled not because it is sensible to do so but because such conduct is thought to be rightful or morally correct. To give a promise, for example, is to be under a moral obligation to carry it out, regardless of the consequences which breaking the promise would entail.

In a sense, rights and obligations are the reverse sides of the same coin. To possess a right usually places someone else under an obligation to uphold or respect that right. In that sense, the individual rights discussed in the previous section place heavy obligations upon the state. If the right to life is meaningful, for instance, government is subject to an obligation to maintain public order and ensure personal security. 'Negative' rights entail an obligation on the part of the state to limit or constrain its power; 'positive' rights oblige the state to manage economic life, provide a range of welfare services and so on. However, if citizens are bearers of rights alone and all obligations fall upon the state, orderly and civilised life would be impossible: individuals who possess rights but acknowledge no obligations would be lawless and unrestrained. Citizenship, therefore, entails a blend of rights and obligations, the most basic of which has traditionally been described as 'political obligation', the duty of the citizen to acknowledge the authority of the state and obey its laws.

The only political thinkers who are prepared to reject political obligation out of hand are philosophical anarchists such as Robert Paul Wolff (1970), who insist upon absolute respect for individual autonomy. Others, however, have been more interested in debating not whether political obligation exists, but the grounds upon which it can be advanced. The classic explanation of political obligation is found in the idea of a 'social contract', the belief that that there are clear rational and moral grounds for respecting state authority. Other thinkers, however, have gone further and suggested that obligations, responsibilities and duties are not merely contractual but are instead an intrinsic feature of any stable society.

Nevertheless, few theorists have been prepared to regard political obligation as absolute. What they disagree about, however, is where the limits of political obligation can be drawn. At what point can the dutiful citizen be released from his or her obligation to obey the state and exercise, by contrast, a right of rebellion?

Contractual obligations

Social contract theory is as ancient as political philosophy itself. Some form of social contract can be found in the writings of Plato (see p. 22); it was the cornerstone of seventeenth- and eighteenth-century thinkers like Hobbes (see p. 124), Locke and Rousseau (see p. 243); and it has resurfaced in modern times in the writings of theorists such as John Rawls (see p. 299). A 'contract' is a formal agreement between two or more parties. Contracts, however, are a specific kind of agreement, entered into voluntarily and on mutually agreed terms. To enter into a contract is, in effect, to make a promise to abide by its terms; it therefore entails a moral as well as sometimes a legal obligation. A 'social contract' is an agreement made either amongst citizens, or between citizens and the state, through which they accept the authority of the state in return for benefits which only a sovereign power can provide. However, the basis of this contract and the obligations it entails have been the source of profound disagreement.

The earliest form of social contract theory was outlined starkly in Plato's *Crito*. After his trial for corrupting the youth of Athens, and facing certain death, Socrates explains his refusal to escape from prison to his old friend Crito. Socrates points out that by choosing to live in Athens and by enjoying the privileges of being an Athenian citizen, he had, in effect, promised to obey Athenian law, and he intended to keep his promise even at the cost of his own life. From this point of view, political obligation arises out of the benefits derived from living within an organised community. The obligation to obey the state is based upon an implicit promise made by the simple fact that citizens choose to remain within its borders. This argument, however, runs into difficulties. In the first place, it is not easy to demonstrate that natural-born citizens have made a promise or entered into an agreement, even an implicit one. The only citizens who have made a clear promise and entered into a 'contract of citizenship' are naturalised citizens, who may even have signed a formal oath to that effect. Moreover, citizens living within a state may claim either that they receive no benefit from it and are therefore under no obligation, or that the state's influence upon their lives is entirely brutal and repressive. Socrates' notion of political obligation is unconditional in that it does not take into account how the state is formed or how it behaves. Finally, Socrates appears to have assumed that citizens dissatisfied with one state would easily be able to take up residence in another. In practice, this may be difficult or impossible: emigration can be restricted by the exercise of force, as was the case with the Soviet Jews, by economic circumstances, and, of course, by immigration regulations imposed by other states.

The social contract theories of the seventeenth and eighteenth centuries, discussed in greater depth in Chapter 3, advance, by contrast, a more conditional basis for political obligation. Thinkers such as Hobbes and Locke were concerned to explain how political authority arose amongst human beings who are morally free and equal. In their view, the right to rule had to be based upon the consent of the governed. This they explained by analysing the nature of a hypothetical society without government, a so-called 'state of nature'. Their portrait of the state of nature was distinctly unattractive: a barbaric civil war of all against all, brought about by the unrestrained pursuit of power and wealth. They therefore suggested that rational individuals would be prepared to enter into an agreement, a social contract, through which a common authority could be established and order guaranteed. This contract was clearly the basis of political obliga-tion, implying as it did a duty to respect law and the state. In very few cases, however, did contractarian theorists believe that the social contract was a historical fact, whose terms could subsequently be scrutinised and examined. Rather, it was employed as a philosophical device through which theorists could discuss the grounds upon which citizens should obey their state. The conclusions they arrived at, however, vary significantly.

In *Leviathan* ([1651] 1968), Thomas Hobbes argued that citizens have an absolute obligation to obey political authority, regardless of how govern-ment may behave. In effect, Hobbes believed that though citizens were obliged to obey their state, the state itself was not subject to any reciprocal obligations. This was because Hobbes believed that the existence of any state, however oppressive, is preferable to the existence of no state at all, which would lead to a descent into chaos and barbarism. Clearly, Hobbes's views reflect a heightened concern about the dangers of in-stability and disorder, perhaps resulting from the fear and insecurity he himself experienced during the English Civil War. However, it is difficult to accept his belief that any form of protest, any limit upon political obligation, would occasion the collapse of all authority and the re-establishment of the state of nature. For Hobbes, citizens are confronted by a stark choice between absolutism and anarchy.

An alternative and more balanced view of political obligation is found in the writings of John Locke. Locke's ([1690] 1965) account of the origins of political obligation involve the establishment of two contracts. The first, the social contract proper, was undertaken by all the individuals who form a society. In effect, they volunteered to sacrifice a portion of their liberty in order to secure the order and stability which only a political community can offer. The second contract, or 'trust', was undertaken between a society and its government, through which the latter was authorised to protect the natural rights of its citizens. This implied that obedience to government was conditional upon the state fulfilling its side of the contract. If the state became a tyranny against the individual, the individual could exercise the right of rebellion, which is precisely what Locke believed had occurred in the 'Glorious Revolution' of 1688, which overthrew the Stuart dynasty. However, in Locke's account, rebellion consists of the removal by a society of its government rather than the dissolution of the social contract and a return to the state of nature.

A very different form of social contract theory was developed by Jean-Jacques Rousseau in *The Social Contract* ([1762] 1969). Whereas Hobbes and Locke had assumed human beings to be power-seeking and narrowly self-interested, Rousseau held a far more optimistic view of human nature. He was attracted by the notion of the 'noble savage' and believed that the roots of injustice lay not in the human individual but rather in society itself. In Rousseau's view, government should be based upon what he called the 'general will', reflecting the common interests of society as opposed to the 'private will', or selfish wishes of each member. In a sense, Rousseau espoused an orthodox social contract theory in that he said that an individual is bound by the rules of a society, including its general will, only if he himself has consented to be a member of that society. At the same time, however, the general will alone can also be seen as a ground for political obligation. By articulating the general will the state is, in effect, acting in the 'real' interests of each of its members. In this way, political obligation can be interpreted as a means of obeying one's own higher or 'true' self. Such a theory of obligation, however, moves away from the idea of government by consent. Being blinded by ignorance and selfishness, citizens may not recognise that the general will embodies their 'real' interests. In such circumstances, Rousseau acknowledged that citizens should be 'forced to be free'; in other words they should be forced to obey their own 'true' selves.

Natural duty

Social contract theories of whatever kind share the common belief that there are rational or moral grounds for obeying state authority. They therefore hold that political obligation is based upon individual choice and decision, upon a specific act of voluntary commitment. Such voluntaristic theories are, however, by no means universally accepted. Some point out, for instance, that many of the obligations to which the individual is subject do not, and often cannot, arise out of contractual agreements. Not only does this apply in most cases to political obligation, but it is even more clear in relation to social duties, like those of children towards parents, which arise long before the children have any meaningful ability to enter into a contract. In addition, social contract theories are based upon individualistic assumptions, implying that society is a human creation or artefact, fashioned by the rational undertakings of independent individuals. This may fundamentally misconceive the nature of society and fail to recognise the degree to which society helps to shape its members and invest them with duties and responsibilities.

There are two principal alternatives to contract theory as a ground of political obligation. The first of these encompasses theories that are usually described as teleological, from the Greek *telos*, meaning a purpose or goal. Such theories suggest that the duty of citizens to respect the state and obey its commands is based upon the benefits or goods which the state provides. This can be seen in any suggestion that political obligation arises from the fact that the state acts in the common good or public interest, perhaps presented in terms of Rousseau's general will. The most influential teleological theory has been utilitarianism (see p. 360), which implies, in simple terms, that citizens should obey government because it strives to achieve 'the greatest happiness for the greatest number'.

The second set of theories, however, relate to the idea that membership of a particular society is somehow 'natural', in which case political obligation can be thought of as a natural duty. To conceive of political obligation in this way is to move away from the idea of voluntary behaviour. A duty is a task or action that a person is *bound* to perform for moral reasons; it is not just a morally preferable action. Thus the debt of gratitude which Socrates claimed he owed Athens did not allow him to challenge or resist its laws, even at the cost of his own life. The idea of natural duty has been particularly attractive to conservative thinkers (see p. 138), who have stressed the degree to which all social groups, including political communities, are held together by the recognition of mutual obligations and responsibilities.

Conservatives have traditionally shied away from doctrines like 'the Rights of Man', not only because they are thought to be abstract and worthless but also because they treat the individual as pre-social, implying that human beings can be conceived of outside or beyond society. By contrast, conservatives have preferred to understand society as organic, and to recognise that it is shaped by internal forces beyond the capacity of any individual to control. Human institutions such as the family, the church and government have not therefore been constructed in accordance with individual wishes or needs but by the forces of natural necessity which help to sustain society itself. Individuals are therefore supported, educated, nurtured and moulded by society, and as a result inherit a broad range of responsibilities, obligations and duties. These include not merely the obligation to obey the law and respect the liberties of others, but also wider social duties such as to uphold established authority and, if appropriate, to shoulder the burden of public office. In this way, conservatives argue that the obligation of citizens towards their government has the same character as the duty and respect that children owe their parents.

The cause of social duty has also been taken up by socialist and social democratic (see p. 312) theorists. Socialists have traditionally underlined the need for community and cooperation, emphasising that human beings are essentially sociable and gregarious creatures. Social duty can therefore be understood as the practical expression of community; it reflects the responsibility of every human being towards every other member of society. This may, for instance, incline socialists to place heavier responsibilities upon the citizen than liberals would be prepared to do. These could include the obligation to work for the community, perhaps through some kind of public service, and the duty to provide welfare support for those who are not able to look after themselves. A society in which individuals possess only rights but recognise no duties or obligations would be one in which the strong may prosper but the weak would go to the wall. Such a line of argument can even be discerned amongst communitarian anarchists. Although classical anarchists such as Proudhon (see p. 168), Bakunin (1814–76) and Kropotkin (see p. 169) rejected the claims of political authority, they nevertheless recognised that a healthy society demanded sociable, cooperative and respectful behaviour from its members. This amounts to a theory of 'social' obligation that in some ways parallels the more traditional notion of political obligation.

Limits of political obligation

Political obligation denotes not a duty to obey a particular law but rather the citizen's duty to respect and obey the state itself. When the limits of political obligation are reached, the citizen is not merely released from a duty to obey the state but, in effect, gains an entitlement: the right to rebel. A rebellion is an attempt to overthrow state power, usually involving a substantial body of citizens as well as, in most cases, the use of violence. Although any major uprising against government can be described as a rebellion, the term is often used in contrast to revolution to describe the attempt to overthrow a government rather than replace an entire political regime. Rebellion can be justified in different ways. In some cases, the act of rebellion reflects a belief that government does not, and never has, exercised legitimate authority. This can be seen, for example, in the case of colonial rule, where government amounts to little more than domination:

it is imposed by force and maintained by systematic coercion. The rebellion in India against British rule, and indeed the national liberation struggles that have taken place throughout Asia and Africa, did not seek justification in terms of political obligation. Quite simply, no duty to obey the colonial ruler had ever been acknowledged, so no limit to obligation had been reached. In the case of the American Revolution of 1776, however, the rebellion of the 13 former British colonies was justified explicitly in terms of a right of rebellion rooted in a theory of political obligation.

The American revolutionaries drew heavily upon the ideas John Locke had developed in *Two Treatises on Civil Government* ([1690] 1965). Locke had emphasised that political obligation was conditional upon respect for natural rights. On these grounds he gave support to the English 'Glorious Revolution' which overthrew Stuart rule and established a constitutional monarchy under William and Mary. The American Declaration of Independence, was imbued with classic social contract principles. In the first place, it portrays government as a human artefact, created by men to serve their purposes; the powers of government are therefore derived from the 'consent of the governed'. However, the contract upon which government is based is very specific: human beings are endowed with certain 'inalienable rights' including the right to 'life, liberty, and the pursuit of happiness', and it is the purpose of government to secure and protect these rights. Clearly, therefore, political obligation is not absolute; citizens have an obligation to obey government only so long as it respects these fundamental rights. When government becomes an 'absolute despotism', the Declaration of Independence states that 'it is the right of the people to alter or abolish it, and to institute a new government'. In other words, the limits of political obligation have been reached and citizens have a right, indeed a duty, to rebel against such a government and to 'provide new guards for their future security'.

Such Lockian principles are rooted very deeply in liberal ideas and assumptions. Social contract theories imply that since the state is created by an agreement amongst rational individuals it must serve the interests of all citizens and so be neutral or impartial. By the same token, if the state fails in its fundamental task of protecting individual rights it fails all its citizens and not just certain groups or sections. Conservatives, by contrast, have been far less willing to acknowledge that political obligation is conditional. Authoritarian conservatives, following Hobbes, warn that any challenge to established authority risks the complete collapse of orderly existence. This is what led Joseph de Maistre (see p. 165), a fierce critic of the French Revolution, to suggest that politics is based upon a willing and complete subordination to 'the master'. According to this view, the very notion of a limit to political obligation is dangerous and insidious.

Although modern conservatives embrace constitutionalism and democracy, they often fear protest, rebellion and revolt, and are not unmindful of the benefits which strong government brings.

Marxists and anarchists, however, have a very different attitude towards political obligation. Classical Marxists discount any idea of a social contract and believe instead that the state is an instrument of class oppression; it is a 'bourgeois state'. The function of the state is therefore not to protect individual rights so much as to defend or advance the interests of the 'ruling class'. Indeed, Marxists have traditionally regarded social contract theories as 'ideological' in the sense that they serve class interests by concealing the contradictions upon which capitalism and all class societies are based. In this light, the notion of political obligation is a myth or delusion whose only purpose is to reconcile the proletariat to its continued exploitation. Although anarchists may be prepared to accept the notion of 'social' obligation, the idea of 'political' obligation is, in their view, entirely unfounded. If the state is an oppressive, exploitative and coercive body, the idea that individuals may have a moral obligation to accept its authority is quite absurd. Political obligation, in other words, amounts to nothing more than servitude.

Citizenship

As already noted, the concept of citizenship is rooted in the political thought of Ancient Greece. Citizenship has also been one of the central themes of the republican political tradition. In its simplest form, a 'citizen' is a member of a political community who is endowed with a set of rights and a set of obligations. Citizenship therefore represents a relationship between the individual and the state, in which the two are bound together by reciprocal rights and obligations. However, the precise nature of this relationship is the subject of considerable argument and dispute. For example, some view citizenship as a legal status which can be defined objectively, while others see it as an identity, a sense of loyalty or belonging. Difficult issues are also raised by the relationship between citizenship and the individual's other identities, such as nationality, ethnicity, religion and class membership. The most contentious question, however, relates to the precise nature of citizen's rights and obligations, and the balance between the two. Although citizenship often appears to be 'above politics' in the sense that most, if not all, theorists are prepared to endorse it, in practice there are a number of competing concepts of citizenship. The most important of these have been social citizenship and active citizenship.

Republicanism

Republican political thought can be traced back to the ancient Roman Republic, its earliest version being Cicero's defence of mixed government developed in *The Republic*. It was revived in Renaissance Italy as a model for the organisation of Italian city-states that supposedly balanced civic freedom against political stability. Further forms of republicanism were born out of the English, American and French revolutions. Although republican ideas subsequently fell out of fashion as a result of the spread of liberalism (see p. 29), and the emphasis upon freedom as privacy and non-interference, there has been growing interest in 'civic republicanism' since the 1960s, particularly amongst communitarian thinkers (see p. 34).

Republicanism is most simply defined in contrast to monarchy. However, the term republic suggests not merely the absence of a monarch but, in the light of its Latin root, *res publica*, it implies a distinctively public arena and popular rule. The central theme of republican political theory is a concern with a particular form of freedom. In the view of Pettit (1997), republican freedom combines liberty in the sense of protection against arbitrary or tyrannical government with full and active participation in public and political life. Republican thinkers have discussed this view of freedom either in relation to moral precepts or institutional structures. The moral concern of republicanism is expressed in a belief in civic virtue, understood to include public spiritedness, honour and patriotism. Above all, it is linked to a stress upon public activity over private activity, as articulated in the twentieth century in the work of Hannah Arendt (see p. 368). The institutional focus of republicanism has shifted its emphasis over time. Whereas classical republicanism was usually associated with government that mixed monarchical, aristocratic and democratic elements, the American and French revolutions reshaped republicanism by applying it to whole nations rather than small communities, and by considering the implications of modern democratic government.

Republican political theory has the attraction that it offers an alternative to individualistic liberalism. In espousing a form of civic humanism, it attempts to re-establish the public domain as the source of personal fulfilment, and thus to resist the privatisation and marketisation of politics as encouraged, for instance, by rational choice theory (see p. 246). However, the weakness of republicanism is that it may be theoretically unclear and its political prescriptions may be uncertain. Republican theory has been criticised either because it subscribes to an essentially 'positive' theory of freedom (which is the characteristic position of 'civic republicanism'), or because it attempts, perhaps incoherently, to straddle the 'negative/positive' freedom divide. Politically, republicanism may be associated with a wide variety of political forms, including parliamentary government within a constitutional monarchy, radical democracy and divided government achieved through federalism and the separation of powers.

→

Key figures

Niccolò Machiavelli (see p. 54)   Machiavelli helped to revive a form of republicanism that was based upon an uncritical admiration of the Roman Republic. He argued not only that a republic is the best way of reconciling tensions between patricians and the people, but also stressed the importance of patriotic virtue in maintaining political stability. Machiavelli identified liberty with self-government and saw military and political participation as an important means of ensuring human fulfilment.

Charles-Louis de Secondat Montesquieu (1689–1755)   A French political philosopher, Montesquieu championed a form of parliamentary liberalism that was based upon the writings of Locke (see p. 269) and, to some extent, a misreading of English political experience. Montesquieu emphasised the need to resist tyranny by fragmenting government power, particularly through the device of the separation of powers. The separation of powers proposes that government be divided into three separate branches, the legislature, the executive and the judiciary. Montesquieu's most important work is *The Spirit of the Laws* (1748).

Thomas Paine (1737–1809)   A British-born writer and revolutionary, Paine was a fierce opponent of the monarchical system and a fervent supporter of the republican cause. He developed a radical strand within liberal thought that fused an emphasis upon individual rights with a belief in popular sovereignty. He also attacked established religion and subscribed to an egalitarianism that laid down an early model for the welfare state and the redistribution of wealth. Paine's most important writings include *Common Sense* (1776), *Rights of Man* (1791–2) and *Age of Reason* (1794).

Benjamin Constant (1767–1830)   A French politician and writer, Constant is best known as a supporter of constitutionalism and for his analysis of liberty. He distinguished between the 'liberty of the ancients' and the 'liberty of the moderns', identifying the former with the ideas of direct participation and self-government, and the latter with non-interference and private rights. Whereas Rousseau (see p. 243) and the Jacobins had emphasised ancient liberty, Constant recommended a balance between ancient and modern liberty achieved through representation and constitutional checks. Constant's main work is *Principles of Politics* (1815).

James Madison (see p. 232)   Madison was an important exponent of constitutional republicanism. His principal concern was to devise institutions through which factional rivalry could be contained and political liberty ensured. The central feature of this was an attempt to ensure that 'power is a check to power'. On this basis, Madison outlined a powerful defence of pluralism and divided government, supporting the adoption into the US Constitution of principles such as federalism, bicameralism and separation of powers.

→

Republicanism continued

Further reading

Lerner, R. *The Thinking Revolutionary: Principle and Practice in the New Republic.* Ithaca, NY: Cornell University Press, 1987.
Oldfield, A. *Citizenship and Community: Civic Republicanism and the Modern World.* London and New York: Routledge, 1990.
Pettit, p. *Republicanism: A Theory of Freedom and Government* Oxford: Oxford University Press, 1997.

Elements of citizenship

To define the citizen simply as 'a member of a political community' is hopelessly vague. One attempt to refine the notion of citizenship is to define its legal substance, by reference to the specific rights and obligations which a state invests in its members. 'Citizens' can therefore be distinguished from 'aliens'. The most fundamental right of citizenship is thus the right to live and work in a country, something which 'aliens' or 'foreign citizens' may or may not be permitted to do, and then only under certain conditions and for a limited period. Citizens may also be allowed to vote, stand for election and enter certain occupations, notably military or state service, which may not be open to non-citizens. However, legal citizenship only designates a formal status, without in any way indicating that the citizen *feels* that he or she is a member of a political community. In that sense, citizenship must always have a subjective or psychological component: the citizen is distinguished by a frame of mind, a sense of loyalty towards his or her state, even a willingness to act in its defence. The mere possession of legal rights does not in itself ensure that individuals will feel themselves to be citizens of that country. Members of groups that feel alienated from their state, perhaps because of social disadvantage or racial discrimination, cannot properly be thought of as 'full citizens', even though they may enjoy a range of formal entitlements. Not uncommonly, such people regard themselves as 'second class citizens', if not as 'third class citizens'.

Undoubtedly, however, citizenship is linked to the capacity to enjoy a set of rights. The classic contribution to the study of citizenship rights was undertaken by T.H. Marshall in 'Citizenship and Social Class' (1963). Marshall defined citizenship as 'full membership of a community' and attempted to outline the process through which it was achieved. Though modelled exclusively on British experience, Marshall's analysis has had far broader influence in discriminating between the various rights of citizenship. In Marshall's view, the first rights to develop were 'civil rights', broadly defined as 'rights necessary for individual freedom'. These include freedom of speech, assembly, movement, conscience, the right to equality before the law, to own property, enter into contracts and so forth. Civil rights are therefore rights exercised within civil society, and their existence depends upon the establishment of limited government, government that respects the autonomy of the individual. Secondly, there are 'political rights' which provide the individual with the opportunity to participate in political life. The central political rights are obviously the right to vote, to stand for election and to hold public office. The provision of political rights clearly requires the development of universal suffrage, political equality and democratic government. Finally, Marshall identified a range of 'social rights' which guarantee the citizen a minimum social status. These rights are diverse but, in Marshall's opinion, include the right to basic economic welfare, social security and what he described, rather vaguely, as the right 'to live the life of a civilised being according to the standards prevailing in society'. The provision of social rights requires the development of a welfare state and an extension of state responsibilities into economic and social life.

Marshall's attempt to break down citizenship into three 'bundles of rights' – civil, political and social – has nevertheless been subject to criticism. The idea of social rights has, for instance, been ferociously attacked by the New Right, an issue that will be more fully examined in connection with social citizenship. In addition, other sets of rights may also be added to Marshall's list. Although he included the right to own property under the heading of civil rights, Marshall did not acknowledge a broader range of economic rights demanded in particular by the trade union movement, such as the right of union membership, the right to strike and picket, and possibly the right to exercise some form of control within the workplace. Feminist theorists (see p. 60) have argued that full citizenship should also take account of gender inequality and grant an additional set of women's rights and, more specifically, a set of reproduction rights, the right to contraception, the right to abortion and so on. Furthermore, because Marshall's work was developed with the nation-state in mind, it failed to take account of the growing significance of the international dimension of citizenship. One of the features of the Treaty of European Union (Maastricht treaty) was that it established a common citizenship for people in all fifteen member states. It established the right to freedom of movement within the EU and with it the right to vote and hold public office wherever the citizen lives. In the same way, attempts to enshrine the doctrine of human rights in international law, as in the UN Declaration, have started to make the notion of global citizenship a meaningful idea.

Nevertheless, citizenship cannot narrowly be understood as a 'citizenship of entitlements', however those entitlements may be defined. Citizenship necessarily makes demands of the individual in terms of duties and responsibilities. To some extent, the obligations of the citizen can be said to match and, perhaps, balance the rights of citizenship. For example, the citizen's right to enjoy a sphere of privacy and personal autonomy surely implies an obligation to respect the privacy of fellow citizens. Similarly, political rights could be said to entail not merely the right to participate in political life but also the duty to do so. In Ancient Greece, this was reflected in the willingness of citizens to hold public office if selected by lot or rota. In modern societies, it can be found in the obligation to undertake jury service and, in countries like Australia, Belgium and Italy, in a legal obligation to vote. Social rights, in turn, could be said to imply an obligation to pay the taxes which finance the provision of education, healthcare, pensions and other benefits. Such duties and obligations must be underpinned by what Derek Heater (1990) called 'civic virtue', a sense of loyalty towards one's state and a willing acceptance of the responsibilities that living within a community entails. This is why citizenship is frequently linked with education: civic virtue does not develop naturally but, like an understanding of the rights of citizenship, must be inculcated and encouraged. In a wide range of countries, 'education for citizenship' is a significant feature of public educational provision, whereas in others it is left in the hands of voluntary organisations. In Britain, for instance, the promotion of civic virtue is largely undertaken by private organisations like the Prince of Wales Trust and the Speaker's Commission on Citizenship.

Finally, it must be recognised that citizenship is merely one of a number of identities which the individual possesses. This is what Heater termed 'multiple citizenship', an idea that acknowledges that citizens have a broader range of loyalties and responsibilities than simply to their nation-state. This can take into account the geographical dimension of citizenship, allowing citizens to identify with supranational bodies and even with the global community, as well as with their particular region or locality. Moreover, citizenship may not always correspond with national identity. In multinational states like Britain it may be possible for each constituent nation to foster a sense of patriotic loyalty, but at the same time for a unifying civic identity to survive. In the same way, racial, ethnic and cultural groups possess their own identities and also make specific demands upon their members. By acknowledging that the individual's relationship to the state is merely one of a number of meaningful identities, liberal democracies can be said to subscribe to the notion of 'limited citizenship'. These other areas of life are, and should remain, in this sense, 'non-political'. By contrast, totalitarian states like Nazi Germany, in which the individual's responsibilities to the state are absolute and unlimited, can be said to practise 'total citizenship'.

Social citizenship

The idea of social citizenship arose out of the writings of T.H. Marshall and the emphasis he placed upon social rights. For Marshall, citizenship was a universal quality enjoyed by all members of the community and therefore demanded *equal* rights and entitlements. The principle of equality had long been accepted in respect of civil and political rights. Few, for instance, would deny that genuine citizenship requires political equality in the form of one person one vote, and one vote one value. The distinctive feature of Marshall's work, however, was the stress it placed upon the relationship between citizenship and the achievement of social equality. In Marshall's view, citizenship is ultimately a social status. Citizens have to enjoy freedom from poverty, ignorance and despair if they are to participate fully in the affairs of their community, an idea embodied in the concept of social rights. Marshall therefore believed that citizenship is incompatible with the class inequalities typically found in a capitalist system; citizenship and social class are 'opposing principles'. This is not to say that Marshall believed citizenship to be irreconcilable with all forms of social inequality, but only those directly generated by the capitalist market. This is why the idea of social citizenship is associated not with the abolition of capitalism but with the development of a welfare state to alleviate poverty and hardship, and guarantee its citizens at least a social minimum. Indeed, Marshall was quite willing to acknowledge that citizenship itself would generate a range of inequalities as the achievement of greater equality of opportunity allowed material differences to reflect natural inequalities amongst humankind.

During the twentieth century, social citizenship has been accepted more widely and the notion of social rights has become part of the currency of political argument and debate. Civil rights movements no longer confine themselves to legal or political demands, but also readily address social issues. The US civil rights movement in the 1960s, for instance, campaigned for urban development and improved job and educational opportunities for blacks, as well as for their right to vote and hold political office. Groups such as women, ethnic minorities, the poor and the unemployed, commonly regard themselves as 'second class citizens' because social disadvantage prevents their full participation in the life of the community. Moreover, the inclusion in the UN Universal Declaration of Human Rights of a battery of social rights invested the idea of social citizenship with the authority of international law. However, there can be little doubt that the principal means through which social citizenship has been established is by the progressive expansion of the welfare state. In Marshall's view, social rights were inextricably bound up with welfare provision and the capacity of the welfare state to ensure that all citizens enjoy a 'modicum of economic welfare and security'.

The link between social citizenship and the welfare state is not, however, always clear. In the first place, the struggle for social rights has by no means been the only cause of burgeoning welfare provision; the need for a healthy, educated and productive workforce has at times been at least as important. The welfare state is, furthermore, at best a means to an end, a way of creating the social conditions that enable all citizens to participate meaningfully and effectively in the life of their community. As such, the welfare state is not the only means of achieving social citizenship, a fact which Marshall himself acknowledged in pointing out that the growth of trade unionism had also helped to establish social rights. Finally, the welfare state has sometimes been attacked as an inadequate vehicle for the establishment of social citizenship. For example, social welfare may only provide a 'safety net', ameliorating the worst incidents of deprivation and hardship, but not seriously tackle the problem of economic inequality or provide the basis for active political participation. Indeed, it has sometimes been suggested that welfare provision actually favours the affluent and privileged sections of society more than the poor and deprived, in which case it serves to entrench class inequalities and restrict citizenship.

The principal advocates of social citizenship have been social democrats (see p. 312), socialists and modern liberals (see p. 29). They have insisted upon the vital need for 'positive' rights, delivered through government intervention, in addition to traditional 'negative' rights like freedom of speech and freedom of assembly. The case for social rights is based upon the belief that economic inequality is more a product of the capitalist economy than it is a reflection of natural differences amongst human beings. For modern liberals, social disadvantages like homelessness, unemployment and sickness not only thwart personal development but also undermine a sense of citizenship. Full citizenship therefore requires equality of opportunity, the ability of each citizen to rise or fall according to his or her own talents and hard work.

Social democrats have regarded economic and social rights not merely as legitimate rights of citizenship but as the very foundations of a civilised life. Individuals who lack food, shelter or a means of material subsistence will set very little store by their right to enjoy freedom of speech or exercise their freedom of religious worship. Social democrats have been attracted to the idea of social citizenship because it gives all citizens a meaningful 'stake' in society. In addition, by upholding the right to work, the right to health care, the right to education and so on, social citizenship advances the cause of material equality. Marxists, on the other hand, have traditionally been less sympathetic towards the idea of social citizenship. Classical Marxists believe that social equality requires not just the growth of social welfare to alleviate poverty and hardship but the abolition of the capitalist class system itself, a conclusion that T.H. Marshall most certainly did not accept. However, modern Marxists or neo-Marxists have moved some way towards a reconciliation with citizenship, seeing the idea of universal rights and obligations as an important statement of egalitarian principles.

The sternest critics of social citizenship have, however, been on the political right. Right-wing libertarians (see p. 340) have been firm opponents of the idea of social rights and believe that social welfare is fundamentally misconceived. Various lines of attack have been adopted, usually drawing inspiration from the individualism and free market philosophy of classical liberalism. Some have argued that the doctrine of rights and entitlements, and in particular social rights, has encouraged citizens to have an unrealistic view of the capacities of government. The result of this has been a relentless growth in the responsibilities of government which, by pushing up taxes and widening budget deficits, has severely damaged economic prospects. In addition, it has been argued that the notion of social citizenship has undermined enterprise and individual initiative, creating the impression that the state will always 'pick up the bill'. The welfare state has thus created a 'culture of dependency'. Furthermore, an empirical onslaught, led by writers such as George Gilder (1982) and Charles Murray (1984), has suggested that welfare initiatives, such as President Johnson's 'War on Poverty' in the United States, have invariably been counter-productive. Rather than alleviating hardship and promoting full citizenship, such programmes have entrenched disadvantages by creating a permanent underclass. Such issues are examined more fully in Chapter 10 in relation to welfare.

Active citizenship

The citizenship debate has not only revolved around the question of social rights but has also thrown up rival conceptions of citizenship, notably what has been called 'active citizenship'. The idea of the 'active citizen' developed out of an emerging neo-conservative model of citizenship, outlined first in the United States but soon taken up by politicians on the other side of the Atlantic. In a series of speeches in 1988 and 1989, for example, the then British Home Secretary, Douglas Hurd, proclaimed the virtues of active citizenship and suggested that the community is confronted by the twin problems of a lack of social or community responsibility and a debilitating dependence upon the state. Although the New Right dismisses Marshall's work and condemns the idea of social citizenship, it chose not to abandon the concept of citizenship so much as to reinvent it. However, since the New Right has drawn upon two contrasting traditions – economic liberalism and social conservatism – active citizenship has two faces. On one hand, it represents a classical liberal emphasis upon self-reliance and 'standing on one's own two feet'; on the other, it underlines a traditionally conservative stress upon duty and responsibility.

The liberal New Right, or neo-liberalism, is committed to rigorous individualism; its overriding goal is to 'roll back the frontiers of the state'. As noted earlier, in its view the relationship between the individual and the state has become dangerously unbalanced. Government intervention in economic and social life has allowed the state to dwarf, even dominate, the citizen, robbing him or her of liberty and self-respect. The essence of active citizenship, from this point of view, is enterprise, hard work and self-reliance. This ideal is firmly rooted in nineteenth-century liberalism, most clearly reflected in the concept of 'self-help', advocated by writers such as Samuel Smiles ([1859] 1986). Neo-liberals believe that individual responsibility makes both economic and moral sense. In economic terms, active citizenship relieves the burden that social welfare imposes upon public finances and community resources. Self-reliant individuals will work hard because they know that at the end of the day there is no welfare state to pick up the bill. In moral terms, active citizenship promotes dignity and self-respect because individuals are forced to support themselves and their own families.

It is questionable, however, whether self-reliance can in any proper sense be said to constitute a theory of citizenship. At heart, citizenship is based upon membership of, and participation in, a community; it refers to the political, or at least public, face of individual life. By attempting to redress the balance between the state and civil society, the New Right is concerned to expand the bounds of 'private' existence at the expense of the 'public' responsibilities of state and government. The 'good citizen' may certainly be hardworking and independent, but is it possible to suggest that these essentially 'private' qualities are the ones upon which citizenship is based? Even when this model of citizenship accepts a need for public services its stress is upon efficiency, cost-cutting and consumer responsiveness. In effect, this is to conceive of the citizen as a consumer, as someone who purchases goods or services, on this occasion from the state, in the hope of satisfying essentially personal needs. Where this model therefore fails is in establishing how the citizen can be regarded as a member of his or her community.

However, the other face of the New Right, the conservative New Right or neo-conservatism, undoubtedly advocates a close relationship between the state and the individual citizen. What distinguishes the neo-conservative concept of citizenship is its emphasis upon civil obligations and its rejection of entitlement-based concepts of citizenship. Most neo-conservatives, for instance, would gladly endorse the words of John F. Kennedy, used in his presidential inaugural address in January 1961: 'Ask not what your country can do for you – ask what you can do for your country'. Neo-conservatives believe that Marshall's 'citizenship of entitlement' has created a society in which individuals know only their rights and do not recognise their duties or responsibilities. Such a society is fraught with the dangers of permissiveness and social fragmentation. Unrestrained liberty will lead to selfishness, greed and a lack of respect for both social institutions and fellow human beings. As neo-conservatives see it, they are attempting to redress this imbalance. Lawrence Mead (1982), for instance, proposed that citizenship should include not just a 'right to work' but also a 'duty to work', a belief reflected in the idea of 'workfare'. Workfare is a system through which the receipt of unemployment benefit is dependent upon the willingness to undertake work within the community. Entitlements have to be 'earned'. Margaret Thatcher endorsed this underlying principle in saying, 'There is no such thing as entitlement, unless someone has first met an obligation'. This was precisely the reasoning that underpinned the introduction in Britain of the 'poll tax', which, unlike other forms of local government taxation, had the virtue that it extended the responsibility for financing local services to all citizens. The replacement of higher education grants with a system of student loans, now used in a growing number of countries, including the United States, Australia and Britain, and the introduction of tuition fees also bears out a desire to strengthen civil obligations. Students have a duty to pay for education; they do not merely have a right of access to it.

This version of active citizenship has nevertheless also had its fair share of criticism. It can be argued, in the first place, that it is in danger of replacing one imbalance with an imbalance of a new kind: the emphasis upon civic duty may displace a concern for rights and entitlements. If entitlements do not belong to citizens as a right but are only allocated by government itself, what limits can be placed upon political obligation? What checks can be established to the powers of the state? Moreover, just as social citizenship is linked to the attempt to modify class inequalities, active citizenship may be turned into a philosophy of 'pay your way' which would simply reinforce existing inequalities. For instance, making students pay for higher education through a system of loans may simply disadvantage those from less prosperous backgrounds or discourage students from taking up financially less rewarding careers. In the same way, workfare can stigmatise the unemployed by implying that they, rather than the government, are responsible for their own misfortune. It can, further, be argued that an emphasis upon civil obligations places far heavier burdens upon women than upon men. Because women are still expected to take prime responsibility for domestic or family life, they are bound to be penalised by any attempt to shift responsibility for the conduct of children, or for the care of the elderly and sick, on to the family.

Finally, a 'citizenship of obligations' is in danger of intruding into private responsibilities, so threatening individual liberty. Whereas the liberal New Right views the individual as self-sufficient and morally autonomous, the conservative New Right views the individual very much as a citizen but one shouldering a potentially unlimited number of responsibilities. Some of these responsibilities, such as the obligation to obey the law and pay taxes, are widely accepted and usually unquestioned; however, others may be considerably more controversial. How far should the citizen's duties extend? In some cases, the citizen's obligation to the state may intrude into the most private areas of life. In Nazi Germany, for instance, healthy German citizens were exhorted to bear children for the Fatherland, abortion and contraception were prohibited, and adultery, for Aryan males at least, was openly encouraged. The Chinese government, on the other hand, has for a number of years established a legal obligation upon parents to have only a single child.

Summary

1   The relationship between individuals and the state – citizenship – is established by the allocation of rights and obligations to each. Particular emphasis in modern politics is placed upon the doctrine of human rights, fundamental and universal rights thought to be applicable to all people and in all societies. Although human rights are believed to transcend ideological divisions, there is considerable debate about who is entitled to them and what these rights might be.

2   Political obligation refers to the duty of citizens to acknowledge the authority of the state and obey its laws. Some argue that it arises from a voluntary agreement, or contract, from which citizens can be released; others believe that it reflects the benefit which the state brings; still others view it as a natural duty akin to respect for parents or elders.

3   Social citizenship is based upon the belief that citizens are entitled to social rights and not merely civil and political rights. A minimum social status has been seen as the basis for full participation in the life of the community. Critics, however, point out that this may both undermine individual responsibility and lead to an ever-expanding social budget.

4 The rival idea of active citizenship has two features. It implies that citizens should, as far as possible, be self-reliant and avoid dependency upon the state; and it underlines the importance of obligations, arguing that entitlements have to be earned. However, the first may mean that citizenship is privatised, while the second may invest the state with potentially unlimited powers.

Further reading

Barbalet, J.M. *Citizenship*. Milton Keynes: Open University Press, 1988; and Minneapolis: University of Minnesota Press, 1989.

Dworkin, R. *Taking Rights Seriously*, rev. edn. London: Duckworth, 1990.

Flathman, R. *Political Obligation*. New York: Atheneum, 1972.

Freeden, M. *Rights*. Milton Keynes: Open University Press and Minneapolis: University of Minnesota Press, 1991.

Heater, D. *Citizenship: The Civil Ideal in World History, Politics and Education* London and New York: Longman, 1990.

Lessnoff, M. *Social Contract*. London: Macmillan and Atlantic Highlands, NJ: Humanities Press, 1986.

Midgley, M. *Animals and Why They Matter*. New York: Penguin, 1983.

Pateman, C. *The Problem of Political Obligation*. New York: John Wiley, 1979.

Waldron, J. (ed.). *Theories of Rights*. Oxford: Oxford University Press, 1984.

Chapter 8

Democracy, Representation and the Public Interest

Introduction
Democracy
Representation
The public interest
Summary
Further reading

Introduction

Since the dawn of political thought the question 'Who should rule?' has been a recurrent issue of argument and debate. It was on this basis, for example, that Aristotle classified governments according to whether they were ruled by one person, a small group, or the many. In the twentieth century, however, the question has elicited a single, almost universally accepted, response: the people should govern. Perhaps no other political ideal is accorded the unquestioning approval, even reverence, currently enjoyed by democracy. Whether they are liberals, socialists, conservatives, communists or even fascists, politicians everywhere are eager to proclaim their democratic credentials and to commit themselves to the democratic ideal. And yet it is its very popularity that makes democracy a difficult concept to understand. When a term means anything to anyone it is in danger of becoming entirely meaningless. Democracy may now be nothing more than a 'hurrah word', endlessly repeated by politicians, but denoting little of substance.

In reality, a number of competing models of democracy have developed in different historical periods and in various parts of the world. These have included direct and indirect democracy, political and social democracy, pluralist and totalitarian democracy and so on. What forms of government can reasonably be described as 'democratic', and why? Moreover, why is democracy so widely valued, and can it be regarded as an unqualified good? Modern ideas of democracy are, however, rarely based upon the classical idea of popular self-government. Rather, they are founded on the belief that politicians in some sense 'represent' the people and act on their behalf. This raises questions about what representation means and how it is accomplished. What, for instance, is being represented: the

220

views of the people, their best interests, or the various groups which make up the people? Is representation a necessary feature of democracy, or is it merely a substitute for it? Finally, democratic governments claim to rule in the national or public interest. If ordinary citizens no longer govern themselves, at least government takes place in their interest, for their benefit. However, what is meant by the 'public interest'? And can the people ever be said to have a single, collective interest? Even if such a collective interest exists, how can it in practice be defined?

Democracy

The term democracy and the classical conception of democratic rule are firmly rooted in Ancient Greece. Like other words that end in 'cracy' – such as autocracy, aristocracy and bureaucracy – democracy is derived from the ancient Greek word *kratos*, meaning 'power' or 'rule'. Democracy therefore means 'rule by the demos', demos standing for 'the many' or 'the people'. In contrast to its modern usage, democracy was originally a negative or pejorative term, denoting not so much rule by all, as rule by the propertyless and uneducated masses. Democracy was therefore thought to be the enemy of liberty and wisdom. While writers such as Aristotle (see p. 68) were prepared to recognise the virtues of popular participation, they nevertheless feared that unrestrained democracy would degenerate into a form of 'mob rule'. Indeed, such pejorative implications continued to be attached to democracy until well into the twentieth century.

Democratic government has, however, varied considerably over the centuries. Perhaps the most fundamental distinction is between democratic systems, like those in Ancient Greece, that are based upon direct popular participation in government, and those that operate through some kind of representative mechanism. This highlights two contrasting models of democracy: direct democracy and representative democracy. Moreover, the modern understanding of democracy is dominated by the form of electoral democracy that has developed in the industrialised West, often called liberal democracy. Despite its undoubted success, liberal democracy is only one of a number of possible models of democracy, and one whose democratic credentials have sometimes been called into question. Finally, the near universal approval which democracy currently elicits should not obscure the fact that the merits of democracy have been fiercely debated over the centuries and that, in certain respects, this debate has intensified in the late twentieth century. In other words, democracy may have its vices as well as its virtues.

Democracy

Although the democratic political tradition can be traced back to Ancient Greece, the cause of democracy was not widely taken up by political thinkers until the nineteenth century. Until then, democracy was generally dismissed as rule by the ignorant and unenlightened masses. Now, however, it seems that we are all democratic. Liberals, conservatives, socialists, communists, anarchists and even fascists have been eager to proclaim the virtues of democracy and to demonstrate their democratic credentials.

This emphasises the fact that the democratic tradition does not advance a single and agreed ideal of popular rule, but is rather an arena of debate in which the notion of popular rule, and ways in which it can be achieved, is discussed. In that sense, democratic political thought addresses three central questions. First, who are the people? As no one would extend political participation to *all* the people, the question is: on what basis should it be limited – in relation to age, education, gender, social background and so on? Second, how should the people rule? This relates not only to the choice between direct and indirect democratic forms, but also to debates about forms of representation and different electoral systems. Third, how far should popular rule extend? Should democracy be confined to political life, or should democracy also apply, say, to the family, the workplace, or throughout the economy?

Democracy, then, is not a single, unambiguous phenomenon. In reality, there are a number of theories or models of democracy, each offering its own version of popular rule. There are not merely a number of democratic forms and mechanisms but also, more fundamentally, quite different grounds on which democratic rule can be justified. Classical democracy, based upon the Athenian model, is characterised by the direct and continuous participation of citizens in the processes of government. Protective democracy is a limited and indirect form of democratic rule designed to provide individuals with a means of defence against government. As such, it is linked to natural rights theory and utilitarianism (see p. 360). Developmental democracy is associated with attempts to broaden popular participation on the basis that it advances freedom and individual flourishing. Such ideas were taken up by New Left thinkers in the 1960s and 1970s in the form of radical or participatory democracy. Finally, people's democracy, rooted in orthodox Marxism (see p. 81), interprets democracy in terms of the pursuit of social equality brought about by the collectivisation of wealth. It thus stands in contrast to 'capitalist' or 'bourgeois' democracy.

Key figures

Jean-Jacques Rousseau (see p. 243)   Rousseau viewed democracy as the most important means through which humans can achieve freedom or autonomy, in the sense of 'obedience to a law one prescribes to oneself'. He was a strenuous critic of the practice of elections and insisted that citizens are only

→

'free' when they participate directly and continuously in shaping the life of their community. For Rousseau, this ultimately meant obedience to the general will, although he was less clear about the precise mechanisms through which the general will would emerge.

Alexis de Tocqueville (1805–59) A French politician, historian and political theorist, Tocqueville developed a highly ambiguous analysis of democracy based upon the experience of the United States. He associated democracy with the advance of egalitarianism and recognised its value in promoting the welfare of the masses and in encouraging a spirit of self-reliance. However, he is best known as a critic of majoritarianism, arguing that popular elections do not guarantee that wise and experienced people hold public office and warning against the tyranny of 'public opinion', by which he meant the ill-informed views and prejudices of the masses. Such ideas had considerable impact upon his friend, J.S. Mill (see p. 258). Tocqueville's most influential work is his epic *Democracy in America* (1835–40).

Joseph Schumpeter (1883–1950) A Moravian-born US economist and sociologist, Schumpeter developed an analysis of capitalism that emphasised its bureaucratic tendencies and its growing resemblance to socialism. His theory of democracy offered an alternative to the 'classical doctrine', which was based upon the idea of a shared notion of the common good; it portrayed the democratic process as an arena of struggle between power-seeking politicians intent upon winning the people's vote. His view that political democracy is analogous to an economic market had considerable influence upon later rational choice theories (see p. 246). Schumpeter's most important political work is *Capitalism, Socialism and Democracy* (1942).

Crawford Brough Macpherson (1911–87) A Canadian political theorist, Macpherson developed a leftist form of liberalism that reflects the influence of Marxism. He portrayed early liberalism as a form of possessive individualism, intrinsically linked to market society. His critique of liberal democracy stressed liberalism's pre-democratic features and acknowledged its bias in favour of capitalism. Nevertheless, he argued that the basic liberal democratic principle of equal liberty could ultimately be realised, but only within conditions of participatory democracy and in a non-market social environment. Macpherson's major works include *The Political Theory of Possessive Individualism* (1962), *Democratic Theory* (1973) and *The Life and Times of Liberal Democracy* (1977).

Robert Dahl (1915–) A US political scientist, Dahl is a leading exponent of pluralist theory. He contrasts modern democratic systems with the classical democracy of Ancient Greece, using the term 'polyarchy' to refer to rule by the many, as distinct from rule by all citizens. His empirical studies led him to conclude that the system of competitive elections prevents any permanent elite from emerging and ensures wide, if imperfect, access to the political process.

→

Democracy continued

His later writings reflect a growing awareness of the tension between democracy and the power of major capitalist corporations. Dahl's major works include *A Preface to Democratic Theory* (1956), *Who Governs?* (1963), *Dilemmas of Pluralist Democracy* (1982) and *A Preface to Economic Democracy* (1985).

Further reading

Birch, A. H. *The Concepts and Theories of Modern Democracy.* London and New York: Routledge, 1993.
Bobbio, N. *The Future of Democracy: A Defence of the Rules of the Game.* Minneapolis: University of Minnesota Press, 1987.
Dahl, R. *Democracy and its Critics.* New Haven, CT: Yale University Press, 1989.

Direct and indirect democracy

In the Gettysburg Address, delivered at the time of the American Civil War, Abraham Lincoln extolled the virtues of what he called 'government of the people, by the people, and for the people'. In so doing, he defined between two contrasting notions of democracy. The first, 'government*by* the people', is based upon the idea that the public participates in government and indeed governs itself: popular self-government. The second, 'government *for* the people', is linked to the notion of the public interest and the idea that government benefits the people, whether or not they themselves rule. The classical conception of democracy, which endured well into the nineteenth century, was firmly rooted in the ideal of popular participation and drew heavily upon the example of Athenian democracy. The cornerstone of Athenian democracy was the direct and continuous participation of all citizens in the life of their*polis* or city-state. As described in Chapter 3, this amounted to a form of government by mass meeting, and each citizen was qualified to hold public office if selected to do so by lot or rota. Athenian democracy was therefore a system of 'direct democracy' or what is sometimes referred to as 'participatory democracy'. By removing the need for a separate class of professional politicians, the citizens themselves were able to rule directly, obliterating the distinction between government and the governed and between the state and civil society. Similar systems of 'town-meeting democracy' continue to be practised at a local level in some parts of the United States, notably in New England, and in the communal assemblies employed in Switzerland.

The town meeting is, however, not the only means through which direct democracy can operate. The most obvious of these is the plebiscite or referendum, a popular vote on a specific issue which enables electors to make decisions directly, instead of selecting politicians to do so on their behalf. Referendums are widely used at every level in Switzerland, and are employed in countries such as Ireland to ratify constitutional amendments. Britain held a referendum in 1975 on continued membership of the then European Community, in 1979 on establishing devolved assemblies in Scotland and Wales, and since the election of the Blair government in 1997 referendums have been held on Scottish and Welsh devolution, the Northern Ireland peace deal and the introduction of a London mayor. In the United States, referendums have increasingly been used in local politics in the form of 'propositions' or popular initiatives. A form of direct democracy has also survived in modern societies in the practice of selecting juries on the basis of lot or rota, as public offices were filled in Athenian times. Advocates of direct democracy further point out that the development of modern technology has opened up broader possibilities for popular participation in government. In particular, the use of so-called interactive television could enable citizens to both watch public debates and engage in voting without ever leaving their homes. Experiments with such technology are already under way in some local communities in the United States.

Needless to say, modern government bears little resemblance to the Athenian model of direct democracy. Government is left in the hands of professional politicians who are invested with the responsibility for making decisions on behalf of the people. Representative democracy is, at best, a limited and indirect form of democracy. It is limited in the sense that popular participation is both infrequent and brief, being reduced to the act of voting every few years, depending on the length of the political term. It is indirect in the sense that the public is kept at arm's length from government: the public participates only through the choice of who should govern it, and never, or only rarely, exercises power itself. Representative democracy may nevertheless qualify as a form of democracy on the grounds that, however limited and ritualised it may appear, the act of voting remains a vital source of popular power. Quite simply, the public has the ability to 'kick the rascals out', a fact that ensures public accountability. Although representative democracy may not fully realise the classical goal of 'government *by* the people', it may nevertheless make possible a form of 'government *for* the people'.

Some advocates of representative democracy acknowledge its limitations, but argue that it is the only practicable form of democracy in modern conditions. A high level of popular participation is possible within relatively small communities, such as Greek city-states or small towns, because face-to-face communication can take place between and amongst citizens. However, the idea of government by mass meeting being conducted in modern nation-states containing tens, and possibly hundreds of millions of citizens is frankly absurd. Moreover, to consult the general public on each and every issue, and permit wide-ranging debate and discussion, threatens to paralyse the decision-making process and make a country virtually ungovernable. The most fundamental objection to direct democracy is, however, that ordinary people lack the time, maturity and specialist knowledge to rule wisely on their own behalf. In this sense, representative democracy merely applies the advantages of the division of labour to politics: specialist politicians, able to devote all their time and energy to the activity of government, can clearly do a better job than would the general public. Nevertheless, since the 1960s there has been a revival of interest in classical democracy and, in particular, in the idea of participation. This reflects growing disenchantment with the bureaucratic and unresponsive nature of modern government, as well as declining respect for professional politicians, who have increasingly been viewed as self-serving careerists. In addition, the act of voting is often seen as a meaningless ritual that has little impact upon the policy process, making a mockery of the democratic ideal.

Liberal democracy

Bernard Crick (1983) has pointed out that democracy is the most promiscuous of political terms. In the sense that the word means different things to different people, democracy is an example of an 'essentially contested' concept. No settled model of democracy exists, only a number of competing models. Nevertheless, a particular model or form of democracy has come to dominate thinking on the matter, to the extent that many in the West treat it as the only feasible or meaningful form of democracy. This is liberal democracy. It is found in almost all advanced capitalist societies and now extends, in one form or another, into parts of the former communist world and the developing world. Indeed, in the light of the collapse of communism, the US New Right theorist, Francis Fukuyama (1992), proclaimed the worldwide triumph of liberal democracy, describing it as the 'end of history', by which he meant the struggle between political ideas. Such triumphalism, however, should not obscure the fact that, despite its attractions, liberal democracy is not the only model of democratic government, and, like all concepts of democracy, it has its critics and detractors.

The 'liberal' element in liberal democracy emerged historically some time before such states could genuinely be described as democratic. Many

Western states, for instance, developed forms of constitutional government in the nineteenth century, at a time when the franchise was still restricted to propertied males. In fact, women in Switzerland did not get the vote until 1971. A liberal state is based upon the principle of limited government, the idea that the individual should enjoy some measure of protection from the state. From the liberal perspective, government is a necessary evil, always liable to become a tyranny against the individual if government power is not checked. This leads to support for devices designed to constrain government, such as a constitution, a Bill of Rights, an independent judiciary and a network of checks and balances amongst the institutions of government. Liberal democracies, moreover, respect the existence of a vigorous and healthy civil society, based upon respect for civil liberties and property rights. Liberal democratic rule therefore typically co-exists with a capitalist economic order.

However, although these features may be a necessary precondition for democracy, they should not be mistaken for democracy itself. The 'democratic' element in liberal democracy is the idea of popular consent, expressed in practice through the act of voting. Liberal democracy is thus a form of electoral democracy, in that popular election is seen as the only legitimate source of political authority. Such elections must, however, respect the principle of political equality; they must be based upon universal suffrage and the idea of 'one person one vote'. For this reason, any system that restricts voting rights on grounds of gender, race, religion, economic status or whatever, fails the democratic test. Finally, in order to be fully democratic, elections must be regular, open and, above all, competitive. The core of the democratic process is the capacity of the people to call politicians to account. Political pluralism, open competition between political philosophies, movements, parties and so on, is thus thought to be the essence of democracy.

The attraction of liberal democracy is its capacity to blend elite rule with a significant measure of popular participation. Government is entrusted to professional politicians, but these politicians are forced to respond to popular pressures by the simple fact that the public put them there in the first place, and can later remove them. Joseph Schumpeter summed this up in *Capitalism, Socialism and Democracy* ([1942] 1976) by describing the democratic method as 'that institutional arrangement for arriving at political decisions in which individuals acquire the power to decide by means of a competitive struggle for the people's vote'. Thus the virtues of elite rule – government by experts, the educated or well-informed – are balanced against the need for public accountability. Indeed, such a view implies that in liberal democracies political power is ultimately wielded by voters at election time. The voter exercises the same power in the political market as the consumer does in economic markets. This process of accountability is strengthened by the capacity of citizens to exert direct influence upon government through the formation of cause groups and interest groups. Liberal democracies are therefore described as pluralist democracies: within them political power is widely dispersed amongst a number of competing groups and interests, each of which has access to government.

Nevertheless, liberal democracy does not command universal approval or respect. Its principal critics have been elitists, Marxists (see p. 81) and radical democrats. Elitists are distinguished by their belief that political power is concentrated in the hands of the few, the elite. Whereas classical elitists believed this to be a necessary and, in many cases, desirable feature of political life, modern elitists have developed an essentially empirical analysis and usually regretted the concentration of political power. In a sense, Schumpeter advanced a form of democratic elitism in suggesting that, though power is always exercised by an elite, competition amongst a number of elites ensures that the popular voice is heard. In the view of C. Wright Mills (1956), however, industrialised societies like the United States are dominated by a 'power elite', a small cohesive group that commands 'the major hierarchies and organisations of modern society'. Such a theory suggests that power is institutional in character and largely vested in the non-elected bodies of the state system, including the military, the bureaucracy, the judiciary and the police. Mills argued, in fact, that the means for exercising power are more narrowly concentrated in a few hands in such societies than at any earlier time in history. From this perspective, the principle of political equality and the process of electoral competition upon which liberal democracy is founded are nothing more than a sham.

The traditional Marxist critique of liberal democracy has focused upon the inherent tension between democracy and capitalism. For liberals and conservatives, the right to own property is almost the cornerstone of democratic rule since it provides an essential guarantee of individual liberty. Democracy can only exist when citizens are able to stand on their own two feet and make up their own minds; in other words, capitalism is a necessary precondition for democracy. Orthodox Marxists have fiercely disagreed, arguing that there is inherent tension between the political equality which liberal democracy proclaims and the social inequality which a capitalist economy inevitably generates. Liberal democracies are thus 'capitalist' or 'bourgeois' democracies, manipulated and controlled by the entrenched power of private property. Such an analysis inclined revolutionary Marxists such as Lenin (see p. 82) and Rosa Luxemburg (see p. 83) to reject the idea that there can be a 'democratic road' to socialism. An alternative tradition nevertheless recognises that electoral democracy gives the working masses a voice and may even be a vehicle for far-reaching social change. The German socialist leader Karl Kautsky (1854–1938) was an exponent of this view, as have been modern Euro-communists. However, even when socialists have embraced the ballot box, they have been critical of the narrow conception of political equality as nothing more than equal voting rights. If political power reflects the distribution of wealth, genuine democracy can only be brought about through the achievement of social equality or what early Marxists termed 'social democracy'.

Finally, radical democrats have attacked liberal democracy as a form of facade democracy. They have returned to the classical conception of democracy as popular self-government, and emphasised the need for popular political participation. The ideal of direct or participatory democracy has attracted support from Karl Marx (see p. 373) most anarchist thinkers, and from elite theorists such as Tom Bottomore (1993) and Peter Bachrach (1967). The essence of the radical democracy critique is that liberal democracy has reduced participation to a meaningless ritual: casting a vote every few years for politicians who can only be replaced by electing another set of self-serving politicians. In short, the people never rule, and the growing gulf between government and the people is reflected in the spread of inertia, apathy and the breakdown of community. Radical democrats therefore underline the benefits that political participation brings, often by reference to the writings of Rousseau (see p. 243) and J.S. Mill (see p. 258). While they suggest no single alternative to liberal democracy they have usually been prepared to endorse any reforms through which grass-roots democracy can be brought about. These include not only the use of referendums and information technology, already discussed, but also the radical decentralisation of power and the wider use of activist and campaigning pressure groups rather than bureaucratic and hierarchic political parties.

Virtues and vices of democracy

In modern politics there is a strange and perhaps unhealthy silence on the issue of democracy. So broad is respect for democracy that it has come to be taken for granted; its virtues are seldom questioned and its vices rarely exposed. This is very different from the period of the English, American and French revolutions, which witnessed fierce and continual debate about the merits of democracy. Indeed, in the nineteenth century, when democracy was regarded as a radical, egalitarian and even revolutionary creed, no issue polarised political opinion so dramatically. The present unanimity about democracy should not, however, disguise the fact that democrats have defended their views in very different ways at different times.

Until the nineteenth century, democracy, or at least the right to vote, was usually regarded as a means of protecting the individual against over-mighty government. Perhaps the earliest of all democratic sentiments was expressed in Aristotle's question *Quis custodiet custodes?* – Who will guard the Guardians? Seventeenth-century social contract theorists also saw democracy as a way in which individuals could check government power. In the eyes of John Locke (see p. 269), for instance, the right to vote was based upon natural rights and, in particular, the right to property. If government, through taxation, possessed the power to expropriate prop-erty, citizens were entitled to protect themselves, which they did by controlling the composition of the tax-making body. In other words, there should be 'no taxation without representation'. To limit the franchise to property owners would not, however, qualify as democracy by twentieth-century standards. The more radical notion of universal suffrage was advanced by utilitarian theorists like Jeremy Bentham (see p. 361). In his early writings Bentham advocated an enlightened despotism, believing that this would be able to promote 'the greatest happiness'. However, he subsequently came to support universal suffrage in the belief that each individual's interests were of equal value and that only they could be trusted to pursue their own interests.

A more radical case for democracy is, however, suggested by theorists who regard political participation as a good in itself. As noted earlier, Jean-Jacques Rousseau and John Stuart Mill have usually been seen as the principal exponents of this position. For Rousseau, democracy was a means through which human beings achieved freedom or autonomy. Individuals are, according to this view, only free when they obey laws which they themselves have made. Rousseau therefore extolled the merits of active and continuous participation in the life of their community. Such an idea, however, moves well beyond the conventional notion of electoral democracy and offers support for the more radical ideal of direct democracy. Rousseau, for example, derided the practice of elections employed in England, arguing that 'the people of England are only free when they elect their Member of Parliament; as soon as they are elected, the people are slaves, they are nothing'. Although Mill did not go so far, remaining an advocate of electoral democracy, he nevertheless believed that political participation was beneficial to both the individual and society. Mill proposed votes for women and the extension of the franchise to include all except illiterates, on educational grounds, suggesting that it would foster amongst individuals intellectual development, moral virtue and practical understanding. This, in turn, would create a more balanced and harmonious society and promote 'the general mental advancement of the community'.

Other arguments in favour of democracy are more clearly based upon its advantages for the community rather than for the individual. Democracy can, for instance, create a sense of social solidarity by giving all members a stake in the community by virtue of having a voice in the decision-making process. Rousseau expressed this very idea in his belief that government should be based upon the 'general will', or common good, rather than upon the private or selfish will of each citizen. Political participation therefore increases the feeling amongst individual citizens that they 'belong' to their community. Very similar considerations have inclined socialists and Marxists to support democracy, albeit in the form of 'social democracy' and not merely political democracy. From this perspective, democracy can be seen as an egalitarian force standing in opposition to any form of privilege or hierarchy. Democracy represents the community rather than the individual, the collective interest rather than the particular.

Even as the battle for democracy was being waged, however, strident voices were raised against it. The most fundamental argument against democracy is that ordinary members of the public are simply not competent to rule wisely in their own interests. The earliest version of this argument was put by Plato (see p. 22) who advanced the idea of rule by the virtuous, government being carried out by a class of philosopher-kings, the Guardians. In sharp contrast to democratic theorists, Plato believed in a radical form of natural inequality: human beings were born with souls of gold, silver or bronze, and were therefore disposed towards very different stations in life. Whereas Plato suggested that democracy would deliver bad government, classical elitists, such as Pareto (1848–1923), Mosca (1857–1941) and Michels (1876–1936), argued that it was simply impossible. Democracy is no more than a foolish delusion because political power is always exercised by a privileged minority, an elite. In *The Ruling Class* ([1896] 1939), Mosca proclaimed that in all societies 'two classes of people appear – a class that rules and a class that is ruled'. In his view, the resources or attributes that are necessary for rule are always unequally distributed and, further, a cohesive minority will always be able to manipulate and control the masses, even in a parliamentary democracy. Pareto suggested that the qualities needed to rule conform to one of two psychological types: 'foxes', who rule by cunning and are able to manipulate the consent of the masses; and 'lions', whose domination is typically based upon coercion and violence. Michels proposed that elite rule followed from what he called 'the iron law of oligarchy'. This states that it is in the nature of all organisations, however democratic they may appear, for power to concentrate in the hands of a small group of dominant figures, who can organise and make decisions, rather than in the hands of the apathetic rank and file.

A further argument against democracy sees it as the enemy of individual liberty. This fear arises out of the fact that 'the people' is not a single entity but rather a collection of individuals and groups, possessed of differing opinions and opposing interests. The 'democratic solution' to conflict is a recourse to numbers and the application of majority rule – the rule of the majority, or greatest number, should prevail over the minority. Democracy, in other words, comes down to the rule of the 51 per cent, a prospect which Alexis de Tocqueville (see p. 223) famously described as 'the tyranny of the majority'. Individual liberty and minority rights can thus both be crushed in the name of the people. A similar analysis was advanced by J.S. Mill. Mill believed not only that democratic election was no way of determining the truth – wisdom cannot be determined by a show of hands – but that majoritarianism would also damage intellectual life by promoting uniformity and dull conformism. A similar view was also expressed by James Madison at the US Constitutional Convention at Philadelphia in 1787. Madison argued that the best defence against such tyranny was a network of checks and balances, creating a highly fragmented system of government, often referred to as the 'Madisonian system'.

In other cases, a fear of democracy has sprung not so much from the danger of majority rule as from the nature of the majority in most, if not

James Madison (1751–1836)

US statesman and political theorist. Madison was a Virginian who was a keen advocate of American nationalism at the Continental Congress, 1774 and 1775. He helped to set up the Constitutional Convention in 1778, and played a major role in writing the Constitution. Madison served as Jefferson's secretary of state, 1801–9, and was the fourth president of the United States, 1809–17.

Madison's best known political writings are his contributions to *The Federalist* (1787–8), which campaigned for constitutional ratification. He was a leading proponent of pluralism and divided government, believing that 'ambition must be made to counteract ambition'. He therefore urged the adoption of federalism, bicameralism and the separation of powers. Madisonianism thus implies a strong emphasis upon checks and balances as the principal means of preventing tyranny. Nevertheless, when in office, Madison was prepared to strengthen the powers of national government. His views on democracy, often referred to as 'Madisonian democracy', stressed the need to resist majoritarianism by recognising the existence of diversity or multiplicity in society, and highlighted the need for a disinterested and informed elite independent from competing individual and sectional interests. Madison's ideas have influenced liberal, republican and pluralist thought.

all, societies. Echoing ancient reservations about popular rule, such theories suggest that democracy places power in the hands of those least qualified to govern: the uneducated masses, those likely to be ruled by passion and instinct rather than wisdom. In *The Revolt of the Masses* ([1930] 1961), for instance, Ortega Y Gasset warned that the arrival of mass democracy had led to the overthrow of civilised society and the moral order, paving the way for authoritarian rulers to come to power by appealing to the basest instincts of the masses. Whereas democrats subscribe to egalitarian principles, critics such as Gasset tend to embrace the more conservative notion of natural hierarchy. For many, this critique is particularly directed at participatory forms of democracy, which place little or no check upon the appetites of the masses. J.L. Talmon (1952), for example, argued that in the French Revolution the radically democratic theories of Rousseau made possible the unrestrained brutality of The Terror, a phenomenon Talmon termed 'totalitarian democracy'. Many have seen similar lessons in the plebiscitary forms of democracy which developed in twentieth-century fascist states, which sought to establish a direct and immediate relationship between the leader and the people through rallies, marches, demonstrations and other forms of political agitation.

Representation

Modern democratic theories are closely bound to the idea of representation. As stressed earlier, when citizens no longer rule directly, democracy is based upon the claim that politicians serve as the people's representatives. However, what does it mean to say that one person 'represents' another? In ordinary language, to represent means to portray or make present, as when a picture is said to represent a scene or person. In politics, representation suggests that an individual or group somehow stands for, or on behalf of, a larger collection of people. Political representation therefore acknowledges a link between two otherwise separate entities – government and the governed – and implies that through this link the people's views are articulated or their interests are secured. The precise nature of this link is, nevertheless, a matter of deep disagreement, as is the capacity of representation ever to ensure democratic government.

In practice, there is no single, agreed model of representation but rather a number of competing theories, each based upon particular ideological and political assumptions. Representatives have sometimes been seen as people who 'know better' than others, and can therefore act wisely in their interests. This implies that politicians should not be tied like delegates to the views of their constituents, but should have the capacity to think for themselves and use personal judgement. For many, however, elections are the basis of the representative mechanism, elected politicians being able to call themselves representatives on the grounds that they have been mandated by the people. What this mandate means and how it authorises politicians to act, is however a highly contentious matter. Finally, there is the altogether different idea that a representative is not a person acting on behalf of another, but one who is typical or characteristic of a group or society. Politicians are representatives, then, if they resemble their society in terms of age, gender, social class, ethnic background and so forth. To insist that politicians are a microcosm of society is to call for radical changes in the personnel of government in every country of the world.

Representatives or delegates?

In his famous speech to the electors of Bristol in 1774 Edmund Burke (see p. 139) informed his would-be constituents that 'your representative owes you, not his industry only, but his judgement; and he betrays, instead of serving you, if he sacrifices it to your opinion'. For Burke, the essence of representation was to serve one's constituents by the exercise of 'mature judgement' and 'enlightened conscience'. In short, representation is a moral duty: those with the good fortune to possess education and understanding should act in the interests of those who are less fortunate. In Burke's view, this position was justified by the fear that if MPs acted as ambassadors who took instructions directly from their constituents, Parliament would become a battleground for contending local interests, leaving no one to speak on behalf of the nation. 'Parliament', Burke emphasised, 'is a deliberative assembly of one nation, with one interest, that of the whole'.

A similar position was adopted in the nineteenth century by J.S. Mill, whose ideas constitute the basis of the liberal theory of representation. Though a firm believer in extending the franchise to working-class men, and an early advocate of female suffrage, Mill nevertheless rejected the idea that all political opinions are of equal value. In particular, he believed that the opinions of the educated are worth more than those of the uneducated or illiterate. This encouraged him, for instance, to propose a system of plural voting, allocating four or five votes to holders of learned diplomas or degrees, two or three to skilled or managerial workers, a single vote to ordinary workers and none at all to those who are illiterate. In addition, like Burke, he insisted that, once elected, representatives should think for themselves and not sacrifice their judgement to their constituents. Indeed, he argued that rational voters would wish for candidates with greater understanding than they possess themselves, ones who have had specialist knowledge, extensive education and broad experience. They will want politicians who can act wisely on their behalf, not ones who merely reflect their own views.

Although developed on a very different ideological basis, V.I. Lenin (see p. 82) also advanced the idea that politicians should act as representatives rather than delegates. As a Marxist revolutionary, Lenin was anxious that the exploited masses, the proletariat, achieved class consciousness and realised its revolutionary destiny. However, he warned that, deluded by bourgeois ideas and theories, the proletariat may never, by its own efforts, recognise the fact of its own exploitation: it may never become a revolutionary class. Thus Lenin pointed out the need for a revolutionary party, a vanguard party, composed of the most class-conscious elements within the proletariat. In effect, the revolutionary party should lead and guide the proletarian class, helping them to realise their revolutionary destiny. Lenin, moreover, acknowledged that the vanguard party would, in part, be distinguished from the proletariat by its level of education and by the presence within the party of a number of bourgeois intellectuals, like Lenin himself.

This theory of representation portrays professional politicians as representatives in so far as they are an educated elite. It is based upon the belief that knowledge and understanding are unequally distributed in society, in the sense that not all citizens are capable of perceiving their own best interests. If politicians therefore act as delegates, who, like ambassadors, receive instructions from a higher authority without having the capacity to question them, they may succumb to the irrational prejudices and ill-formed judgements of the masses. On the other hand, to advocate representation in preference to delegation is also to invite serious criticism. In the first place, the basic principles of this theory have anti-democratic implications: if politicians should think for themselves rather than reflect the views of the represented because the public is ignorant, poorly educated or deluded, surely it is a mistake to allow them to choose their representatives in the first place. Indeed, if education is the basis of representation, it could be argued that government should be entrusted to non-elected experts, selected, like the Mandarins of Imperial China, on the basis of examination success. Mill, in fact, did accept the need for a non-elected executive on such grounds. Furthermore, the link between representation and education is questionable. Whereas education may certainly be necessary to aid an understanding of intricate political and economic issues, it is far less clear that it helps politicians to make moral judgements about the interests of others. There is little evidence, for example, to support the belief which underpinned J.S. Mill's theory, and by implication those of Burke and Lenin, that education gives people a broader sense of social responsibility and a greater willingness to act altruistically.

The most serious criticism of this theory of representation is, however, that it grants representatives considerable latitude in controlling the lives of others. In particular, there is a danger that to the degree to which politicians are encouraged to think for themselves they may become insulated from popular pressures and end up acting in their own selfish interests. In this way, representation could become a substitute for democracy. This fear had traditionally been expressed by radical democrats such as Tom Paine (see p. 209). As a keen advocate of the democratic doctrine of popular sovereignty, Paine actively involved himself in both the American and French revolutions. Unlike Rousseau, however, he recognised the need for some form of representation. Nevertheless, the theory of representation he advocated in *Common Sense* ([1776] 1987) came close to the ideal of delegation. Paine proposed 'frequent interchange' between representatives and their constituents in the form of regular elections designed to ensure that 'the elected might never form to themselves an interest separate from the electors'. In addition to frequent elections, radical democrats have also supported the idea of popular initiatives, a system through which the general public can make legislative proposals, and the right of recall, which entitles the electorate to call unsatisfactory elected officials to account and ultimately to remove them. From this point of view, the democratic ideal is realised only if representatives are bound as closely as possible to the views of the represented.

Elections and mandates

For most people, representation is intimately tied up with elections, to such an extent that politicians are commonly referred to as representatives simply because they have been elected. This does not, however, explain how elections serve as a representative mechanism, or how they link the elected to the views of the electors. An election is a device for filling public offices by reference to popular preferences. That being said, electoral systems are widely divergent, some being seen as more democratic or representative than others. It is difficult, for instance, to argue that non-competitive elections, in which only a single candidate is placed before the electorate, can be regarded as democratic, since there is no electoral choice and no opportunity to remove office-holders. However, there are also differences amongst competitive electoral systems. In countries such as Britain, the United States, New Zealand and India, plurality systems exist, based upon the 'first-past-the-post' rule – the victorious candidate needs only acquire more votes than any single rival. Such systems do not seek to equate the overall number of seats won by each party with the number of votes it gains in the election. Typically, plurality systems 'over-represent' large parties and 'under represent' smaller ones. In the 1983 British general election, for example, the Alliance gained 26 per cent of the vote but won only 3.4 per cent of the seats of the House of Commons. By contrast, proportional electoral systems, used throughout continental Europe, employ various devices to ensure a direct, or at least closer, relationship between the votes cast for each party and the seats eventually won.

Regardless of the system employed, there are problems in seeing any form of election as the basis of representation. An election is only representative if its results can be interpreted as granting popular authority for particular forms of government action. In other words, an election must have a meaning. The most common way of imposing meaning upon an election result is to interpret it as providing a 'mandate' for the winning candidate or party, an idea that has been developed into a theory of representation, the so-called doctrine of the mandate. A mandate is an authoritative instruction or command. The doctrine of the mandate is based, first of all, upon the willingness of parties or candidates to set out their policy proposals through speeches or by the publication of manifestos. These proposals are, in effect, electoral promises, indicating what the party or candidate is committed to doing if elected. The act of voting can thus be understood as the expression of a preference from amongst the various policy programmes on offer. Victory in the election is therefore a reflection of the popularity of one set of proposals over its rivals. In this light, it can be argued that the winning party or candidate not only enjoys a popular mandate to carry out its manifesto pledges but has a duty to do so. The act of representation thus involves politicians remaining faithful to the policies upon which they were elected, which, in turn, provides an obvious justification for strict party discipline.

The great merit of the mandate doctrine is that it seems to impose some kind of meaning upon an election, and so offers popular guidance to those who exercise government power. However, the doctrine also has its drawbacks. For example, the doctrine acts as a straightjacket, limiting government policies to those positions and proposals the party took up during the election, and leaves politicians with no capacity to adjust policies in the light of ever-changing circumstances. The doctrine is therefore of no value in relation to events like international and economic crises which crop up unexpectedly. As a result, the more flexible notion of a 'mandate to rule' has sometimes been advanced in place of the conventional 'policy mandate'. The idea of a mandate to rule is, however, hopelessly vague and comes close to investing politicians with unrestricted authority simply because they have won an election.

It has, furthermore, been suggested that the doctrine of the mandate is based upon a highly questionable model of electoral behaviour. Specifically, it portrays voters as rational creatures, whose political preferences are determined by issues and policy proposals. In reality, there is abundant evidence to suggest that many voters are poorly informed about political issues and possess little knowledge of the content of manifestos. To some extent, voters are influenced by 'irrational' factors, such as the personality of party leaders, the image of parties, or habitual allegiances formed through social conditioning. Indeed, modern electoral campaigns fought largely on television have strengthened such tendencies by focusing upon personalities rather than policies, and upon images rather than issues. In no way, therefore, can a vote for a party be interpreted as an endorsement of its manifesto's contents or any other set of policies. Moreover, even if voters are influenced by policies, it is likely that they will be attracted by certain manifesto commitments, but may be less interested in or even opposed to others. A vote for a party cannot therefore be taken as an endorsement of its entire manifesto. Apart from those rare occasions when an election campaign is dominated by a single, overriding issue, elections are inherently vague and provide no reliable guide about which policies led one party to victory and others to defeat.

Finally, countries with plurality electoral systems have the further problem that governments can be formed on the basis of a plurality of votes rather than an overall majority. For instance, Bill Clinton was elected US president in 1992 on the basis of 43 per cent of the popular vote, and in 1997 the Blair government in Britain gained an overall majority in the House of Commons of 179 seats with only 44 per cent of the vote. When more voters oppose the elected government or administration than support it, it seems frankly absurd to claim that it enjoys a mandate from the people. On the other hand, proportional systems, which tend to lead to the formation of coalition governments, also get in the way of mandate democracy. In such cases, government policies are often hammered out through post-election deals negotiated by coalition partners. In the process, the policies which may have attracted support in the first place may be amended or traded-off as a compromise package of policies is constructed. It is not therefore possible to assume that all those who voted for one of the coalition parties will be satisfied by the eventual government programme. Indeed, it can be argued that such a package enjoys no mandate whatsoever because no set of voters has been asked to endorse it.

Characteristic representation

A final theory of representation is based less upon the manner in which representatives are selected than on whether or not they typify or resemble the group they claim to represent. This notion of representation is embodied in the idea of a 'representative cross-section', employed by market researchers and opinion pollsters. To be 'representative' in this sense it is necessary to be drawn from a particular group and to share its characteristics. A representative government would therefore be a microcosm of the larger society, containing members drawn from all groups and sections in society, in terms of social class, gender, religion, ethnicity, age and so forth, and in numbers that are proportional to their strength in society at large.

This theory of representation has enjoyed support amongst a broad range of theorists and political activists. It has, for instance, been accepted by many socialists, who believe that an individual's beliefs, attitudes and values tend to be shaped by their social background. Thus people's views can, in most cases, be traced back to their class origins, family circumstances, education, occupation and so on. This is why socialists have long believed that an obstacle to democracy exists in the fact that the political elite – ministers, civil servants, judges, police and military chiefs – are drawn disproportionately from the ranks of the privileged and prosperous. Because the working classes, the poor and the disadvantaged are 'underrepresented' in the corridors of power, their interests tend to be marginalised or ignored altogether. Feminist theorists (see p. 60) also show sympathy for this notion of representation, suggesting that patriarchy, dominance by the male sex, operates in part through the exclusion of women from the ranks of the powerful and influential in all sectors of life. Groups such as the National Organisation of Women (NOW) in the United States have therefore campaigned to increase the number of women in political and professional life. Anti-racist campaigners similarly argue that prejudice and bigotry is maintained by the 'under-representation' of racial minorities in government and elsewhere. Civil rights groups, particularly in the United States, have made an increase in minority representation in public life a major objective.

This theory of representation is based upon the belief that only people who are drawn from a particular group can genuinely articulate its interests. To represent means to speak for, or on behalf of, others, something that is impossible if representatives do not have intimate and personal knowledge of the people they represent. In its crudest form, this argument suggests that people are merely conditioned by their backgrounds and are incapable of or unwilling to understand the views of people different from themselves. In its more sophisticated form, however, it draws a distinction between the capacity to empathise or 'put oneself in the shoes of another' through an act of imagination, and, on the other hand, direct and personal experience of what other people go through, something which engages a deeper level of emotional response. This implies, for example, that although the so-called 'New Man' or 'profeminist' male, may sympathise with women's interests and support the principle of sexual equality, he will never be able to take women's problems as seriously as women do themselves. Men will therefore not regard the crime of rape as seriously as do women, since they are far less likely to be a victim of rape. In the same way, white liberals may show a laudable concern for the plight of ethnic minorities but, never having experienced racism, their attitude towards it is unlikely to match the passion and commitment that many members of minority communities feel. Similarly, those who come from affluent and secure backgrounds may never fully appreciate what it means to be poor or disadvantaged.

Nevertheless, the belief that representatives should resemble the represented, and that government should be a microcosm of the people, is by no means universally accepted. Many, in fact, regard it as a positive threat to democracy rather than as a necessary precondition. It could be argued, first, that people simply do not want to be ruled by politicians like themselves. Nowhere in the world can government be described as a representative cross-section of the governed and, ironically, the countries that have come closest to this ideal, orthodox communist regimes, were one-party states. Moreover, if politicians are selected on the basis that they are typical or characteristic of the larger society, government itself may simply reflect the limitations of that society. What is the advantage, for instance, of government resembling society when the majority of the population is apathetic, ill-informed and little educated? Critics of this idea of representation point out, as J.S. Mill emphasised, that good government requires politicians to be drawn from the ranks of the educated, the able and the successful.

A further danger is that this theory sees representation in exclusive or narrow terms. Only a woman can represent women; only a black can represent other blacks; only a member of the working class can represent the working classes, and so forth. If all representatives are concerned to advance the interests of the sectional groups from which they come, who is prepared to defend the common good or advance the national interest? Indeed, this form of representation may simply be a recipe for social division and conflict. In addition to this, characteristic representation must confront the problem of how its objective is to be achieved. If the goal is to make government a microcosm of the governed, the only way of achieving this is to impose powerful constraints upon electoral choice and individual freedom. For instance, political parties may have to be forced to select a quota of female and minority candidates; or certain constituencies may be set aside for candidates from particular backgrounds; or, more dramatically, the electorate may have to be divided on the basis of class, gender, race and so on, and only allowed to vote for candidates from their own group.

The public Interest

When the opportunity for direct popular participation is limited, as it is in any representative system, the claim to rule democratically is based upon the idea that, in some way, government serves the people or acts in their interests. Politicians in almost every political system are eager to claim that they work for the 'common good', or in the 'public interest'. Indeed, the constant repetition of such phrases has devalued them, rendering them almost meaningless. Too often the notion of the public interest serves merely to give a politician's views or actions a cloak of moral respectability. Yet the notion of a collective or public interest has played a vital role in political theory, and constitutes a major plank of the democratic ideal, in the form of 'government *for* the people'. The idea of a public interest has, however, been subjected to stern and often hostile scrutiny, especially in the late twentieth century. It has been pointed out, for example, that it is difficult, and perhaps impossible, to distinguish between the private interests of each citizen and what can be thought of as their collective or public interests. In the view of some commentators, the concept itself is misleading or simply incoherent. Moreover, attention has been given to how the public interest can in practice be defined. This has precipitated debate about what has been called the 'dilemma of democracy', and led to the suggestion that, though democratic rule may be desirable, no constitutional and electoral mechanism may exist through which it can be brought about.

Private and public interests

Political argument often turns on whether a particular action or policy is thought to be in somebody's interest, with little or no attention being paid to what that interest might be, or why it should be regarded as important. In its broadest sense, an 'interest' denotes some kind of benefit or advantage; the public interest is, then, what is 'good' for the people. However, what does this 'good' consist of, and who can define it? Interests may be nothing more than wishes or desires, defined subjectively by each individual for himself or herself. If so, interests have to be consciously acknowledged or manifest in some form of behaviour. Sociologists, for example, identify interests as the *'revealed* preferences' of individuals. On the other hand, an interest can be thought of as a need, requirement or even necessity, of which the individual may personally be entirely unconscious. This suggests the distinction, discussed in Chapter 5, between 'felt' or subjective interests and genuine or 'real' interests which have some objective basis.

The problem of defining interests runs through any discussion of the public interest, shrouding the issue in ideological debate and disagreement. Those who insist that all interests are 'felt' interests, or revealed preferences, hold that individuals are the only, or best, judges of what is good for them. By contrast, theorists who employ the notion of 'real' interests may argue that the public is incapable of identifying its own best interests because it is ignorant, deluded or has in some way been manipulated. In *Political Argument* (1990), however, Brian Barry attempted to bridge the gap between these two concepts by defining a person's interests as 'that which increases his or her opportunities to get what he or she wants'. This accepts that interests are 'wants' that can only be defined subjectively by the individual, but suggests that those individuals who fail to select rational or appropriate means of achieving their ends cannot be said to recognise their own best interests.

What are called 'private' interests are normally thought to be the selfish, and usually materialistic, interests of particular individuals or groups. This idea is based upon long-established liberal beliefs about human nature: individuals are separate and independent agents, each bent upon advancing his or her perceived interests. In short, individuals are egoistical and self-interested. Such a notion of private interests is inevitably linked to conflict, or at least competition. If private individuals act rationally, they can be assumed to prefer their own interests to those of others, to strive above all for their own 'good'. Socialists, however, have tended to reject such a notion. Rather than being narrowly self-interested, socialists believe human beings to be sociable and gregarious, bound to one another by the existence of a common humanity. The belief that human nature is essentially social has profound implications for any notion of private interests. To the extent that individuals are concerned about the 'good' of their fellow human beings, their private interests become indistinguishable from the collective interests of all. In other words, socialists challenge the very distinction between private and public interests, a position that inclines them towards a belief in natural social harmony, rather than conflict and competition.

Most political theorists, however, have accepted that a distinction can be drawn between private interests and the public interest. Any concept of the public interest must, in the first place, be based upon a clear understanding of what 'public' means. 'The public' stands for *all* members of a community, not merely the largest number or even overall majority. Whereas private interests are multiple and competing, the public interest is indivisible; it is that which benefits each and every member of the public. However, there are two, rather different, conceptions of what might constitute the public interest, the first of which is based upon the idea of shared or common interests. From this viewpoint, individuals can be said to share an interest if they perceive that the same action or policy will benefit each of them, in the sense that their interests overlap. The public interest therefore constitutes those private interests which all members of the community hold in common. An obvious example of this would be defence against external aggression, a goal which all citizens could reasonably be expected to recognise as being of benefit to them.

The alternative and more radical notion of the public interest is based not so much upon shared private interests as upon the interests of the public as a collective body. Instead of seeing the public as a collection of individuals, whose interests may or may not overlap, this view portrays the public as a collective entity possessed of distinct common interests. The classical proponent of this idea was Rousseau, who advanced it in the form of the 'general will'. In *The Social Contract* ([1762] 1969), Rousseau defined the general will as that 'which tends always to the preservation and welfare of the whole'. The general will therefore represents the collective interests of society; it will benefit all citizens, rather than merely private individuals. Rousseau thus drew a clear distinction between the general will and the selfish, private will of each citizen. The general will is,

---

Jean-Jacques Rousseau (1712–78)

Geneva-born French moral and political philosopher, perhaps the principal intellectual influence upon the French Revolution. Rousseau was entirely self-taught. He moved to Paris in 1742, and became an intimate of leading members of the French Enlightenment, especially Diderot. His autobiography, *Confessions* (1770), examines his life with remarkable candour and demonstrates a willingness to expose his faults and weaknesses.

Rousseau's writings, ranging over education, the arts, science, literature and philosophy, reflect a deep belief in the goodness of 'natural man' and corruption of 'social man'. His political teaching, summarised in *Émile* (1762) and developed in *Social Contract* (1762), advocates a radical form of democracy which has influenced liberal, socialist, anarchist and, some would argue, fascist thought. Rousseau departed from earlier social contract theories in being unwilling to separate free individuals from the process of government. He aimed to devise a form of authority to which the people can be subject without losing their freedom. He proposed that government be based upon the 'general will', reflecting the collective good of the community as opposed to the 'particular', and selfish, will of each citizen. Rousseau believed that freedom consists in political participation, obedience to the general will, meaning that he was prepared to argue that individuals can be 'forced to be free'. Rousseau envisaged such a political system operating in small, relatively egalitarian communities united by a shared civil religion.

in effect, what the people would wish if they were to act selflessly. The problem with such a notion of the public interest is that, so long as they persist in being selfish, it cannot be constructed on the basis of the revealed preferences of individual citizens. It is possible, in other words, that citizens may not recognise the general will as their own, even though Rousseau clearly believed that it reflected the 'higher' interests of each and every member of society.

Is there a public interest?

Despite the continued popularity of terms such as the 'common good' and the 'national interest', the idea of a public interest has been subject to growing criticism. Critics have suggested not only that politicians are prone to using such terms cynically but also that the concept itself may simply not stand up: the public may not have a collective interest. The principal advocates of such a view have subscribed to individualist or classical liberal creeds. Jeremy Bentham (see p. 361), for example, developed a moral and political philosophy on the basis that individuals sought to maximise what he called 'utility', calculated in terms of the quantity of pleasure over pain experienced by each individual. In other words, only individuals have interests, and each individual alone is able to define what that interest is. From this perspective, any notion of a public interest is bogus; the interests of the community are at best what Bentham called 'the sum of the interests of the several members who compose it'. The notion of a public interest as shared private interests therefore makes little sense simply because each member of the community will strive for something different: a collection of private interests does not add up to a coherent 'public interest'.

Individualists suggest that the issues over which all, or even most, citizens would agree, such as the need for public order or for defence against external aggression, are few and far between. Even when there is general agreement about a broad goal, such as maintaining domestic order, there will be profound differences about how that goal can best be achieved. For instance, is order more likely to be promoted by social equality and respect for civil liberty, or by stiff penalties and strict policing? Bentham's views contrast even more starkly with Rousseau's alternative notion of the public interest as the collective interests of the community. The idea of the general will is meaningless quite simply because collective entities like 'society', the 'community' and the 'public' do not exist. The nearest Bentham came to acknowledging the public interest was in his notion of general utility, defined as 'the greatest happiness for the greatest number'. However, this formula merely accepts that public policy should be designed to satisfy the 'greatest number' of private interests, not that it can ever serve the interests of all members of the public.

Similar ideas have been developed by modern pluralist theorists, who view politics in terms of competition between various groups and interests. The emergence of organised groups is explained by 'rational choice' (see p. 246) or 'public choice' theorists in terms of rational, self-interested behaviour. Individuals who may be powerless when they act separately can nevertheless exert influence by acting collectively with others who share a similar interest. Such an analysis, for example, can explain the emergence of trade unionism: the threat of strike action by a single worker can be disregarded by an employer, but an all-out strike by the entire workforce cannot be. This interpretation acknowledges the existence of shared interests and the importance of collective action. However, it challenges the conventional idea of a public interest. Interest groups are 'sectional' pressure groups, representing a section or part of society, ethnic or religious groups, trade unions, professional associations, employer's groups and so on. Each sectional group has a distinctive interest, which it seeks to advance through a process of campaigning and lobbying. This leaves no room, however, for a public interest: each group places its interest before those of the whole society. Indeed, the pluralist view of society as a collection of competing interests does not allow for society itself to have any collective interests.

Despite growing criticism, the concept of a public interest has not been abandoned by all theorists. Its defence takes one of two forms. The first rejects the philosophical assumptions upon which the individualist attack is based. In particular, this questions the image of human beings as being resolutely self-interested. It is clear, for example, that Rousseau regarded selfishness not as a natural impulse but as evidence of social corruption; human beings are, in Rousseau's view, essentially moral, even noble, creatures, whose genuine character is revealed only when they act as members of the community. Socialists uphold the idea of the public interest on the same grounds. The concept of the public interest, from a socialist perspective, gives expression to the fact that individuals are not separate and isolated creatures vying against one another, but social animals who share a genuine concern about fellow human beings and are bound together by common human needs. Nevertheless, it is also possible to defend the concept of the public interest from the perspective of rational choice theory, without relying upon socialist assumptions about human nature.

The notion of a public interest can only be dispensed with altogether if there is reason to believe that the pursuit of self-interest genuinely works to the benefit of at least the 'greatest number' in society. In reality, there are

Rational choice theory

Rational choice theory, with its various sub-divisions including public choice theory, social choice theory and game theory, emerged as a tool of political analysis in the 1950s and gained greater prominence from the 1970s onwards. Sometimes called formal political theory, it draws heavily upon the example of economic theory in building up models based upon procedural rules, usually about the rationally self-interested behaviour of individuals. Most firmly established in the United States, and associated in particular with the so-called Virginia School, rational choice theory has been used to provide insights into the actions of voters, lobbyists, bureaucrats and politicians. It has had its broadest impact upon political analysis in the form of what is called institutional public choice theory.

Using a method that dates back to Hobbes (see p. 124) and is employed in utilitarian theorising (see p. 360), rational choice theorists assume that political actors consistently choose the most efficient means to achieve their various ends. In the form of public choice theory, it is concerned with the provision of so-called public goods, goods that are delivered by government rather than the market, because, as with clean air, their benefit cannot be withheld from individuals who choose not to contribute to their provision. In the form of game theory, it has developed more from the field of mathematics than from the assumptions of neo-classical economics, and entails the use of first principles to analyse puzzles about individual behaviour. The best-known example of game theory is the 'prisoner's dilemma', which demonstrates that rationally self-interested behaviour can be generally less beneficial than cooperation.

Supporters of rational choice theory argue that it has introduced greater rigour into the discussion of political phenomena, by allowing political analysts to develop explanatory models in the manner of economic theory. By no means, however, has the rational choice approach to political analysis been universally accepted. It has been criticised for overestimating human rationality in that it ignores the fact that people seldom possess clear sets of preferred goals and rarely make decisions in the light of full and accurate knowledge. Furthermore, in proceeding from an abstract model of the individual, rational choice theory pays insufficient attention to social and historical factors, failing to recognise, amongst other things, that human self-interestedness may be socially conditioned, and not innate. Finally, rational choice theory is sometimes seen to have a conservative value bias, stemming from its initial assumptions about human behaviour.

$\longrightarrow$

Key figures

James Buchanan (1919–) A US economist, Buchanan used public choice theory to defend the free market and argue in favour of a minimal state. He developed the idea of constitutional economics to explain how different constitutional arrangements can affect a nation's social and economic development. This led to an analysis of the defects and economic distortions of democracy which emphasises, for instance, the ability of interest groups to make gains at the expense of the larger community. He supports tough constitutional limitations to keep the political market under control and prevent the expansion of state powers. Buchanan's main works include *Fiscal Theory and Political Economy* (1960), *The Calculus of Consent* (1962) and *Liberty, Market and the State* (1985).

Anthony Downs (1930–) A US economist and political analyst, Downs developed a theory of democracy based upon the assumptions of economic theory. His 'spatial model' of political behaviour, a sub-set of rational choice theory, presupposes a 'policy space' in which political actors, candidates and voters can measure where they stand in relation to other political actors. Influenced by Schumpeter (see p. 223), Downs portrayed parties as vote-maximising machines, anxious to develop whatever policies offer the best prospect of winning power. On this basis, he explained both the behaviour of political parties and the features of particular party systems. Downs' key political work is *An Economic Theory of Democracy* (1957).

Mancur Olson (1932–98) A US political scientist, Olson used public choice theory to analyse groups' behaviour. He argued that people join interest groups only to secure 'public goods'. As individuals can become 'free riders' by reaping the benefits of group action without incurring the cost of membership, there is no guarantee that the existence of a common interest will lead to the formation of an organisation to advance or defend that interest. Olson questioned pluralist assumptions about the distribution of group power, and suggested that strong networks of interest groups can threaten a nation's economic performance. His best-known works include *The Logic of Collective Action* (1968) and *The Rise and Decline of Nations* (1982).

Further reading

Barry, B. and Hardin, R. (eds) *Rational Man and Irrational Society?* Beverly Hills, CA: Sage, 1982.

Dunleavy, P. *Democracy, Bureaucracy and Public Choice: Economic Explanations in Political Science.* Hemel Hempstead: Harvester Wheatsheaf, 1991.

Self, P. *Government by the Market.* London: Macmillan, 1993.

persuasive reasons for believing that the unrestrained pursuit of self-interest tends ultimately to be self-defeating and that a society guided by private interests alone is doomed to frustration and unhappiness. This can be explained through reference to what economists call 'public goods', goods or services from which all individuals derive benefit but which none has an incentive to produce. Environmental concerns such as energy conservation and pollution demonstrate very clearly the existence of a public interest. The avoidance of pollution and the conservation of finite energy resources are undoubtedly public goods in that they are vital for both human health and, possibly, the long-term survival of the human species. Nevertheless, self-interested human beings may rationally choose to despoil the environment or waste vital resources. Private firms, for example, may pump poisonous waste into rivers and the sea on the grounds that it would clearly be more expensive to dispose of it in an environmentally friendly way, and also because each firm calculates that its waste alone is unlikely to cause serious damage. Obviously, if all firms act in the same way and for the same reasons, the result will be environmental devastation: the seas and rivers will die, disease will spread and everyone will suffer.

The idea of public goods thus highlights the existence of public or collective interests that are distinct from the private interests of either individuals or groups. It could be argued that these constitute the 'real' interest of the individuals concerned rather than their 'felt' interests. However, following Barry, this can perhaps be seen as a case of individuals and groups demonstrating that they do not recognise their own best interests. All people acknowledge the need for a clean and healthy environment, but, left to their own devices, they do not act to secure one. In such circumstances, the public interest can only be safeguarded by government intervention, designed to curb the pursuit of private interests for the collective benefit of the whole society.

Dilemmas of democracy

The drawback of any concept of the public interest derived from an abstract notion like the general will is that by distancing government from the revealed preferences of its citizens it allows politicians to define the public interest in almost whatever way they please. This danger was most grotesquely illustrated by the 'totalitarian democracies' which developed under fascist dictators such as Mussolini and Hitler, in which the democratic credentials of the regime were based upon the claim that 'the Leader', and the leader alone, articulated the genuine interests of the people. In this way, fascist leaders identified a 'true' democracy as an absolute dictatorship. In reality, however, no viable form of democratic rule can be based exclusively upon a claim to articulate the public interest – that claim must be subject to some form of public accountability. In short, no definition of the public interest is meaningful unless it corresponds at some point and in some way to the revealed preferences of the general public. This correspondence can only be ensured through the mechanism of popular elections.

One of the most influential attempts to explain how the electoral process ensures government in the public interest was undertaken by Anthony Downs in *An Economic Theory of Democracy* (1957). Downs explained the democratic process by drawing upon ideas from economic theory. He believed that electoral competition creates, in effect, a political market, in which politicians act as entrepreneurs bent upon achieving government power, and individual voters behave rather like consumers, voting for the party whose policies most closely reflect their preferences. Downs believed that a system of open and competitive elections serves to guarantee democratic rule because it places government in the hands of the party whose philosophy, values and policies most closely correspond to the preferences of the largest group of voters. Moreover, democratic competition creates a powerful incentive for the emergence of a policy consensus, in that parties will be encouraged to shift their policies towards the 'centre ground', in the hope of appealing to the largest possible number of electors. Although the 'economic theory of democracy' does not contain an explicit concept of the public interest, it is, nevertheless, an attempt to explain how electoral competition ensures that government pays regular attention to the preferences of at least a majority of the enfranchised population. This, indeed, may serve as at least a rough approximation of the public interest.

Downs's model of democratic politics was not meant to be an exact description of the real world, but rather, like economic theories, a sufficiently close approximation to help us understand how such a system works. Nevertheless, it has its limits. In the first place, it assumes a relatively homogeneous society, forcing parties to develop moderate or centrist policies that will have broad electoral appeal. Clearly, in societies deeply divided on racial or religious lines, or by social inequality, party competition may simply ensure government in the interests of the largest sectional group. Furthermore, as a general tendency, it could be argued that party competition shifts politics away from any notion of the public interest since it encourages parties to frame policies which appeal to the immediate private and sectional interests of voters rather than to their more abstract, shared interests. For example, parties are noticeably reluctant to propose tax increases that will discourage the use of finite fossil fuels, or to tackle problems like global warming and ozone depletion, because such policies, though in the long-term public interest, will not win votes at the next election.

Downs's model may also be based upon questionable assumptions about the rationality of the electorate and the pragmatic nature of electoral politics. As discussed in the previous section, voters may be poorly informed about political issues and their electoral preferences may be shaped by a range of 'irrational' factors like habit, social conditioning, the image of the party and the personality of its leader. Similarly, parties are not always prepared to construct policies simply on the basis of their electoral appeal; to some extent, they attempt to shape the political agenda and influence the values and preferences of ordinary voters. The workings of the political market can, for instance, be distorted as effectively by party propaganda as the economic market is by the use of advertising. Finally, the responsiveness of the political market to voters' preferences may also be affected by the level of party competition, or lack of it. In countries such as Japan and Britain where single parties have enjoyed long periods of uninterrupted power, the political market is distorted by strong monopolistic tendencies. Two-party systems, as exist in the United States, Canada, New Zealand and Australia, can be described as duopolistic. Even the multi-party systems of continental Europe can be seen, at best, as oligopolistic, since coalition partners operate rather like cartels in that they try to restrict competition and block entry into the market.

A further, and some would argue more intractable, problem is that no constitutional or elective mechanism may be able reliably to give expression to the collective or public interest. Downs's 'economic' version of democratic politics operates on the assumption that voters only have a single preference because traditional electoral systems offer them a single vote. However, in the complex area of government policy, where a wide range of policy options are usually available, it is reasonable to assume that voters will have a scale of favoured options which could be indicated through a preferential voting system. The significance of such preferences was first highlighted in the field of welfare economics by Kenneth Arrow, whose *Social Choice and Individual Values* (1963) discussed the problem of 'transitivity'. This suggests that when voters are able to express a number of preferences it may be impossible to establish which option genuinely enjoys public support. Take, for instance, the example of an election in which candidate A gains 40 per cent of the vote, candidate B receives 34 per cent, and candidate C gets 26 per cent. In such a situation it is clearly possible to argue that no party represents the public interest because none receives an overall majority of votes – though candidate A could obviously make the strongest claim to do so on the grounds of achieving a plurality, more votes than any other single candidate. Nevertheless, the situation may become still more confused when second preferences are taken into account.

Let us assume that the second preferences of all candidate A supporters go to candidate C; the second preferences of candidate B favour candidate A; and the second preferences of candidate C go to candidate B. This creates a situation in which each candidate could claim to be preferred by a majority of voters. The combined first and second preferences for candidate A add up to 74 per cent (40 per cent plus B's 34 per cent); candidate B could claim 60 per cent support from the electorate (34 per cent plus C's 26 per cent); and candidate C could claim 66 per cent support (26 per cent plus A's 40 per cent). In other words, an examination of the second or subsequent preferences of individual voters can lead to the problem of 'cyclical majorities' in which it is difficult, and perhaps impossible, to arrive at a collective choice which could reasonably be described as being in the public interest. Although A's claim to office may still be the strongest, it is severely compromised by the majorities that B and C also enjoy. Arrow described this as the 'impossibility theorem'. It suggests that even if the concept of a public interest is meaningful and coherent, it may be impossible to define that interest in practice through any existing constitutional or electoral arrangements.

The implications of Arrow's work for democratic theory are profound and depressing. If no reliable link can be made between individual preferences and collective choices, two possibilities are available. The first option, proposed by James Buchanan and Gordon Tulloch in *The Calculus of Consent* (1962), is that the range of issues decided by collective choice should be extremely limited, leaving as many as possible in the hands of free individuals. Buchanan and Tulloch propose that collective decisions are only appropriate where policies elicit unanimous agreement, at least amongst elected representatives, a position which would be consistent with only the most minimal state. The alternative is to accept that, since election results cannot speak for themselves, politicians who use the term 'public interest' always impose their own meaning upon it. All references to the public interest are therefore, to some extent, arbitrary. Nevertheless, this latitude is not unlimited because there is the possibility of calling politicians to account at the next election. For this point of view, the democratic process may simply be a means of reducing this arbitrary element by ensuring that politicians who claim to speak *for* the public must ultimately be judged *by* the public.

Summary

1   A number of models of democracy can be identified. The principal distinction is between the classical ideal of direct democracy, in which people literally govern themselves – government *by* the people – and more modern forms of representative democracy, in which professional politicians govern on behalf of the people – government *for* the people.

2   The most successful form of democracy has been liberal democracy, founded upon the twin principles of limited government and popular consent expressed at election time. The strength of liberal democracy is that by upholding individual liberty and making possible a high degree of popular responsiveness it is able to maintain political stability.

3   Representation means, broadly, acting on behalf of others, but opinions differ about how this is best achieved. Some argue that representatives should think for themselves, exercising their own wisdom or judgement; others believe that representatives have a mandate from the voters to fulfil their election pledges; still others think that representatives must resemble or be drawn from the group they aim to represent.

4   All notions of democracy are based, to some degree, upon the idea that government can and does act in the public interest, the common or collective interests of society. But individualists and pluralists have questioned whether there is any such thing as public interest separate from the private interests of citizens. Others have doubted if there exists an electoral or constitutional mechanism through which the public interest can in practice be defined.

Further reading

Arblaster, A. *Democracy*. Milton Keynes: Open University Press and Minneapolis: University of Minnesota Press, 1994.

Birch, A.H. *Representation*. London: Macmillan, 1972 and New York: Praeger, 1971.

Bogdanor, V. and Butler, D. *Democracy and Elections: Electoral Systems and Their Consequences*. Cambridge: Cambridge University Press, 1983.

Dahl, R. *Dilemmas of Pluralist Democracy*. New Haven, CT.: Yale University Press, 1982.

Flathman, R. *The Public Interest*. New York: John Wiley, 1966.

Harrop, M. and Miller, W. *Elections and Voters: A Comparative Introduction*. London: Macmillan and New York: New Amsterdam, 1987.

Held, D. *Models of Democracy*. Oxford: Polity and Stanford: Stanford University Press, 1996.

Schultze, C. *The Public Use of Private Interest*. Washington, DC: Brookings Institute, 1977.

Chapter 9

![line]

Freedom, Toleration and Liberation

Introduction
Freedom
Toleration
Liberation
Summary
Further reading

Introduction

The principle of freedom has customarily been treated by political thinkers with a degree of reverence that borders on religious devotion. Political literature is littered with proclamations that humankind should break free from some form of enslavement. Rousseau lamented that 'Man is born free but is everywhere in chains'; Marx concluded the *Communist Manifesto* with the words, 'Workers of the world unite. You have nothing to lose but your chains'; and the American Declaration of Independence proclaims that human beings are 'endowed by their Creator with certain unalienable rights'. Yet the popularity of freedom is often matched by confusion about what the term actually means, and why it is so widely respected. Is freedom, for instance, an unconditional good, or does it have costs or drawbacks? How much freedom should individuals and groups enjoy? At the heart of such questions, however, lies a debate about precisely what it means to be 'free'. Does freedom mean being left alone to act as one chooses, or does it imply some kind of fulfilment, self realisation or personal development?

Confusion is also caused by the fact that freedom is often associated with a range of other terms, notably liberty, rights, toleration and liberation. Most people treat 'freedom' and 'liberty' as interchangeable terms and they will be regarded as synonymous in what follows. The confusion between 'freedom' and 'rights' stems from the tendency to speak of a right of freedom, as in the right to freedom of speech, the right to freedom of religious worship, and so on. Nevertheless, a clear analytical distinction must be made between a right, as an entitlement to act or be treated in a particular way, and that to which one is entitled, which may involve the exercise of what is called freedom. The case of 'toleration' is, however, different: there is a sense in which toleration can be thought of as a manifestation of freedom. As the willingness to put up with actions or opinions with which we may disagree, toleration affords individuals a broader opportunity to act as they please or choose. In the eyes of many, toleration is an essential precondition for

→

253

harmony and social stability, guaranteeing that we can live together without encroaching upon one another's rights and liberties. Others warn, however, that toleration can also go too far, encouraging people to tolerate the intolerable and threatening the very basis of social existence. How far should toleration go, and where should the limits of toleration be set? In the twentieth century, moreover, a new language of freedom has emerged in the growth of so-called 'liberation' movements, proclaiming the need for national liberation, women's liberation, sexual liberation and so forth. The idea of liberation seems to promise a more complete and 'inner' fulfilment than more conventional terms like liberty and emancipation imply. However, why have oppressed groups been drawn to the idea of liberation, and does the idea of liberation in any sense represent a distinctive and coherent form of freedom?

Freedom

Freedom is a difficult term to discuss because it is employed by social scientists and philosophers as commonly as by political theorists. In each case the concern with freedom is rather different. In philosophy, freedom is usually examined as a property of the will. Do individuals possess 'free will' or are their actions entirely determined? Clearly, the answer to this question depends upon one's conception of human nature and, more importantly, the human mind. In economics and sociology, freedom is invariably thought of as a social relationship. To what extent are individuals 'free agents' in social life, able to exercise choice and enjoy privileges in relation to others? By contrast, political theorists often treat freedom as an ethical ideal or normative principle, perhaps as the most vital such principle. In many cases, however, they separate the definition of what freedom is from questions about its value, allowing them to employ an essentially social-scientific definition of the term. Nevertheless, as a popular political slogan 'freedom' undoubtedly functions as an ideal – but it is one which cries out for analytical attention and clarity.

Perhaps the best way of giving shape to freedom is by distinguishing it from 'unfreedom'. Most people are willing, for instance, to accept a difference between 'liberty' and what is called 'licence'. However, where that distinction should be drawn is the source of considerable controversy. Furthermore, it is by no means clear what we mean by the term 'freedom'. For example, by highlighting the various forms which freedom can take, political thinkers have long treated freedom as an 'essentially contested' concept. In the early nineteenth century, the French liberal Benjamin Constant (see p. 209) distinguished between what he called 'the liberty of the ancients', by which he meant direct and collective participation in political life, and 'the liberty of the moderns', which referred to independence from government and from the encroachment of others. The most influential attempt to do this in the twentieth century was undertaken by Isaiah Berlin in his essay 'Two Concepts of Liberty' ([1958] 1969). Berlin (see p. 30) claimed to identify a 'positive' concept of freedom and a 'negative' concept of freedom. In everyday language, this has sometimes been understood as a distinction between being 'free to' do something, and being 'free from' something.

Such a distinction has, however, been widely criticised. For instance, the difference between freedom *to* and freedom *from* is merely a confusion of language: each example of freedom can be described in both ways. Being 'free to' gain an education is equivalent to being 'free from' ignorance; being 'free from' excessive taxation simply means being 'free to' spend one's money as one wishes. In 'Negative and Positive Freedom' (1972) G.C. MacCallum went further and proposed a single, value-free concept of freedom in the form: 'X is free from Y to do or be Z'. MacCallum's formula helps to clarify thought about freedom in a number of ways. In the first place, it suggests that the apparently deep question 'Are we free?' is meaningless, and should be replaced by a more complete and specific statement about what we are free from, and what we are free to do. For instance, it brings out the fact that while we may be free from one obstacle, like physical assault, we are not free from others, such as laws which prevent us assaulting fellow citizens. Similarly, we can be free from the same obstacle, Y, in this case the law, to do one thing – smoke tobacco – but not another, like smoking marijuana. Finally, it helps to explain how people disagree about freedom. Most commonly, this occurs over what can count as an obstacle to freedom, what can count as Y. For example, while some argue that freedom can only be restricted by physical or legal obstacles, others insist that a lack of material resources, social deprivation and inadequate education may be a cause of unfreedom.

Liberty and licence

The term freedom crops up more frequently in the writings and speeches of politicians than perhaps any other political principle. Indeed, it is almost universally accepted as being morally 'good', and its opposites – oppression, imprisonment, slavery or unfreedom – are regarded as undesirable, if not as morally 'bad'. In its simplest sense, freedom means to do as one wishes or act as one chooses. In everyday language, for example, being 'free' suggests the absence of constraints or restrictions, as in freedom of speech: an unchecked ability to say whatever one pleases. However, few people are prepared to support the removal of all restrictions or constraints upon the individual. As R.H. Tawney (see p. 313) pointed out, 'The freedom of the pike is death to the minnows'.

Only anarchists, who reject all forms of political authority as unnecessary and undesirable, are prepared to endorse unlimited freedom. Others insist upon a distinction between two kinds of self-willed action, between 'liberty' and 'licence'. This distinction can nevertheless create confusion. For example, it implies that only morally correct conduct can be dignified with the title 'freedom' or 'liberty'. However, as many political theorists employ a value-free or social-scientific understanding of such terms, they are quite prepared to accept that certain freedoms – such as the freedom to murder – should be constrained. In that sense, the liberty/licence distinction merely begs the question: which freedoms are we willing to approve, and which ones are we justified in curtailing?

'Licence' means the abuse of freedom; it is the point at which freedom becomes 'excessive'. Whereas liberty is usually thought to be wholesome, desirable and morally enlightening, licence is oppressive, objectionable and morally corrupt. There is, however, deep ideological controversy about the point at which liberty starts to become licence. Libertarians, for instance, seek to maximise the realm of individual freedom and so reduce to a minimum those actions which are regarded as licence. Although both socialists and liberals have at times been attracted to libertarianism (see p. 340), in the late twentieth century it has increasingly been linked to the defence of private property and the cause of free market capitalism. Right-wing libertarians such as Robert Nozick (see p. 320) and Milton Friedman see freedom in essentially economic terms and advocate the greatest possible freedom of choice in the marketplace. An employer's ability to set wage levels, alter conditions of work, and to decide who to employ or not employ, can therefore be seen as manifestations of liberty. On the other hand, socialists have often regarded such behaviour as licence, on the grounds that the freedom of the employer may mean nothing more than misery and oppression for his or her workers. Fundamentalist socialists may go so far as to portray all forms of private property as licence since they inevitably lead to the exploitation of the poor or propertyless. Clear ethical grounds must therefore be established in order to distinguish between what can be commended as liberty and what should be condemned as licence.

The problem with establishing the desirable realm of liberty is that there are a bewildering number of grounds upon which freedom can be upheld. In much liberal political thought (see p. 29), freedom is closely related to the notion of rights. As pointed out earlier, this occurs because the tendency is to treat freedom as a right or entitlement. Indeed, the two concepts become almost fused, as when 'rights' are described as 'liberties'. One of the attractions of a rights-based theory of freedom, whether these are thought to be 'natural', 'human' or 'civil' rights, is that it enables a clear distinction to be made between liberty and licence. In short, liberty means acting according to or within one's rights, whereas licence means to act beyond one's rights or, more particularly, to abuse the rights of others. For example, employers are exercising liberty when they are acting on the basis of their rights, derived perhaps from the ownership of property or from a contract of employment, but are straying into the realm of licence when they start to infringe upon the rights of their employees.

However, this distinction becomes more complex when it is examined closely. In the first place, rights are always balanced against one another, in the sense that most actions can have adverse consequences for other people. In this sense, freedom is a zero-sum game: when one person, an employer, gains more freedom, someone else, an employee, loses it. It is impossible, therefore, to ensure that the rights of all are respected. More serious, however, is the problem of defining who has rights and why. As emphasised in Chapter 7, individual rights are the subject of deep political and ideological controversy. For example, whereas most liberals and conservatives insist that the right to property is a fundamental human right, many socialists and certainly communists would disagree. In the same way, socialists and modern liberals uphold the importance of social rights, like the right to health care and education, while supporters of the New Right have argued that individuals alone are responsible for such matters.

An alternative means of distinguishing between liberty and licence was proposed by J.S. Mill (see p. 258). As a libertarian who believed that individual freedom was the basis for moral self-development, Mill proposed that individuals should enjoy the greatest possible realm of liberty. However, as discussed in Chapter 6, Mill also recognised that unrestrained liberty could become oppressive, even tyrannical. In *On Liberty* ([1859] 1972), Mill proposed a clear distinction between 'self-regarding' actions and 'other-regarding' actions, suggesting that each individual should exercise sovereign control over his or her own body or life. The only justification for constraining the individual, Mill argued, was in the event of 'harm' being done to others. In effect, the 'harm principle' indicates the point at which freedom becomes 'excessive', the point at which liberty becomes licence.

Although this distinction may appear to be clear and reliable, the notion of 'harm' being more concrete than the idea of 'rights', it nevertheless provokes controversy. This largely centres upon what is meant by 'harm'. If the principle is understood, as Mill intended it to be, to refer merely to physical harm, it allows a very broad range of actions to be regarded as liberty. Mill was clearly prepared to allow individuals absolute freedom to think, write and say whatever they wish, and also to allow them to undertake harmful actions, so long as they are self-regarding. Mill would not, therefore, have tolerated any form of censorship or restrictions upon

---

John Stuart Mill (1806–73)

British philosopher, economist and politician. Mill was subjected to an intense and austere regime of education by his father, the utilitarian theorist James Mill, graphically described in his *Autobiography* (1873). This resulted in a mental collapse at the age of 20, after which he developed a more human philosophy influenced by Coleridge and the German Idealists. He founded and edited the *London Review* and was MP for Westminster, 1865–8.

Mill's work was crucial to the development of liberalism because it straddled the divide between classical and modern theories. In *On Liberty* (1859) he advanced an eloquent defence of freedom based upon the principle that the only justification for restricting individual freedom is to prevent 'harm to others'. His opposition to collectivist tendencies and traditions, including those embodied in majoritarian democracy, was rooted in a commitment to 'individuality'. His essay, *Utilitarianism* (1861), was designed to outline the basic themes of the utilitarian tradition (see p. 360), but departed from them in emphasising the difference between 'higher' and 'lower' pleasures. In *Considerations on Representative Government* (1861), Mill discussed the representative and electoral mechanisms he believed would balance broader participation against the need for an intellectual and moral elite. *The Subjection of Women* (1869), written in collaboration with his wife Harriet Taylor, proposed that women should enjoy the same rights and liberties as men, including the right to vote.

---

the use of dangerous drugs. However, if the notion of 'harm' is broadened to include psychological, moral and even spiritual harm, it can be used to classify a far more extensive range of actions as licence. For example, the portrayal of violence, pornography or blasphemy on television may be regarded as morally harmful in the sense that it is corrupting and offensive. The same confusion occurs when 'harm' is taken to include economic or social disadvantage. For instance, the imposition of a pay freeze by an employer may not harm his or her employees in a physical sense but undoubtedly harms their interests.

Most attempts to distinguish between liberty and licence refer in some way to the principle of equality. If liberty is thought to be a fundamental value, surely it is one to which all human beings are entitled. Thus, those who employ a rights-based theory of freedom invariably acknowledge the importance of 'equal rights'; and Mill insisted that the 'harm principle' applied equally to all citizens. This implies that another way of distinguishing between liberty and licence is through the application of the principle of equal liberty. In other words, liberty becomes licence not when the rights of another are violated, or when harm is done to others, but when liberty is unequally shared out. John Rawls (see p. 299) expressed this in the principle that each person is entitled to the greatest possible liberty compatible with a like liberty for all. On the face of it, most liberal democracies respect the principle of equal liberty, reflected in the fact that, at least in theory, political, legal and social rights are available to all citizens. However, the doctrine of equal liberty is bedevilled by problems about how freedom is defined. If freedom consists of exercising a set of formal rights, the task of measuring freedom and ensuring that it is equally distributed is easy: it is necessary simply to ensure that no individual or group enjoys special privileges or suffers from particular disadvantages. This can be achieved by the establishment of formal equality, equality before the law. The matter becomes more complicated, however, if freedom is understood not as the possession of formal rights but as the opportunity to take advantage of these rights. Modern liberals and social democrats (see p. 312), for example, argue that the principle of equal liberty points to the need to redistribute wealth and resources in society. Such disagreements go to the very heart of the debate about the nature of freedom and, in particular, to the difference between negative and positive conceptions of freedom.

Negative freedom

Freedom has been described as 'negative' in two different senses. In the first, law is seen as the main obstacle to freedom. Such a view is negative in the sense that freedom is limited only by what others deliberately prevent us from doing. Thomas Hobbes (see p. 124), for instance, described freedom as the 'silence of the laws'. This contrasts with 'positive' freedom, as modern liberals and socialists use the term, which focuses upon the *ability* to act, and so, for instance, sees a lack of material resources as a source of unfreedom. Isaiah Berlin ([1958] 1969), on the other hand, used the term in a different way. He defined negative freedom as 'an area within which a man can act unobstructed by others'; freedom therefore consists of a realm of unimpeded action. To so define negative freedom is, however, to include within its bounds the socialist view outlined above. What is in question is not the nature of freedom so much as the obstacles which impede that freedom – laws or social circumstances. As a result, Berlin used the term positive freedom to refer to autonomy or self-mastery, an idea that will be discussed more fully in the next section.

Although some have portrayed negative conceptions of freedom as value-free, it is difficult to deny that they have clear moral and ideological implications. If freedom refers, in some way, to the absence of external constraints upon the individual, a commitment to liberty implies that definite limits be placed upon both law and government. Law, by definition, constrains individuals and groups because, through the threat of punishment, it forces them to obey and to conform. To advocate that freedom should be maximised does not, however, mean that law should be abolished, but only that it should be restricted to the protection of one person's liberty from the encroachments of others. This is what John Locke (see p. 269) meant when he suggested that law does not restrict liberty so much as defend or enlarge it. Government should similarly be restricted to a 'minimal' role, amounting in practice to little more than the maintenance of domestic order and personal security. For this reason, advocates of negative freedom have usually supported the minimal state and sympathised with *laissez-faire* capitalism. This is not to say, however, that state intervention in the form of economic management or social welfare can never be justified, but only that it cannot be justified in terms of freedom. In other words, theorists who conceive of freedom in negative terms always recognise a trade-off between equality and social justice on the one hand, and individual liberty on the other.

The notion of negative freedom has often been portrayed in the form of 'freedom of choice'. For example, in *Capitalism and Freedom* (1962) by Milton Friedman, 'economic freedom' consists of freedom of choice in the marketplace – the freedom of the consumer to choose what to buy, the freedom of the worker to choose a job or profession, the freedom of a producer to choose what to make and who to employ. According to Friedman, this vital freedom is found only in free market capitalist economies, in which 'freedom' in effect means the absence of government interference. The attraction of 'choice' to theorists of freedom is that it highlights an important aspect of individual liberty. To choose implies that the individual makes a voluntary or unhindered selection from amongst a range of alternatives or options. Consequently, it is reasonable to assume that a choice reflects a person's preferences, wants or needs. Quite simply, they are in a position to act otherwise if they so wish. When workers, for instance, select one job rather than another this surely indicates that that job is the one which best satisfies the inclinations and interests of the worker concerned. However, if freedom is reflected in the exercise of choice, the options available to the individual must be reasonable ones. What might be considered a 'reasonable' option may in practice be difficult to establish. For example, at times of high unemployment, or when most available jobs are poorly paid, is it possible to regard a worker's choice of a job as a voluntary and self-willed action? Indeed, classical Marxists (see p. 81) argue that since workers have no other means of subsistence they are best thought of as 'wage slaves': the likely alternative to work is poverty and destitution.

To conceive of freedom in negative terms, as the absence of external interference, links freedom very closely to the idea of privacy. Privacy is a deeply respected principle in Western societies, and is regarded by many as a core liberal-democratic value. Privacy suggests a distinction between a 'private' or personal realm of existence, and some kind of 'public' world. Advocates of negative freedom often regard this private sphere of life, consisting very largely of family and personal relationships, as a realm within which people can 'be themselves'. It is an arena in which individuals should therefore be left alone to do, say and think whatever they please. Any intrusion into the privacy of a person is, in this sense, an infringement of their liberty. To prize negative freedom is clearly to prefer the 'private' to the 'public', and to wish to enlarge the scope of the former at the expense of the latter. For example, a commitment to negative freedom could provide the basis for arguing that education, the arts, social welfare and economic life should be entirely 'private' and so be left to individuals to determine as they see fit. A very different tradition of political thought, however, sees public life not as a realm of duty and unfreedom, but as an arena within which cooperation, altruism and social solidarity are promoted. From this point of view, the demand for privacy may simply reflect a flight from social responsibility into isolation, insularity and selfishness.

The case for negative freedom is based very firmly upon faith in the human individual and, in particular, in human rationality. Free from interference, coercion and even guidance, individuals are able to make their own decisions and fashion their own lives. The result of this will be, as Bentham (see p. 361) put it, the greatest happiness for the greatest number, simply because individuals are the only people who can be trusted to identify their own interests. Any form of paternalism, however well intentioned, robs the individual of responsibility for his or her own life, and so infringes upon liberty. This is not, of course, to argue that left to their own devices individuals will not make mistakes, both intellectual and moral, but simply to say that if they are in a position to learn from their mistakes they have a better opportunity to develop and grow as human beings. In short, morality can never be taught or imposed; it can only arise through voluntary action. In sharp contrast, however, opponents of negative freedom have suggested that it amounts to 'freedom to starve'. When individuals are simply 'left alone' they may be prey to economic misfortune or the arbitrary justice of the market; they may be in no position to make rational or informed choices. Such a line of thought has led to the emergence of a rival, 'positive' conception of freedom.

Positive freedom

As indicated earlier, positive freedom, no less than negative freedom, can be understood in two ways. For Berlin, positive freedom consists of 'being one's own master'. It is therefore equivalent to democracy – a people is said to be free if it is self-governing, and unfree if it is not. Thus freedom is concerned with the question 'By whom am I governed?' rather than 'How much am I governed?'. Indeed, a *demos* that imposes many restrictive laws on itself may be positively free but negatively quite unfree. In its other sense, however, positive freedom relates to the ideas of self-realisation and personal development. Being likened to the capacity of human beings to act and fulfil themselves, this conception of freedom is more concerned with the distribution of material or economic resources. It is often seen as the antithesis of negative freedom in that, instead of justifying the contraction of state power, it is more commonly linked to welfarism and state intervention. The notion of positive freedom therefore encompasses a broad range of theories and principles, whose political implications are diverse and sometimes contradictory. In effect, freedom may be positive in that it stands for effective power, self-realisation, self-mastery or autonomy, or moral or 'inner' freedom.

One of the earliest critiques of negative freedom was developed by modern liberals in the late nineteenth century who found the stark injustices of industrial capitalism increasingly difficult to justify. Capitalism had swept away feudal obligations and legal restrictions but still left the mass of working people subject to poverty, unemployment, sickness and disease. Surely such social circumstances constrained freedom every bit as much as laws and other forms of social control. Behind such an argument, however, lies a very different conception of freedom, often traced back to the ideas of J.S. Mill. Although Mill appeared to endorse a negative conception of freedom, the individual's sovereign control over his or her own body and mind, he nevertheless asserted that the purpose of freedom was to encourage the attainment of individuality. 'Individuality' refers to the distinctive and unique character of each human individual, meaning that freedom comes to stand for personal growth or self-development. One of the first modern liberals openly to embrace a 'positive' conception of freedom was the British philosopher T.H. Green (1836–82), who defined freedom as the ability of people 'to make the most and best of themselves'. This freedom consists not merely in being left alone but in having the effective power to act, shifting attention towards the opportunities available to each human individual. It is a form of freedom that has been eagerly adopted by modern social democrats, including Bryan Gould (1985) and Roy Hattersley (1985).

In the hands of modern liberals and social democrats, this conception of freedom has provided a justification for social welfare. The welfare state, in other words, enlarges freedom by 'empowering' individuals and freeing them from the social evils that blight their lives – unemployment, homelessness, poverty, ignorance, disease and so forth. However, to define freedom as effective power is not to abandon negative freedom altogether.

All liberals, even modern ones, prefer individuals to make their own decisions and to expand the realm of personal responsibility. The state, therefore, only acts to enlarge liberty when it 'helps individuals to help themselves'. Once social disadvantage and hardship are abolished, citizens should be left alone to take responsibility for their own lives. Nevertheless, this doctrine of positive freedom has also been roundly criticised. Some commentators, for example, see it simply as a confusion in the use of language. Individuality, personal growth and self-development may be *consequences* of freedom, but they are not freedom itself. In other words, freedom is here being mistaken for 'power' or 'opportunity'. Moreover, other critics, particularly amongst the New Right, have argued that this doctrine has given rise to new forms of servitude since, by justifying broader state powers, it has robbed individuals of control over their own economic and social circumstances. This critique is discussed at greater length in Chapter 10, in relation to welfare.

Freedom has also been portrayed in the form of self-realisation or self-fulfilment. Freedom in this sense is positive because it is based upon want-satisfaction or need-fulfilment. Socialists, for example, have traditionally portrayed freedom in this way, seeing it as the realisation of one's own 'true' nature. Karl Marx (see p. 373), for instance, described the true realm of freedom as the 'development of human potential for its own sake'. This potential could be realised, Marx believed, only by the experience of creative labour, working together with others to satisfy our needs. From this point of view, Robinson Crusoe, who enjoyed the greatest possible measure of negative freedom since no one else on his island could check or constrain him, was a stunted and unfree individual, deprived of the social relationships through which human beings achieve fulfilment. This notion of freedom is clearly reflected in Marx's concept of 'alienation'. Under capitalism, labour is reduced to being a mere commodity, controlled and shaped by de-personalised market forces. In Marx's view, capitalist workers suffer from alienation in that they are separated from their own genuine or essential natures: they are alienated from the product of their labour; alienated from the process of labour itself; alienated from their fellow human beings; and, finally, alienated from their 'true' selves. Freedom is therefore linked to the personal fulfilment which only un-alienated labour can bring about.

There is no necessary link, however, between this conception of positive freedom and the expanded responsibilities of the state. Indeed, this form of freedom could be perfectly compatible with some form of negative freedom: the absence of external constraints may be a necessary condition for the achievement of self-realisation. In the case of anarchism, for example, the call for the abolition of all forms of political authority casts freedom in starkly negative terms, but the accompanying belief in cooperation and social solidarity gives it also a strongly positive character. For Marx, unalienated labour would only be possible within a classless, communist society in which the state, and with it all forms of political authority, had 'withered away'. Advocates of negative freedom, however, may nevertheless firmly reject this and other conceptions of positive freedom. By imposing a model of human nature upon the individual – assuming, in this case, sociable and cooperative behaviour – such ideas do not allow people simply to seek fulfilment in whatever way they may choose.

A final conception of positive freedom links the idea of liberty to the notions of personal autonomy and democracy. This is clearly reflected in the writings of Rousseau (see p. 243), who in *The Social Contract* ([1762] 1969) described liberty as 'obedience to a law one prescribes to oneself'. In Rousseau's view, freedom means self-determination, the ability to control and fashion one's own destiny. In other words, citizens are only 'free' when they participate directly and continuously in shaping the life of their community. This is the essence of what Berlin called 'positive freedom' and Constant referred to as 'the liberty of the ancients'. Both, however, argued that this conception of freedom is a serious threat to personal independence and civil liberty in the modern, negative sense, even though some republican theorists (see p. 208) have attempted to balance the claims of negative freedom against those of positive freedom. For Rousseau, freedom ultimately meant obedience to the general will, in effect, the common good of the community. In that sense, Rousseau believed the general will to be the 'true' will of each individual citizen, in contrast to their 'private' or selfish will. By obeying the general will, citizens are therefore doing nothing other than obeying their own 'true' natures. It follows, therefore, that those who refuse to obey the general will, so denying their own 'true' wills, should be compelled to do so by the community; they should, in Rousseau's words, be 'forced to be free'. Rousseau thus distinguished between a 'higher' and a 'lower' self, and identified freedom with moral or 'inner' liberty: a freedom from internal constraints like ignorance, selfishness, greed and so forth.

A very similar tradition of freedom can be found in the religious idea that 'perfect freedom' means doing the will of God, submitting to our 'moral' nature, rather than indulging our 'immoral' drives, inclinations and passions. However, such a conception of freedom may also be compatible with gross violations of what is generally taken to be political liberty. If citizens can be 'forced to be free', for instance, they are no longer in a position to determine for themselves what is freedom and what is unfreedom. The danger of any notion of 'inner' or 'higher' freedom is that it places the definition of freedom in the hands of another. The most grotesque manifestation of this conception of freedom is found in fascist theory, where the community is portrayed as an indivisible organic whole, its interests being articulated by a single all-powerful leader. In such circumstances, 'true' freedom comes to mean absolute submission to the will of the leader.

Toleration

Debate about the proper realm of individual freedom often centres upon the idea of toleration. How far should we tolerate the actions of our neighbours, and when, if ever, are we justified in constraining what they might do, think or say? By the same token, what kind of behaviour, opinions and beliefs should society be prepared to put up with? Toleration is both an ethical ideal and a social principle. On the one hand, it represents the goal of personal autonomy, but on the other hand, it establishes a set of rules about how human beings should interact with each another. In neither case, however, does toleration simply mean allowing people to act in whatever way they please. Toleration is a complex principle, whose meaning is often confused with related terms such as 'permissiveness' and 'indifference'. However, like freedom, the value of tolerance is often taken for granted; it is regarded as little more than a 'good thing'. What is the case for toleration, what advantages or benefits does it bring either society or the individual? Nevertheless, toleration is rarely considered to be an absolute ideal: at some point a line must be drawn between actions and views that are acceptable and ones that are simply 'intolerable'. What are the limits of toleration? Where should the line be drawn?

Toleration and permissiveness

In everyday language, tolerance, the quality of being tolerant, is often understood to mean a willingness to 'leave alone' or 'let be', with little reflection upon the motives that lie behind such a stance. Indeed, from this point of view, toleration suggests inaction, a refusal to interfere or willingness to 'put up with' something. Toleration, however, refers to a particular form of inaction, based upon moral reasoning and a specific set of circumstances. In particular, toleration must be distinguished from permissiveness, blind indifference and willing indulgence. For example, a parent who simply ignores the unruly behaviour of his or her children, or a passer-by who chooses not to interfere to apprehend a mugger, cannot be said to be exhibiting 'tolerance'.

Permissiveness refers to a social attitude in which permission is given for people to act as they think best. To 'permit' means simply to allow, and in that sense it is morally neutral since no judgement is being made about the behaviour in question. For example, to give permission for a speech to be made, a meeting to be held or a demonstration to take place, implies neither approval nor disapproval of what is to be said or done; the speech, meeting or demonstration are neither 'good' nor 'bad'. A permissive stance can stem from one of two positions. The first is a belief in moral relativism, the idea that there are no absolute values or standards, implying that ethics is a matter of personal judgement for each human being. From this point of view, for example, homosexuality can be regarded as morally correct in that the freely-chosen behaviour of the people concerned makes it so. The alternative position, however, is one which regards large areas of life as being morally indifferent. In this case, a permissive attitude to homosexuality may simply reflect the belief that there is nothing morally wrong with it; it is not a matter about which moral judgements should be made.

It has often been suggested that the social morality of the 1960s was characterised by permissiveness. This was evident in changing attitudes towards various forms of behaviour, from premarital sex and homosexuality to the use of drugs. In many cases, the argument for the relaxation of social norms and moral codes was clearly permissive. The emerging gay and lesbian movement, for instance, argued that an individual's sexual preference is entirely a matter of personal choice, homosexuality and heterosexuality being equally valid in moral terms. The youth culture of the period demanded that matters such as dress, personal appearance and private morality should be left to the individual. By refusing to accept the authority of established moral or religious principles, the permissive ethic can be said to have spawned a form of 'moral anarchy'. However, only anarchists are consistently prepared to support permissiveness because only they are willing to leave *all* moral decisions in the hands of the individual. For anarchists, permissiveness represents the ideal of personal and moral autonomy. Other thinkers are less willing to endorse permissiveness in relation to behaviour that affects other people or society at large. Conservative theorists (see p. 138) in particular have feared that 'moral anarchy' deprives individuals of vital moral guidance and leaves society without a bedrock of common ethical beliefs.

Toleration, by contrast, has been more closely associated with the liberal tradition, though it finds support amongst socialists and some conservatives. Toleration resembles permissiveness in that it is a refusal to interfere with, constrain or check the behaviour or beliefs of others. However, it differs from permissiveness in that this non-interference exists in spite of the fact that the behaviour and beliefs in question are disapproved of, or simply disliked. Tolerantion, in other words, is not morally neutral; it does not reflect either moral indifference or moral relativism. In that sense, toleration is a form of forbearance, it exists when there is a clear capacity to impose one's views on another but a deliberate refusal to do so. Putting up with what cannot be changed is clearly not toleration. It would be absurd, for example, to describe a slave as tolerant of his servitude simply because he or she chooses not to rebel. Similarly, a battered wife who stays with her abusive husband out of fear can hardly be said to tolerate his behaviour.

Although toleration means forbearance, a refusal to impose one's will on others, it does not mean non-interference. The fact that a moral judgement is made leaves the opportunity open for influence to be exerted over others, but only in the form of rational persuasion. There is undoubtedly a difference, for example, between 'permitting' a person to smoke and 'tolerating' their smoking. In the latter case, the fact that smoking is disapproved of, or disliked, may be registered, and an attempt made to persuade the person to stop or even give up smoking. However, toleration demands that forms of persuasion be restricted to rational argument and debate, because once some form of cost or punishment is imposed, even in the form of social ostracism, the behaviour in question is being constrained. It is difficult, for instance, to argue that smoking is being tolerated if it could lead to the loss of friendship, damage to career prospects, or if it can only take place in a restricted area. In fact, these are better examples of intolerant behaviour.

Intolerance refers, quite obviously, to a refusal to accept the actions, views or beliefs of others. Not only is there moral disapproval or simple dislike, but there is also some kind of attempt to impose constraints upon others. However, the term intolerance undoubtedly has pejorative connotations. Whereas 'tolerance' (the quality of being tolerant) is usually thought to be laudable and even enlightened – a tolerant person is patient, forgiving and philosophical – 'intolerance' suggests an unreasoned and unjustified objection to the views or actions of another, bringing it close to bigotry or naked prejudice. Intolerance suggests an objection to that which should have been tolerated. Thus laws which discriminate against people on grounds of race, colour, religion, gender or sexual preference, are often described as intolerant. The apartheid system which developed in South Africa is clearly therefore an example of racial intolerance; while the imposition of dress codes upon women and their exclusion from professional and public life in fundamentalist Islamic states can be described as sexual intolerance. On the other hand, there is also a sense in which tolerance can imply weakness or simply a lack of moral courage. If something is 'wrong', surely it should be stopped. This aspect of tolerance is conveyed by the term 'intolerable', meaning that something should no longer be accepted and, indeed, *can* no longer be accepted. There are, quite simply, no grounds for tolerating the intolerable. In certain circumstances, therefore, intolerance may not only be defensible – it may even be a moral duty.

The case for toleration

Toleration is one of the core values of Western culture and may even be its defining one. Indeed, it is commonly believed that human and social progress is tied up with the advance of toleration and that intolerance is somehow 'backward'. For example, it is widely argued that as Western societies have abandoned restrictions upon religious worship, ceased to confine women to subordinate social roles, and tried to counter racial discrimination and prejudice, they have thereby become more 'socially enlightened'. As the climate of toleration has spread from religious to moral and political life, it has enlarged the realm of what is usually taken to be individual liberty. The cherished civil liberties which underpin liberal-democratic political systems – freedom of speech, association, religious worship and so forth – are all, in effect, guarantees of toleration. Moreover, although it may be impossible to legislate bigotry and prejudice out of existence, the law has increasingly been used to extend toleration rather than constrain it, as in the case of legislation prohibiting discrimination on grounds of race, religion, gender and sexual preference. What this does not demonstrate, however, is why toleration has been so highly regarded in the first place.

The case for toleration first emerged during the Reformation of the sixteenth and seventeenth centuries, a time when the rising Protestant sects challenged the authority of the Pope and the established Catholic church. Preaching the new and radical doctrine of 'individual salvation', Protestantism generated a strong tradition of religious dissent, reflected in the work of writers such as John Milton (1608–74) and John Locke. In *A Letter Concerning Toleration* ([1689] 1963), Locke advanced a number of arguments in favour of toleration. He suggested, for instance, that as the proper function of the state is to protect life, liberty and property, it has no right to meddle in 'the care of men's souls'. However, Locke's central argument was based upon a belief in human rationality. 'Truth' will only emerge out of free competition amongst ideas and beliefs and must therefore be left to 'shift for herself'. Religious truth can only be established by the individual for himself or herself; it cannot be taught, and should not be imposed by government. Indeed, Locke pointed out that even if religious truths could be known, they should not be imposed upon dissenters because religious belief is ultimately a matter of personal faith.

Locke's argument amounts to a restatement of the case for privacy, and has been widely accepted in liberal democracies within which the distinction between public and private life is regarded as vital. Toleration should be extended to all matters regarded as 'private' on the grounds that, like religion, they fall within a realm of personal faith rather than revealed

John Locke (1632–1704)

English philosopher and politician. Born in Somerset, Locke studied medicine at Oxford before becoming secretary to Anthony Ashley Cooper, first Earl of Shaftesbury. His political views were developed against the background of, and were shaped by, the English Revolution.

Locke was a consistent opponent of absolutism (see p. 164) and is often portrayed as the philosopher of the 'Glorious Revolution' of 1688, which established a constitutional monarchy in England. He is usually seen as a key thinker of early liberalism. His *Two Treatises of Civil Government* (1690) used social contract theory to emphasise the importance of natural rights, identified as the right to 'life, liberty and estate (property)'. As the purpose of government is to protect such rights, government should be limited and representative; however, the priority he accorded property rights prevented him from endorsing political equality or democracy in the modern sense. His *A Letter Concerning Toleration* (1689) defends freedom of religious conscience on the grounds that rulers are always uncertain about the meaning of true religion; but he allowed that religion could be constrained if it threatened order, which meant, Locke argued, not extending toleration to atheists or Roman Catholics.

truth. Many would argue, therefore, that moral questions should be left to the individual to decide simply because no government is in a position to define 'truth', and even if it were it would have no right to impose it upon its citizens. In 'public' affairs, however, where the interests of society are at stake, there is a clearer case for limiting toleration. Locke, for example, was not prepared to extend the principle of toleration to Roman Catholics, who, in his view, were a threat to national sovereignty since they gave allegiance to a foreign Pope.

Perhaps the most famous defence of toleration was made in the nineteenth century in J.S. Mill's *On Liberty* ([1859] 1972). For Mill, toleration was of fundamental importance to both the individual and society. Whereas Locke outlined a distinctive case for toleration in itself, Mill saw toleration as little more than one face of individual liberty. At the heart of Mill's case for toleration lies a belief in individuals as autonomous agents, free to exercise sovereign control over their own lives and circumstances. Autonomy, in his view, is an essential condition for any form of personal or moral development; it therefore follows that intolerance, restricting the range of individual choice, can only debase and corrupt the individual. Mill was, for this reason, particularly fearful of the threat to autonomy posed by the spread of democracy and what he called 'the despotism of custom'. The greatest threat to individual freedom lay not in restrictions imposed by formal laws but in the influence of public opinion in a majoritarian age. Mill feared that the spread of 'conventional wisdom' would promote dull conformity and encourage individuals to submit their rational faculties to the popular prejudices of the age. As a result, he extolled the virtues of individuality and even eccentricity.

In Mill's view, toleration is not only vital for the individual but it is also an essential condition for social harmony and progress. Toleration provides the necessary underpinning for any balanced and healthy society. As with other liberals, Mill subscribed to an empiricist theory of knowledge, which suggests that 'truth' will only emerge out of constant argument, discussion and debate. If society is to progress, good ideas have to displace bad ones, truth has to conquer falsehood. This is the virtue of cultural and political diversity: it ensures that all theories will be 'tested' in free competition against rival ideas and doctrines. Moreover, this process has to be intense and continuous because no final or absolute truth can ever be established. Even democratic elections provide no reliable means of establishing truth because, as Mill argued, the majority may be wrong. The intellectual development and moral health of society therefore demand the scrupulous maintenance of toleration. Mill expressed this most starkly by insisting that if the whole of society apart from a single individual held the same opinion, they would have no more right to impose their views upon the individual than the individual would have to impose his or her views upon society.

Limits of toleration

Although widely regarded in Western societies as an enlightened quality, toleration is rarely regarded as an absolute virtue. Toleration should be limited simply because it can become 'excessive'. This is particularly clear in relation to actions that are abusive or damaging. No one would advocate, for instance, that toleration should be extended to actions which, in Mill's words, do 'harm to others'. However, what people believe, what they say or may write about, raises much more difficult questions. One line of argument, usually associated with the liberal tradition, suggests that what people think and the words they use are entirely their own business. Words, after all, do no harm. To interfere with freedom of conscience, or freedom of expression, is simply to violate personal autonomy. On the other hand, it is possible to argue that both the individual and society may be endangered by the failure to set limits to what people can say or believe. For example, toleration itself may need to be protected from intolerant ideas and opinions. In addition, it is possible that words themselves may be harmful, either in the sense that they can cause anxiety, alarm or offence, or in that they may foster aggressive or damaging forms of behaviour.

Political toleration is usually regarded as an essential condition for both liberty and democracy. Political pluralism, the unrestricted expression of all political philosophies, ideologies and values, ensures that individuals are able to develop their own views within an entirely free market of ideas, and that political parties compete for power on a level playing field. However, should toleration be extended to the intolerant? Should parties which reject political pluralism and which, if elected to power, would ban other parties and suppress open debate, be allowed to operate legally? The basis for banning such parties is surely that toleration is not granted automatically, it has to be earned. In that sense, all moral values are reciprocal: only the tolerant deserve to be tolerated, only political parties which accept the rules of the democratic game have a right to participate in it. The danger of failing to appreciate this point was dramatically underlined by the example of Hitler and the German Nazis. The Weimar Republic, created in 1918, remodelled Germany on liberal democratic lines; it introduced a highly proportional electoral system and permitted unrestricted political competition. Despite the failed Munich *putsch* of 1923, which demonstrated the anti-constitutional character of the Nazis, Hitler was soon able to portray himself once again as a respectable and democratic politician. This charade was, however, exposed within weeks of Hitler coming to power in 1933, as he set about banning other parties, manipulating elections and eventually constructing a one-party Nazi dictatorship. By contrast, the Federal Republic of Germany, born after the war, took steps to protect itself from excessive toleration, taking upon itself the power to ban anti-constitutional parties and by depriving parties with less than 5 per cent support of representation in the Bundestag.

On the other hand, to ban political parties or suppress the expression of political views, even in defence of toleration, may simply contribute to the disease itself. Intolerance in the name of toleration is certainly ambiguous and may be impossible. In the first place, political intolerance of any kind can lead to witch-hunts and stimulate a climate of suspicion and paranoia. In the United States in the 1950s, for instance, Senator Joseph McCarthy's 'Un-American Activities Committee' aimed to root out card-carrying communists, whose political allegiances were to Moscow rather than Washington, and whose Marxist-Leninist principles made them sympathetic towards Soviet-style single party rule. However, the definition of what was 'un-American' expanded to encompass democratic socialists, left liberals and progressives of all kinds, and McCarthyism came to resemble the kind of political intolerance it was designed to fight. In practice, to define terms such as 'extremist', 'undemocratic', 'anti-constitutional' and so forth, is notoriously difficult. Moreover, it is often argued that to ban parties for the expression of bigoted, insulting or offensive views does little to combat them, but, by driving them underground, may actually help them to grow stronger. Intolerance cannot be combated by intolerance; the best way of tackling it is to expose it to criticism and defeat it in argument. At the heart of such an argument lies faith in the power of human reason: if the competition is fair, good ideas will push out bad ones. The problem is, however, as demonstrated by the history of Weimar Germany, that at times of economic crisis and political instability 'bad' ideas can possess a remarkable potency.

The issue of censorship raises similar questions about the limits of toleration. The traditional liberal position is that what a person reads or watches, and how a person conducts his or her personal life and sexual relationships, is entirely a matter of individual choice. No 'harm' is done to anyone – so long as only 'consenting adults' are involved – or to society. Others argue, however, that tolerance amounts to nothing more than the right to allow that which is 'wrong'. Mere disapproval of immorality is no way of fighting evil. Such a view was, for example, advanced in the United States in the 1980s by groups such as Moral Majority and by a growing number of neo-conservative critics, who warned that a society that is not bound together by a common culture and shared beliefs faces the likely prospect of decay and disintegration. This position, however, is based upon the assumption that there exists an authoritative moral system – in this case, usually fundamentalist Christianity – which is capable of distinguishing between 'right' and 'wrong'. In the absence of an objective definition of 'evil', society is in no position to save the individual from moral corruption. In modern multi-cultural and multi-religious societies it has to be doubted that any set of values can be regarded as authoritative. To define certain values as 'established', 'traditional' or 'majority' values may simply be an attempt to impose a particular moral system upon the rest of society.

A specific ground for censorship is sometimes suggested in the notion of offence. For example, the portrayal of sex and violence in literature, television and the cinema is sometimes regarded as an 'obscenity' in the sense that it provokes disgust and outrages accepted standards of moral decency. The 'Rushdie affair', however, has highlighted the particular importance of religious offence, and raised questions which strain the conventional understanding of toleration. In 1989 the Iranian religious leader, Ayatollah Khomeini (see p. 103), issued a *fatwa* or religious order sentencing to death the British author Salman Rushdie for the publication of his book *The Satanic Verses*. The basis for the *fatwa* was that the book offends against the most cherished of Islamic principles, the sacred image of the Prophet Mohammed. From the traditional liberal viewpoint, this action amounts to a gross violation of both Rushdie's rights as a human individual and the principle of tolerance. It is no more defensible to forbid the criticism of religious ideas than it is to enforce religious views upon others.

However, although liberals firmly believe that to prohibit a book, speech or idea on the grounds that it is 'wrong' is unacceptable, they may nevertheless not be insensitive to the offence which has been caused. There is little doubt in this case, for instance, that, regardless of its contents, the book is regarded by Muslims in many parts of the world as a threat to the very foundation of Islamic culture and self-respect. Some have suggested, as a result, that when offence goes to the core of a community's identity it may provide grounds for limiting toleration. At the same time, of course, what Islamic fundamentalists have called for offends against the most fundamental principles of Western culture. What this conflict perhaps highlights, therefore, is the incompatibility of the liberal-democratic principle of tolerance and any form of religious fundamental-ism.

A final argument in favour of censorship is based upon the belief that what people read, hear or think is likely to shape their social behaviour. In the case of pornography, for example, an unlikely alliance has been forged between feminist groups concerned about violence against women, and neo-conservatives who support what has been called the 'New Puritanism'. Both groups believe that the debased and demeaning portrayal of women in newspapers, on television and in the cinema has contributed to a rise in the number of rapes and other crimes against women. Such a link between the expression of views and social behaviour has long been accepted in the case of racism. The incitement of racial hatred has been made illegal in Britain and many other liberal democracies on the grounds that it encourages, or at least legitimises, racist attacks and creates a climate of genuine apprehension within minority communities. However, unlike racist literature which may openly call for attacks upon minority groups, the link between the portrayal of women in the media, in advertising and throughout popular culture, and the abusive or criminal behaviour of men, may be more difficult to establish. The processes at work in the latter case are largely insidious and unconscious, not easily susceptible to empirical investigation.

Liberation

Since the 1960s, the term 'liberation' has increasingly been used to describe both political movements and the goal they strive for. The fight against colonialism in the developing world was often portrayed as a struggle for 'national liberation'. The feminist movement was reborn as the women's liberation movement, and came to embrace the goal of 'sexual liberation'. Radical priests in Latin America who denounced social inequality and political oppression, embraced what they called Liberation Theology. At first sight, liberation merely seems to be a synonym for freedom; after all, to 'liberate' means to free or to escape. However, the term is more than just a fashionable slogan. It denotes a particular form of political liberty and a distinctive style of political movement. Liberation implies not merely the removal of constraints upon the individual or even the promotion of individual self-development, but rather the overthrow of what is seen as an all-encompassing system of subjugation and oppression. Liberation marks nothing less than a historic break with the past: the past represents oppression and unfreedom, while the future offers the prospect of complete human satisfaction. The term liberation therefore tends to possess a quasi-religious character in that, whether it refers to an oppressed nation, ethnic group, gender or an entire society, it offers a vision of human life as entirely satisfying and completely fulfilling.

Although liberation movements, which proclaim the possibility of complete emancipation from a pervasive 'system of exploitation', are usually regarded as a modern development, the roots of the idea lie in a much older tradition of political millenarianism. Literally, this means a belief in the 'millennium', the establishment on earth of a thousand-year 'Kingdom of God'. Millenarian sects and movements, such as the Diggers of the English Civil War and the Shakers and Mormons of nineteenth-century United States, often espoused political beliefs and values as well as religious doctrines. They sought, in other words, to establish an entirely new system of living. For instance, under the leadership of Gerrard Winstanley the Diggers argued not only for the overthrow of clerical privilege but also for a crude type of communism. Although modern liberation movements may not embrace millenial beliefs, or, with the exception of Liberation Theology, openly endorse religious doctrines, they nevertheless practise a highly moralistic style of politics. Existing society is rejected as fundamentally corrupt, and a utopian future is eagerly anticipated. This is why many conservatives and some liberals see liberation politics as positively dangerous, believing that it turns the rationalist principle of individual freedom into a quasi-mystical doctrine.

National liberation

Nationalist movements have been in existence since the early nineteenth century. Traditionally, the goal of nationalism has been the establishment of national self-determination, brought about either through unification or by the overthrow of foreign rule. The goal of 'national liberation', however, is of more modern origin and reflects the emergence of the new and more radical style of nationalist politics embraced by self-styled 'liberation fronts' and linked to the ideas of anticolonialism (see p. 102). For example, in 1954, under the leadership of Ahmed Ben Bella, an Algerian National Liberation Front was founded to fight the French; a Vietnamese National Liberation Front was formed in 1960 by groups opposed, first, to French rule and, subsequently, to United States involvement; and 1964 saw the formation of the Palestine Liberation Organisation (PLO), an umbrella organisation which campaigned against Israel for the formation of a secular Palestinian state. By adopting the goal of national liberation such groups were setting themselves apart from more traditional forms of nationalism, both conservative nationalism, which tended to be insular and backward-looking, and liberal nationalism, which campaigned for the limited goals of independence and national unification. National liberation, by contrast, fused nationalist and socialist goals: 'liberation' stood not just for independence but also for full economic and social emancipation. Indeed, the goal of national liberation moved nationalism beyond its traditional political objective – the formation of a nation-state – by holding out the prospect of social revolution, cultural renewal and even psychological regeneration.

National liberation movements have typically embraced some form of revolutionary socialism, usually Marxism. On the surface, nationalism and Marxism share little in common except mutual antipathy. Marxism, for instance, espouses a form of internationalism, and has usually regarded nationalism as, at best, a deviation from the class struggle, if not as a form of 'bourgeois ideology'. Nevertheless, Marxism exerted a powerful appeal in the third world, both because it offered an analysis of oppression and exploitation that helped to make sense of the colonial experience, and because it held out the prospect of fundamental social change. The form of Marxism adopted was usually Marxism-Leninism, the attraction of which was theoretical as well as practical. In theoretical terms, Lenin's unbending commitment to a revolutionary road to socialism coincided with the belief of many third world nationalists that colonialism could only be overthrown by a violent uprising, an 'armed struggle'. Moreover, Lenin (see p. 82) had been the first Marxist thinker to draw attention to the economic roots of colonialism. In *Imperialism, the Highest Stage of Capitalism* ([1916] 1970) he portrayed imperialism as a form of economic exploitation through which capitalist countries maintained profit levels by exporting capital to the developing world and by gaining the benefits of cheap labour and raw materials. In practical terms, the adoption of Marxist-Leninist principles was encouraged, in the 1960s and 1970s at least, by the inducement of financial and military support from the Soviet Union. National liberation thus came to mean much more than simply the overthrow of colonial rule: it promised an end to all forms of oppression, colonial, social and economic, and so held out the prospect of full economic and political emancipation.

The idea of national liberation also has an important cultural dimension. Colonial oppression is often thought to operate as much through cultural stereotypes and values as through political control, military power and economic manipulation. Colonialism is so difficult to root out because, in a sense, it has been 'internalised'; colonised peoples find it difficult to challenge or throw off colonial rule because they have been indoctrinated by a culture of inferiority, passivity and subordination. Such an analysis has been particularly evident within the black liberation movement in the United States and elsewhere. Stokely Carmichael (1968), for example, one of the Black Power leaders of the 1960s, proclaimed that he was fighting in the US and throughout the third world a 'system of international white supremacy coupled with international capitalism'. The root of this system, however, was what Carmichael called 'cultural imposition', a process through which the oppressed are encouraged to regard their oppression as natural, inevitable and unchallengeable. The first step to rebelling against this all-pervasive oppression is therefore an 'inner' refusal, a form of cultural renewal. As a result, the black nationalist movement has often stressed the need for 'consciousness raising' and a rediscovery of pride in its black or Afro-Caribbean roots. Such ideas led the Jamaican political thinker and activist, Marcus Garvey (see p. 103), to found the African Orthodox Church in an effort to inculcate a distinctive black consciousness, and in the 1960s led to the growth of the Black Muslim movement under the leadership of Malcolm X.

The 'inner' or psychological dimension of national liberation was emphasised by the Algerian revolutionary and psychiatrist, Frantz Fanon (see p. 103). In *The Wretched of the Earth* (1962), written in the light of the Algerian liberation struggle, Fanon developed a powerful critique of the psychological impact of colonialism. In Fanon's view, colonialism has created a culture of subordination which renders colonial peoples politically impotent and incapable of rebellion. He argued that the only way to break through this impotence and passivity was through the regenerative experience of violence: only by killing or attacking the colonial master can the slave regain a sense of pride, power and purpose. In this way, therefore, 'national liberation' ultimately proclaims the need for a revolution of the human psyche.

Sexual liberation

As with nationalist movements, the feminist or women's movement (see p. 60) first emerged in the nineteenth century. During that period and for the early part of the twentieth century it was principally concerned with liberal values such as equal rights and with the goal of political emancipation, in particular, the quest for female suffrage. This is usually referred to as 'first wave' feminism. During the 1960s, however, a more radical and militant wing of the feminist movement emerged, styling itself the women's liberation movement. In one sense, the idea of 'women's liberation' came to stand broadly for any action that would improve the social role of women. However, at the same time the use of the term 'liberation' indicated a more radical, even revolutionary, analysis of female oppression, and the development of a new style of politics. It is these radical theories that have given modern or 'second wave' feminism its distinctive character.

Radical feminists differ from their predecessors in believing that women are not merely disadvantaged by a lack of rights or opportunities, or by economic inequality, but are confronted by a system of sexist oppression which pervades every aspect of life, political, economic, social, personal and sexual. This system of oppression is often described as 'patriarchy', literally the 'rule of the father' but is usually taken to describe the dominance of men and subordination of women in society at large. For radical feminists such as Kate Millett (see p. 61), patriarchy has been a social constant; it is found in all societies, contemporary and historical. Moreover, patriarchy is the most pervasive and fundamental form of political oppression, gender inequality running deeper than class exploitation, racial discrimination and so forth. To call for 'women's liberation' is therefore to demand not just political reform but a social, cultural and personal revolution: the overthrow of patriarchy.

Radical feminists have emphasised the degree to which patriarchy is rooted in a process of cultural domination. In *Patriarchal Attitudes* ([1970] 1987), Eva Figes drew attention to the prevalence of patriarchal values and beliefs in modern culture, philosophy, morality and religion. Kate Millett's *Sexual Politics* ([1970] 1990) highlights the sexist character, even misogyny, of much modern literature, and analyses the process of 'conditioning' through which from a very early age boys and girls are encouraged to conform to very specific gender identities. In Millet's view, male domination is reproduced in each generation by the family, 'patriarchy's chief institution', which systematically prepares boys for the role of domination and accustoms girls to accepting subordination. This is why modern feminists insist that 'the personal is the political'. At the very least, the goal of liberation means a re-examination of traditional family roles and a redistribution of domestic and child-rearing responsibilities. For some radical feminists, it may require the outright abolition of the family and a wholesale social revolution. This revolution, however, seeks to address not merely economic, social and political issues but also opens up the prospect of personal development and, above all, sexual fulfilment.

The idea of 'sexual liberation' has developed out of the writings of the Austrian psychiatrist and founder of psychoanalysis, Sigmund Freud (1856–1939). Freud's writings were noted amongst other things for the stress he placed upon the role of sexuality or what he came to call the 'pleasure principle'. In his view, the desire for sexual gratification was the most powerful of all human drives, other activities like work, sport and intellectual enquiry being the result of sublimated sexual energy. For Freud himself, sublimation was the very foundation of an ordered and civilised society: without it human beings would simply embark upon unrestrained sexual fulfilment, leaving all other considerations to one side. Later thinkers, however, drew more radical conclusions from Freud's work.

One of Freud's collaborators, Wilhelm Reich (1897–1957), invented the term 'sexual politics' to describe what he believed to be a struggle within society between freedom and authority. Reich argued that by misdirecting sexual energy, in his view the life-force itself, the authoritarian structures that pervade modern society had created psychic damage and personal unhappiness. In *The Function of the Orgasm* ([1948] 1973), Reich went on to advocate unrestricted sexual freedom, and towards the end of his life he claimed to have devised a machine that could capture and accumulate the sexual life-force, called 'orgone', from the environment. The idea of sexual liberation was further advanced by Herbert Marcuse (see p. 281). Marcuse's *Eros and Civilisation* ([1955] 1969), developed a scathing attack on contemporary society by, in effect, turning Freudianism on its head. In Marcuse's view, modern industrial society is characterised by 'sexual repression', brought about not by the need for social order but by capitalism's desire for a disciplined and obedient workforce. Marcuse argued that there was a biological basis for socialism in the form of the need to liberate the sexual or libidinal instinct from repressive capitalism. Ultimately, sexual liberation would involve the re-sexualisation of the whole body and the rediscovery of what Freud had called 'polymorphous perversity'.

Such ideas have had considerable impact upon those sections of the women's movement that see patriarchy as an all-encompassing system of female subordination. Patriarchy, in other words, is reflected not merely in the social and political subjection of women but also in their sexual repression. In *The Female Eunuch* ([1970] 1985), Germaine Greer suggested that male domination had had a devastating effect upon the personal quality of women's lives. Women had effectively been 'castrated' by the cultural myth of the 'eternal feminine', which demanded that they be passive, submissive and asexual creatures. As a result, women's liberation would be marked by personal and sexual emancipation in that they would for the first time be able to seek gratification as active and autonomous human beings. Similar ideas have also been developed by the gay and lesbian movement. Radical lesbians, for instance, have sometimes pointed out what in their view are the inadequacies of heterosexual relationships. They argue that heterosexual sex is implicitly oppressive because penetration is a symbol of male domination. The nature of women's sexuality has also been the subject of analysis and debate. For example, in her essay 'The Myth of the Vaginal Orgasm' (1973), Anne Koedt took issue with Freud's notion that only through intercourse could women experience a 'mature' orgasm, highlighting instead the importance of the clitoris in the achievement of female sexual fulfilment.

Politics of liberation

In the 1960s, 'liberation' was a demand made not only on behalf of specific groups – colonial peoples, women, gays and lesbians – but also in relation to the entire society. The quest for liberation was the rallying cry of a broad collection of groups broadly classified as the New Left. Although the New Left lacked theoretical and organisational coherence, embracing movements as diverse as feminism, environmentalism, student activism and anti-Vietnam War protest, it was distinguished by its rejection of both 'old left' alternatives on offer. Soviet-style state socialism in Eastern Europe was regarded as authoritarian and oppressive; Western social democracy was thought to be hopelessly compromised, lacking both vision and principles. By contrast, the New Left adopted a radical style of political activism which extolled the virtues of popular participation and direct action. The revolutionary character of this new political style was clearly revealed by the events of May 1968 in France, the month-long rebellion by students and young workers.

Many in the New Left were attracted by the revolutionary character of Marxist thought, but strove to remodel and revise it to make it applicable to advanced industrial societies that had achieved a high level of material affluence. Whereas orthodox Marxists had developed an economic critique of capitalism, emphasising the importance of exploitation, economic inequality and class war, the New Left, influenced by critical theory and anarchist ideas, underlined the way in which capitalism had produced a system of ideological and cultural domination. The enemy was therefore no longer simply the class system or a repressive state but rather 'the system', an all-encompassing process of repression that operated through the family, the educational system, conventional culture, work, politics and so on. In this context, 'political liberation' came to mean nothing less than a negation of the existing society, a radical break or, as Marcuse described it, a 'leap into the realm of freedom – a total rupture'. Once again, 'liberation' held out the prospect of cultural, personal and psychological revolution and not merely political change; at the same time it

Critical theory

Critical theory refers to the work of the so-called Frankfurt School, the Institute of Social Research, which was established in Frankfurt in 1923, relocated in the United States in the 1930s, and was re-established in Frankfurt in the early 1950s. The Institute was dissolved in 1969. Two phases in the development of critical theory can be identified. The first was associated with the theorists who dominated the Institute's work in the pre-war and early post-war period, notably Horkheimer, Adorno and Marcuse. The second phase stems from the work of the major post-war exponent of critical theory, Habermas.

Critical theory does not and has never constituted a unified body of work. However, certain general themes tend to distinguish Frankfurt thinkers as a school. The original intellectual and political inspiration for critical theory was Marxism (see p. 81). However, critical theorists were repelled by Stalinism, criticised the determinist and scientistic tendencies in orthodox Marxism, and were disillusioned by the failure of Marx's predictions about the inevitable collapse of capitalism. Frankfurt thinkers therefore developed a form of neo-Marxism that focused more heavily upon the analysis of ideology than upon economics and no longer treated the proletariat as the revolutionary agent. They also blended Marxist insights with the ideas of thinkers such as Kant (see p. 117), Hegel (see p. 4), Weber and Freud. Critical theory is characterised by the attempt to extend the notion of critique to all social practices by linking substantive social research to philosophy. In so doing, it not merely looks beyond the classical principles and methodology of Marxism but also cuts across a range of traditionally discrete disciplines, including economics, sociology, philosophy, psychology and literary criticism.

Critical theory has itself attracted criticism, however. First-generation Frankfurt thinkers in particular were criticised for advancing a theory of social transformation that was often disengaged from the on-going social struggle. Moreover, they were accused of over-emphasising the capacity of capitalism to absorb oppositional forces, and thus of underestimating the crisis tendencies within capitalist society. On the other hand, critical theory has brought about important political and social insights through the cross-fertilisation of academic disciplines and by straddling the divide between Marxism and conventional social theory. It has also provided a continuingly fertile and imaginative perspective from which the problems and contradictions of existing society can be explored.

Key figures

Max Horkheimer (1895–1973) A German philosopher and social psychologist, Horkheimer pioneered the interdisciplinary approach that was to become characteristic of critical theory. His principal concern was to analyse the psychic and ideological mechanisms through which class societies contain conflict. He explained totalitarianism in terms of the psychological, racial and

→

political tendencies of liberal capitalism, and argued that the advent of 'mass society' and the dominance of the 'culture industry' had made old ideological divisions irrelevant and threatened permanently to subordinate individual freedom. Horkheimer's major works include *Studies on Authority and the Family* (with Erich Fromm) (1936), *Dialectic of Enlightenment* (with Theodor Adorno) (1944) and *The Eclipse of Reason* (1974).

Herbert Marcuse (1898–1979)   A German political philosopher and social theorist, Marcuse portrayed advanced industrial society as an all-encompassing system of repression, which subdues argument and debate and absorbs all forms of opposition. Against this 'one-dimensional society', he held up the unashamedly utopian prospect of personal and sexual liberation, looking not to the conventional working class as a revolutionary force but to groups such as students, ethnic minorities, women and workers in the third world. Marcuse had a major influence on the New Left of the 1960s. His most important works include *Reason and Revolution* (1941), *Eros and Civilisation* (1958) and *One-Dimensional Man* (1964).

Theodor Adorno (1903–69)   A German philosopher, sociologist and musicologist, Adorno made important contributions to the critique of mass culture. With Horkheimer, he developed a new socio–cultural theory that centred on the advance of 'instrumental reason' rather than the Marxist idea of class struggle. Adorno interpreted culture and mass communication as political instruments through which dominant ideologies are imposed upon society, producing conformism and paralysing individual thought and behaviour. He also helped to provide the theoretical basis for a psychological theory of authoritarianism. Adorno's best known writings include *The Authoritarian Personality* (with others) (1950), *Minima Moralia* (1951) and *Negative Dialectics* (1966).

Jürgen Habermas (1929–)   A German philosopher and social theorist, Habermas is the leading exponent of the 'second generation' of the Frankfurt School. Habermas' work ranges over epistemology, the dynamics of advanced capitalism, the nature of rationality, and the relationship between social science and philosophy. He has highlighted the 'crisis tendencies' in capitalist society that result from tensions between capital accumulation and democracy. His analysis of rationality has developed critical theory into what has become a theory of 'communicative action'. Habermas's main works include *Towards Rational Society* (1970), *Legitimation Crisis* (1973) and *The Theory of Communicative Competence* (1984).

Further reading

Bottomore, T. *The Frankfurt School.* London: Horwood, 1984.
Held, D. *Introduction to Critical Theory.* London: Hutchinson, 1980.
Jay, M. *The Dialectical Imagination.* Boston: Little, Brown and London: Heinemann, 1973.

created the image of a fully satisfying and personally fulfilling society of the future.

Herbert Marcuse was probably the most influential thinker within the New Left. Not only did Marcuse develop a biological critique of capitalism in terms of sexual repression, but he also tried to explain how conventional society had effectively contained criticism and questioning. In *One-Dimensional Man* (1964) he argued that, far from being tolerant and democratic, advanced industrial civilisation had a totalitarian character. The capacity of advanced capitalism to 'deliver the goods' through relentless technological progress had turned human beings into unquestioning and unthinking consumers, creating a 'society without opposition'. For Marcuse, 'liberation' meant liberation from the 'comfortable servitude' of affluent society, not through a retreat into a kind of inner-worldly aestheticism but through the rediscovery of 'genuine' human needs and satisfactions. Marcuse was also scathing about the liberal democratic freedoms enjoyed in Western societies. In his view, the battery of individual rights and liberties of which liberal societies are so proud amount to nothing more than 'repressive tolerance'. By giving the impression of choice and individual freedom without offering human beings the prospect of genuine fulfilment, Western societies merely create a seductive and compelling form of oppression.

If conventional society is regarded as a repressive 'system', liberation from it requires the creation of an entirely new culture and an alternative lifestyle, a 'counter culture'. One of the distinctive features of the New Left was a willingness to endorse and support cultural and social movements which fundamentally rejected 'repressive technocratic society'. This was evident in the emergence of radical feminism and in the growth of ecologism (see p. 196). In the same way, there was greater interest in non-Western societies and values. In some cases this was linked to support for national liberation struggles in the developing world; in other cases it led to interest in Eastern mysticism in the form of Hinduism, Buddhism, Taoism and Zen. Similarly, a more sympathetic attitude was adopted to the use of so-called 'consciousness-expanding' drugs, endorsed by writers such as Aldous Huxley (1894–1963) and Timothy Leary. Within the counter-culture of the 1960s an openly permissive ethic reigned, distinguishing it from the liberal tolerance that prevailed in conventional society. Although such movements were primarily social, cultural or even religious in character, many in the New Left nevertheless regarded them as intensely 'political' in that they constituted a form of resistance to an essentially repressive civilisation. In that way, counter-cultural views and movements provided the basis for the liberated society of the future.

As with other forms of liberation, political liberation had an important psychological dimension. This was most clearly addressed in the work of psychiatrists such as R.D. Laing (1927–89) and David Cooper, who styled their work 'anti-psychiatry'. Particularly influential in the 1960s and early 1970s, they were interested in challenging the conventional understanding of mental illness. In their view, it was society rather than the individual that was 'insane', in that social, personal and sexual repression had come to be regarded as 'normal'. People who were classified as 'mentally ill' were not, they argued, insane, but were rather simply people who still struggled to hang on to their sanity in an insane world. In that light, conventional psychiatry, concerned as it is with 'curing' mental illness and preparing the sick for a return to conventional society, can be seen as being positively oppressive. In the view of anti-psychiatrists such as David Cooper (1967), the family lay at the heart of this system of repression in that it enforces conformity and obedience on children, thus preparing them for the demands of an insane world. From the perspective of anti-psychiatry, 'liberation' means the establishment of personal autonomy, a goal that can only be achieved when the family, together with the other institutions of conventional society, are finally abolished.

Summary

1   In its simplest sense, freedom means the absence of constraints or restrictions. Few, however, believe that freedom should be absolute; they recognise the distinction between liberty and licence. Nevertheless, it is unclear whether liberty becomes licence when rights are abused, when harm is done to others or when freedom is unequally shared out.

2   Although a formal or neutral definition of freedom is possible, negative and positive conceptions of freedom have commonly been advanced. Negative freedom means non-interference, the absence of external constraints, usually understood to mean law or some kind of physical constraint. Positive freedom is conceived variously as autonomy or self-mastery, as personal self-development and as some form of moral or 'inner' freedom.

3   Toleration refers to forbearance, the willingness to put up with actions or opinions with which we disagree. It can be defended on grounds of privacy, personal development and in the belief that it will promote progress and social harmony. Limits may, however, be placed on tolerance when it threatens social cohesion, the security of particular groups or provides a platform for political extremism.

4   Liberation constitutes a radical notion of freedom: the overthrow of an all-encompassing system of oppression, offering the prospect of complete human satisfaction. In the twentieth century, liberation movements have fought against colonial rule, against sexual and racial oppression, and against the pervasive manipulation that supposedly exists in advanced industrial societies.

Further reading

Gray, J. and Pelczynski, Z. (eds). *Conceptions of Liberty in Political Philosophy.* London: Athlone, 1984.

Gray, T. *Freedom.* London: Macmillan and Atlantic Highlands, NJ: Humanities Press, 1990.

Harris, N. *National Liberation.* Harmondsworth: Penguin, 1990; and New York: St Martin's Press, 1991.

King, P. *Toleration.* London: Frank Cass, 1998.

Marcuse, H. *An Essay on Liberation.* Boston MA: Beacon and Harmondsworth: Penguin, 1972.

Mendus, S. *Toleration and the Limits of Liberalism.* London: Macmillan and Atlantic Highlands, NJ: Humanities Press, 1989.

Millett, K. *Sexual Politics.* New York: Simon & Schuster, 1990.

Wolff, R.P., Marcuse, H. and Moore, B. *A Critique of Pure Tolerance.* London: Cape and Boston MA: Beacon, 1969.

Chapter 10

Equality, Social Justice and Welfare

Introduction
Equality
Social justice
Welfare
Summary
Further reading

Introduction

The idea of equality is perhaps the defining feature of modern political thought. Whereas classical and medieval thinkers took it for granted that hierachy is natural or inevitable, modern ones have started out from the assumption that all human beings have equal moral worth. Nevertheless, few political principles are as contentious as equality, or polarise opinion so effectively. Many, for example, see the political spectrum itself, the distinction between left and right, as a reflection of differing attitudes towards equality. While left-wingers are thought to be broadly committed to equality, right-wingers are more dubious about it and may even be openly hostile. Yet there is also a sense in which we are all egalitarians now. So remorseless has been the advance of egalitarianism that few, if any, modern thinkers would not be prepared to subscribe to some form of it, be it in relation to legal rights, political participation, life-chances or opportunities, or whatever. The modern battle about equality is therefore fought not between those who support the principle and those who reject it, but between different views about where and how equality should be applied. For example, should the law treat all citizens equally, or are there grounds for special provisions? Are all political views of equal value, or should the opinions of certain people carry extra weight? Should people simply have an equalopportunity to rise or fall in society, or should they enjoy equal economic and social circumstances?

The issue of equality has provoked particularly intense debate when it has been applied to the distribution of wealth or income in society, what is commonly referred to as 'social justice'. How should the cake of society's resources be cut? What distribution of material rewards can be considered just or defensible? Whereas some insist that an equal, or at least more equal, distribution of rewards and benefits is desirable, others argue that justice demands that natural differences amongst humankind should be reflected in the way society treats them. Questions about social justice, however, are invariably linked to the issue

285

of welfare. In almost all parts of the world the cause of equality and social justice has been associated with calls for the growth of social welfare, for the state's responsibilities to be expanded to include the social well-being of its citizens. During the twentieth century, in fact, a 'welfare consensus' emerged, embracing socialists, liberals and conservatives, which saw welfare provision as the cornerstone of a stable and harmonious society. In the late twentieth century, however, this consensus has broken down, leaving welfare at the heart of a bitter ideological dispute that, in many ways, echoes earlier political battles over equality. What are the attractions of the welfare state? And why has the principle of welfare come to be so stridently criticised?

Equality

The earliest use of the term 'equal', still widely used in everyday language, was to refer to identical physical characteristics. In this sense, two cups can be said to contain 'equal' quantities of water; a runner is said to 'equal' the 100-metre world record; and the price of a bottle of expensive wine may 'equal' the cost of a television set. In political theory, however, a clear distinction is made between equality and ideas such as 'uniformity', 'identity' and 'sameness'. Although critics of equality have sometimes tried to ease their task by reducing equality to simple uniformity, linking it thereby to regimentation and social engineering, no serious political thinker has ever advocated *absolute* equality in all things. Equality is not the enemy of human diversity, nor is its goal to make everyone alike. Indeed, egalitarians (from the French *égalité*) may accept the uniqueness of each human individual, and perhaps also acknowledge that people are born with different talents, skills, attributes and so on. Their goal, though, is to establish the legal, political or social conditions in which people will be able to enjoy equally worthwhile and satisfying lives. Equality, in other words, is not about blanket uniformity, but rather is about 'levelling' those conditions of social existence which are thought to be crucial to human well-being. However, equality is in danger of degenerating into a mere political slogan unless it is possible to answer the question 'equality of what?'. In what should people be equal, when, how, where and why?

Equality is a highly complex concept, there being as many forms of equality as there are ways of comparing the conditions of human existence. For instance, it is possible to talk about moral equality, legal equality, political equality, social equality, sexual equality, racial equality and so forth. Moreover, the principle of equality has assumed a number of forms, the most significant of which have been formal equality, equality of opportunity and equality of outcome. Although the ideas of equal opportunities and equal outcome developed out of an original commitment to formal equality, there are times when they point in very different directions. For instance, supporters of legal equality may roundly denounce equality of opportunities when this implies discrimination in favour of the poor or disadvantaged. Similarly, advocates of social equality may attack the notion of equal opportunities on the grounds that it amounts to the right to be unequal. Egalitarianism thus encompasses a broad range of views, and its political character has been the subject of deep disagreement.

Formal equality

The earliest notion of equality to have had an impact on political thought is what can be called 'foundational equality', suggesting that all people are equal by virtue of a shared human essence. Such an idea arose out of the natural rights theories that dominated political thought in the seventeenth and eighteenth centuries. The American Declaration of Independence, for example, declares simply that, 'All men are created equal', and the French Declaration of the Rights of Man and Citizen states that, 'Men are born and remain free and equal in rights'. However, what form of equality did such high-sounding declarations endorse? Certainly they did not constitute descriptive statements about the human condition, the eighteenth century being a period of ingrained social privilege and stark economic inequality. These were, rather, normative assertions about the moral worth of each human life. Human beings are 'equal' in the simple sense that they are all 'human'. They are 'born' or 'created' equal, they are 'equal in the sight of God'. But what does this form of equality imply in practice?

In the early modern period, foundational equality was most definitely not associated with the idea of equal opportunities, still less with any notion of equal wealth and social position. Writers such as John Locke (see p. 269) saw no contradiction in endorsing the idea that 'all men are created equal' at the same time as defending absolute property rights and the restriction of the franchise to property owners – to say nothing of the exclusion of the entire female sex from the category of 'human beings'. 'Men' are equal only in the sense that all human beings are invested with identical natural rights, however these might be defined. The idea that all human beings are possessors of equal rights is the basis of what is usually called 'formal equality'. Formal equality implies that, by virtue of their common humanity, each person is entitled to be treated equally by the rules of social practice. As such, it is a procedural rule which grants each person equal freedom to act however they may choose and to make of their lives whatever they are capable of doing, without regard to the opportunities, resources or wealth they start with.

The most obvious, and perhaps most important, manifestation of formal equality is the principle of legal equality, or 'equality before the law'. This holds that the law should treat each person as an individual, showing no regard to their social background, religion, race, colour, gender and so forth. Justice, in this sense, should be 'blind' to all factors other than those relevant to the case before the court, notably the evidence presented. Legal equality is thus the cornerstone of the rule of law, discussed in Chapter 6. The rule of law seeks to ensure that all conduct, of both private citizens and state officials, conforms to a framework of law, and only to law. In the United States, this is reflected in the constitutional principle of 'equal protection', according to which in similar circumstances people must be treated in a similar way. This principle has been used to advance the cause of civil rights, most famously in the Supreme Court case *Brown* v. *Board of Education* (1954), which declared that racial segregation in American schools was unconstitutional.

The principle of formal equality is, however, essentially negative: it is very largely confined to the task of eradicating special privileges. This was evident in the fact that calls for formal equality were first made in the hope of breaking down the hierarchy of ranks and orders which had survived from feudal times; its enemy was aristocratic privilege. It also explains why formal equality meets with near universal approval, enjoying support from conservatives (see p. 138) and liberals (see p. 29) no less than from socialists. Indeed, this is one form of equality seldom thought to be in need of justification: privileges granted to one class of persons on grounds of 'accidents of birth' like gender, colour, creed or religion, are now widely regarded as simple bigotry or irrational prejudice. This was evident in the worldwide condemnation of the apartheid system in South Africa. Nevertheless, many regard formal equality as a very limited notion, one which, if left on its own, may be incapable of fostering genuine equality. For example, legal equality grants each person an equal right to eat in an expensive restaurant, in the sense that no one is excluded on grounds of race, colour, creed, gender or whatever, but entirely fails to address their capacity to exercise this right, their money. This is what the French novelist Anatole France meant when in *The Red Lily* he ridiculed 'the majestic equality of the law which forbids rich and poor alike to steal bread and to sleep under bridges'.

These limitations can be seen in relation to both racial and sexual equality. Formal equality requires that no one should be disadvantaged on grounds of their race or gender and would be consistent, for instance, with laws prohibiting such discrimination. However, merely to ban racial discrimination does not necessarily counter culturally ingrained or 'institutionalised' racism, nor does it address the economic or social disadvantages from which racial minorities may suffer. Karl Marx (see p. 373) examined this problem in his essay 'On the Jewish Question' ([1844] 1967). Marx belittled attempts to bring about Jewish 'political emancipation' through the acquisition of equal civil rights and liberties, advocating instead 'human emancipation', the emancipation not only of the Jews but of all people from the tyranny of class oppression. Marxists have accepted that capitalism has brought about a form of equality in that the marketplace judges people not according to social rank or any other individual peculiarities, but solely in terms of their market value. However, the existence of private property generates class differences which ensure that individuals have starkly different market values. This is why Marxists have portrayed legal equality as 'market' or 'bourgeois' equality, and argued that it operates as little more than a facade, serving to disguise the reality of exploitation and economic inequality.

The struggle for sexual equality has also involved the call for legal equality or 'equal rights'. Early feminists such as Mary Wollstonecraft and J.S. Mill (see p. 258) advanced their arguments in terms of liberal individualism: gender, in their view, is irrelevant to public life because

---

Mary Wollstonecraft (1759–97)

British social theorist and feminist. Drawn into radical politics by the French Revolution, Wollstonecraft was part of a creative and intellectual circle that included her husband, the anarchist William Godwin (see p. 341). She died giving birth to her daughter, Mary, who later married the poet Shelley and wrote *Frankenstein*.

Wollstonecraft developed the first systematic feminist critique some 50 years before the emergence of the female suffrage movement. Her feminism, which was influenced by Lockian liberalism as well as by the democratic radicalism of Rousseau (see p. 243) (even though she objected to his exclusion of women from citizenship), was characterised by a belief in reason and a radical humanist commitment to equality. In *A Vindication of the Rights of Men* (1790) she criticised the structures and practices of British government from the standpoint of what she called the 'rights of humanity'. Her best known work, *A Vindication of the Rights of Women* (1792), emphasised the equal rights of women on the basis of the notion of 'personhood'. She claimed that the 'distinction of sex' would become unimportant in political and social life as women gained access to education and were regarded as rational creatures in their own right. However, Wollstonecraft's work did not merely stress civil and political rights but developed a more complex analysis of women as the objects and subjects of desire, and also presented the domestic sphere as a model of community and social order.

each 'person' is entitled to the same rights in education, law, politics and so on. Wollstonecroft, for instance, argued that women should be judged as human beings, 'regardless of the distinction of sex'. However, although women have gone a long way to achieving 'formal' equality with men in many modern societies, significant cultural, social and political inequalities nevertheless persist. Many modern feminists (see p. 60) have, as a result, been inclined to move beyond the liberal idea of equal rights to endorse more radical notions of equality. Socialist feminists, for example, seek to advance the cause of greater social equality. They highlight the economic inequalities which enable men to be 'breadwinners' while women remain either unwaged housewives or are confined to low-paid and poor-status occupations. Radical feminists, for their part, argue that formal equality is inadequate because it applies only to public life and ignores the fact that patriarchy, 'rule by the male', is rooted in the unequal structure of family and personal life. Meaningful sexual equality therefore requires that women enjoy not only equal legal rights, but are also equal to men in economic, social and domestic life.

Equality of opportunity

The more radical notion of equal opportunities is often thought to have followed naturally from the idea of formal equality. Despite links between the two, they can have very different implications, and, as will become apparent later, a consistent application of equality of opportunity may be in danger of violating the principle of formal equality. The idea of equal opportunities can be found in the writings of Plato (see p. 22), who proposed that social position should be based strictly upon individual ability and effort, and that the educational system should offer all children an equal chance to realise their talents. The concept is widely endorsed by modern ideologies and is embraced as a fundamental principle by political parties of almost every shade of opinion. Social democrats (see p. 312) and modern liberals believe that equal opportunity is the cornerstone of social justice, and modern conservatives, late converts to the cause, now extol the virtues of what they call a 'classless society', meaning a society based upon individual effort not, as Marx used the term, one based upon collective ownership.

Formal equality pays attention to the status people enjoy either as human beings or in the eyes of the law; it does not address their 'opportunities', the circumstances in which they live and the chances or prospects available to them. Equality of opportunity is concerned principally with initial conditions, with the starting point of life. Very often sporting metaphors are employed to convey this sense, such as an 'equal start' in life, or that life should be played on a 'level playing field'. To confine equality to the initial circumstances of life, however, can have radically inegalitarian implications. Advocates of equal opportunities do not expect all runners to finish a race in line together simply because they left the starting blocks at the same time. Indeed, in the eyes of many, it is precisely the 'equal start' to the race which legitimises its unequal outcome, the difference between winning and losing. Unequal performance can be put down, quite simply, to differences in natural ability. In effect, the principle of equal opportunities comes down to 'an equal opportunity to become unequal'. This is because the concept distinguishes between two forms of equality, one acceptable, the other unacceptable. Natural inequality, arising from personal talents, skills, hard work and so on, is considered to be either inevitable or morally 'right'; in Margaret Thatcher's words there is a 'right to be unequal'. However, inequalities that are bred by social circumstances, such as poverty, homelessness or unemployment, are morally 'wrong', because they allow some to start the race of life halfway down the running track while other competitors may not even have arrived at the stadium.

Equality of opportunity points towards an inegalitarian ideal, but a very particular one, a meritocratic society. Meritocracy means rule by a talented or intellectual elite, merit being defined in Michael Young's (1961) formula as IQ + effort. In a meritocratic society, both success and failure are 'personal' achievements, reflecting the simple fact that while some are born with skills and a willingness to work hard, others are either untalented or lazy. Not only is such inequality morally justified but it also provides a powerful incentive to individual effort by encouraging people to realise whatever talents they may possess. However, the idea of meritocracy relies heavily upon the ability clearly to distinguish between 'natural' and 'social' causes of inequality. Psychologists such as Hans Eysenck (1973) and Arthur Jensen (1980) championed the cause of natural inequality and advocated the use of IQ tests which they claimed could measure innate intelligence. Such ideas, for example, lay behind the introduction of selection in British schools through the use of the so-called 'Eleven-plus' examination. In practice, however, performance in such tests and examinations is influenced by a wide range of social and cultural factors which contaminate any estimate of 'natural' ability. Selection in British schools, for example, produced a clear bias in favour of children from middle-class homes, whose parents had themselves usually done well at school. The problem is that if natural talent cannot reliably be disentangled from social influences the very idea of 'natural inequality' may have to be abandoned. Moreover, if wealth and social position cannot be regarded simply as a personal achievement, the notion of equal opportunities may have to give way to a still more radical concept of equality.

The attraction of equality of opportunity is nevertheless potent. In particular, it offers the prospect of maximising an equal liberty for all. Equal opportunities means, put simply, the removal of obstacles that stand in the way of personal development and self-realisation, a right that should surely be enjoyed by all citizens. Many applications of the principle are no longer controversial. It is widely accepted, for instance, that careers should be open to talent and that promotion should be based upon ability. However, some have argued that a rigorous and consistent application of the principle may lead to widespread state intervention in social and personal life, threatening individual liberty and perhaps violating the principle of formal equality. For example, the family could be regarded as one of the major obstacles to the achievement of equal opportunities. Through the inheritance of wealth and the provision of different levels of parental encouragement, social stability and material affluence, the family ensures that people do not have an equal start in life. To push equality of opportunity to its extreme would mean contemplating the banning of inheritance and regulating family life through a wide range of compensatory programmes. In this sense, there may be a trade-off between equality and freedom, with the need for a balance to be struck between the demand to equalise opportunities on the one hand, and the need to protect individual rights and liberties on the other.

One particularly difficult issue which the principle of equal opportunities leads to is that of reverse or 'positive' discrimination. This is a policy, in an early form associated with 'affirmative action' on race issues in the United States, which discriminates in favour of disadvantaged groups in the hope of compensating for past injustices. Such a policy can clearly be justified in terms of equal opportunities. When racial minorities, for example, are socially underprivileged, merely to grant them formal equality does not give them a meaningful opportunity to gain an education, pursue a career or enter political life. This was recognised, for instance, in the US Supreme Court case *Regents of the University of California* v. *Bakke* (1978), which upheld the principle of reverse discrimination in educational admissions. In this sense, reverse discrimination operates rather like the handicap system in golf to ensure fair and equal competition between unequal parties. Some argue that this application of the principle amounts to different but equal treatment and so conforms to the strictures of formal equality. Others, however, suggest that unequal treatment, albeit in an attempt to compensate for previous disadvantage, must of necessity violate the principle of equal rights. In the Bakke case, for example, a student was denied a university place by the admission of other candidates with poorer educational records than his own.

Equality of outcome

The idea of an equality of outcome is the most radical and controversial face of egalitarianism. Whereas equal opportunities requires that significant steps are taken towards achieving greater social and economic equality, far more dramatic changes are necessary if 'outcomes' are to be equalised. This is a goal which uncovers a fundamental ideological divide: socialists, communists and some anarchists regard a high level of social equality as a fundamental goal, while conservatives and liberals believe it to be immoral or unnatural.

A concern with 'outcomes' rather than 'opportunities' shifts attention away from the starting point of life to its end results, from chances to rewards. Equality of outcome implies that all runners *finish* the race in line together, regardless of their starting point and the speed at which they run. As such, equality of outcomes not merely differs from formal equality and equal opportunities but may positively contradict them. Although it is sometimes unclear whether 'outcome' refers to resources or to levels of welfare or fulfilment, the demand for equal outcomes is most commonly associated with the idea of material equality, an equality of social circumstances, living conditions and possibly even wages. For many, however, material equality is merely one of a number of desirable goals, and a trade-off must be negotiated between social equality and concerns such as individual liberty and economic incentives. J.J. Rousseau (see p. 243) is often seen as a spokesperson for this school of thought. Though no socialist in the sense that he was a keen advocate of private property, Rousseau ([1762] 1969) nevertheless recognised the dangers of social inequality in proposing that 'no citizen shall be rich enough to buy another and none so poor as to be forced to sell himself'. This principle is consistent with the modern idea of a redistribution of wealth from rich to poor, which has more to do with reducing social inequalities than with achieving any abstract goal of social equality. In that sense, when modern social democrats advocate equality they are referring to the modest idea of 'distributive' equality rather than any radical goal of 'absolute' equality. Although they recognise material equality to be desirable, they acknowledge the need for some measure of inequality, to provide, for instance, an incentive to work.

Fundamentalist socialists, however, believe a far higher degree of social equality to be both possible and desirable. Marx, for instance, disparaged the very idea of equality, seeing it as a 'bourgeois' right, a right to inequality. He therefore drew a clear distinction between equal, or at least more equal, property ownership, and his own goal, the common ownership of productive resources. To advocate the abolition of all forms of private property, however equally distributed, is, in effect, to endorse the idea of 'absolute' social equality. Perhaps the most famous experiment in radical egalitarianism took place in China, under the so-called 'Cultural Revolution' (1965–8). During this period, not only did militant Red Guards denounce wage differentials and all forms of privilege and hierarchy, but even competitive sports like football were banned.

Advocates of equality of outcome, whether in its moderate or radical sense, usually argue that it is the most vital form of equality, since without it other forms of equality are a sham. Equal legal and civil rights are, for example, of little benefit to citizens who do not possess a secure job, a decent wage, a roof over their head and so forth. Moreover, the doctrine of equal opportunities is commonly used to defend material inequalities by creating the myth that these reflect 'natural' rather than 'social' factors. Although defenders of social equality rarely call upon the concept of 'natural' equality, they commonly argue that differences among human beings more often result from unequal treatment by society than they do from unequal natural endowment. For example, success in IQ tests and other forms of educational assessment are, they would argue, as much a reflection of social background, good schooling and stimulating teaching, as they are an indication of natural ability.

Equality of outcome can also be justified on the grounds that it is a prerequisite for securing individual liberty. As far as the individual is concerned, a certain level of material prosperity is essential if people are to lead worthwhile and fulfilled lives, an expectation to which each of us is surely entitled. Rousseau feared that material inequality would lead, in effect, to the enslavement of the poor and deprive them of both moral and intellectual autonomy. At the same time, inequality would corrupt the rich, helping to make them selfish, acquisitive and vain. Furthermore, a high level of social equality is sometimes regarded as vital for social harmony and stability. In *Equality* ([1931] 1969), R.H. Tawney (see p. 313) argued that social equality constitutes the practical foundation for a 'common culture', one founded upon the unifying force of 'fellowship'. By contrast, he castigated equality of opportunity as the 'tadpole philosophy': all may start out from the same position but are then left to the vagaries of the market; some will succeed but many will fail. Generations of socialist thinkers have therefore regarded social equality as the basis for spontaneous cooperation and genuine community.

Critics, however, point out that the pursuit of equality of outcome leads to stagnation, injustice and, ultimately, tyranny. Stagnation results from the fact that social 'levelling' serves to cap aspirations and remove the incentive for enterprise and hard work. To the extent that a society moves towards the goal of social equality it will therefore pay a heavy price in terms of sterility and inertia. The economic cost of equality is, however, less forbidding than the moral price that has to be paid. This is a lesson which New Right thinkers such as Friedrich Hayek (see p. 341) and Keith Joseph (1979) were at pains to teach. In their view, the socialist principle of equality is based on little more than social envy, the desire to have what the wealthy already possess. Policies that aim to promote equality by redistributing wealth do little more than rob the rich in order to pay the poor. The simple fact is, Hayek argued, that people are very different, they have different aspirations, talents, dispositions and so forth, and to treat them as equals must therefore result in inequality. This is what Joseph portrayed as the contradiction that lies at the heart of the concept of equality. As Aristotle (see p. 68) said, injustice arises not only when equals are treated unequally, but also when unequals are treated equally.

It may be a sad fact, but not all people can run at the same speed; some will be faster, some stronger, some will have more stamina. Equality of outcome can thus be seen as an 'unnatural' result which can only be achieved by massive interference and the violation of any notion of a 'fair' race. Faster runners will have to be handicapped, perhaps run further than slower runners, start after them, or be forced to negotiate a series of obstacles. In short, talent is penalised and an equal result is achieved by a process of 'levelling downwards'. To achieve equality of outcome in society at large would require a similarly extensive system of manipulation, often derided as 'social engineering'. The drive for equality is therefore carried out at the expense of individual liberty. This is why the New Right portrays egalitarianism in such a sinister light, arguing that it is always accompanied by the growth of regimentation, discrimination and coercion. In their view, it was no coincidence, for example, that the militant egalitarianism of the Cultural Revolution was accompanied by chaos, social paralysis and the deaths of an estimated 400 000 people.

Social justice

The term 'social justice' is beset by political controversy. For some, it is inextricably linked to egalitarianism and acts as little more than a cipher for equality. As a result, the political right recoils from using the term, except in a negative or derogatory sense. Hayek, for instance, regarded social justice as a 'weasel word', a term used intentionally to evade or mislead. In their view, social justice tends to be a cloak for the growth of state control and government interference. Social democratic and modern liberal thinkers, on the other hand, treat social justice more favourably, believing that it refers to the attempt to reconstruct the social order in accordance with moral principles, the attempt to rectify social injustice. However, there is no necessary link, either political or logical, between social justice and the ideas of equality and state control. As will become apparent later, all theories of social justice can be used to justify inequality, and some are profoundly inegalitarian.

A distinctive concept of 'social justice', as opposed to the more ancient ideal of 'justice', first emerged in the early nineteenth century. It is 'social' in the sense that it is concerned not with legal penalties and punishments so much as with social well-being. Social justice thus stands for a morally defensible distribution of benefits or rewards in society, evaluated in terms of wages, profits, housing, medical care, welfare benefits and so forth. Social justice is therefore about 'who *should* get what'. For example, when, if ever, do income differentials become so wide they can be condemned as 'unjust'? Or, on an international level, are there grounds for arguing that the unequal distribution of wealth between the prosperous and industrialised North and the developing South is 'immoral'? In the view of some commentators, however, the very notion of social justice is mistaken. They argue that the distribution of material benefits has nothing whatsoever to do with moral principles like justice, but can only be evaluated in the light of economic criteria such as efficiency and growth. Hayek's antipathy towards the term can, for example, be explained by his belief that justice can only be evaluated in terms of individual considerations, in which case broader 'social' principles are meaningless.

Most people, nevertheless, are unwilling to reduce material distribution to mere economics, and indeed many would argue that this is perhaps the most important area in which justice must be seen to be done. The problem, however, is that political thinkers so seldom agree about what is a just distribution of material rewards. Like justice itself, social justice is an 'essentially contested' concept, there being no universally agreed notion of what is socially just. In *Social Justice* (1976), David Miller accepted that the concept is essentially contested and socially relative, but tried to identify a number of contrasting principles of justice. These are 'to each according to his *needs*', 'to each according to his *rights*' and 'to each according to his *deserts*'.

According to needs

The idea that material benefits should be distributed on the basis of need has most commonly been proposed by socialist thinkers, and is sometimes regarded as the socialist theory of justice. Its most famous expression is found in *Critique of the Gotha Programme* ([1875] 1968), in which Karl Marx proclaimed that a fully communist society will inscribe on its banners the formula, 'From each according to his ability, to each according to his needs!'. It would be a mistake, however, to reduce socialist conceptions of social justice to a simplistic theory of need-satisfaction. Marx himself, for example, distinguished between the distributive principle that was appropriate to full communism and the one which should be adopted in the transitional 'socialist' society. Marx accepted that capitalist practices could not be swept away overnight, and that many of them, such as material incentives, would linger on in a socialist society. He therefore recognised that under socialism labour would be paid according to its individual contribution and that this would vary according to the worker's physical or mental capacities. In effect, in Marx's view, the 'socialist' principle of justice amounted to 'to each according to his*work*'. The criterion of need can be said to be the basis of the 'communist' principle of justice, because, according to Marx, it is appropriate only to a future society of such material abundance that questions about the distribution of wealth become almost irrelevant.

Needs differ from both wants and preferences. A 'need' is a necessity, it *demands* satisfaction; it is not simply a frivolous wish or a passing fancy. For this reason, needs are often regarded as 'basic' to human beings, their satisfaction is the foundation of any fully human life. While 'wants' are a matter of personal judgement, shaped by social and cultural factors, human needs are objective and universal, belonging to all people regardless of gender, nationality, religion, social background and so forth. The attraction of a needs-based theory of social justice is that it addresses the most fundamental requirements of the human condition. Such a theory accepts as a moral imperative that all people are entitled to the satisfaction of basic needs because, quite simply, worthwhile human existence would otherwise be impossible. Attempts to identify human rights are, for instance, often grounded in some notion of basic needs. One of the most influential attempts to identify such needs was undertaken by the psychologist Abraham Maslow (1908–70), who proposed that there is a 'hierarchy of needs'. The most basic of these needs are physiological considerations like hunger and sleep, which are followed by the need for safety, belonging and love, then there is the need for self-esteem, and finally what Maslow referred to as 'self-actualisation'. In *A Theory of Human Need* (1991), Len Doyal and Ian Gough identify physical health and autonomy as objective and universal needs, arguing that they are the essential preconditions for participation in social life.

Any needs-based theory of social justice clearly has egalitarian implications. If needs are the same the world over, material resources should be distributed so as to satisfy at least the basic needs of each and every person. This means, surely, that every person is entitled to food and water, a roof over his or her head, adequate health care and some form of personal security. To allow people, wherever in the world they may live, to be hungry, thirsty, homeless, sick or to live in fear, when the resources exist to make them otherwise is therefore immoral. The need criterion thus implies that those in the prosperous West have a moral obligation to relieve suffering and starvation in other parts of the world. Indeed, it suggests a clear case for a global redistribution of wealth. In the same way, it is unjust to afford equally sick people unequal health care. Distribution according to need therefore points towards the public provision of welfare services, free at the point of delivery, rather than towards any system of private provision which would take account of the ability to pay. Nevertheless, a needs-based theory of justice does not in all cases lead to an equal distribution of resources because needs themselves may sometimes be unequal. For example, if need is the criterion, the only proper basis for distributing health care is ill-health. The sick should receive a greater proportion of the nation's resources than the healthy, simply because they are sick.

Distribution according to human needs has, however, come in for fierce attack, largely because needs are notoriously difficult to define. Conservative and sometime liberal thinkers have tended to criticise the concept of 'needs' on the grounds that it is an abstract and almost metaphysical category, divorced from the desires and behaviour of actual people. They argue that resource allocation should instead correspond to the more concrete 'preferences' which individuals express, for instance, through market behaviour. It is also pointed out that if needs exist they are in fact conditioned by the historical, social and cultural context in which they arise. If this is true, the notion of universal 'human' needs, as with the idea of universal 'human' rights, is simply nonsense. People in different parts of the world, people brought up in different social conditions, may have different needs. Finally, the idea that the needs of one person constitute a moral imperative upon another, encouraging him or her to forego material benefits, is based upon particular moral and philosophical assumptions. The most obvious of these is that human beings have a social responsibility for one another, a belief normally linked to the notion of a common humanity. Whilst such a belief is fundamental to socialism and many of the world's major religions, it is foreign to many conservatives and classical liberals, who see human beings as essentially self-striving.

Although the ideas of need and equality have often gone hand in hand, modern egalitarian theories have sometimes drawn upon a broader range of arguments. The most influential of these, John Rawls' *A Theory of Justice* (1971), has helped to shape both modern liberal and social democratic concepts of social justice. Though not strictly a needs theorist, Rawls nevertheless employs an instrumental notion of needs in his idea of primary goods. These are conceived of as the universal means for the attainment of human ends. The question of social justice therefore concerns how these primary goods, or needs-resources, are to be distributed. Rawls proposed a theory of 'justice as fairness'. This is based upon the maintenance of two principles:

1. Each person is to have an equal right to the most extensive liberty compatible with a similar liberty for others.
2. Social and economic inequalities are to be arranged so that they are both:
   (a) to the greatest benefit of the least advantaged; and
   (b) attached to positions and offices open to all under conditions of fair equality of opportunity.

The first principle reflects a traditional liberal commitment to formal equality, the second, the so-called 'difference principle', points towards a significant measure of social equality. By no means, however, does this justify absolute social equality. Rawls fully recognises the importance of material inequality as an economic incentive. Nevertheless, he makes an important presumption in favour of equality in that he insists that material inequalities are only justifiable when they work to the advantage of the less well-off. This is a position compatible with a market economy in which wealth is redistributed through the tax and welfare system up to the point that this becomes a disincentive to enterprise and so disadvantages even the poor. Rawls' egalitarianism is, however, based upon a kind of social contract theory rather than any evaluation of objective human needs. He imagines a hypothetical situation in which people, deprived of knowledge

John Rawls (1921–)

US academic and political philosopher. His major work, *A Theory of Justice* (1971), is regarded as the most important work of political philosophy written in English since the Second World War. It has influenced modern liberals and social democrats alike, and is sometimes credited with having re-established the status of normative political theory.

Rawls employed the device of the social contract to develop an ethical theory which represents an alternative to utilitarianism (see p. 360). His theory of 'justice as fairness' is based upon principles that he believed people would support if they were placed behind a veil of ignorance which deprived them of knowledge of their own social position and status. He proposed that social inequality is justified only if it works to the benefit to the least advantaged (in that it strengthens incentives and enlarges the size of the social cake). This presumption in favour of equality is rooted in the belief that people cooperating together for mutual advantage should have an equal claim to the fruits of their cooperation and should not be penalised as a result of factors, such as gender, race and genetic inheritance, over which they have no control. Redistribution and welfare are therefore 'just' because they conform to a widely held view of what is fair. Rawls developed a similar justification for the principles of equal liberty and equality of opportunity. In *Political Liberalism* (1993), he somewhat modified the universalist presumptions of his early work.

about their own talents and abilities, are confronted by a choice between living in an egalitarian society or an inegalitarian one. In Rawls's view, people are likely to opt to live in an egalitarian society simply because, however enticing the prospect of being rich might be, it would never counterbalance the fear people have of being poor or disadvantaged. Thus Rawls starts out by making traditionally liberal assumptions about human nature, believing individuals to be rationally self-interested, but concludes that a broadly egalitarian distribution of wealth is what most people would regard as 'fair'.

According to rights

The late twentieth century has witnessed a right-wing backlash against the drift towards egalitarianism, welfarism and state intervention. New Right theories, such as those propounded by Robert Nozick (see p. 320) in *Anarchy, State and Utopia* (1974), have rejected both the needs-based principle of justice and any presumption in favour of equality. Instead, they have championed a principle of justice based upon the idea of 'rights', 'entitlements' or, in some cases, 'deserts'. In so doing, the New Right has built upon a tradition of distributive thought dating back to Plato and Aristotle, which suggests that material benefits should in some way correspond to personal 'worth'. This was also the cornerstone of the classical liberal concept of social justice, advocated by writers such as John Locke and David Hume (1711–76). Just as the concept of 'needs' provides the foundation for a socialist principle of justice, so 'rights' has usually served as the basis for a rival, liberal principle of justice.

'Rights' are moral entitlements to act or be treated in a particular way. In distributive theory, however, rights have usually been regarded as entitlements that have in some way been 'earned', usually through hard work and the exercise of skills or talents. This can be seen, for instance, in the classical liberal belief that the right to own property is based upon the expenditure of human labour. Those who work hard are *entitled* to the wealth they produce. In that sense, rights-based theories are not so much concerned with 'outcomes' – who has what – as with *how* that outcome is arrived at. Rights-based theories are thus based upon a theory of procedural justice. By contrast, needs-based theories are concerned with substantive justice because they focus upon outcomes, not upon how those outcomes are achieved. Rights theories are therefore properly thought of as non-egalitarian rather than inegalitarian: they endorse neither equality nor inequality. According to this view, material inequality is only justified if talents and the willingness to work are unequally distributed amongst humankind. This contrasts with Rawls's theory of justice which, though he claims it to be procedural, has broadly egalitarian outcomes built into its major principles.

The most influential modern rights-based theory of justice is that of Robert Nozick, often interpreted as a response to Rawls's theories. Nozick distinguished between historical principles of justice and end-state principles. Historical principles relate to past circumstances or historical actions that have created differential entitlements. In his view, end-state principles like social equality and human needs are irrelevant to the distribution of rewards. Nozick's objective was to identify a set of historical principles through which we can determine if a particular distribution of wealth is just. He suggested three 'justice preserving' rules. First, wealth has to be justly acquired in the first place, that is, it should not have been stolen and the rights of others should not have been infringed. Secondly, wealth has to be justly transferred from one responsible person to another. Thirdly, if wealth has been acquired or transferred unjustly this injustice should be rectified.

These rules can clearly be used to justify gross inequalities in the distribution of wealth and rewards. Nozick rejects absolutely the idea that there is a moral basis for redistributing wealth in the name of equality or 'social justice', a term of which he, in common with most libertarian theorists, is deeply suspicious. If wealth is transferred from rich to poor, either within a society or between societies, it is only as an act of private charity, undertaken through personal choice rather than moral obligation. On the other hand, Nozick's third principle, the so-called 'rectification principle', could have dramatically egalitarian implications, especially if the origin of personal wealth lies in acts of duplicity or corruption. It also, for instance, brings the global distribution of wealth into question by casting a shadow over that portion of the wealth of the industrialised West which derives from conquest, plunder and enslavement in Africa, Asia and Latin America.

There have, nevertheless, been a number of major objections to any rights-based theory. Any exclusively procedural theory of justice is, for instance, forced to disregard end-state conditions altogether. This may, in practice, mean that circumstances of undeniable human suffering are regarded as 'just'. A just society may be one in which the many are unemployed, destitute or even starving, while the few live in luxury – providing, of course, that wealth has been acquired and transferred justly. Furthermore, any historical theory of justice, such as Nozick's, must explain how rights are acquired in the first place. The crucial first step in Nozick's account is the assertion that individuals can acquire rights over natural resources, yet he fails to demonstrate how this comes about. An additional objection to rights-based theories of justice is that they are grounded in what C.B. Macpherson (see p. 223) called 'possessive individualism'. Individuals are seen to be the sole possessors of their own talents and capacities, and on this basis they are thought to be morally entitled to own whatever their talents produce. The weakness of such a notion is that it abstracts the individual from his or her social context, and so ignores the contribution which society has made to cultivating individual skills and talents in the first place. Some would go on to argue further that to treat individuals in this way is, in effect, to reward them for selfishness and actually to promote egoistical behaviour.

According to deserts

It is common to identify two major traditions of social justice, one based upon needs and inclined towards equality, the other based upon some consideration of merit and more inclined to tolerate inequality. In practice, however, merit-based theories are not all alike. The idea of distributing benefits according to rights, discussed in the last section, relates distribution to entitlements that arise out of historical actions like work, and are in some cases established in law. Deserts-based theories undoubtedly resemble rights-based theories in a number of ways, notably in rejecting any presumption in favour of equality. Nevertheless, the idea of deserts suggests a rather different basis for material distribution. While the notion of 'needs' has usually been understood as a socialist principle, and 'rights' has often been linked to liberal theories, the idea of 'deserts' has commonly been employed by conservative thinkers intent upon justifying not an abstract concept of 'social justice' but what they regard as the more concrete idea of 'natural justice'. However, the ideological leanings of deserts theories are difficult to tie down because of the broad, even slippery, nature of the concept itself.

A 'desert' is a just reward or punishment, reflecting what a person is 'due' or 'deserves'. In this wide sense, all principles of justice can be said to be based upon deserts, justice itself being nothing more than giving each person what he or she is 'due'. It is possible, therefore, to encompass both needs-based and rights-based theories within the broader notion of just deserts. For example, it can be said that the hungry 'deserve' food, and that the worker is 'due' a wage. Nevertheless, it is possible to identify a narrower concept of deserts. This is related to the idea of innate or moral worth, that people should be treated in accordance with their 'inner' qualities. For example, the theory that punishment is a form of retribution is based upon the idea of deserts because the wrong-doer is thought to 'deserve' punishment not simply as a result of his actions but in view of the quality of evil lying within him or her. Conservatives have been attracted to the notion of deserts precisely because it appears to ground justice in the 'natural order of things' rather than in principles dreamt up by philosophers or social theorists. To hold that justice is somehow rooted in nature, or has been ordained by God, is to believe that its principles are unalterable and inevitable.

The concept of natural justice has been prominent in conservative attempts to defend free-market capitalism. Theorists who write within the liberal tradition, such as Locke or Nozick, have usually enlisted principled arguments about property rights to justify the distribution of wealth found in such economies. By contrast, conservative thinkers have often followed Edmund Burke (see p. 139) in regarding the market order as little more than the 'laws of nature' or the 'laws of God'. Although Burke accepted the classical economics of Adam Smith (see p. 340) which suggested that intervention in the market would result in inefficiency, he also believed that government regulation of working conditions or assistance for the poor amounts to interference with Divine Providence. If the prevailing distribution of wealth, however unequal, can be regarded as 'the natural course of things', it is also, in Burke's view, 'just'. Herbert Spencer (1820–1904), the British social philosopher, also developed a theory of distributive justice that relies heavily upon 'natural' factors. Spencer was concerned to develop a new social philosophy by relying on ideas developed in the natural sciences by Charles Darwin (1809–82). In Spencer's view, people, like animals, were biologically programmed with a range of capacities and skills which determined what they were able to make of their lives. In *The Principle of Ethics* ([1892–3] 1982), he therefore argued that 'each individual ought to receive the benefits and the evils of his own nature and consequent conduct', a formula that underpinned his belief in the 'survival of the fittest'. In other words, there is little point in defining justice in terms of abstract concepts such as 'needs' or 'rights' when material benefits simply reflected the 'natural' endowments of each individual.

When material distribution reflects 'the workings of nature' there is little purpose in, or justification for, human beings interfering with it, even if this means tolerating starvation, destitution and other forms of human suffering. Some have employed precisely this argument in criticism of attempts to mount famine or disaster relief. Although the more fortunate may like to feel they can relieve the suffering of others, if in doing so they are working against nature itself their efforts will ultimately be to no avail and may even be counter-productive. An early exponent of such a view was the British economist Thomas Malthus (1766–1834), who warned that all attempts to relieve poverty were pointless. In *An Essay on the Principles of Population* ([1798] 1971), he argued that all improvements in living conditions tend to promote increases in population size which then quickly outstrip the resources available to sustain them. War, famine and disease are therefore necessary checks upon population size; any attempt by government, however well-intentioned, to relieve poverty will simply court disaster.

The idea that justice boils down to natural deserts has, however, been subject to severe criticism. At best, this can be regarded as a harsh and unforgiving principle of justice, what is sometimes referred to as 'rough justice'. Material circumstances are put down to the roll of nature's dice: the fact that some countries possess more natural resources and a more hospitable climate than others is nobody's fault, and nothing can be done about it. The simple fact is that some are lucky, and others are not. Many would argue, however, that this is not a moral theory at all, but rather a way of avoiding moral judgements. There is no room for justice in nature, and to base moral principles upon the workings of nature is simply absurd. Indeed, to do so is to distort our understanding of both 'justice' and 'nature'. To portray something as 'natural' is to suggest that it has been fashioned by forces beyond human control, and possibly beyond human understanding. In other words, to suggest that a particular distribution of benefits is 'natural' is to imply that it is inevitable and unchallengeable, not that it is morally 'right'. Moreover, what in the past may have appeared to be unalterable may no longer be so. Modern, technologically advanced societies undoubtedly possess a greater capacity to tackle problems such as poverty, unemployment and famine, which Burke and Malthus had regarded as 'natural'. To portray the prevailing distribution of material resources in terms of 'natural deserts' may therefore be no more than an attempt to find justification for ignoring the suffering of fellow human beings.

Welfare

In the twentieth century, debate about equality and social justice has often focused on the issue of welfare. In its simplest form, 'welfare' refers to happiness, prosperity and well-being in general; it implies not mere physical survival but some measure of health and contentment as well. As such, 'general well-being' is an almost universally accepted political ideal: few political parties would wish to be associated with the prospect of poverty and deprivation. Although there is clearly room to debate what in fact constitutes 'well-being', 'prosperity' or 'happiness', what gives the concept of welfare its genuinely contentious character is that it has come to be linked to a particular means of achieving general well-being: collectively provided welfare, delivered by government through what is called the welfare state. The welfare state is linked to the idea of equality in that, in broad terms, it aims to secure a basic level of equal well-being for all citizens. In many cases it is also seen as one of the basic requirements of social justice, at least from the perspective of needs theorists. Nevertheless, there is a sense in which welfare is a narrower concept than either equality or social justice. Whereas theories of social justice usually relate to how the whole cake of society's resources is distributed, the notion of welfare is more concerned with providing a minimum quality of life for all, accepting that much wealth and income is distributed through the market.

In political debate, welfare is invariably a collectivist principle, standing for the belief that government has a responsibility to promote the social well-being of its citizens. This principle of welfare is sometimes termed 'social welfare'. However, two other principles of welfare have been employed, each of which continues to be relevant to ideological debate. The first is the individualist theory of welfare, which holds that general well-being is more likely to result from the pursuit of individual self-interest, regulated by the market, than it is from any system of public provision. This notion of 'welfare individualism', is rooted in the classical economics of Adam Smith but has been revived by New Right thinkers such as Hayek and Friedman. Secondly, there is the idea that public welfare should be provided for but only through a system of private charity. This theory acknowledges that welfare cannot simply be left in the hands of self-striving individuals, but balks at the coercion necessarily involved in state provision. Advocated by traditional conservatives and some classical liberals, the idea of 'charitable welfare' places a heavy stress upon social duty and altruism.

Welfare and poverty

The term welfare state came into being in the twentieth century to describe the broader social responsibilities of government. However, the term is used in at least two contrasting senses, one broad, the other narrow. The broad meaning, in the form of '*a* welfare state', draws attention to the provision of welfare as a prominent, if not the predominant, function of the state. This is how William Temple, Archbishop of York, first used the term in English in 1941 to distinguish Western 'welfare states', orientated around the promotion of social well-being, from what he called the 'power states' of Nazi Germany and Stalinist Russia. This is also the sense in which modern welfare states can be contrasted with the minimal or 'nightwatchman' states of the nineteenth century, whose domestic functions were largely confined to the maintenance of domestic order. More commonly, however, the term is used in the form of *the* welfare state' to describe the policies and, more specifically, the institutions through which the goal of welfare is delivered. Thus institutions like the social security system, health service and public education are often referred to collectively as 'the welfare state'. This is also the sense in which it is possible to refer to the welfare state expanding or diminishing as government either assumes broader social responsibilities or relinquishes them.

It is sometimes difficult, however, to determine which institutions and policies can be said to be part of the welfare state in the narrow sense, because a very wide range of public policies can be said to have a 'welfare' goal. The most common image of the welfare state is of positive welfare provision, the delivery of services like pensions, benefits, housing, health and education, which the market either does not provide or does not provide adequately. In this sense, the welfare state is an attempt to supplement or, in some cases, replace a system of private provision. This was the form of welfare state constructed in the postwar period in Britain, modelled on the Beveridge Report (1942), and subsequently adopted throughout much of Western Europe. Such a system of positive welfare provision was developed most fully in countries such as Sweden and Germany in the early postwar period. However, welfare provision can also be negative, in the sense that it attempts to promote social well-being not by the provision of services but through the regulation of market behaviour. For example, any attempt by government to influence working conditions – legal protection for trade unions in industrial action, minimum wage legislation and regulations about health and safety – can be said to serve a welfare purpose.

The status of education and its relationship to welfare has also been the cause of confusion. It is sometimes argued that not being directly related to material well-being, education is different from services like pensions, benefits and health, and is therefore not part of the welfare state. Nevertheless, there is undoubtedly an indirect link between education and prosperity, better educated citizens being able to command higher wages and to enjoy greater social security than less well-educated ones. Moreover, if welfare is related to broader goals such as the promotion of 'happiness', it is clearly not exclusively concerned with material provision. For these various reasons, it is often difficult to determine if a state *is*, or *has*, a welfare state. This problem is particularly apparent in the United States. On the one hand, the United States clearly does not possess the developed and comprehensive institutions found in certain European states; on the other, however, a wide range of benefits are available in the form of social insurance, based upon the Social Security Act (1935), Medicare and Medicaid, the food stamps programme and so forth. Indeed, following Gosta Esping-Anderson (1990), it is possible to identify three distinct forms of welfare provision found in developed industrialised states. The United States, Canadian and Australian systems can be described as liberal (or limited) welfare states since they aim to provide little more than a 'safety net' for those in need. In countries such as Germany, conservative (or corporate) welfare states provide a more extensive range of services but depend heavily on the 'paying in' principle and link benefit closely to jobs. Social democratic (or Beveridge) welfare states, such as the classical Swedish and the original British system, are, by contrast, based upon universal benefits and the maintenance of full employment.

All systems of welfare, however, are concerned with the question of poverty. Although welfare states may address broader and more ambitious goals, the eradication of poverty is their most fundamental objective. However, what is 'poverty'? On the face of it, poverty means being deprived of the 'necessities of life', sufficient food, fuel and clothing to maintain 'physical efficiency'. In its original sense, this was seen as an *absolute* standard, below which human existence became difficult to sustain. According to this view, poverty hardly exists in developed industrialised states like the United States, Canada, Britain and Australia; even the poor in such countries live better than much of the world's population. However, to regard as 'poor' only those who are starving is to ignore the fact that poverty may also consist in being deprived of the standards, conditions and pleasures enjoyed by the majority in society. This is the notion of *relative* poverty, defined by Peter Townsend (1974) as not having 'the living conditions and amenities which are customary, or at least widely encouraged and approved, in the society to which they belong'. In this sense, the poor are the 'less well-off' rather than the 'needy'. By such a standard, for example, the US Government estimated in 1981 that 14 per cent of American citizens (about 30 million people) lived below the 'poverty line'. The concept of relative poverty, however, raises important political questions because it establishes a link between poverty and inequality, and in so doing suggests that the welfare state's task of eradicating poverty can only be achieved through the redistribution of wealth and the promotion of social equality. The definition of poverty is therefore one of the most contentious issues in the area of welfare provision.

In all bar state socialist countries the welfare state has existed alongside a continuing system of private welfare, delivered through the market. 'Private' health care, education and pensions are available in even the most highly developed social welfare systems. Apart from right-wing libertarians such as Nozick, who dismiss all forms of public welfare, and fundamentalist socialists, who reject any kind of private provision, it is widely accepted that there should be a balance between collective and individual provision. The most crucial of all welfare issues, therefore, is where that balance should be struck: what should people be able to rely upon the state to do, and what should they be expected to do for themselves? However, there are also a number of other questions about how any welfare system should operate. Should welfare benefits and services be 'universal', available to all citizens regardless of means, or should they be 'targeted' on the less well-off or needy? Should welfare be financed, at least in part, through a system of insurance or charges, or should it be non-contributory? Should welfare services be provided in kind or through a system of cash payments which people can then use as they see fit? Finally, should the welfare state function as a 'safety net' concerned only to guarantee minimum standards and redress the worst instances of poverty, or should it aim to achieve wider goals, such as the redistribution of wealth and the promotion of equal opportunities?

In praise of welfare

Welfarism is the belief that social well-being is properly the responsibility of the community and that this responsibility should be met through government. In the postwar period a 'welfare consensus' developed in most liberal democracies, which saw parties of the left, right and centre competing to establish their welfarist credentials, only disagreeing with one another on matters of detail like funding, structure and organisation. Without doubt, this consensus was underpinned by powerful electoral factors, as a large body of voters recognised that the welfare state provided social safeguards which free market capitalism could never match. Nevertheless, welfarism is by no means a coherent philosophy. Although liberals, conservatives and socialists have each recognised its attractions, they have often been drawn to welfare by different considerations and have endorsed different systems of welfare provision.

One of the earliest reasons for interest in social welfare had more to do with national efficiency than with principles like justice and equality. When a country's workforce is sickly and undernourished it is in no position to build up a prosperous economy, still less to develop an effective army. It is therefore no coincidence that in countries like Germany and Britain the foundations of the welfare state were laid during a period of international rivalry and colonial expansion, the period leading up to the outbreak of the First World War. The first modern welfare state developed in Germany in the 1880s under Chancellor Bismarck, featuring a system of medical and accident insurance, sick pay and old age pensions. Britain's response, under the Asquith Liberal Government after 1906, was dictated by growing apprehension about German power, highlighted by the discovery during the Boer War (1899–1902) that a large proportion of working-class conscripts were unfit for military service. Although such motives have little to do with altruism and compassion, it can clearly be argued that in the long run a healthy and productive workforce is beneficial for the whole of society. Indeed, it is often suggested that the growth of social welfare is linked to a particular stage of economic development. Whereas early industrialisation makes use of a largely unskilled, unthinking manual workforce, further industrial progress requires educated and trained workers, who are capable of understanding and utilising modern technology. It is the function of the welfare state to bring such a workforce into existence.

Welfare has also been linked to the prospect of social cohesion and national unity. This concern has been close to the heart of conservative thinkers, who have feared that grinding poverty and social deprivation will generate civil unrest and, possibly, revolution. Such considerations helped to advance the cause of social reform in mid-nineteenth-century Britain, often associated with the Conservative statesman, Benjamin Disraeli. Disraeli was acutely aware that industrial progress brought with it the danger of strife and social bitterness, the prospect of Britain being divided into 'two nations: the Rich and the Poor'. As Prime Minister, Disraeli therefore introduced a programme of social reforms, including improvements in housing conditions and hygiene, which contrasted sharply with the *laissez-faire* policies still advocated by the Liberal Party. Similar motives also influenced the advance of welfare provision in Germany. Bismarck, for example, believed he was confronting a 'Red menace', and supported welfare in a deliberate attempt to wean the masses away from socialism by improving their living and working conditions. This conservative welfare tradition is based upon a combination of prudence and paternalism. It is undoubtedly concerned to alleviate material hardship, but only to the point where the working masses cease to pose a threat to the prosperous minority. Moreover, this form of welfarism is entirely compatible with the survival of hierarchy: it can be seen as an attempt to uphold social inequality rather than eradicate it. Welfare paternalism is based upon neo-feudal principles like *noblesse oblige*, which imply that it is the duty of the privileged and prosperous to 'look after' those less fortunate than themselves – not to bring to them up to their level.

The liberal case for welfare, by contrast, has very largely been based upon political principles, and in particular the belief that welfare can broaden the realm of freedom. Although early liberals feared that social reform would sap initiative and discourage hard work, modern liberals have seen it as an essential guarantee of individual self-development. Such a theory was advanced in the late nineteenth century by the so-called New Liberals, people such as T.H. Green (1836–82), Leonard Hobhouse (1864–1929) and J.A. Hobson (1858–1940), whose views created the intellectual climate which made the Asquith reforms possible. The central idea of liberal welfarism is the desire to safeguard individuals from the social evils which can blight their lives, evils such as deprivation, unemployment, sickness and so on. *The Beveridge Report* (1942), the blueprint for a modern welfare state in Britain, described its purpose as to protect citizens from the 'five giants' of want, disease, ignorance, squalor and idleness, and to extend this protection 'from the cradle to the grave'.

Very similar motives influenced the introduction of social welfare in the United States in the 1930s, under Franklin Roosevelt's 'New Deal'. The high point of this New Deal liberalism was reached in the 1960s with Lyndon Johnson's 'War on Poverty', an ambitious programme of education, job training and urban renewal projects. While firmly aware of the benefits that welfare can bring to society, liberal welfarism is nevertheless rooted in a commitment to individualism and equality of opportunity. This is reflected in support for a contributory system of welfare provision which preserves a measure of individual responsibility and serves to counter dependency. The War on Poverty, for instance, tried to stimulate communities to mobilise their own resources and involve the poor themselves in the operation of its projects. The ultimate goal of welfare, from this perspective, is to enable individuals to make their own moral decisions, to help individuals to help themselves. Once deprivation has been alleviated, liberals hope that individuals will once again be able to take responsibility for their own economic and social circumstances and 'stand on their own two feet'.

The socialist or social democratic case for welfare, however, goes further. Although social democratic politicians have increasingly come to adopt the language of liberal welfarism in taking up the cause of individual liberty, they have traditionally based their support for welfare upon two more radical principles: communitarianism (see p. 34) and equality. Social democrats have, for example, seen the welfare state as a practical application of communitarian values, believing that its function is to promote the spontaneous bonds of sympathy and compassion which characterise a genuine community. In other words, the welfare state should not merely be concerned with ameliorating conflict or relieving individual hardship, but should actively strengthen a sense of responsibility for other human beings. In the *Gift Relationship* (1970), for example, Richard Titmuss suggested that the welfare state is, in essence, an ethical system, based upon *reciprocal* obligations. People should receive welfare as if it is a gift from a 'stranger', as an expression of human sympathy and mutual affection. Its ultimate purpose is therefore to strengthen social solidarity. As a demonstration that such welfare principles are practical as well as morally attractive, Titmuss pointed to the success of systems of blood donation by comparison with ones where blood is bought and sold.

Social democratic theorists have also linked welfare to the goal of equality, believing it to be a necessary counter-weight to the injustices and 'inhumanity' of market capitalism. Indeed, modern socialism is largely based upon the merits of welfarism. For instance, in *The Future of*

Socialism (1956), Anthony Crosland identified socialism with progress towards equality rather than with the fundamentalist goal of common ownership. The welfare state, according to this revisionist socialist view, is a redistributive mechanism: it transfers wealth from rich to poor through a system of welfare benefits and public services, financed by progressive taxation. The merit of such a system is that it consciously addresses the problem of 'relative' poverty and also seeks to remove the stigma attached to welfare by insisting that as far as possible benefits are universal and not 'means tested'. Nevertheless, it is clear that the welfare state can never bring about absolute social equality; its goal is rather to 'humanise' capitalism by reducing distributive inequalities. As such, though, social democratic welfarism is dedicated not merely to fostering equal opportunities but also to bringing about a greater measure of equality of outcome.

Welfare under attack

The welfare consensus which underpinned a steady rise in the social budget has come under growing pressure since the 1970s. The expansion of welfare provision that occurred in the 1950s and 1960s had been made possible by a period of sustained economic growth, the so-called 'long boom'. The onset of recession in the 1970s, however, precipitated a fiscal crisis of the welfare state. As levels of economic growth declined, governments throughout the world were confronted with the problem of how to sustain their welfare programmes at a time when tax revenues were falling. This boiled down to two options: one, push up taxes; two, cut the welfare budget. Against this background, New Right theories emerged which suggested that welfare had not only been responsible for unacceptable levels of taxation but is also an affront to individualism and personal responsibility. Nevertheless, anti-welfarism is every bit as ideologically diverse as welfarism. In addition to socialists who warn that the welfare state seldom helps those for whose benefit it was created, there is a long-standing Marxist critique of welfare which sees it as little more than a prop of the capitalist system.

New Right criticisms of welfare range over moral, political and economic considerations. The centrepiece of the New Right's libertarian critique is, however, the idea that the welfare state in effect enslaves the poor by creating dependency and turning them into 'welfare junkies'. In the United States this took the form of a backlash against the welfare reforms of the 1960s. George Gilder's *Wealth and Poverty* (1982) and Charles Murray's *Losing Ground* (1984) were amongst the most influential attempts to portray welfare as counter-productive. Job creation programmes, for instance, had only pushed up unemployment by weakening individual initiative; and classifying people as 'unemployed', 'handicapped'

Social democracy

The term social democracy has been defined in a number of different ways. Originally used by Marxists to distinguish between the narrow goal of political democracy and the more fundamental objectives of socialism, social democracy came, by the early twentieth century, to be associated with a reformist rather than a revolutionary road to socialism. However, the modern use of the term was shaped by the tendency of democratic socialist parties to abandon the goal of abolishing capitalism and embrace the more modest objective of reforming or humanising capitalism. Social democracy, then, stands for a balance between the market and the state, a balance between the individual and the community. The chief task of social democratic theory has therefore been to establish a compromise between, on the one hand, an acceptance of capitalism as the only reliable mechanism for generating wealth, and on the other, a desire to distribute wealth in accordance with moral, rather than market, principles.

The characteristic emphasis of social democratic thought is a concern for the underdog in society, the weak and vulnerable. This can, in most cases, be seen as a development of the socialist tradition, either being shaped by attempts to revise or update Marxism (see p. 81) or emerging out of ethical or utopian socialism. Such developments usually involved the re-examination of capitalism and the rejection of the Marxist belief that the capitalist mode of production is characterised by systematic class oppression. Nevertheless, social democracy lacks the theoretical coherence of Marxism and may, anyway, not be firmly or exclusively rooted in socialism. In particular, social democrats have drawn so heavily upon modern liberal ideas such as positive freedom and equality of opportunity that it has become increasingly difficult to distinguish between social democracy and liberalism (see p. 29). This can be seen in the influence of Rawls (see p. 299) upon social democratic thought. More recent developments within social democracy have involved an accommodation with principles such as community, social partnership and moral responsibility, reflecting parallels between modern social democracy and communitarianism (see p. 34).

The attraction of social democracy is that it has kept alive the humanist tradition within socialist thought, offering an alternative to the dogmatism and narrow economism of orthodox Marxism. Its attempt to achieve a balance between efficiency and equality has been, after all, the centre ground towards which politics in most developed societies has tended to gravitate, regardless of whether socialist, liberal or conservative governments are in power. From the Marxist perspective, however, social democracy amounts to a betrayal of socialist principles, an attempt to prop up a defective capitalist system in the name of socialist ideals. Nevertheless, social democracy's central weakness is its lack of firm theoretical roots. Although social democrats have an enduring commitment to equality and social justice, the kind and extent of equality they support and the specific meaning they have given to social

→

justice have constantly been revised. For instance, to the extent that social democracy has been recast as a defence of community, it can be said to have assumed an essentially conservative character. Instead of being a vehicle for social transformation, it has developed into a defence of duty and responsibility, and so serves to uphold established institutions and ways of life.

Key figures

Eduard Bernstein (1850–1932)   A German socialist politician and theorist, Bernstein was responsible for the first systematic revision of Marxism. He drew attention to the failure of Marx's predictions about the collapse of capitalism, pointing out that economic crises were becoming less, not more acute. Bernstein rejected revolution and called for alliances with the liberal middle class and the peasantry, emphasising the possibility of a gradual and peaceful transition to socialism. He later abandoned all semblance of Marxism and developed a form of ethical socialism based upon neo-Kantianism. Bernstein's most significant work is *Evolutionary Socialism* (1898).

Richard Henry Tawney (1880–1962)   A British social philosopher and historian, Tawney championed a form of socialism firmly rooted in a Christian social moralism unconnected with Marxist class analysis. The disorders of capitalism, he argued, derived from the absence of a 'moral ideal', leading to unchecked acquisitiveness and widespread material inequality. The project of socialism is therefore to build a 'common culture' that will provide the basis for social cohesion and solidarity. Tawney's major works include *The Acquisitive Society* (1921), *Equality* (1931) and *The Radical Tradition* (1964).

Anthony Crosland (1918–77)   A British politician and socialist theorist, Crosland built on Bernstein in attempting to give social democracy a theoretical basis. He argued that capitalism no longer needs to be abolished as the ownership of wealth has become divorced from its control, and major economic decisions are made by salaried managers rather than by the bourgeoisie of old. The task of socialism is thus to promote equality, by which Crosland meant narrow distributive inequalities, rather than to restructure the system of ownership. Crosland's best known works include *The Future of Socialism* (1956) and *Socialism Now* (1974).

Further reading

Clarke, P. *Liberals and Social Democrats*. Cambridge: Cambridge University Press, 1978.

Crick, B. *Socialism*. Milton Keynes: Open University Press, 1987.

Sassoon, D. *One Hundred Years of Socialism*. London: Fontana, 1997.

or 'disadvantaged' merely convinced them that they were 'victims of circumstance'. In this way, a welfare-dependent underclass had come into existence, lacking the work ethic, self-respect and the supportive structures of conventional family life. Murray's solution to this problem was that welfare responsibilities be transferred from central government to local communities, emphasising, as far as possible, individual and community initiative.

By suggesting that the less well-off can, and should, be responsible for their own lives, the New Right revived the idea of the 'undeserving poor'. In its extreme form, this implies that the poor are simply lazy and inadequate, those who are more interested in living off the charity of others than in working for themselves. However, in its more sophisticated form, it implies that regardless of the causes of poverty, only the individual can get himself or herself out of it; society cannot be held responsible. Welfare should therefore be provided in such a way as to promote and reward individual responsibility. The welfare state, for instance, should be nothing more than a safety net, designed to relieve 'absolute' poverty, and benefits should be 'targeted' at cases of genuine deprivation. When welfare is turned into a system of rights or entitlements, people are sucked into dependency rather than encouraged to get out of it. The New Right has consequently placed a heavy stress upon civil obligations, believing that welfare in some way has to be 'earned'. This is why many in the New Right have been attracted by the idea of 'workfare', which forces those in receipt of state support to work for their benefit. Such ideas have also informed the 'welfare to work' reforms of the Blair government in Britain. A further proposal, popularised by the US economist Milton Friedman, is that all forms of welfare be replaced by a 'negative income tax'. This would mean that all those below a certain income would *receive* money from the tax authorities instead of having to *pay* tax (as those above this level have to do). The virtue of such a system is that it greatly extends choice for those in need and encourages them to be more responsible for improving their circumstances. In the same vein, Friedman endorsed the idea that poorer families should receive a 'voucher' which could be used to purchase some or all of their children's schooling.

The New Right also objects to welfare on a variety of other grounds. The welfare state has, for example, been blamed for both declining levels of economic growth and high inflation. Electoral pressures allowed welfare expenditure to spiral upwards out of control, creating the problem of government 'overload'. This, however, penalised those in work or in business, who were crushed by an ever-higher tax burden. Whilst benefits themselves create an incentive to idleness, the taxes needed to finance them constitute a disincentive to enterprise. To make matters worse, rising levels of public spending pumped more money into the economy, so pushing up prices. The New Right has therefore been interested in squeezing the welfare budget by cutting benefits and encouraging a shift towards private welfare provision. For both ideological and economic reasons, the New Right favours the privatisation of welfare in areas like education, health care, pensions and so forth. Where privatisation is ruled out by electoral constraints, they have pressed ahead with reforms designed to make state provision conform to market principles. This is best seen in the 'internal markets' which now operate in education and health in Britain. In turn, though, the New Right claims that the stimulus to economic performance gained by privatisation and reform will bring benefit to all social groups, including the poor. This is what has been called 'trickle down' economics. Welfare cuts may initially widen inequalities but by promoting an 'enterprise culture' will ensure that the economic cake itself expands, pushing up general living standards.

A different attack upon the welfare state has come from socialists who accept the egalitarian principles embodied in welfare but argue that in practice they are seldom realised. In *The Strategy of Equality* (1982), Julian Le Grand examined the consumption of welfare services by different social groups and discovered that, ironically, the prosperous and educated often fare better than the poor and needy. In areas like health care, rail subsidies, tax benefits for home-owners, secondary and, particularly, higher education, the middle classes are often better placed to benefit than the working classes because they are usually better educated and informed and have the opportunity to take advantage of the service. Le Grand therefore concluded that in some cases welfare tends to deepen social inequality rather than diminish it. The economist James O'Connor has also pointed out that the welfare system tends to uphold economic inequalities. In *The Fiscal Crisis of the State* (1973), he suggested that welfare programmes consist either of 'social capital' or 'social expenses'. Social capital directly or indirectly serves the interests of private corporations by using tax money to provide benefits and insurance to workers, thus lowering labour costs and increasing productivity. Social expenses include those benefits, for example for the unemployed, that are not directly related to production but nevertheless benefit corporate capitalism by ensuring social stability.

Orthodox Marxists have taken the socialist analysis further and reject the whole idea of 'humanising' capitalism through the expansion of social welfare. According to this view, capitalism is a system of class exploitation; it cannot be reformed, it can only be abolished. The role of welfare in this process is to stabilise capitalism and so perpetuate exploitation. The welfare state supports capitalism in at least two ways. First, it meets the productive needs of the economic system: strong, healthy and well-trained workers. In this respect, Marxists acknowledge that the long-term interests of capitalism have won out over the short-term desire of businessmen and industrialists to slash welfare in order to cut taxes. Secondly, by cushioning the effects of the capitalist system and alleviating the worst incidents of hardship, the welfare state has prevented the proletariat from achieving revolutionary class consciousness. The working masses have been placated; they have not been emancipated. The welfare state therefore serves as an agent of social control because it allows an ideology of 'welfare capitalism' to disguise the realities of class oppression. Indeed, many Marxists would regard the idea of welfare as a trap, encouraging people to think about social development narrowly in terms of the relief of poverty and hardship. To do so is to treat poverty as an isolated problem and abstract it from the economic system that in their view is its real cause.

Summary

1   A commitment to equality may take one of three contrasting forms. Formal or foundational equality holds that all human beings are of equal moral worth and is reflected in a commitment to legal and political equality. Equality of opportunity is concerned with equalising the starting point of life in order to allow natural inequalities to flourish. Equality of outcome seeks to achieve equal, or at least more equal, circumstances of life, social equality.

2   Social justice refers to a defensible or just distribution of material rewards. Fundamental differences exist between those who believe that distribution should be broadly egalitarian because it aims to satisfy human needs; those who argue that it should reflect individual merits, rights based upon talent and the willingness to work; and those who suggest that it is determined by innate and unchangeable factors, the natural deserts of individuals and groups.

3   Welfare is the idea of a basic level of equal well-being for all citizens, a minimum quality of life for all. Although some believe that this goal can best be achieved through individual self-reliance and hard work or by a system of private charity, it is invariably achieved in practice through collectively provided welfare services delivered by government, the welfare state. Forms of welfare provision however vary considerably.

4   The principle of welfare has been supported by a broad ideological consensus, ranging from paternalistic conservatives to parliamentary socialists. Amongst the virtues that it has been identified with are that it promotes national efficiency, fosters social cohesion, helps individuals to develop their potential, and tends to narrow social inequalities. Critics, however, have attacked welfare, on the one hand, for creating dependency and promoting inefficiency and, on the other, for ameliorating inequalities rather than abolishing them.

Further reading

Barker, J. *Arguing for Equality.* London and New York: Verso, 1987.

Barry, N. *Welfare.* Milton Keynes: Open University Press and Minneapolis: University of Minnesota Press, 1998.

Bedau, H. A. (ed.). *Justice and Equality.* Englewood Cliffs, NJ: Prentice-Hall, 1971.

Goodin, R. *Reasons for Welfare: The Political Theory of the Welfare State* Princeton: Princeton University Press, 1988.

Miller, D. *Social Justice.* Oxford and New York: Oxford University Press, 1976.

Pettit, P. *Judging Justice: An Introduction to Contemporary Political Philosophy* London and Boston, MA: Routledge & Kegan Paul, 1980.

Rae, D. *Equalities.* Cambridge, MA: Harvard University Press, 1981.

Wicks, M. *A Future for All: Do We Need a Welfare State?* Harmondsworth: Penguin, 1987.

Chapter 11

Property, Planning and the Market

Introduction
Property
Planning
The market
Summary
Further reading

Introduction

At almost every level, politics is intertwined with economics. Election results are often thought to be determined by economic factors: at times of prosperity, governments are likely to be re-elected, but during recessions they face defeat. It is little surprise therefore that party politics is invariably dominated by economic issues. Parties compete against each other by promising higher rates of economic growth, increased prosperity, lower inflation and so forth. The influence of economics has been no less significant in political theory. For almost two hundred years, ideological debate revolved around a battle between socialism and capitalism, a clash between two rival economic philosophies. This struggle was regarded as fundamental to the political spectrum itself, left-wing ideas being broadly socialist, right-wing ones being sympathetic towards capitalism. In effect, this tendency reduced politics to a debate about the ownership of property and the desirability of one economic system over another. Should property be owned by private individuals and be used to satisfy personal interests? Or should it be owned collectively, by either the community or the state, and be harnessed to the common good?

Questions about property are closely related to conflicting models of economic organisation, notably the rival economic systems that dominated much of twentieth-century history: central planning and market capitalism. At times, politics has been simplified to a choice between planning and the market. Forms of planning have been adopted in a wide range of countries, but the principle was applied most rigorously in orthodox communist states. What are the strengths or attractions of the planning process? But why, also, has planning often failed or been abruptly abandoned? In many respects, the rival idea of the market achieved ascendency in the late twentieth century, being championed not only by liberal and conservative thinkers but by a growing number of socialists as well. What is it that has made market-based systems of economic organisation so successful? But why, nevertheless, has there been a continual need for government to intervene in economic life to supplement or regulate the market?

Property

The most common misunderstanding in any discussion of property is the everyday use of the term to refer to inanimate objects or 'things'. Property is in fact a social institution, and so is defined by custom, convention and, in most cases, by law. To describe something as 'property' is to acknowledge that a relationship of *ownership* exists between the object in question and the person or group to whom it belongs. In that sense, there is a clear distinction between property and simply making use of an object as a possession. For example, to pick up a pebble from a beach, to borrow a pen, or drive away someone else's car, does not establish ownership. Property is thus an established and enforceable claim to an object or possession; it is a 'right' not a 'thing'. The ownership of property is therefore reflected in the existence of rights and powers over an object and also the acceptance of duties and liabilities in relation to it. From this point of view, property may confer the ability to use and dispose of an object, but it may also involve the responsibility to conserve or repair it.

The range of objects that can be designated as property has varied considerably. Primitive societies, like those of the native Americans, may have little or no conception of property. In such societies, inanimate objects, and especially land, are thought to belong to nature; human beings do not *own* property, they are at best its custodians. The modern notion of property dates from the seventeenth and eighteenth centuries and stems from the growth in Western societies of a commercialised economy. As material objects increasingly came to be regarded as economic resources – as the 'means of production' or as 'commodities' capable of being bought or sold – the question of ownership became absolutely vital. The natural world was turned into 'property' to enable it to be exploited for human benefit. Nevertheless, property has not only been restricted to material objects. Human beings, for instance, have been thought of as property, most obviously in the institution of slavery but also in legal systems which have regarded wives as the 'chattels' of their husbands. However, different forms of property have developed, depending upon who or what was entitled to make a claim of ownership: private property, common property and state property. Each form of property has radically different implications for the organisation of economic and social life, and each has been justified by reference to very particular moral and economic principles.

Private property

So deeply is the notion of private property embedded in Western culture that it is not uncommon for all property to be thought of as 'private'. Nevertheless, private property is a distinctive form of property, defined by

---

Robert Nozick (1938–)

US academic and political philosopher. Nozick's major work, *Anarchy, State and Utopia* (1974) is widely seen as one of the most important contemporary works of political philosophy, and has had a profound influence upon New Right theories and beliefs.

Nozick's work is often interpreted as a response to the ideas of John Rawls (see p. 299), and is seen, more broadly, as part of a right-wing backlash against the postwar growth in state power. He developed a form of libertarianism (see p. 340) that draws upon the ideas of Locke (see p. 269) and was influenced by nineteenth-century US individualists such as Spooner and Tucker. At its core is an entitlement theory of justice that takes certain rights to be inviolable, and rejects the notion that social justice requires that a society's income and wealth be distributed according to a particular pattern. In particular, Nozick argues that property rights should be strictly upheld, provided that wealth has been justly acquired in the first place or has been justly transferred from one person to another. In short, 'whatever arises from a just situation by just steps is itself just'. On this basis, he rejects all forms of welfare and redistribution as theft. Nozick nevertheless supports a 'minimal state', which he believes would inevitably develop from a hypothetical state of nature. Some of the conclusions of *Anarchy, State and Utopia* were moderated in *The Examined Life* (1989).

C.B. Macpherson (1973) as the right of an individual or institution to 'exclude others' from the use or benefit of something. The 'right to exclude' does not, of course, necessarily deny access. Someone else can use 'my' car – but only with my permission. The notion of property as 'private' developed in the early modern period and provided a legal framework within which commercial activity could take place. Private property thus became the cornerstone of the growing market or capitalist economic order.

Liberal (see p. 29) and conservative (see p. 138) theorists have been the most committed defenders of private property, but its justification has taken a number of forms. One of the earliest arguments in favour of private property was advanced in the seventeenth century by natural rights theorists such as John Locke (see p. 269). A very similar position has been adopted in the twentieth century by right-wing libertarians such as Robert Nozick. The basis of this argument is a belief in 'self-ownership', that each individual has a right to own his or her own person or body. If, as Locke argued, each person has exclusive rights over his or her self, it follows that they have an exclusive right to the product of their own labour, what they personally have crafted, produced or created. Property rights are therefore based upon the idea that inanimate objects have been 'mixed' with human labour and so become the exclusive property of the labourer. This argument justifies not only exclusive property rights but also unlimited ones; individuals have an absolute right to use or dispose of property in whatever way they wish. This is evident in Nozick's theory of distribution, discussed in Chapter 10. According to Nozick, providing property has been acquired or transferred 'justly', there is no justification for infringing property rights, whether in the cause of social justice or in the interests of the larger society. Such a position, for example, sets very clear limits to the capacity of government to regulate economic life or even to tax its citizens.

Often linked to the idea of natural rights is the justification of private property as an incentive to labour. Found in Aristotle (see p. 68) and developed by utilitarian (see p. 360) and economic theorists, this defence of private property is based less upon moral principles than it is on the promise of economic efficiency. In short, it is only the possibility of acquiring and consuming wealth, in the form of private property, which encourages people to work hard and develop the skills and talents they were born with. Economists point out, moreover, that through the mechanism of market competition private property ensures that economic resources are attracted to their most efficient use, ensuring a productive and growing economy. Such an argument is based upon the belief that human beings are self-seeking and that work is regarded as essentially instrumental. In other words, work is at best a means to an end. The driving force behind productive activity is simply the desire for material consumption. Individuals will only be encouraged to devote their time and energy to work if there is the compensating prospect of acquiring material wealth.

Private property has also been linked to the promotion of important political values, notably individual liberty. Property ownership gives citizens a degree of independence and self-reliance, enabling them to 'stand on their own two feet'. By contrast, the propertyless can easily be manipulated and controlled, either by the wealthy or by government. Thus, even political theorists who feared the emergence of economic inequality, such as Jean-Jacques Rousseau (see p. 243), the anarchist Pierre-Joseph Proudhon (see p. 169) and modern social democrats (see p. 312), have been unwilling to contemplate the abolition of private property. This argument has, however, been put particularly forcefully by free-market economists, such as Friedrich Hayek (see p. 341). In *The Road to Serfdom* ([1944] 1976) Hayek portrayed property ownership as the most fundamental of civil liberties, and argued that personal freedom can only reign within a capitalist economic system. In his view, government intervention in economic life necessarily escalates to the point where all aspects of social existence are brought under state control. In effect, any encroachment upon private property contains the seeds of totalitarian oppression.

In addition to its economic and political advantages, private property also brings social and personal benefits. Private property, for instance, promotes a range of important social values. Property owners have a 'stake' in society, an incentive to maintain order, be law-abiding and behave respectfully. Conservatives have, as a result, praised the notion of a 'property-owning democracy'. In pursuit of this goal, in the 1980s and 1990s, governments in Britain expanded share ownership by privatising nationalised industries. However, this argument also has modestly egalitarian implications. It may justify, for example, heavier taxation of the rich in order to extend property ownership to a disadvantaged 'underclass', which may otherwise remain a constant threat to social stability. A final justification for private property sees property not as an economic resource or as consumable wealth, but rather as a source of personal fulfilment. Property has been seen as both a source of personal security and as an extension of an individual's personality. Property provides security because it gives people 'something to fall back on'. However, the enjoyment and satisfaction which property ownership brings is as much a psychological fact as it is an economic one. There is a sense, for instance, in which people 'realise' themselves, even 'see' themselves, in what they own – their cars, houses, books and the like.

The case against private property has usually been advanced by socialists, though modern liberals and conservatives have also at times recognised the need to limit property rights. The most common approach has been to view private property not as the cornerstone of liberty, but as a fundamental threat to it. One version of this argument warns that unfettered property rights can lead to a grossly unequal distribution of wealth, allowing property to become a means of controlling, even enslaving, others. This idea was expressed most graphically in Proudhon's ([1840] 1970) famous dictum, 'Property is Theft'. What Proudhon meant by this was not so much that individuals have no right to property but simply that the accumulation of wealth in private hands can allow the rich to exploit and oppress the poor. The Marxist argument, however, is more radical. Marx (see p. 373) adopted a labour theory of value, based upon the writings of Locke. This implied that the value of a good reflects the quantity of labour expended in its manufacture. Whereas Locke believed that property rights could be traced to an initial act of labour, Marx saw a stark distinction between those who own wealth, the bourgeoisie, and those whose labour is responsible for its creation, the proletariat. In the process of accumulating wealth, the bourgeoisie extracts what Marx called 'surplus value' from the labour of the proletariat. In other words, private property inevitably leads to exploitation and class oppression. In the *Communist Manifesto* ([1848] 1976), Marx was therefore able to sum up the theory of communism in a single phrase: 'Abolition of private property'.

A further Marxist argument against private property is linked to the idea of alienation. In common with many socialists, Marx believed that labour is of intrinsic human value and not merely of instrumental value: work is important *in itself*, not simply because of what it produces. Work has the potential to be a genuinely fulfilling and creative experience. It can foster skills, talents and sensibilities within the individual, as well as strengthen social solidarity by encouraging cooperation and collective effort. Private property, however, serves to alienate the worker. As explained in Chapter 9, the worker is alienated from the product of his labour, from the process of labour, from fellow workers and, ultimately, from himself or herself. In this way, Marx articulated the fundamentalist socialist belief that private property is corrupting and de-humanising. In promoting selfishness and greed, private property is an obstacle to the realisation of our common humanity. This is an analysis which classical anarchists such as Bakunin (1814–76) and Kropotkin (see p. 169) were also prepared to echo.

Although conservatives have typically defended private property, they have traditionally not supported absolute property rights. In particular, conservative thinkers accept that property rights may have to be constrained in the cause of stability and continuity. In the tradition of Edmund Burke (see p. 139), property has been seen not merely as a reflection of the labour of the present generation but also of the energies and hard work of many earlier generations, passed down to us through the institution of inheritance. In this sense, property links one generation to the next, providing a sense of security and belonging based upon continuity. Such an argument implies that property can never be seen as the exclusive and absolute right of any individual. Rather, property owners are 'stewards', invested with the duty to preserve and perhaps enlarge wealth for the benefit of future generations. This is the sense in which Lord Stockton, formerly Harold Macmillan, criticised the policy of privatisation as 'selling off the family silver'. Moreover, this argument underlines the degree to which property ownership entails duties or responsibilities, and not merely rights. Property, from this perspective, is viewed essentially as a privilege, gained not by individual hard work but through the accident of birth. As a result, property ownership is thought to entail a range of obligations, not least to those who have the misfortune to be poor or propertyless.

Common property

Despite the common misconception of property as private property, the common or collective ownership of wealth has a history which long predates modern socialist thought. Plato (see p. 22) recommended that amongst the philosopher-kings who should be entrusted to rule, property should be owned in common; and Thomas More's *Utopia* ([1516] 1965) portrays a society without private property, in some respects pre-figuring ideas later developed in the *Communist Manifesto*. Whereas private property is based upon the right to exclude others from use, common property can be defined, in Macpherson's words, as 'the right not to exclude others'. In other words, a right of access to property is shared by the members of a collective body and no member is entitled to detach a portion from the common wealth and exclude others, thereby establishing 'private' domain over it. This does not necessarily mean, however, that no one is excluded from use of common property. The right of common ownership may be restricted to the members of a workers' cooperative, a commune or locality. For example, access to common land may be restricted to people designated as 'commoners', 'non-commoners' being excluded, just as the free use of 'public' facilities like libraries, museums and schools may not be extended to 'non-citizens'. In other cases, common ownership may be universal in the sense that no human being is, or can be, excluded from use, as has sometimes been advocated in the case of land. Although a modern corporation or joint stock company exhibits one of the characteristics of common property, being owned by a collective body, its shareholders, it is nevertheless better thought of as an example of institutionalised private property. Since shares can be bought and sold, an individual can detach his or her portion from the whole, something which common property does not allow.

The case in favour of collective property has usually been advanced by socialists, communists and communitarian anarchists. At the heart of this usually lies a theory of labour, but one very different from Locke's. Locke believed that the right to private property could be traced to the labour of an independent and specifiable individual. Supporters of common property, on the other hand, have typically regarded labour as a social and collective activity, depending in almost all cases upon group cooperation rather than independent effort. It follows, therefore, that the wealth so produced should be owned in common and should be used to promote the collective good. Any system of private property simply institutionalises robbery. Common property has also been justified on grounds of social cohesion and solidarity. When property is owned in common, anti-social instincts like selfishness, greed and competition are kept at bay, while social harmony and a sense of collective identity is strengthened. Plato, for instance, believed common ownership to be essential because it would ensure that the class of rulers would act as a united and selfless whole. Socialists have typically seen common property as a way of ensuring that *all* citizens are full members of society, in which case it harnesses the collective energies of the community rather than the narrow and selfish drives of the individual.

Common property has also been sternly criticised. Critics allege that in robbing the individual of a 'private' domain of personal possessions, common ownership creates a de-personalised and insecure social environment. Some socialists have implicitly acknowledged this problem in drawing a distinction between productive property, the 'means of production', which they believe should be collectively owned, and personal property, the 'means of consumption', which can still remain in private hands. Others argue that common property is inherently inefficient in that it fails to provide individuals with a material incentive to work and to realise their talents. A final problem with collective property is that it embodies no mechanism for restricting access to scarce resources, except a reliance upon natural good sense and cooperation. This is sometimes explained by reference to what is called 'the tragedy of the commons'. Before the enclosure of land, all commoners had an unrestricted right of access to it, being able to graze as many animals as they wished. The problem was that in many cases land was over-grazed and became unproductive, a tragedy which affected all commoners. Systems of private property ownership get round this problem by allowing the market to ration scarce resources through the price mechanism. Where systems of common ownership have been introduced, however, access to scarce resources has usually been restricted by the imposition of some form of political authority. Thus common ownership has often in practice taken the form of state ownership.

State property

The notions of common property and state property are often confused. Terms such as 'public ownership' or 'social ownership' appear to refer to property owned collectively by all citizens, but in practice usually describes property that is owned and controlled by the state. 'Nationalisation' similarly implies ownership by the nation but through a system of state control. Nevertheless, state property constitutes a form of property distinct from both private and common property, though, confusingly, it exhibits characteristics of each. The resemblance between state property and common property is borne out by the fact that unlike private corporations the state acts in the name of the people and supposedly in the public interest. A distinction is sometimes made therefore between the ownership and control of state property: ownership, nominally at least, is in the hands of 'the people', while control clearly rests with the government of the day. In other respects, however, state property is more akin to private property. Ordinary citizens, for instance, have no more right of access to state property such as police cars than they do to any other private vehicle.

Moreover, state institutions like schools, public libraries and government offices guard their property no less jealously than private corporations. However, the extent of state property ownership varies considerably from society to society. All states own some range of property to enable them to carry out their basic legislative, executive and judicial functions, but in some countries state property may encompass an extensive range of economic resources and even entire industries. In the case of state collectivisation, as found in orthodox communist regimes such as the Soviet Union, all economic resources – the means of production, distribution and exchange – was designated as 'socialist state property'.

Arguments for state property have often drawn upon those which also favour common ownership. For instance, if state property is regarded as 'public' it reflects the fact that collective social energy was expended in its production, and, unlike private property, it promotes cooperation and cohesion rather than conflict and competition. However, state property may also be said to enjoy advantages to which common property cannot aspire. In particular, the state can act as a mechanism through which access to, and the use of, scarce resources is controlled, thereby avoiding 'the tragedy of the commons'. In the case of state property, however, the right of access to economic resources is limited not for private gain but in the long-term interests of the community. Moreover, unlike common property, state property can be organised along rational and efficient lines. This is usually made possible by some form of planning system, capable both of establishing economic targets and of allocating resources so as to ensure that these targets are met. The nature and merits of planning are considered in greater depth in the next section.

State property is, however, also subject to severe criticism. Advocates of common ownership normally point out that state property is neither 'public' nor 'social' in any meaningful sense. When resources are controlled by state officials they may engender precisely the same alienation as occurs in the case of private property. There is little evidence, for example, that workers in nationalised industries feel in any way closer to the service they provide, or more in control of the process of work, than do those who work for a privately owned company. In addition, state property has often been linked to centralisation, bureaucracy and inefficiency. Whereas private property leaves the organisation of economic life to the vagaries of the market, and common ownership relies upon the sociable and cooperative instincts of ordinary people, state property places its faith in a centralised and supposedly rational system of economic planning. However, all too frequently planning systems have become hopelessly unwieldy and inherently inefficient. Massive numbers of state officials are needed to direct the economy and there is a strong tendency for them to get out of touch with both the needs of the economy and the wishes of the consumer. Furthermore, there is the danger that the state can develop interests separate from those of the people themselves. In such cases, state property can be used to benefit bureaucrats and state officials rather than advance the common good.

Planning

The need for some kind of economic organisation arises out of the simple fact of scarcity: while human needs and wants are infinite, the material resources available to satisfy them clearly are not. In a world of abundant wealth and general prosperity economics would be irrelevant; but in circumstances of scarcity economic issues threaten to dominate all others, political ones included. As already noted, the heart of the economic question has traditionally been posed as a choice between two fundamentally different economic systems – socialism or capitalism – and therefore between two rival mechanisms for allocating resources within the economy: the plan or the market. However, the idea of planning is often poorly understood, being linked in many people's minds to the machinery of central planning once found in the Soviet Union. Yet planning has assumed a wide variety of forms, having been employed by developing countries in the third world as well as by some advanced industrialised states. Moreover, although some have argued that historical developments have entirely discredited the planning process, it is difficult to see how economic activity can be undertaken without some element of planning.

The planning process

To 'plan' is to draw up a scheme or devise a method for achieving a specified goal. In effect, it is to think before one acts. All forms of planning must therefore have two essential features. In the first place, planning is a purposeful activity; planning presupposes the existence of clear and definable objectives, something that it is desirable to achieve or accomplish. These goals may be highly specific, as in the case of the output targets set in Soviet-style central planning, or they may be broader and more generalised, for example, an increase in economic growth, a reduction in unemployment and so on. Secondly, planning is a rational activity. It is based upon the assumption that economic and social problems are capable of being solved through the exercise of human reason and ingenuity. At the heart of economic planning therefore lies a belief that the problem of scarcity can best be overcome by a rational mechanism for allocating resources, geared to established human goals. This 'rational mechanism' undoubtedly involves the exercise of some kind of control over economic life, the production, distribution and exchange of goods and services. However, the means for doing this and the range of control exerted over the economy differs considerably from one system of planning to the next.

The idea of planning has traditionally been associated with socialist economics, and particularly with Marxism (see p. 81). However, Marx never laid down a blueprint for the organisation of a future socialist society and, believing that it was impossible to envisage in detail how a historically different society would work, he restricted himself to a number of broad principles. His central belief was that private property should be abolished and replaced by a system of collective or social ownership. In Marx's view, capitalism was a system of 'commodity production', in which goods and services were produced in response to market pressures, a system of 'production for exchange'. By contrast, a socialist economy would be based upon the principle of 'production for use', and would dispense altogether with market transactions and indeed the need for a money economy. In other words, under socialism the economy would serve the material needs of society, a requirement that presupposes some kind of planning arrangement. Unfortunately, Marx did not specify what form that arrangement would take. What is certain, however, is that neither Marx nor Engels envisaged the emphasis upon central control and large-scale production which characterised the planning process in the Soviet Union. Marx consistently supported broad popular participation at every level in society, and his prediction that the state would 'wither away' as full communism was established suggests support for common property and self-management rather than for state collectivisation.

There is little doubt that the planning process reached its highest stage of development in the Soviet Union, a model later adopted by state socialist regimes in Eastern Europe and elsewhere. In his famous phrase Lenin (see p. 82) described communism as 'Soviet power plus electrification', indicating a broad commitment to modernisation and the task of bringing the economy under democratic control. In the early years of the Soviet regime, however, economic policy was largely shaped by strategic and political considerations. The near economic collapse of the Civil War period, 1918–21, dictated the introduction of 'war communism', which involved widespread nationalisation and the forceable requisitioning of grain surpluses. The 'New Economic Policy', announced in 1921, encouraged the emergence of a mixed economy as Lenin sought to stimulate recovery by permitting the reintroduction of private enterprise in agriculture and small-scale industry. However, the announcement by Stalin in 1928 of the First Five Year Plan, and the collectivisation of Soviet agriculture started the next year, led to the construction of a centrally planned economy. With the exception of private plots of land, supposedly for the personal use of peasants, all economic resources came under the control of the state.

Under Stalin a 'command economy' was established, which involved a system of so-called 'directive planning' operating through a hierarchy of party and state institutions. Overall control of economic policy lay in the hands of the highest organs of the Communist Party, the Central Committee and the Politburo. A complicated network of planning agencies and committees, operating under Gosplan, the State Planning Committee, was responsible for drawing up Five Year Plans. These set production targets for the entire economy and in the process allocated resources to each enterprise, controlled trade and fixed prices, wage levels, taxes and subsidies. The execution of these plans was placed in the hands of powerful economic ministries, which were responsible for particular sectors of the economy and directly controlled Soviet enterprises like banks, factories, shops, and state and collective farms. Soviet-style central planning placed unquestioning faith in the notion that society could be organised on rational lines, and was prepared, when necessary, to imitate US capitalism. For example. the giant steel town of Magnito Gorsk was modelled upon Gary, Indiana, and work in Soviet enterprises was organised on the basis of Taylorism, according to the pioneering time and motion studies undertaken by F.W. 'Speedy' Taylor of the Bethlehem Steel Corporation.

In other countries, however, planning has been seen as a way of supplementing the market rather than replacing it. In such cases, a system of so-called 'indicative planning' has developed in which plans do not establish directives instructing enterprises what to produce and how much to produce, but rather seek to influence the economy indirectly. Economists sometimes refer to this form of government intervention as economic 'management' to distinguish it from Soviet-style 'planning'; nevertheless, it still seeks to exercise a purposeful and rational influence over the organisation of economic life. After 1945 state intervention became increasingly commonplace in the West as governments sought to meet a broad range of economic objectives: maintaining a high level of economic growth, controlling inflation, boosting international trade, ensuring full employment and a fair distribution of wealth, and so forth. In countries such as Britain and France this led to the nationalisation of strategic industries and the construction of mixed economies, allowing government to exert growing influence over economic life.

Formal systems of planning were also set up. In Britain, faltering steps were taken in this direction under the National Plan, drawn up in 1966 by the ill-fated Department of Economic Affairs. However, in France and the Netherlands in particular, more developed and far more successful systems were introduced. A form of planning was also applied in Japan, clearly distinguishing it from the free-market model of economic development found in the United States. The 'economic miracle' Japan experienced in the 1950s and 1960s was overseen by the Ministry of International Trade and Industry, which guided the investment policies of private industry, helped to identify growth industries and targeted export markets. A similar system of careful government intervention to promote export-led growth was adopted elsewhere in East Asia, notably in Hong Kong, Singapore, South Korea and Taiwan. India, however, developed a system of planning that drew unashamedly from Soviet experience. Shortly after independence in 1947, an Indian Planning Commission was set up which, with the assistance of expert institutions such as the Ministry of Finance and the Reserve Bank of India, drew up Five Year Plans. Although these gave the Indian government considerable influence over investment and trade, they did not amount to direct control over the private sector of the economy. Moreover, all plans were subject to approval and amendment in the Indian parliament, the Lok Sabha.

Promise of planning

The attraction of planning rests upon economic, political and moral considerations. Central to these arguments is the fact that planning is a rational process, implying that no economic problem is beyond human ingenuity to solve. In short, planning places the economy firmly in human hands, rather than leaving it to the impersonal and sometimes capricious whims of the market. This is particularly important in establishing overall economic goals – what to produce, and how much to produce. Being relieved of the drive for profit, planners are able to organise a system of 'production for use' geared to the satisfaction of human needs, instead of a system of 'production for exchange' that responds only to market forces.

Although human needs are highly complex and infinitely variable, especially in the areas of consumer taste and popular fashion, there is broad agreement about what constitutes the basic necessities of life. These surely include shelter, a subsistence diet, primary health care and basic education. Unlike capitalist countries, state socialist regimes orientated their economies around the satisfaction of such needs. Although the central planning systems employed in the Soviet Union and throughout Eastern Europe failed dismally in their attempt to produce Western-style consumer goods, they were nevertheless successful in eradicating homelessness, unemployment and absolute poverty, problems which continue to blight the inner cities in some advanced capitalist countries. Despite chronic economic backwardness, Cuba, for example, has a literacy rate of over 98 per cent and a system of primary health care that compares favourably with those in many Western states. Such achievements require not only that economic resources are channelled into the construction industry, agriculture and the building of schools and hospitals, but also that the prices of basic necessities are subsidised and controlled by the planning process, delivering cheap food and affordable housing, as well as free education and health care.

'Planning for need' also offers the prospect of efficiency. Having decided what to produce, planning offers a rational solution to the problem of how to produce, distribute and exchange the goods and services that are desired. In this respect, planning draws on the experience of capitalist firms which have long organised production on rational lines. Although private corporations respond to external market conditions, their internal organisation is planned and directed by a team of senior managers, whose task is to ensure the efficient use of resources. In a sense, Soviet planning was an attempt to transfer this mechanism of rational control from the private corporation to the entire economy. This was evident in the eagerness of Soviet planners to apply management techniques such as Taylorism which had developed in the capitalist West. In this way, planning was able to avoid some of the irrationalities of market capitalism. For instance, planning systems can avoid the scourge of unemployment and the gross waste of economic resources which this represents. Unemployment means that the most vital of all resources, human labour, lies idle while important social needs, such as the building of houses or the improvement of schools and hospitals, go unmet.

A system of planning also means that the economy can be organised in line with long-term goals rather than short-term profit. This has been particularly important in developing economies where market pressures can seriously distort economic prospects, as the dependence of many third world countries upon cash crops clearly demonstrates. Soviet economic development in the 1930s was largely based upon the priority planners gave to building up heavy industries and the steel industry in particular, seeing these as the basis for both national security and future economic progress. By 1941, the central planning system had created a sufficiently strong industrial base to enable the Soviet Union to withstand the Nazi invasion. Similarly, in the 1950s, Japanese planners rejected the advice of economists to concentrate resources in traditional, labour-intensive industries like agriculture in which Japan had a 'comparative advantage', but instead promoted capital-intensive industries like steel, automobiles, electrical and electronic goods, which they believed, correctly as it turned out, were to become the industries of the future.

The political case for planning largely rests upon the prospect of bringing the economy under political and therefore democratic control. Market capitalism strives to separate economics from politics in the sense that the economy is driven by internal, market forces not by government regulation. The economy is therefore accountable to the owners of private businesses, in whose interests decisions are taken, rather than to the public. Planning, by contrast, can be seen as a means of creating a democratic economy. Undoubtedly, the image of planning has been tainted by its association with the authoritarian political structures of orthodox communism. Planning has thus been portrayed as a step towards the construction of a Soviet-style 'command economy'. However, it would appear that there is no necessary link between planning and authoritarianism. Indicative planning, as has been practised in countries such as France, Germany and the Netherlands, is carried out in stable parliamentary democracies in which economic decisions are open to genuine public scrutiny, argument and debate. From this point of view, planning can perhaps be seen as a means through which the anti-democratic tendencies of the market can be tamed.

A moral case can, finally, be made out in favour of planning. As an alternative to private enterprise, planning, in whatever form, attempts to serve public or collective interests rather than particular or selfish ones. That actual systems of planning have failed in this respect, notably the Soviet system of central planning, may have more to do with political circumstances than with the planning process itself. If the planning mechanism is subject to open and democratic accountability and thus addresses genuine human needs, it will give all citizens a 'stake' in their economy. Planning can therefore foster social solidarity and strengthen the bonds of community, in contrast to capitalism which encourages only self-striving and avarice. There is, moreover, a clear link between planning and egalitarianism, which helps to explain why planning has been so attractive to socialists. Planning goes hand in hand with the collective ownership of wealth, ensuring that a planned economy is not debilitated by class conflict which pits the interests of property owners against those of the masses. A planned economy is also likely to be characterised by a more egalitarian system of distribution, as material rewards start to reflect social needs rather than individual productivity. In this sense, planning is based upon a theory of motivation quite foreign to advocates of market capitalism. Insofar as planning strengthens social bonds and counteracts selfishness, it creates a moral incentive to work based upon the betterment of the community rather than the well-being of the private individual.

Perils of planning

Despite its attractions, planning undoubtedly has a number of serious drawbacks. Indeed, planning has never stood alone as a principle of economic organisation, but has always been sustained by market 'impurities'. This is perfectly obvious in the capitalist West where planning has sought to sustain market capitalism by compensating for its failures rather than trying to replace it. However, market impurities also existed in the Soviet Union. For example, private consumption was never controlled, allowing a measure of consumer choice to survive; except in wartime, a market in labour was tolerated; peasant's 'private plots' supplied almost half the potatoes and 15 per cent of the vegetables in the Soviet Union; and thriving 'black' markets developed in goods which the official Soviet system failed to produce. Furthermore, when planned economies have been reformed this has invariably meant making concessions to market competition. This was seen as early as 1921 with the introduction of Lenin's New Economic Policy. In the postwar period, a form of 'market socialism' developed in Yugoslavia and Hungary, which strove to decentralise economic decision-making and permitted the emergence of small capitalist enterprises. In turn, Yugoslav and Hungarian experience influenced Gorbachev's attempts to reform the ailing Soviet economy in the late 1980s. Under the slogan *Perestroika*, or 'restructuring', Gorbachev legalised private cooperatives and single-proprietor businesses, and set about dismantling what he called the 'command-administrative apparatus' by encouraging state enterprises to become self-managing and self-financing.

The central problems that have confronted planned economies have been economic inefficiency and low growth. While the gap between the Soviet Union and the capitalist West continued to diminish until the 1950s, allowing Khrushchev to predict that the Soviet Union would 'bury the West', thereafter growth levels declined to the point that in the early 1980s the Soviet economy was actually shrinking. There is no doubt that the sluggish performance of centrally planned economies, particularly in contrast to an increasingly affluent West, was a major factor contributing to the 'collapse of communism' in the revolutions of 1989–91. One of the first attempts to develop a critique of planning was undertaken by Friedrich Hayek in *The Road to Serfdom* ([1944] 1976). In an analysis elaborated in later writings, Hayek suggested that planning was inherently inefficient because planners were confronted by a range and complexity of information that was simply beyond their capacity to handle. Central planning means making 'output' decisions about what each and every enterprise is to produce, and therefore also 'input' decisions which allocate resources to them. However, given that there were over 12 million products in the Soviet economy, some of which came in hundreds, if not thousands, of varieties, the volume of information within the planning system was frankly staggering. Economists have, for example, estimated that even a relatively small central planning system is confronted by a range of options which exceeds the number of atoms in the entire universe. However competent and committed the planners may be and however well-served by modern technology, any system of central planning is therefore doomed to inefficiency.

A further explanation of the poor economic performance of planned economies is their failure to reward or encourage enterprise. An egalitarian system of distribution may be attractive in moral or ideological terms, but does little to promote economic efficiency. Although centrally planned economies achieved full employment, they typically suffered from high levels of absenteeism, low productivity and a general lack of innovation and enterprise. All Soviet workers, for example, had a job, but it was more difficult to ensure that they actually worked. This problem was acknowledged in the Soviet Union where an initial emphasis upon moral incentives, based upon medals and social prestige, soon gave way to a system of differential wage levels and material rewards, albeit one more egalitarian than in capitalist countries. Some have gone further, however, and argued that to the extent that incentives exist in planned economies these tend to inhibit growth rather than stimulate it. Because the overriding goal in such an economy is to fulfil planning targets, industrial managers are encouraged to underestimate their productive capacity in the hope of being set more achievable output targets. In the same way, planners themselves are likely to set modest targets since promotion, prestige and other rewards are linked to the successful completion of the plan. The planning machine is thus biased in favour of low growth.

Planning systems have also been criticised for their disregard of consumer tastes and preferences. Although planners have employed questionnaires and surveys, neither is as sensitive to consumer pressures as the capitalist price mechanism. Some goods are clearly, in Alec Nove's (1982) term, more 'plannable' than others, in that estimates of likely demand can be made with a reasonable degree of accuracy. This applies, for instance, in the case of electricity. However, modern consumer goods are less 'plannable' since demand for them is more easily influenced by changing tastes and emerging needs. This perhaps accounts for the tendency of planning systems to address basic social needs while ignoring more sophisticated consumer appetites. For example, although planned economies conquered the problem of homelessness, they did so by providing dreary and impersonal tenement accommodation. Agriculture similarly concentrated upon the production of staple foodstuffs, with little attention being given to developing a varied and interesting diet. Moreover, when enterprises are geared to the completion of production targets there is no incentive for them to consider the quality of the goods being produced. Quite simply, production targets can be achieved even though the goods made are never sold and never used.

Finally, planning has been attacked on political and moral grounds. Planned economies have, in particular, been associated with bureaucracy, privilege and corruption. In the absence of market competition, planners are able to enforce their own preferences and values upon society at large. This can lead to 'the tyranny of the planners', as economic and social priorities are determined 'from above' without the wishes of ordinary people being understood, still less being taken into account. Centrally planned economies have certainly suffered from the problem of bureaucratisation as vast armies of state officials, estimated at over 20 million in the Soviet Union, came to enjoy privileges and rewards which set them apart from the mass of the population. Milovan Djilas (1957), at one time a confidante of Tito in Yugoslavia but later imprisoned, termed this sprawling state bureaucracy the 'New Class', drawing parallels between its position and the privileges enjoyed by the capitalist class in Western societies. At the very least, the concentration of economic power in the hands of state officials and industrial managers fostered widespread corruption, a problem that became endemic in the Soviet Union. The fiercest attack upon planning was, however, undertaken by free market economists such as Hayek, who argued that it contains the seeds of totalitarian oppression. Once economic life is regulated, all other aspects of human existence will be brought under state control. Without doubt, the introduction of central planning in the Soviet Union was accompanied by brutal political oppression, with an estimated 20 million people dying as a result of the famines, purges, show trials and executions of the period. In Hayek's view, there was a causal link between these events. In effect, Gosplan led to the gulags, the labour camps.

The market

The alternative to some form of rational organisation of economic life is to rely upon the spontaneous and unregulated workings of the market. A market, as everyone knows, is a place where goods are bought or sold, such as a fish market or a meat market. In economic theory, however, the term 'market' refers not so much to a geographical location as to the commercial activity which takes place therein. In that sense, a market is a system of commercial exchange in which buyers wishing to acquire a good or service are brought into contact with sellers offering the same for purchase. Although transactions can obviously take the form of barter, a system of good-for-good exchange, commercial activity more usually involves the use of money serving as a convenient means of exchange.

The market has usually been regarded as the central feature of a capitalist economy. Capitalism is, in Marx's words, a 'generalised system of commodity production', a 'commodity' being a good or service produced for exchange, that is, possessed of a market value. The market is therefore the organisational principle which operates within capitalism, allocating resources, determining what is produced, setting price and wage levels and so forth. Indeed, many have regarded the market as the source of capitalism's dynamism and success. This success has even converted a growing number of socialists who have come to advocate a form of regulated capitalism or even a system of market socialism. Nevertheless, although the market has achieved particular prominence in the late twentieth century, in the view of some having vanquished its principal rival, its attractions are by no means universally accepted.

The market mechanism

The earliest attempts to analyse the workings of the market was undertaken by the Scottish economist, Adam Smith (see p. 340), in *The Wealth of Nations* ([1776] 1930). Though significantly refined and elaborated by subsequent thinkers, Smith's work still constitutes the basis for much academic economic theory. Smith attacked constraints upon economic activity, such as the survival of feudal guilds and mercantilist restrictions on trade, arguing that as far as possible the economy should function as a self-regulating market. He believed that market competition would act as an 'invisible hand', helping, as if by magic, to organise economic life without the need for external control. As he put it, 'It is not from the benevolence of the butcher, the brewer, or the baker, that we expect our dinner, but from their regard to their own interest'. Although Smith did not subscribe to the crude view that human beings are blindly self-interested, and indeed in *The Theory of Moral Sentiments* ([1759] 1976) developed a complex theory of motivation, he nevertheless emphasised that by pursuing our own ends we unintentionally achieve broader social goals. In this sense, he was a firm believer in the idea of natural order. This notion of unregulated social order, arising out of the pursuit of private interests, was also expressed in Bernard Mandeville's *The Fable of the Bees* ([1714] 1924), which emphasises that the success of the hive is based upon the bees giving in to their 'vices', that is, their passionate and egoistical natures.

Smith suggested that wealth is created through a process of market competition. Later economists have developed this idea into the model of 'perfect competition'. This assumes that in the economy there are an infinite number of producers and an infinite number of consumers, each possessed of perfect knowledge about what is going on in every part of the economy. In such circumstances, the economy will be regulated by the price mechanism, responding as it does to 'market forces', usually referred to as the forces of demand and supply. 'Demand' is the willingness and ability to buy a particular good or service at a particular price; 'supply' refers to the quantity of a good or service that will be available for purchase at a particular price. Prices thus reflect the interaction between demand and supply. If, for example, the demand for motor cars increases, more cars will be wanted for purchase than are available to be bought. When demand exceeds supply, the market price will rise, encouraging producers to step up their output. Similarly, new and cheaper methods of producing television sets will increase supply and allow prices to fall, thereby encouraging more people to buy televisions. Although decision-making in such an economy is highly decentralised, lying in the hands of an incalculable number of producers and consumers, these are not random decisions. An unseen force is at work within the market serving to ensure stability and balance – Adam Smith's 'invisible hand'. Ultimately, market competition tends towards equilibrium because demand and supply will tend to come into line with one another. The price of shoes will, for instance, settle at the level where the number of people willing and able to buy shoes equals the number of shoes available for sale, and will only change when the conditions of demand or supply alter.

A market economy is nothing more than a vast network of commercial relationships, in which both consumers and producers indicate their wishes through the price mechanism. The clear implication of this is that government is relieved of the need to regulate or plan economic activity; economic organisation can simply be left to the market itself. Indeed, if government interferes with economic life, it runs the risk of upsetting the delicate balance of the market. In short, the economy works best when left alone by government. In its extreme form, this leads to the doctrine of *laissez-faire*, literally meaning 'to leave to be', suggesting that the economy should be entirely free from the influence of government. However, only anarcho-capitalists believe that the market can in all respects replace government. Most free-market economists follow Adam Smith in acknowledging that the government has a vital, if limited, role to play.

This, in almost all cases, involves the acceptance that only a sovereign state can provide a stable social context within which the economy can operate, specifically by deterring external aggression, maintaining public order and enforcing contracts. In this respect, free-market economics merely restates the need for a minimal or 'nightwatchman' state. Its proponents may also acknowledge, however, that government has a legitimate economic function, though one largely confined to the maintenance of the market mechanism. For example, government must police the economy to prevent competition being restricted by unfair practices like price agreements and the emergence of 'trusts' or monopolies. Moreover, government is responsible for ensuring stable prices. A market economy relies above all on 'sound money', in other words, a stable means of exchange. Government therefore controls the supply of money within the economy, thereby keeping inflation at bay.

Miracle of the market

The dynamism and vigour of the market has been amply demonstrated by the worldwide dominance of Western capitalist states. Although economic growth in industrialised capitalist states has been by no means consistent, these are the only countries that have come close to achieving the goal of general prosperity. This lesson was not lost on the former communist states of Eastern Europe which, once state socialism was overthrown, speedily introduced market reforms. Indeed, in the late twentieth century the market has achieved a renewed ascendancy and succeeded in converting some of its former critics. Many conservatives, for example, abandoned their pragmatic 'middle way' economic principles, and came instead to embrace the libertarian convictions of the New Right. A growing number of socialists, whose fundamentalist principles reject both private property and competition, came to acknowledge the market as the only reliable mechanism for creating wealth. As socialists sought a social democratic accommodation with the capitalist market, they were forced to revise and modify their goals and, in some cases, to develop entirely new market-based economic models.

The principal attraction of the market has been as a mechanism for creating wealth. This is a task it accomplishes by generating an unrelenting thirst for enterprise, innovation and growth, and by ensuring that resources are put to their most efficient use. The market is a gigantic and highly sophisticated communication system, constantly sending messages or 'signals' from consumers to producers, producers to consumers and so on. The price mechanism, in effect, acts as the central nervous system of the economy, transmitting signals in terms of fluctuating prices. For example, a rise in the price of saucepans conveys to consumers the message 'buy fewer saucepans', while producers receive the message 'produce more saucepans'. The market is thus able to accomplish what no rational allocation system could possibly achieve because it places economic decision-making in the hands of individual producers and individual consumers.

As a result, a market economy can constantly adapt to changes in commercial behaviour and in economic circumstance. In particular, economic resources will be used efficiently not because of a blueprint drawn up by a committee of planners, but simply because resources are drawn to their most profitable use. New and expanding industries will, for instance, win out against old and inefficient ones, as healthy profit levels attract capital investment and labour is drawn by the prospect of high wages. In this way, producers are encouraged to calculate costs in terms of 'opportunity costs', that is in terms of the alternative uses to which each factor of production could be put. Only a market economy is therefore capable of meeting the criterion of economic efficiency proposed in the early twentieth century by Vilfredo Pareto (1848–1923), that resources are allocated in such a way that no possible change could make someone better off and no one worse off.

Efficiency also operates at the level of the individual firm, once again dictated by the profit motive. The market effectively decentralises economic power by allowing vital decisions about what to produce, how much to produce, and at what price to sell, to be made separately by each business. However, capitalist enterprises operate in a market environment which rewards the efficient and punishes the inefficient. In order to compete in the marketplace, firms must keep their prices low and so are forced to keep costs down. Market disciplines therefore help to eradicate the waste, overmanning and low productivity which, by contrast, can be tolerated within a planning system. There is no doubt that in certain respects the market imposes harsh disciplines – the collapse of failed businesses and the decline of unprofitable industries – but in the long run this is the price that has to be paid for a vibrant and prosperous economy. This is precisely why viable forms of market socialism are so difficult to construct. As once practised in Yugoslavia and Hungary, market socialism tried to encourage self-managing enterprise to operate competitively in a market environment. In theory, this offered the best of both worlds: market competition to promote hard work and efficiency, and common ownership to prevent exploitation and inequality. However, such enterprises were reluctant to accept market disciplines because self-management dictates that they respond first and foremost to the interests of the workforce. This is why free-market economists have usually argued that only hierarchically organised private businesses are capable of responding consistently to the dictates of the market.

Market economies are characterised not only by efficiency and high growth but also by responsiveness to the consumer. In a competitive market, the crucial output decisions – what to produce, and in what quantity – are taken in the light of what consumers are willing and able to buy. In other words, the consumer is sovereign. The market is thus a democratic mechanism, ultimately governed by the purchase decisions or 'votes' of individual consumers. This is reflected in the bewildering variety of consumer products available in capitalist economies and the range of choice confronting potential purchasers. Moreover, consumer sovereignty creates an unrelenting drive for technological innovation and advance by encouraging firms to develop new products and improved methods of

Libertarianism

Libertarian political thought is characterised by the strict priority given to liberty (understood in negative terms) over other values, such as authority, tradition and equality. Libertarians thus seek to maximise the realm of individual freedom and minimise the scope of public authority, typically seeing the state as the principal threat to liberty. This anti-statism differs from classical anarchist doctrines in that it is based upon an uncompromising individualism that places little or no emphasis upon human sociability or cooperation.

The two best known libertarian traditions are rooted in, respectively, the idea of individual rights and *laissez-faire* economic doctrines. Libertarian theories of rights generally stress that the individual is the owner of his or her person and thus that people have an absolute entitlement to the property that their labour produces. Libertarian economic theories emphasise the self-regulating nature of the market mechanism and portray government intervention as always unnecessary and counter-productive. Although all libertarians reject government's attempts to redistribute wealth and deliver social justice, a division can nevertheless be drawn between those libertarians who subscribe to anarcho-capitalism and view the state as an unnecessary evil, and those who recognise the need for a minimal state, sometimes styling themselves as 'minarchists'. The relationship between libertarianism and liberalism (see p. 29) is complex and contested. Some view libertarianism as an outgrowth of classical liberalism. Most, however, argue that liberalism, even in its classical form, refuses to give priority to liberty over order and therefore does not exhibit the hostility to the state that is the defining feature of libertarianism. On the other hand, New Right thinking within conservatism (see p. 138) contains an unmistakable libertarian emphasis.

Libertarian theories are founded on an extreme faith in the individual and in freedom. Their virtue is that they provide a constant reminder of the oppressive potential that resides within all the actions of government. However, criticisms of libertarianism fall into two general categories. One sees the rejection of any form of welfare or redistribution as an example of capitalist ideology, linked to the interests of the business community and private wealth. The other highlights the imbalance in a libertarian philosophy that allows it to stress rights but ignore responsibilities, and which values individual effort and ability but fails to take account of the extent to which these are the product of the social environment.

Key figures

Adam Smith (1723–90) A Scottish economist and philosopher, Smith developed the free-market economic theories upon which much of libertarianism is based. A classical liberal rather than a libertarian, Smith's theory of motivation tried to reconcile human self-interestedness with

→

unregulated social order. He was a strong critic of mercantilism and made the first systematic attempt to explain the workings of the economy in market terms, emphasising the role of the 'invisible hand' of market competition. Smith was nevertheless aware of the limitations of *laissez-faire*. His best known works include *The Theory of Modern Sentiments* (1759) and *The Wealth of Nations* (1776).

William Godwin (1756–1836)   A British philosopher and novelist, Godwin developed a thorough-going critique of authoritarianism that amounted to the first full exposition of anarchist beliefs. His extreme form of liberal rationalism readjusted traditional social contract theory in portraying government as the source of, not cure for, disorder in society. He relied upon a theory of human perfectibility based on education and social conditioning. Though an individualist, he believed that humans are capable of genuinely disinterested benevolence. Godwin's chief political work is*Enquiry Concerning Political Justice* (1773).

Max Stirner (1806–56)   A German philosopher, Stirner developed an extreme form of individualism based upon egoism. Stirner saw egoism as a philosophy that places the individual self at the centre of the moral universe, implying that individual action should be unconstrained by law, social convention or moral and religious principles. Such a position points clearly in the direction of atheism and individualist anarchism, even though Stirner gave little attention to the nature of the stateless society. His most important political work is *The Ego and His Own* (1845).

Friedrich Hayek (1899–1992)   An Austrian economist and political philosopher, Hayek was the most influential of modern free-market theorists. An exponent of the so-called Austrian School, he was a firm believer in individualism and market order, and an implacable critic of socialism. He portrayed the market as the only means of ensuring economic efficiency, and attacked government intervention as implicitly totalitarian. Hayek was a classical liberal rather than a conventional libertarian, supporting a modified form of traditionalism and upholding an Anglo-American version of constitutionalism. Hayek's best known works include *The Road to Serfdom* (1948), *The Constitution of Liberty* (1960) and *Law, Legislation and Liberty* (1979).

Robert Nozick (see p. 320)   Nozick is the most important modern libertarian philosopher. His rights-based theory of justice, developed in response to the ideas of John Rawls (see p. 299), rejects all policies of welfare and redistribution, and advocates the decriminalisation of 'victimless crimes' such as prostitution and drug-taking. He nevertheless rejects anarchist beliefs on the grounds that competition between private protection agencies will inevitably lead to the re-establishment of some form of minimal state.

→

Libertarianism continued

Murray Rothbard (1926–95) A US economist and political activist, Rothbard was a leading theorist of modern anarcho–capitalism. He combined a belief in an unrestricted system of *laissez-faire* capitalism with a 'basic libertarian code of the inviolate right of person and property' and, on that basis, rejected the state as a 'protection racket'. In Rothbard's libertarian society of the future there would be no legal possibility for coercive aggression against the person or the property of any individual. His major writings include *Power and Market* (1970), *For a New Liberty* (1973) and *Ethics of Liberty* (1982).

Further reading

Friedman, D. *The Machinery of Freedom*, 3rd edn. New York: Harper & Row, 1989.
Matchan, T.R. (ed.) *The Libertarian Reader*. Totowa, NJ: Rowan & Littlefield, 1982.
Newman, S.L. *Liberalism at Wits' End: The Libertarian Revolt against the Modern State*. Ithaca: Cornell University Press, 1984.

production, so keeping 'ahead of the market'. The market has been the dynamic force behind the most sustained period of technological progress in human history, from the emergence of the iron and steel industries in the nineteenth century to the development of plastics, electrical and electronic goods in the twentieth century.

Although the market has usually been defended on economic grounds, libertarian theorists insist that it can also be supported for moral and political reasons. For instance, the market can be seen as morally desirable in so far as it provides a mechanism through which people are able to satisfy their own desires. In this sense, market capitalism is justified in utilitarian terms: it leaves the definition of pleasure and pain, and therefore of 'good' and 'bad', firmly in the hands of the individual. This, in turn, is clearly linked to individual liberty. Within the market, individuals are able to exercise freedom of choice: they choose what to buy, they choose where to work, they may choose to set up in business, and if so, choose what to produce, who to employ and so on. Furthermore, market freedom is closely linked to equality. Quite simply, the market is no respecter of persons. In a market economy, people are evaluated on the basis of individual merit, their talent and ability to work hard; all other considerations – race, colour, religion, gender and so on – are simply irrelevant. In addition, it can be argued that far from being the enemy of morality the market tends to strengthen moral standards and, indeed, could not exist outside an ethical context. For example, successful employer–worker relations demand reliability and integrity from both parties, while business agreements and commercial transactions would be very difficult to conclude in the absence of honesty and trust.

Market failures

The success of the market as a system for creating wealth has been widely accepted, even by Karl Marx, who, in the *Communist Manifesto*, acknowledged that capitalism had brought about previously undreamed of technological progress. Nevertheless, the market system has also been severely criticised. Some critics, like Marx himself, have believed the market to be fundamentally flawed and in need of abolition. Others, however, recognise the strengths of the market but warn against its unregulated use. In short, they believe that the market is a good servant but a bad master.

Just as no planning system has ever been 'pure', impurities are present in all market economies. This is evident in individual firms which, though they respond to external market conditions, organise their own production on a rational or planned basis. This element of planning is all the more important when the size of modern, multinational corporations is taken into account, some of which have an annual turnover larger than the national income of many small countries. The most obvious impurity, however, takes the form of government economic intervention, found to some extent in all market-based economies. Indeed, through much of the twentieth century, the predominant economic trend in the capitalist West has been for *laissez-faire* to be abandoned as government assumed ever-wider responsibility for economic and social life. Welfare states were established that affected the workings of the labour market by providing a 'social wage'; governments 'managed' their economies through fiscal and monetary policies; and, in a growing number of cases, government exerted direct influence upon the economy by taking industries into public ownership. Some have gone as far as to suggest that it was precisely this willingness by government to intervene and control, rather than leave the economy to the whim of the market, that explains the widespread prosperity enjoyed in advanced capitalist states.

A major failing of the market is that there are economic circumstances to which it does not, or cannot, respond. The market is not, for instance, able to take account of what economists call externalities or 'social costs'. These are costs of productive activity which affect society in general but are disregarded by the firm that makes them because they are external, they do not show up on its balance sheet. An obvious example of a social cost is pollution. Market forces may encourage private business to pollute even though this damages the environment, threatens other industries and endangers the health of neighbouring communities. Only government intervention can force businesses to take account of social costs, in this case either by prohibiting pollution or by ensuring that the polluter pays for the environmental damage they cause. In the same way, the market fails to deliver what economists refer to as 'public goods'. These are goods which it is in everybody's interest to produce but, because it is difficult or impossible to exclude people from their benefit, are not provided by the market. Lighthouses are a clear example of a public good. Ships coming within sight of a lighthouse are able to respond to its warning, but the owners of the lighthouse have no way of extracting payment for the service received. Because the service is available to all, ships thus have an incentive to act as 'free-riders'. As the market cannot respond, public goods have to be provided by government. Indeed, this argument may justify extensive government intervention since sanitation, public health, transport, education and the major utilities could all be regarded as public goods.

Criticism has also been levelled at the consumer responsiveness of the market and, in particular, its ability to address genuine human needs. This occurs, in the first place, because of a powerful tendency towards monopoly. The internal logic of the market is, by contrast with normal expectations, to reward cooperative behaviour and punish competition. Just as individual workers gain power in relation to their employer by acting collectively, private businesses have an incentive to form cartels, make pricing agreements and exclude potential competitors. Most economic markets are therefore dominated by a small number of major corporations. Not only does this restrict the range of consumer choice, but it also gives corporations, through advertising, the ability to manipulate consumer appetites and desires. As economists such as J.K. Galbraith (1962) have warned, consumer sovereignty may be an illusion. Moreover, it is clear that the market responds not to human needs but to 'effective demand', demand backed up by the ability to pay. The market dictates that economic resources are drawn to what it is profitable to produce. This may, however, mean that vital resources are devoted to the production of expensive cars, high fashion and other luxuries for the rich, rather than to providing decent housing and an adequate diet for the mass of society. Quite simply, the poor have little market power.

Despite Adam Smith's faith in natural order, the market may also be incapable of regulating itself. This was, in essence, the lesson the British economist John Maynard Keynes (1883–1946) outlined in *The General Theory of Employment, Interest and Money* ([1936] 1965). Against the background of the Great Depression, Keynes argued that there were circumstances in which the capitalist market could spiral downwards into deepening unemployment, without having the capacity to reverse the trend. He suggested that the level of economic activity was geared to 'aggregate demand', the total level of demand in the economy. As unemployment grows, market forces dictate a cut in wages which, Keynes pointed out, merely reduces demand and so leads to the loss of yet more jobs. By no means did Keynes reject the market altogether, but what he did insist on was that a successful market economy has to be regulated by government. In particular, government must manage the level of demand, increasing it by higher public spending when economic activity falls, leading to a rise in unemployment, but reducing it when the economy is in danger of 'overheating'. One of the first attempts to apply Keynesian techniques was undertaken by F.D. Roosevelt as part of his New Deal policies in the 1930s. Public works programmes were introduced to re-route rivers, build roads, reclaim land and so forth, the most famous of which were supervised by the Tennessee Valley Authority (TVA). In the early postwar period, Keynesian policies were widely adopted by Western governments and were seen as the key to sustaining the 'long boom' of the 1950s and 1960s.

Finally, a moral and political case has been made out against the market. Neo-conservatives as well as socialists have, for instance, argued that the market is destructive of social values. By rewarding selfishness and greed, the market creates atomised and isolated individuals, who have little incentive to fulfil their social and civic responsibilities. Moral condemnation of the market, however, usually focuses upon its relationship with deep social inequality. Fundamentalist socialists link this to the institution of private property and the unequal power of those who own wealth and those who do not. Nevertheless, an unregulated market will also generate wide income differentials. It is a mistake to believe, for example, that the market is a level playing field on which each is judged according to individual merit. Rather, the distribution of both wealth and income is influenced by factors like inheritance, social background and education. Moreover, rewards reflect market value rather than any consideration of benefit to the larger society. This means, for instance, that sports stars and media personalities are substantially better paid than nurses, doctors, teachers and the like. Any economic system that relies upon material incentives will inevitably generate inequalities. Many of those who praise the market as a means of creating wealth are nevertheless reluctant to endorse it as a mechanism for distributing wealth. The solution is therefore that the market be supplemented by some system of welfare provision, as discussed in Chapter 10.

In addition, the market has been seen as a threat to democracy. Socialists in particular argue that genuine democracy is impossible in a context of economic inequality. Such a view suggests that, far from standing apart from the political process, the market shapes political life in crucial ways. For example, party competition is unbalanced by the fact that pro-business parties are invariably better funded than pro-labour ones. Further, they can usually rely upon more sympathetic treatment from a largely privately owned media. Such biases may reach deep into the state system itself. As the principal source of investment and employment in the economy, private corporations will exert considerable sway over any government, regardless of its manifesto commitments or ideological leanings. Governments are, finally, advised by state officials who, because of their educational and social background, are likely to favour capitalism and the interests of private property. In these various ways, the market serves to concentrate political power in the hands of the few and to counter democratic pressures.

Summary

1   Property is an established and enforceable right to an object or possession. Questions about property ownership have traditionally been fundamental to ideological debate, with liberals and conservatives, on the one hand, defending private property, while socialists and communists have upheld either common or state property, on the other.
2   Planning refers to a rational system of resource-allocation within the economy, which may be used either to supplement the market or, in the case of central planning, to replace it. Whereas its supporters have emphasised that planning can address genuine needs and be orientated around long-term goals, it has also been associated with inefficiency, bureaucracy and centralisation.
3   The market is a system of commercial exchange regulated by an 'invisible hand', the impersonal forces of demand and supply. Market theorists emphasise that, as a self-regulating mechanism which tends towards long-run equilibrium, the market works best when left alone by government.
4   Supporters of the market see it as the only reliable mechanism for creating wealth; its virtues are that it promotes efficiency, responds to consumer wishes and preserves both freedom of choice and political liberty. Opponents, however, point out that the market needs to be regulated because it tends to generate social costs, fails to provide public goods, generates deep social inequalities and may, finally, corrupt the democratic process.

Further reading

Bottomore, T. *Theories of Modern Capitalism*. London: Allen & Unwin, 1985.
Brown, M.B. *Models in Political Economy: A Guide to the Arguments*, 2nd edn. Harmondsworth: Penguin, 1995.
Hodgson, G. *The Democratic Economy: A New Look at Planning, Market and Power*. Harmondsworth: Penguin, 1984.

Lindblom, C. *Politics and Markets: The World's Political–Economic Systems* New York: Basic Books, 1977.

Miller, D. *Market, State and Community: Theoretical Foundations of Market Socialism.* Oxford and New York: Oxford University Press, 1989.

Nove, A. *The Economics of Feasible Socialism.* London and New York: Allen & Unwin, 1983.

Reeve, A. *Property.* London: Macmillan and Atlantic Highlands, NJ: Humanities Press, 1986.

Ryan, A. *The Political Theory of Property.* Oxford: Basil Blackwell, 1984.

Schotter, A. *Free Market Economics: A Critical Appraisal.* New York: St Martin's Press and London: Macmillan, 1989.

Chapter 12

Reaction, Reform and Revolution

Introduction
Reaction
Reform
Revolution
Summary
Further reading

Introduction

Political debate and argument can never be confined to cloistered academics because political theories are ultimately concerned with reshaping and remodelling the world itself. Change lies at the very heart of politics. Many would sympathise, for instance, with Marx's assertion in 'Theses on Feuerbach' ([1845] 1968) that, 'The philosophers have only *interpreted* the world, in various ways; the point, however, is to *change* it'. This concluding chapter examines the difficult questions that arise from the issue of change, and from the inevitable linkage in politics between theory and practice. Yet the desire to change the world raises a number of difficult questions.

In the first place, is change desirable? Does change involve growth or decline, progress or decay; should it be welcomed or resisted? Some have turned their faces firmly against change and longed to return to an earlier, simpler time. Such reactionary views, however, became increasingly unfashionable as the modern idea of progress took root. This implies that human history is marked by an advance in knowledge and the achievement of ever-higher levels of civilisation: all change is for the good. Nevertheless, even if change is to be welcomed, what form should it take? This has usually been posed as a choice between two contrasting notions of change: reform or revolution. On the one hand, reform stands for a gradual and incremental process of change that modifies the circumstances of life without fundamentally altering the nature of society. On the other, revolution refers to a more profound and dramatic upheaval, a far-reaching transformation of society itself. What are the merits of reform, and why has it attracted support from such a broad range of thinkers and movements? But why, nevertheless, have others embraced the idea of revolution, regarding it as the only meaningful form of political change?

Reaction

Reaction literally means to respond to an action or stimulus, to re-act. In politics, reaction suggests a negative attitude to change, often thought to be the characteristic feature of conservative thought. In that sense, conservatism stands, very crudely, for the desire to conserve and therefore to resist change. Such a stance, however, can take at least three different forms. First, reaction can amount to a demand for continuity with the past. In other words, it seeks to eradicate change, usually in the name of custom or tradition. Secondly, reaction can involve an attempt to reclaim the past, in effect, to 'turn the clock back'. Such a position endorses change providing it is backward-looking or regressive, a goal often inspired by the notion of a 'Golden Age'. Thirdly, reaction can recognise the need for change as a means of preservation, adopting a philosophy of 'change in order to conserve'. This implies a belief in 'natural' change. If certain changes are inevitable any attempt to resist them risks precipitating more far-reaching and damaging change.

Defending the status quo

The 'desire to conserve' is the moderate face of reactionary politics. Instead of advocating a lurch backwards into the past, it preaches the need for preservation, the need for continuity with the past. In essence, this amounts to a defence of the status quo, the existing state of affairs. For some, this desire to resist or avoid change is deeply rooted in human psychology. In his essay 'Rationalism in Politics' ([1962] 1991), for example, Michael Oakeshott (see p. 139) argued that to be a conservative is 'to prefer the familiar to the unknown, to prefer the tried to the untried, fact to mystery, the actual to the possible, the limited to the unbounded, the near to the distant, the sufficient to the superabundant, the convenient to the perfect, present laughter to utopian bliss'. By this, Oakeshott did not suggest that the present is in any way perfect or even that it is better than any other condition that might exist. Rather, the present is valued on account of its familiarity, a familiarity that engenders a sense of reassurance, stability and security. Change, on the other hand, will always appear threatening and uncertain: a journey into the unknown. This is why conservative theorists have usually placed so much emphasis upon the importance of custom and tradition.

Customs are long-established and habitual practices. In traditional societies which lack the formal machinery of law, custom often serves as the basis for order and social control. In developed societies, custom has sometimes been accorded the status of law itself in the form of so-called common law. In the English tradition of common law, for example, customs are recognised as having legal authority if they have existed without interruption since 'time immemorial', in theory since 1189 but in practice as far back as can reasonably be established. The reason why custom embodies moral and sometimes legal authority is that it is thought to reflect popular consent: people accept something as rightful because 'it has always been that way'. Custom shapes expectations and aspirations and so helps to determine what people think is reasonable and acceptable: familiarity breeds legitimacy. This is why people's sense of natural fairness is offended when long-established patterns of behaviour are disrupted. They appeal to 'custom and practice', feeling that they have a right to expect things to remain the way they have always been. Much of the defence of custom is, however, closely linked to the particular virtues of tradition.

Tradition, in the words of Edward Shils (1981), encompasses 'anything transmitted or handed down from the past to the present'. Therefore, anything from long-standing customs and practices to an institution, political or social system, or a body of beliefs, can be regarded as a tradition. However, it may be very difficult to determine precisely how long a belief, practice or institution has to survive before it can be regarded as a tradition. Traditions have usually been thought to denote continuity between generations, things that have been transmitted from one generation to the next, but the line between the traditional and the merely fashionable is often indistinct. Whereas the Christian religion is undoubtedly a tradition, having endured for two thousand years, can the same be said of industrial capitalism which only dates back to the nineteenth century, or of the welfare state which first emerged in the early twentieth century? At what point, for instance, did universal adult suffrage become a tradition? Despite these difficulties, however, there is an impressive body of conservative thought that highlights the vital importance of traditional practices and beliefs.

The classic statement of this position is found in the writings of Edmund Burke (see p. 139), and in particular in *Reflections on the Revolution in France* ([1790] 1968). Burke acknowledged that society is founded upon a contract, but not one made only by those who happen to be alive at present. In Burke's words, society is a partnership 'between those who are living, those who are dead and those who are to be born'. Tradition therefore reflects the accumulated wisdom of the past, beliefs and practices that have literally been 'tested by time' and have been proved to have worked. This is what G.K. Chesterton referred to as a 'democracy of the dead'. If those who 'merely happen to be walking around' turn their backs upon tradition they are, in effect, disenfranchising earlier generations – the majority – whose contribution and understanding is simply being ignored. As what Burke called 'the collected reason of ages', tradition provides both the only reliable guide for present conduct and the most valuable inheritance we can pass on to future generations. From Oakeshott's point of view, tradition not merely reflects our attachment to the familiar, but also ensures that social institutions work better because they operate in a context of established rules and practices.

Critics have, nevertheless, viewed custom and tradition in a very different light. Thomas Paine's *The Rights of Man* ([1791–2] 1987) was written in part as a reply to Burke. Paine (see p. 209) argued that Burke had placed 'the authority of the dead over the rights and freedoms of the living'. In other words, to revere tradition merely on the grounds that it has long endured is to enslave the present generation to the past, condemning it to accepting the evils of the past as well as its virtues. In his view, uncritical respect for the past clearly violated modern democratic principles, the central point of which is the right of each generation to make and remake the world as it sees fit. Such a position implies that while the present generation is at liberty to learn from the past, it should not be forced to relive it.

Furthermore, the assertion that values, practices and institutions have only survived because they have worked is highly questionable. Such a view sees in human history a process of 'natural selection': those institutions and practices that have been of benefit to humankind are preserved, while those of little or no value have declined or become extinct. This comes down to a belief in survival of the fittest. Clearly, however, institutions and beliefs may have survived for very different reasons. For instance, they may have been preserved because they have been of benefit to powerful elites or a ruling class. This can perhaps be seen in Britain in the case of the monarchy and the House of Lords. Indeed, to foster reverence for history and tradition may simply be a means of manufacturing legitimacy and ensuring that the masses are pliant and quiescent. In addition, custom and tradition may be an affront to rational debate and intellectual enquiry. To revere 'what is' simply because it marks continuity with the past forecloses debate about 'what could be' and perhaps even 'what should be'. From this perspective, tradition tends to inculcate an uncritical, unreasoned and unquestioning acceptance of the status quo and leave the mind in the thrall of the past. J.S. Mill (see p. 258) referred to this danger as 'the despotism of custom'.

Reclaiming the past

A more radical form of reactionary politics looks not to continuity and preservation, but rather embraces the idea of backward-looking change. Such a style of politics has in fact little to do with tradition because tradition is concerned with the maintenance of a status quo which these radical reactionaries are intent upon destroying. Far from upholding the importance of the familiar and the stable, this form of reaction can, at times, have a revolutionary character. For example, the 'Islamic Revolution' in Iran in 1979 can be regarded as a reactionary revolution in that it marked a dramatic break with the immediate past, designed to prepare the way for the re-establishment of more ancient Islamic principles. This form of reaction is based upon a very clear picture of human history. Whereas traditionalism sees in history the threads of continuity, linking one generation to the next, radical reaction sees a process of decay and corruption. At its heart, therefore, lies the image of an earlier period in history – a Golden Age – from which point human society has steadily declined.

The call for backward-looking change clearly reflects dissatisfaction with the present, as well as distrust of the future. This style of politics, which condemns the existing state of affairs by comparing it to an idealised past can be found in many historical periods. For example, conservatism in continental Europe exhibited a strong reactionary character throughout the nineteenth century and into the twentieth. In countries like France, Germany and Russia, conservatives remained faithful to autocratic and aristocratic principles long after these had been displaced by constitutional and representative forms of government. This was well reflected in the writings of Joseph de Maistre (see p. 165) and in the statecraft of Metternich, both of whom rejected any concession to reformist pressures and strove instead to re-establish an *ancien régime*. Fascist doctrines in the twentieth century also tended to be backward-looking. Mussolini and the Italian Fascists, for instance, glorified the military might and political discipline of Imperial Rome. In the case of Hitler and the Nazis, this was reflected in an idealisation of the 'First Reich', Charlemagne's Holy Roman Empire. Similarly, reactionary leanings can be found in the modern period in the radicalism of the New Right. In embracing the notion of the 'frontier ideology' in the 1980s, Ronald Reagan harked back to the conquest of the American West and the virtues of self-reliance, hard work and adventurousness which he believed it exemplified. In Britain during the same period, Margaret Thatcher extolled the importance of 'Victorian values' such as decency, enterprise and self-help, seeing the mid-nineteenth century as a sort of Golden Age.

The desire to 'turn the clock back' is based upon a simple historical comparison between the past and the present. Forward-looking or progressive reform means a march into an unknown future, with all the uncertainty and insecurity which that must involve. By comparison, the past is known and understood and therefore offers a firmer foundation for remodelling the present. This does not, however, imply blind reverence for history or a determination to maintain institutions and practices simply because they have survived. On the contrary, by breaking with traditionalism, radical reactionaries can adopt a more critical and questioning attitude towards the past, taking from it what is of value to the present and leaving what is not. For example, the New Right recommends the re-establishment of *laissez-faire* economic principles, not on the grounds that they have been 'sanctified by history' but because when applied in the nineteenth century they promoted growth, innovation and individual responsibility. In the same way, if respect for the family and for traditional values did once help to create a more stable, decent and cohesive society, there is a case for renouncing the permissive morality of the present in order to reclaim the values of the past.

However, the prospect of backward-looking change can also have less favourable implications. For instance, the desire to 'turn the clock back' may be based upon little more than nostalgia, a yearning for a mythical past of stability and security. All too often this form of reaction embraces a naive and romanticised image of the past, against which the present appears to be squalid, corrupt or simply charmless. The Golden Age is, at best, a selective portrait of the past and at worst a thoroughly distorted picture of what life was really like. The conquest of the American West, for example, could be linked as easily with the near-genocide of the native Americans as it is with the rugged individualism of the frontier settlers. Equally, 'Victorian values' could stand for grinding poverty, the work-house and child prostitution, instead of decency, respect and a willingness to work.

The very idea of a Golden Age, a utopia located in the past, may simply reflect the desire to escape from present-day problems by seeking comfort in historical myths. Just as modern thinkers have extolled the virtues of the Victorian age, the Victorians lamented the passing of the eighteenth century. In that sense, there never was a Golden Age. Moreover, even if meaningful lessons can be learnt from the past, it is questionable whether these can be applied to the present. Historical circumstances are the product of a complex network of interconnected social, economic, cultural and political factors. To identify a particular feature of the past as admirable does not mean it would necessarily have the same character in the present, even if it could be reproduced in its original form. All institutions and ideas may be specific to the period in which they arise. For instance, although *laissez-faire* policies may have promoted vigorous growth, enterprise and innovation in the nineteenth century, a period of early industrialisation, there is no certainty that it would have the same results if applied to a developed industrial economy.

Change in order to conserve

The final face of reaction is, ironically, a progressive one. Reactionaries have not always set their faces firmly against change, or only endorsed change when it has a regressive character. On some occasions they have accepted that the onward march of history is irresistible. Quite simply, to try to block inevitable change may be as pointless as King Canute's attempt to stop the flow of the tide. More seriously, blinkered reaction that does not recognise that at times change can be natural and inevitable runs the risk of precipitating a still more dramatic upheaval. The motto of this form of progressive conservatism is therefore that reform is preferable to revolution. This amounts to a form of enlightened reaction which recognises that, though it may be desirable to preserve the status quo, an implacable resistance to change is likely to be self-defeating. It is better to be the willow that bends before the storm than the proud oak which risks being uprooted and destroyed.

This progressive form of conservatism is usually linked to the ideas of Edmund Burke. In contrast to the reactionary conservatism widely found in continental Europe, Burke argued that the French monarchy's stubborn commitment to absolutism had helped to precipitate revolution in the first place. 'A state without the means of some change', Burke ([1790] 1968) proclaimed, 'is without the means of its conservation'. This lesson was borne out by the English monarchy which had survived precisely because it had been prepared to accept constitutional constraints upon its power. The 'Glorious Revolution' of 1688, which brought the English Revolution to an end with the establishment of a constitutional monarchy under William and Mary, was a classic example of conservative reform. Similar lessons can be learnt from the 1917 Russian Revolution. The Tsarist regime can, to some extent, be regarded as the architect of its own downfall because of its blinkered refusal to make concessions to the growing movement for political and social reform. Tsar Nicholas II's touching but absurd faith in Divine Right and his refusal to address problems highlighted by the 1905 Revolution, helped to create the social and political conditions which Lenin and the Bolsheviks were able to exploit in 1917. Indeed, while reactionary conservatism often failed to survive the nineteenth century and was finally brought down by its association with fascism in the twentieth century, the Anglo-American tradition of Burkian conservatism has been far more successful. The philosophy of 'change in order to conserve' has, for example, enabled conservatives to come to terms with constitutionalism, democracy, social welfare and economic intervention.

Enlightened reaction is based upon a view of history which differs from both traditionalism and backward-looking reaction. Traditionalism tends to emphasise the stable and unchanging nature of human history, highlighting a continuity with the past; backward-looking reaction has a deeply pessimistic view of history, underpinned by the belief that 'things get worse'. Enlightened reaction, by contrast with the other two, is based upon the idea of inevitable change which because it is 'natural' is neither to be applauded nor regretted, only accepted. This suggests a view of history as being largely beyond human control and dictated by what Burke called 'the pattern of Nature'. For Burke, such a view was closely linked to the belief that human affairs are shaped by the will of God and so are beyond the capacity of humankind to fathom. In the same way, the process of history may simply be too complex and intricate for the human mind adequately to grasp, still less to control. In other words, when the tide of history is flowing, wisdom dictates that human beings swim with it rather than try to swim against it.

Such a position has been taken up at various points in history. In the United States, for instance, commentators like Luis Hartz have suggested that no real conservative tradition can be identified. American political culture was shaped by the struggle for independence and is deeply embued with a commitment to progress, the dream of a limitless future. In such circumstances, conservatives have often been more tolerant of change and less suspicious of reform than their European counterparts; and, lacking a feudal past or an *ancien régime* to restore, they have less easily fallen prey to Golden Age fantasies. Indeed, the term 'conservative' has only been widely used in US party politics since the 1960s. In Canada, the Conservative Party adopted the title Progressive Conservative precisely in order to demonstrate its reforming credentials and distance itself from the image of unthinking reaction. The British tradition of progressive conservatism is usually traced back to Disraeli in the nineteenth century, the so-called One Nation tradition. It reached its peak in the 1950s as the Conservative Party accepted the social democratic reforms of the Attlee government. In continental Europe since 1945, a reformist stance has been adopted by Christian Democratic parties that have attempted to balance a commitment to free enterprise against the need for welfare and social justice.

However, even when it is intended to conserve, change can create difficulties for a conservative. In the first place, there is the problem of distinguishing between 'natural' changes, which if not to be welcomed should at least be accepted, and other forms of change which should still be resisted. This is a much simpler task to accomplish, as Burke did, with the advantage of hindsight. It is much easier to point out that the failure to introduce prudent reform was likely to lead to violent revolution after that revolution has occurred. Quite clearly, it is much more difficult at the time to know which of the many changes being demanded are resistible and which ones are irresistible. A further problem is that, far from promoting stability and contentment, reform may pave the way for more radical change. In some respects, abject poverty is more likely to generate resignation and apathy than revolutionary fervour. On the other hand, improving political or social conditions may heighten expectations and stimulate the appetite for change. This is perhaps what happened in the Soviet Union in the late 1980s, when Gorbachev's reforms merely succeeded in hastening the demise of the regime itself. The idea that revolutions are often linked to 'rising expectations' is discussed more fully in the final section of this chapter, together with other theories of revolution.

Reform

The earliest meaning of 'reform' was literally to re-form, to form again, as when soldiers re-form their lines. This meaning of reform, ironically, has a reactionary character since it implies the recapturing of the past, the restoration of something to its original order. This backward-looking aspect of reform was evident in the use of the term 'Reformation' to describe the establishment of the Protestant churches in the sixteenth century, because its supporters saw it as a movement to restore an older and supposedly purer form of spiritual experience. However, in modern usage, reform is more commonly associated with innovation rather than restoration; it means to make anew, to create a new form, as opposed to returning to an older one. Reform is now inextricably linked to the ideas of progress. For example, to 'reform your ways' means to mend your ways; a 'reformed character' is a person who has abandoned his or her bad habits; and a 'reformatory' is a place which is meant to help correct anti-social behaviour. For this reason, the term 'reform' always carries positive overtones, implying betterment or improvement. Strictly speaking, therefore, it is contradictory to condemn or criticise what is acknowledged to be a reform.

Nevertheless, reform denotes a particular kind of improvement. Reform indicates changes within a person, institution or system which may remove their undesirable qualities but which do not alter their fundamental character: in essence, they remain the same person, institution and system. For instance, to demand the reform of an institution is to call for a reorganisation of its structure, an alteration of its powers or a change of its function, but it is not to propose that the institution itself be abolished or be replaced by a new one. In that sense, reform stands clearly in opposition to revolution: it represents change within continuity. Indeed, in order to advocate reform it is necessary to believe that the person, institution or system in question has within it the capacity to be saved or improved. Political reform therefore stands for changes like the extension of the franchise and institutional adjustments which take place within the existing constitutional structure; social reform, similarly, refers to improvements in public health, housing or living conditions which help to improve the social structure rather than fundamentally alter it. Reform thus amounts to a qualified endorsement of the status quo; it suggests that, provided they are improved, existing institutions, structures and systems are preferable to the qualitatively new ones that could replace them. For this reason, reform stands for incremental improvement rather than a dramatic upheaval, gradual progress rather than a radical departure, evolution rather than revolution.

Progress and reason

Fundamental to any kind of reform is the idea of progress. If reform implies improvement it suggests a forward-looking and optimistic attitude towards change that departs significantly from the ideas of traditionalism and reaction. Progress literally means an advance, a movement forward. The idea that human history is marked by progress originated in the seventeenth century and reflected the growth of rationalist and scientific thought. A belief in progress, the 'forward march of history', subsequently became one of the basic tenets of the Western intellectual tradition. Liberal thinkers, for instance, believed that humankind was progressively emancipating itself from the chains of poverty, ignorance and superstition. In Britain this was manifest in the emergence of the so-called 'Whig interpretation of history', which portrayed history as a process of intellectual and material development. In 1848, for instance, in the first chapter of his immensely successful *History of England*, Thomas Macaulay was able to write that 'The history of our country during the last hundred and sixty years is eminently the history of physical, of moral and of intellectual improvement'. The optimism implied by the idea of progress also influenced socialists who believed that a socialist society would emerge out of, or be built on, the foundations of liberal capitalism. Faith in progress has often amounted to a form of historicism, in that it portrays human history as an inevitable process leading humankind from lower levels of civilisation to higher ones. Not uncommonly, this is reflected in the use of biological metaphors like 'growth' and 'evolution' to describe the process of historical change. However, on what basis is it possible to portray history as remorseless and irresistible progress?

The idea of progress was a product of the scientific revolution and has gone hand in hand with the growth of rationalism. Science provided a rational and reliable form of enquiry through which human beings could acquire objective knowledge of the world around them. As such, it emancipated human beings from the religious doctrines and dogmas that had previously shackled intellectual enquiry and promoted the secularisation of Western thought. Armed with reason, human beings could for the first time not only explain the natural world but also start to understand the society in which they live and interpret the process of history itself. The power of reason gave human beings the capacity to take charge of their own lives and shape their own destinies. When problems exist, solutions can be found; when obstacles block human advance these can be overcome; when defects are identified, remedies are available. Rationalism therefore emancipates humankind from the grip of the past and the weight of custom and tradition. Instead, it is possible to learn from the past, its successes and failures, and move forward. The process of history is thus marked by the accumulation of human knowledge and the deepening of wisdom. Each new generation is able to advance beyond the last.

A belief in inevitable progress is reflected in the tendency to interpret economic, social and political change in terms of 'modernisation' and 'development'. The political and social upheavals through which advanced industrial societies came into existence have, for instance, often been described as a process of modernisation. To be 'modern' means not only being contemporary, being 'of the present', but it also implies an advance in relation to the past, a movement away from the 'old fashioned' or 'out of date'. Political modernisation is usually thought to involve the emergence of constitutional government, the safeguarding of civil liberties and the extension of democratic rights. In short, a 'modern' political system is a liberal democratic one. Social modernisation, in turn, is closely linked to the spread of industrialisation and urbanisation. 'Modern' societies possess efficient industrialised economies and a high level of material affluence. In the same way, Western industrialised societies are often described as 'developed' by comparison with the 'underdeveloped' or 'developing' third world. Such terminology clearly implies that the liberal democratic political systems and industrialised economies typically found in the West mark a higher level of civilisation compared with the more traditional structures found in parts of Africa, Asia and Latin America. In such cases, 'traditional' implies backwardness. Moreover, to describe the process of modernisation in the West as 'development' suggests that it is the likely, if not inevitable, path that non-Western societies will also tread. Human history is therefore portrayed as an onward march with Western societies in the vanguard. They map out a route which other societies are destined to follow.

Faith in the idea of progress is not, however, universal. Many in the developing world, for example, point out that to interpret political and social progress in exclusively Western terms both fails to appreciate the distinctive culture and traditions of non-Western societies and ignores the possibility that there may be other models of development. More fundamentally, the very idea of progress has been called into question. Such a position, usually adopted by conservative theorists, suggests that faith in rationality is often misplaced. As Burke suggested, the world is simply too vast and too complicated for the human mind to fully comprehend. If this is true, 'systems of thought', typically devised by liberal and socialist theorists, will inevitably simplify or distort the reality which they set out to explain. Quite simply, no reliable 'blueprint' exists which enables human beings to remodel or reform their world. Where attempts have been made to improve political and social circumstances, whether through reform or revolution, conservatives often warn, in Oakeshott's words, that 'the cure may be worse than the disease'. Wisdom therefore dictates that human beings should abandon the delusion of progress and base their actions instead upon the firmer ground of experience, history and tradition.

Reform versus revolution

To advocate reform is to prefer evolutionary change to revolutionary change. In biology 'evolution' refers to a process of genetic mutation taking place within each species which either fits the species to survive and prosper within its environment or else fails to do so, in which case the species will die out. This is what Charles Darwin (1809–82) referred to as 'natural selection'. In this way, higher and more complex species, such as humankind, have evolved from lower and more simple ones like the apes. This is, nevertheless, a very gradual process, taking perhaps thousands and maybe millions of years. However, it is precisely the gradual and incremental nature of evolutionary change that has encouraged both liberals and parliamentary socialists to advocate reform rather than revolution.

Liberal reformism is often associated with the utilitarianism (see p. 360) of Jeremy Bentham (see p. 361). This provided the basis for what was called 'philosophic radicalism', which helped to shape many of the most prominent reforms in nineteenth-century Britain. Founded upon the utilitarian assumption that all individuals seek to maximise their own happiness, and applying the goal of general utility – 'the greatest happiness for the greatest number' – the philosophic radicals advocated a wide range of legal, economic and political reforms. Bentham proposed that laws be thoroughly codified and the legal system be put on a soundly rational basis, with no place being found for traditionalist ideas like common law or metaphysical notions, such as 'natural law' and 'natural rights'. In economic life, the philosophic radicals were keen supporters of the classical political economy of Adam Smith (see p. 340) and David Ricardo (1772–1823), and were thus critical of any attempt to constrain the workings of the market through monopoly or protectionism. Their programme of political reform centred upon the demand for greater

Utilitarianism

Utilitarian theory emerged in the late eighteenth century as a supposedly scientific alternative to natural rights theories. In Britain, during the nineteenth century, utilitarianism provided the basis for a wide range of social, political and legal reforms, advanced by the so-called Philosophic Radicals. Utilitarianism provided one of the major foundations for classical liberalism (see p. 29) and remains perhaps the most important branch of moral philosophy, certainly in terms of its impact upon political issues.

Utilitarianism suggests that the 'rightness' of an action, policy or institution can be established by its tendency to promote happiness. This is based upon the assumption that individuals are motivated by self-interest and that these interests can be defined as the desire for pleasure, or happiness, and a wish to avoid pain. Individuals thus calculate the quantities of pleasure and pain that each possible action would generate, and choose whichever course promises the greatest amount of pleasure over pain. Utilitarian thinkers believe that it is possible to quantify pleasure and pain in terms of utility, taking account of their intensity, duration and so forth. Human beings are therefore utility maximisers, who seek the greatest possible pleasure and the least possible pain or unhappiness. The principle of utility can be applied to society at large using the classic nineteenth-century formula of 'the greatest happiness for the greatest number'.

However, utilitarianism has developed into a cluster of theories. Classical utilitarianism is act-utilitarianism, in that it judges an act to be right if its consequences produces at least as much pleasure-over-pain as those of any alternative act. Rule-utilitarianism, rather, judges an act to be right if it conforms to a rule which, if generally followed, would produce good consequences. What is called utilitarian generalisation assesses an act's rightfulness not in terms of its own consequences, but on the basis of its consequences if the act were to be universally performed. Motive-utilitarianism places emphasis upon the intentions of the actor rather than upon the consequences of each action.

The attraction of utilitarianism is its capacity to establish supposedly objective grounds on which moral judgements can be made. Rather than imposing values on society, it allows each individual to make his or her own moral choices as each alone is able to define what is pleasurable and what is painful. Utilitarian theory thus upholds diversity and freedom, and demands that we respect others as pleasure-seeking creatures. Its drawbacks are philosophical and moral. Philosophically, utilitarianism is based upon a highly individualistic view of human nature that is both asocial and ahistorical. It is by no means certain, for instance, that consistently self-interested behaviour is a universal feature of human society. Morally, utilitarianism may be nothing more than crass hedonism, a view expressed by J. S. Mill (see p. 258) in his declaration that he would rather be 'Socrates dissatisfied than a fool satisfied' (although Mill himself subscribed to a modified form of utilitarianism). Utilitarianism has also been criticised for

→

endorsing acts that are widely considered wrong, such as the violation of basic human rights, if they serve to maximise the general utility of society.

Key figures

Jeremy Bentham (1748–1832) A British philosopher and legal reformer, Bentham was the founder of utilitarianism and laid down the basis of philosophical radicalism. His moral and philosophical system, developed as an alternative to natural rights theory, was based upon the belief that human beings are rationally self-interested creatures who calculate pleasure and pain in terms of utility. Using the 'greatest happiness' principle, he developed a justification for *laissez-faire* economics, advocated a wide range of legal and constitutional reforms, and, in later life, supported political democracy in the form of universal manhood suffrage. Bentham's major works include *A Fragment on Government* (1776) and *Principles of Morals and Legislation* (1789).

James Mill (1773–1836) A Scottish philosopher, historian and economist, Mill helped to turn utilitarianism into a radical reform movement. Using Benthamite philosophy, he attacked mercantilism, the church, the established legal system and, especially, the system of aristocratic government. Mill supported what he called 'pure democracy' as the only means of achieving good government, defined as government in the interests of the governed, or at least in the interests of the 'greatest number'. On this basis, he recommended a progressive widening of the franchise, frequent elections and a secret ballot. Mill's best known work is *Essay on Government* (1820).

Peter Singer (1945–) An Australian philosopher, Singer has employed utilitarianism to consider a range of political issues. He has argued in favour of animal welfare on the grounds that an altruistic concern for the well-being of other species derives from the fact that, as sentient beings, they are capable of suffering. Animals, like humans, have an interest in avoiding physical pain, and he therefore condemns any attempt to place the interests of humans above those of animals as 'speciesism'. However, he accepts that altruistic concern does not imply equal treatment, and he does not accord animals rights. Singer has also used utilitarianism to justify increasing assistance from rich to poor countries. Singer's major works include *Animal Liberation* (1975), *Practical Ethics* (1979) and *How Are We to Live?* (1993).

Further reading

Brandt, R. B. *Morality, Utilitarianism and Rights*. Cambridge: Cambridge University Press, 1992.
Goodin, R. *Utilitarianism as a Public Philosophy*. Cambridge: Cambridge University Press, 1995.
Sen, A. and Williams, B. (eds) *Utilitarianism and Beyond*. Cambridge: Cambridge University Press, 1982.

democracy, including a commitment to frequent elections, the secret ballot and universal suffrage. Indeed, the zeal of these liberal reformers ensured that during the nineteenth century Britain was transformed from a hierarchic and aristocratic society into a modern parliamentary democracy.

Socialist reformism, which emerged towards the end of the century, consciously built on these liberal foundations. The Fabian Society, for instance, founded in 1884 and named after the Roman general, Fabius Maximus, famous for the patient and delaying tactics with which he defeated Hannibal, emphasised its faith in 'the inevitability of gradualism'. The Fabians openly rejected the ideas of revolutionary socialism, represented by Marxism (see p. 81), and proposed instead that a socialist society would gradually emerge out of liberal capitalism through a process of incremental and deliberate reform. Such ideas were widely taken up by parliamentary socialists in Europe and elsewhere. In Germany, Eduard Bernstein's (see p. 313) *Evolutionary Socialism* ([1898] 1962) marked the first major critique of orthodox Marxism, and championed the idea of a gradual and peaceful transition from capitalism to socialism. This tradition of socialist reformism constitutes the basis of modern Western social democracy. In *The Future of Socialism* (1956), Anthony Crosland (see p. 313) defined socialism not as the abolition of capitalism and its replacement by a system of common ownership, but as steady progress made towards the goal of equality, a more equitable distribution of rewards and privileges in society. This, he argued, would be brought about through a gradual process of social reform, involving in particular the expansion of the welfare state and the improvement and extension of educational provision.

Reform as a process of evolutionary change has a number of advantages over revolution. In the first place, by bringing about change within continuity, reform can be brought about peacefully and without disrupting social cohesion. Even when the cumulative affect of reform amounts to fundamental change, because it is brought about in a piecemeal fashion, bit by bit, and over an extended period, it is more likely to be acceptable, even to those who are at first unsympathetic. This was apparent in the establishment of political democracy in most Western societies through the gradual extension of the franchise, first to working-class men, and finally to women. By contrast, revolution reflects an attempt forcibly to impose change on society. As such, it dramatically polarises opinions and deepens divisions, and is often accompanied by violence, which may be regarded as morally unacceptable. A second argument in favour of reform is that it is prepared to build upon what already exists, rather than simply discard it. In this way, reform appeals to a pragmatic style of politics in which policy is dictated more by practical circumstances than by abstract theory. To some extent, reform accepts what conservatives have traditionally taught: all theories and systems of thought are liable to be defective. To break completely with the past by bringing about revolutionary change is, in effect, to enter unknown territory without a reliable map for guidance.

Thirdly, reform appeals to the best empirical traditions of scientific enquiry. Reform is an incremental process, it advances by a series of relatively small steps. Modern welfare states, for example, have not been constructed overnight; they are developed over a period of time through reforms which progressively extend the social security system, expand health and education provision and so forth. In the United States, the welfare programme of the 1960s built upon foundations laid under F.D. Roosevelt in the 1930s. Similarly, the Attlee reforms in Britain in the 1940s extended programmes which had been introduced by Asquith before the First World War. The virtue of incrementalism is that it proceeds through a process of 'trial and error'. As reforms are introduced their impact can be assessed and adjustments can be made through a further set of reforms. If progress is founded upon a belief in rationalism, reform is simply a way of bringing about progress through on-going experimentation and observation. Evolutionary change is therefore a means of expanding and refining human knowledge. To rely upon reform rather than revolution is to ensure that our desire to change the world does not outstrip our knowledge about how it works.

The case for revolution, by stark contrast, is that reform is little more than a sham. In effect, reform serves to perpetuate that which it appears to condemn. This has been the analysis of generations of revolutionary socialists, who have seen reformism not so much as a means of achieving social progress but as a prop of the capitalist system. In *Social Reform or Revolution* ([1899] 1937), for instance, Rosa Luxemburg (see p. 82) attacked the reformist drift of German socialism by portraying parliamentary democracy as a form of 'bourgeois democracy'. She castigated electoral politics as a form of 'parliamentary cretinism', which betrayed rather than served the proletariat. Perhaps the most outspoken critic of reformism, V.I. Lenin (see p. 83) argued in *The State and Revolution* ([1917] 1973) that parliamentary elections amounted to nothing more than deciding 'every few years which member of the ruling class is to repress and crush the people through parliament'.

In the view of revolutionaries such as Luxemburg and Lenin, reformism should be condemned on two counts. First, it misses the target: it addresses superficial problems but never fundamental ones. Revolutionary socialists argue that exploitation and oppression are rooted in the institution of private property and thus in the capitalist system. Reformists, on the other hand, have turned their attention to other issues, such as economic security, broader welfare rights and the struggle for political democracy.

Even when such reforms have improved living and working conditions, they have failed to bring about root-and-branch change because the capitalist class system is left intact. Secondly, reform may not only fail to address fundamental problems, it may be part of the problem itself. Revolutionaries have alleged that reform may actually strengthen capitalism, indeed that capitalism's susceptibility to reform has been the secret of survival. From this perspective, the development of political democracy and the introduction of a welfare state have served to reconcile the working masses to their exploitation, persuading them that their society is just and fair. In that sense, perhaps all reform has a conservative character: it serves to bring about change but within an established constitutional or socio-economic framework. Such a line of thought clearly has an appeal that extends well beyond socialism, and has led to the emergence of revolutionary forms of doctrines such as anarchism, nationalism and feminism.

The march of history halted?

The reformist approach to politics is based squarely upon an optimistic assumption: things get better. Instead of simply inheriting wisdom passed down to us from earlier generations, it should be possible to build upon the past and learn from its mistakes. Knowledge and wisdom will thus accumulate with each passing year, and human history will be marked by unceasing progress. Although such progress may be erratic – as when the business cycle moves from boom to slump and back to boom again – the overall direction in which human history is marching is not in doubt. Indeed, liberal and socialist reformers have identified very clear trends which mark the passage from lower levels of civilisation to higher ones. These include the achievement of general prosperity and widespread affluence, the social stability which a just distribution of wealth and resources brings about, and the expansion of individual liberty to promote greater autonomy and personal development. From the viewpoint of modern liberals and social democrats, these benefits have been the result of a series of reforms, through which political power has been dispersed and government has taken greater responsibility for the delivery of social welfare and the regulation of economic life.

Some thinkers have gone as far as to suggest that the onward march of history is an inevitable process, dictated by the irresistible logic of history itself. While Marxists have believed that history is driven forward by class conflict leading inevitably to revolution, gradualists have suggested that reform is also advanced by irresistible forces. Such a view is particularly associated with the Fabian Society and its proclaimed faith in 'the inevitability of gradualism'. In many ways, Fabianism represents the high point of rationalist optimism, building upon the scientific reformism of Bentham and the utilitarians. The Fabians believed that socialist ideas would gradually come to 'permeate' political and intellectual circles as the merits of a rational and more efficient organisation of society became apparent. They believed that, guided by the development of the social sciences, an enlightened political elite, consisting of politicians, civil servants and leading academics, would engineer a more just and prosperous society. What made this process inevitable, however, was the achievement of universal suffrage. It was their belief that the newly enfranchised working masses, the electoral majority in most societies, would recognise that socialism was in their interests and would therefore vote to bring socialist parties to power. In effect, the march of history towards the establishment of a more egalitarian and socially enlightened society was underwritten by the ballot box.

Faith in gradualist reform reached its peak in the 1960s, a period of rising living standards, more generous welfare provision and wider personal freedom. The cause of reform was taken up throughout the industrialised West and was supported by a broad consensus of political forces, including parliamentary socialism, modern liberalism and progressive conservatism. In the United States, for example, enthusiasm for reform was reflected in Lyndon Johnson's 'Great Society' programme, which promoted urban renewal, health care, literacy projects and so on. In Britain, comprehensive education was introduced and higher education rapidly expanded. In Canada, Australia, New Zealand and elsewhere in Western Europe, welfare expenditure reached new levels. Since then, however, there has been evidence that the forward march of history has at least faltered, if not been reversed.

The first indication of a shift in priorities and goals came in the 1970s with the emergence of the New Right. The New Right restated the case for free-market economics and individual responsibility, causes that had long been regarded as unfashionable. The advance of such ideas was evident in many Western countries but was most pronounced in Britain and the United States where in the 1980s the Thatcher and Reagan administrations tried to 'roll back the state' by cutting taxes, reducing economic intervention and holding back welfare spending. In turn, social democratic and modern liberal parties, the principal advocates of reform, have in many cases rethought and revised their policy commitments. The British Labour Party and the US Democratic Party have, for instance, both been at pains to shed their 'tax and spend' images by adopting market-driven and consumer-orientated policies. The generally leftward shift of government policy in the early postwar period, in the direction of economic management, welfarism and social justice, had therefore given way to a rightward drift towards individual responsibility and self-reliance. Emboldened by the collapse of communism in Eastern Europe, the American New Right theorist, Francis Fukuyama (1992), went as far as to suggest that the establishment of liberal capitalism marked 'the end of history'. Drawing upon the Hegelian belief that history marked progress towards a definable end-point, Fukuyama argued that that end-point had been reached in the late 1980s. In his view, history had ended because human beings throughout the world had come to recognise that only a market economic order could deliver general prosperity and only a liberal democratic political system could preserve individual liberty.

Such developments clearly raise questions about the notion of human history as unending progress. The final decades of the twentieth century may, of course, be an aberration, a departure from an underlying trend soon to be reasserted. Nevertheless, a series of economic, political and ecological obstacles appear to stand in the way of further progressive reform. For instance, the economic and social reforms of the early postwar period were underwritten by sustained economic growth, the so-called 'long boom', which generated resources that could be ploughed into public works and public services. The ending of the 'long boom' in the 1970s, and erratic economic performance since, has made such public investment much more difficult to finance, and emphasised the degree to which future reforms are dependent upon favourable economic circumstances. The emergence of a global capitalist system perhaps consolidates this shift by narrowing the scope for progressive action available to national governments. Moreover, there is a sense in which the growing affluence of the 1950s and 1960s has, ironically, worked against further reform by creating a politically active majority who are relatively prosperous and therefore inclined to be conservative. This lesson was underlined by J.K. Galbraith in *The Culture of Contentment* (1992). When most voters were working class and disadvantaged, as the Fabians had assumed, democracy marched hand in hand with reform, but, since the emergence of a 'contented majority', parties have had to show more interest in tax cuts than in welfare spending. Finally, the environmental crisis perhaps demonstrates that there may be ecological limits to growth. Industrial progress has resulted in over-population, widespread pollution and the depletion of finite energy resources. If economic growth is no longer sustainable, the dream of progress towards an ever more prosperous, equitable and enlightened society may have to be reassessed.

Revolution

Revolution represents the most dramatic and far-reaching form of change. In its most common sense, revolution refers to the overthrow and replacement of a system of government, quite distinct from reform or evolution where reform takes place within an enduring constitutional framework. However, the earliest notions of revolution, developed in the fourteenth century, denoted not so much fundamental change as the restoration of proper political order, usually thought of as 'natural' order. This created the idea of revolution as cyclical change, evident in the verb 'to revolve'. Thus, in the case of both the 'Glorious Revolution' (1688) in Britain, which established a constitutional monarchy, and the American Revolution, through which the American colonies gained independence, the revolutionaries themselves believed that they were re-establishing a lost moral order rather than creating an historically new one.

Nevertheless, the association between revolution and fundamental changes also has a long history. The English Revolution of the 1640s and 1650s, which culminated in the 'Glorious Revolution', involved the overthrow of the monarchy and the establishment of the Commonwealth under Oliver Cromwell. The American Revolution not only achieved independence but led to the creation of a constitutional republic, the United States of America. The modern concept of revolution, however, was most clearly influenced by the French Revolution (1789), which set out, openly and deliberately, to destroy the *ancien régime* or old order. The French Revolution became the archetypal model for the European revolutions which broke out in the nineteenth century, like those of 1830 and 1848, and decisively influenced the revolutionary theories of thinkers such as Marx (see p. 373). In the same way, the Russian Revolution (1917), the first 'socialist' revolution, dominated revolutionary theory and practice for much of the twentieth century, providing an example which inspired amongst others the Chinese Revolution (1949), the Cuban Revolution (1959), the Vietnamese Revolution (1972) and the Nicaraguan Revolution (1979).

Competing theories of revolution tend to lean heavily upon particular revolutions to bear out the characteristic features of their model. Hannah Arendt's (see p. 368) *On Revolution* (1963), for example, focused heavily upon the English and American Revolutions in developing the essentially liberal view that revolutions reflect a quest for freedom and so highlight the failings of the existing political system. Marx, on the other hand, looking to the example of the French Revolution, regarded revolution as a stage in the inevitable march of history, reflecting the contradictions which exist in all class society. In reality, however, no two revolutions are alike; each is a highly complex historical phenomenon, containing a mix of political, social and cultural features that is, perhaps, unique. The 'Islamic Revolution' (1979) in Iran, for instance, represented a backward-looking movement attempting to establish theocratic absolutism, quite at odds with the Western idea of revolution as progressive change. The East

---

Hannah Arendt (1906–75)

German political theorist and philosopher. Arendt was brought up in a middle-class Jewish family. She fled Germany in 1933 to escape from Nazism, and finally settled in the United States, where her major work was produced.

Arendt's wide-ranging, even idiosyncratic, writing was influenced by the existentialism of Heidegger (see p. 13) and Jaspers (1883–1969); she described it as 'thinking without barriers'. In *The Origins of Totalitarianism* (1951), which attempted to examine the nature of both Nazism and Stalinism, she developed a critique of modern mass society, pointing out the link between its tendency to alienation and atomisation, caused by the breakdown of traditional norms, and the rise of totalitarian movements. Her most important philosophical work, *The Human Condition* (1958), develops Aristotle (see p. 68) in arguing that political action is the central part of a proper human life. She portrayed the public sphere as the realm in which freedom and autonomy are expressed, and meaning is given to private endeavours. She analysed the American and French revolutions in *On Revolution* (1963), arguing that each had abandoned the 'lost treasure' of the revolutionary tradition, the former by leaving the mass of citizens outside the political arena, the latter by its concentration on the eradication of poverty. In *Eichmann in Jerusalem* (1963), Arendt used the fate of the Nazi war criminal Adolf Eichmann as a basis for discussing the 'banality of evil'.

European revolutions (1989–91), which saw the overthrow or collapse of orthodox communist regimes in the Soviet Union and elsewhere, created the spectacle of a socialist revolution being itself overthrown by a revolution which, to some extent, sought to resurrect pre-socialist principles. Amongst other things, this cast grave doubt on the conventional notion of historical progress.

Revolution may indeed be another example of an 'essentially contested' concept. It may be impossible to decide objectively whether a revolution has taken place since there is no settled definition of 'revolution'. Nevertheless, it is possible to identify a number of features which are characteristic of most, if not all, revolutions. First, revolutions are periods of dramatic and sudden change. Revolutions involve a major upheaval which takes place within a limited time span. When the term 'revolution' is used to describe profound change brought about gradually over a long period of time, as with the Industrial Revolution, it is being used metaphorically. In some cases, however, an initial and sudden upheaval may give way to a longer and more evolutionary process of change. In that sense, the Russian

Revolution started in 1917 but continued until the collapse of the Soviet Union in 1991, its goal of 'building communism' still not having been completed. Secondly, revolutions are usually violent. By challenging the existing regime, revolutionaries are forced to operate outside the existing constitutional framework, which means resorting to an armed struggle or even civil war. There are nevertheless many examples of revolutions brought about with little bloodshed. For example, only three people died in August 1991 as tanks attacked the barricades around the White House, the Russian parliament building, during the failed military *coup* which, by the December, had led to the collapse of the Soviet Union.

Thirdly, revolutions are popular uprisings, usually involving demonstrations, strikes, marches, riots or some other form of mass participation. David Beetham (1991) has suggested that the defining characteristic of revolution is extra-legal mass action, brought about, in effect, by the loss of legitimacy. The level of popular involvement is, however, often difficult to calculate. From one point of view, for example, the Russian Revolution of November 1917 had more the character of a *coup d'état* than a popular revolution, in that power was seized by a tightly knit band of Bolshevik revolutionaries. Nevertheless, this misses the point that the Bolshevik seizure of power was the final act in a process that had started the previous March with the collapse of the Tsarist regime amidst a wave of popular demonstrations. Finally, revolutions bring about fundamental change, not merely the replacement of one governing elite or ruling class by another. A revolution therefore consists of a change in the political *system*, in the very foundations of a society. However, the precise nature of this change is often unclear. For some, revolutions are essentially or exclusively political events; others suggest that any political change only reflects a deeper and more meaningful social transformation; still others insist that the vital element in revolution is some kind of cultural or even psychological renewal.

Political revolution

All revolutions have a political character. Even though revolution may bring about far-reaching social and cultural change, this is always linked to a fundamental transformation of political life. The political change which revolution brings about is, however, root-and-branch change. In this sense, revolutions can be distinguished from both rebellions and *coups d'état*. A rebellion resembles a revolution in that it is an uprising, is usually violent, and is carried out against the established authority of the state. However, by contrast with revolutions, rebellions typically have narrower and more specific goals. In particular, rebellions seek to replace one set of leaders by another one, often drawn from the same class or milieux. An uprising in the army which replaces one group of military leaders by another is therefore a rebellion rather than a revolution. A *coup d'état*, literally the overthrow of the state, involves the seizure of power not through some kind of popular rebellion but by a relatively small and usually conspiratorial band. A *coup d'état* is thus a covert act, carried out with stealth and in secrecy, while both rebellions and revolutions are overt or public acts. Moreover, while a political revolution aims to re-cast the political system itself, destroying and replacing the constitutional framework within which conventional politics operates, a *coup d'état* merely seeks to displace a governing elite or ruling class.

Revolutions are rare but profoundly important events. Their causes, course and consequences are, however, matters of considerable academic disagreement. One of the most influential theories of revolution has developed out of the systems approach to politics, examined in Chapter 3. This views the political system as a self-regulating mechanism which responds to 'inputs', the demands and supports of the larger society, by issuing authoritative decisions or 'outputs'. Such an approach implies that the political system will tend towards long-run stability as the 'outputs' of government are brought into line with the 'inputs' or pressures placed upon it. However, it can also be used to explain revolutions as a form of 'disequilibrium' in the political system, brought about by economic, social, cultural or international changes to which the political system is incapable of responding. For example, in *Revolutionary Change* (1966), Chalmers Johnson argued that revolutions occur in conditions of 'multiple dysfunction' when the political system breaks down under the pressure of competing demands for change. The autocratic Tsarist regime thus proved to be incapable of responding to the mixture of pressures created by early industrialisation, and the dislocation and demoralisation caused by the First World War. Similarly, it can be argued that in the late twentieth century orthodox communist regimes in the Soviet Union and Eastern Europe were unable to deal with the pressures generated by an urbanised, better educated and more politically sophisticated population. However, systems analysis tends to ignore the important subjective or psychological factors that help precipitate revolution.

An alternative theory of revolution has drawn upon the lessons of social psychology, and was perhaps first employed by Alexis de Tocqueville (see p. 223) in an attempt to explain the outbreak of the French Revolution. These ideas have developed into the model of a 'revolution of rising expectations'. In *The Old Regime and the French Revolution* ([1856] 1947), Tocqueville pointed out that revolution rarely results from absolute poverty and gross deprivation, conditions that are more commonly associated with despair, resignation and political inertia. Rather, revolutions tend to break out when a government relaxes its grip after a long period of oppressive rule. As Tocqueville put it, 'the most perilous moment for a bad government is when it seeks to mend its ways'. This had, for example, occurred in France when Louis XVI had summoned the Estates General in 1788. Instead of satisfying demands for political change, this act merely heightened popular expectations which by the following year had achieved a revolutionary fervour.

The classic modern statement of this theory is found in Ted Gurr's *Why Men Rebel* (1970). In Gurr's view, rebellion is the result of 'relative deprivation', brought about by the gap between what people expect to receive, their 'value expectations', and what they actually get, their 'value capability'. The greatest likelihood of revolution therefore occurs when a period of economic and social development, producing rising expectations, is abruptly reversed. This creates a revolutionary gap between expectations and capabilities. In *When Men Revolt and Why* (1971), James Davies explained this in terms of the J-Curve theory of revolutions. The shape of the letter 'J' represents a period of rising expectations which is suddenly brought to a halt. The notion of relative deprivation is significant because it draws attention to the fact that people's perception of their position is more important than their objective circumstances. What is crucial is how people evaluate their condition relative either to the recent past or to what other people have. This latter comparison was, for instance, significant in Eastern Europe in 1989, in that the perceived affluence of the capitalist West was undoubtedly one of the factors that prompted discontent and instability throughout the communist bloc.

A third theory of revolution focuses not on pressures operating within the political system but upon the strengths and weaknesses of the state itself. There is a sense in which a state can withstand any amount of internal pressure so long as it possesses the coercive power to maintain social control, as well as the political will to employ it. This can be seen in the case of regimes like Hitler's Germany, the Soviet Union under Stalin and Saddam Hussein's Iraq, each of which crushed opposition through the exercise of totalitarian terror. In such regimes, political change is more likely to result from a rebellion within the political or military elite than from popular revolution. In a comparative analysis of the French, Russian and Chinese revolutions, Theda Skocpol (1979) advanced a social-structural explanation of revolutions which highlights the international weakness and domestic ineffectiveness of regimes which succumb to breakdown. War and invasion, for instance, have often been the decisive factor in precipitating revolutionary situations, as occurred in China (1911 and 1949) and Russia (1905 and 1917). Confrontation, actual or potential, between a state and economically more developed military rivals can clearly make a regime structurally vulnerable to revolutionary overthrow.

In domestic politics, states become vulnerable to revolution when they are no longer able to count upon the loyalty of their armed forces or no longer possess the resolve and determination to exercise widespread repression. A crucial moment in many revolutions is when, faced with a popular rebellion, elements within the military either mutiny or gradually defect. It is instructive, for example, to compare the brutal but successful suppression of the Chinese student rebellion in Tiananmen Square in June 1989 with the swift and largely bloodless collapse of communist regimes in Eastern Europe in the autumn and winter of the same year. In the latter case, the communist governments chose not to instigate mass repression, either because they doubted the loyalty of their own troops or no longer possessed the political will to resort to violence. A decisive factor in this respect was the unwillingness of the Soviet Union under Gorbachev to step in and suppress these nascent revolutions, as it had earlier done in East Germany (1949), Hungary (1956) and Czechoslavakia (1968).

Social revolution

The profound changes which revolution brings about have sometimes been confined to the political sphere, taking the form of a new regime or constitutional system. The American Revolution, for example, achieved independence for the former British colonies and led to the creation of a constitutional republic, but left the system of ownership and the social structure untouched. In other cases, revolution has precipitated far-reaching social as well as political change. Marxists have in fact gone further and portrayed revolution as an essentially social phenomenon, arguing that political events such as the overthrow and replacement of a constitutional system are best interpreted as a reflection of a deeper social transformation. This theory of 'social revolution' deserves particular attention since it has been the most influential model of revolution during the twentieth century.

In Marx's view, revolution was the 'locomotive of history'. Revolution marks a point of transition from one stage of history to the next, and so reflects a major step in the relentless progress of humankind. The key to revolution in a Marxist sense lies not with changes at a political level – a change of government or establishment of an entirely new regime – but with fundamental social change, the establishment of a new economic system or 'mode of production'. Marx and later Marxists looked to the French Revolution as the archetypal model of revolution in the belief that it marked the transition from a feudal mode of production to a capitalist one; and, in turn, they looked ahead to a socialist revolution that would overthrow capitalism itself. Indeed, Marx at times was uncertain about the

Karl Marx (1818–83)

German philosopher, economist and political thinker, usually portrayed as the father of twentieth-century communism. After a brief career as a university teacher, Marx took up journalism and became increasingly involved with the socialist movement. He moved to Paris in 1843, later spent three years in Brussels and finally, in 1849, settled in London. He worked for the rest of his life as an active revolutionary and writer, supported by his friend and life-long collaborator Friedrich Engels (see p. 82).

Marx's work provides the basis for the Marxist political tradition (see p. 81). It was derived from a synthesis of Hegelian philosophy, British political economy and French socialism. His early writings, known as the *Economic and Philosophical Manuscripts* (1844), outlined a humanist conception of communism based upon the prospect of unalienated labour in conditions of free and cooperative production. The ideas of historical materialism started to take shape in the *German Ideology* (1846) and are given their most succinct expression in *A Contribution to the Critique of Political Economy* (1859). Marx's best known and most accessible work is the *Communist Manifesto* (1848), which summarises his critique of capitalism and highlights its transitional nature by drawing attention to systematic inequality and instability. Marx's classic work is the three-volume *Capital* (1867, 1885 and 1894), which painstakingly analyses the capitalist process of production and is based, some argue, upon economic determinism.

form which any political revolution might take, even speculating towards the end of his life about the possibility of a peaceful transition to socialism through parliamentary action.

In Marxist theory, revolution emerges out of contradictions which exist at a socio-economic level. Revolution reflects, at heart, the conflict between exploiters and exploited; all class societies are thus doomed. Marx believed that revolution marked the point at which the class struggle would develop into open conflict, leading one class to overthrow and displace another. The French Revolution was therefore interpreted as a 'bourgeois revolution', a process through which the rising bourgeoisie overthrew the aristocracy. In the same way, the Russian Revolution was a 'proletarian revolution', setting in motion a process that would culminate in the establishment of full communism. In Marx's view, the epoch of social revolution began when the class system, the 'relations of produc-tion', became a fetter upon the further development of productive techniques and innovation, the so-called 'forces of production'. This would heighten class antagonism, bringing the exploited class – in capitalism, the proletariat – to class consciousness. As the proletariat recognises the fact of its own exploitation, it will become a revolutionary force and will rise spontaneously in revolt. The proletarian revolution would give way to a transitionary period, which Marx referred to as 'socialism' by contrast with the final goal of 'communism'. This phase would be characterised by the 'dictatorship of the proletariat'; the working masses would organise a proletarian state to defend the revolution against the dispossessed bourgeoisie. As class antagonisms abated, however, a classless, communist society would come into existence, allowing the proletarian state to 'wither away'. In bringing an end to the class struggle, the achievement of full communism would also bring an end to history itself, or what Marx described as 'the prehistory of human society'.

There is little doubt that revolutions have not come about as Marx anticipated. Revolution has not occurred, as he expected it would, in the advanced capitalist countries of western and central Europe. Indeed, his belief that the class system would at some point become a 'fetter' constraining the further development of productive forces has proved to be profoundly mistaken; instead, capitalism's seemingly endless appetite for technological innovation has generated a steady, if at times erratic, improvement in living standards and rendered the proletariat politically passive. The Marxist theory of revolution has, nevertheless, had considerable impact in the twentieth century, though not where or how Marx intended. The Russian Revolution, carried out by Lenin and the Bolsheviks, advanced the Marxist theory of revolution in two important senses. In the first place, while classical Marxists portrayed revolution as an inevitable breakdown of class society that would occur when objective conditions were ripe, Lenin seized the point that revolutions have to be *made*. The Bolsheviks seized power in November 1917 even though the supposed 'bourgeois revolution' had only occurred in March and the proletariat was still small and politically unsophisticated. Secondly, Lenin recognised the need for political leadership, at least to guide the working classes towards revolutionary class consciousness. This leadership was provided by a 'revolutionary party', the Bolsheviks, later renamed the Communist Party.

Marxist-Leninist revolutions in the twentieth century have therefore had the character of *coups d'état*. They may have enjoyed widespread popular support but were carried out by dedicated groups of committed revolutionaries, who were prepared to exploit the vulnerability of the established order. A further twentieth-century development in the Marxist theory of revolution is that revolutions have typically occurred in economically backward countries and have looked for support not to the proletariat but rather to a revolutionary peasantry. This was clearly established by the Chinese Revolution, under the leadership of Mao Zedong (see p. 83), which amounted to a peasant revolution carried out in the countryside rather than in large urban areas. Instead of being a philosophy of social revolution, the Marxist-Leninist doctrine has tended to be employed as an ideology of modernisation and industrialisation, particularly attractive to developing countries. Furthermore, third world revolutions have typically fused the quest for social development and the struggle for national liberation in a way not anticipated by either Marx or Lenin. Anti-colonialism (see p. 102) was, for example, a potent force in the outbreak of revolutions in countries like China, Algeria and Vietnam, as well as in countries whose revolutions were in no way linked to Marxism-Leninism, such as Iran.

Cultural revolution

All revolutions seek to bring about cultural and not merely political or social change. They try to root out the values, doctrines and beliefs that supported the old order and establish in their place a set of new ones. The American Revolution, for instance, attempted to overthrow monarchical values and principles and replaced them with a set of liberal–republican ones, expressed in the Declaration of Independence and in the US Constitution. In other cases, however, the process of cultural change has been more formal and deliberate, constituting one of the acknowledged goals of the revolution itself.

This has been particularly evident in Marxist revolutions where 'bourgeois ideology' has been seen as one of the props of the capitalist order, its purpose being to delude the proletariat, rendering it politically passive. A socialist revolution can therefore only succeed if bourgeois values are rooted out and replaced by proletarian ones, a process which may require the suppression of bourgeois political parties and the promotion of an alternative socialist culture through the mass media, educational system and constant agitation and propaganda. In the Soviet Union, for example, this was understood as the goal of constructing 'Socialist Man', citizens who exemplified the socialist principles of community, cooperation and solidarity, and were prepared to put the common good before their own selfish interests. In the final analysis, the fate of the revolution itself depends upon such a cultural transformation because it alone ensures the legitimacy of the new regime. The surprising ease with which the communist regimes of Eastern Europe collapsed between 1989 and 1991 is perhaps evidence of their failure to inculcate a genuinely socialist culture. The swift re-emergence of nationalism, racial-ism and religion demonstrates that, at best, pre-revolutionary and non-socialist values were suppressed, and then only temporarily.

The Nazi seizure of power in 1933 also provides an example of a cultural revolution. From the Marxist perspective, the Nazi takeover would best be described as a counter-revolution rather than a revolution: its purpose, Marxists have argued, was to defend capitalism against the possibility of a proletarian revolution. Nevertheless, although with the obvious exception of the Jewish community the social structure in Germany was little affected by Nazi rule, profound political changes undoubtedly took place. Despite the superficial legality of Hitler's assumption of power, physical intimidation and open violence were widely used against trade unionists, socialists and communists. In little more than a year, Hitler presided over a political revolution through which the constitutional democracy of the Weimar Republic was destroyed and replaced by a one-party Nazi dictatorship. However, the revolution which the Nazis sought to carry through was more cultural than political in character. Their goal was nothing less than a revolution of the human psyche, the creation of a new type of human being, variously described as 'New Man' or 'Fascist Man'. The debilitating values which democracy, socialism and Christianity had spawned were to be replaced by a Nazi culture based upon duty, honour and self-sacrifice. The book-burning ceremony in May 1933, which witnessed the destruction of some 20 000 works by Jewish, socialist and liberal authors, therefore symbolised what the Nazi revolution stood for. The Nazi regime was one of the first to recognise and exploit the potential of modern mass communications for carrying through what, in effect, was an ideological revolution. While 'un-German' ideas were brutally suppressed, 'politically sound' National Socialist theories and values were propagated by Josef Gøbbels and the Nazi propaganda machine.

No discussion of the cultural implications of revolution could, however, be complete without a consideration of the 'Great Proletarian Cultural Revolution' in China. The so-called Cultural Revolution, inaugurated in 1965, marked a radicalisation of the revolution that had commenced in 1949. In common with earlier usages of the term 'revolution', the Cultural Revolution called for a return to the original and fundamental principles of the Chinese revolutionary movement and criticised liberal and 'Khrushchevian' tendencies within the Chinese Communist Party. Although the period between 1965 and 1969 can be interpreted as a power struggle through which Mao Zedong marginalised and eventually removed 'rightist' elements including President Liu Shaoqi and Deng Xiaoping, it also witnessed a profound ideological and cultural upheaval. Mao's principal instrument was the Red Guards, gangs of fanatical students, armed with 'The Little Red Book' containing the *Thoughts of Chairman Mao*. Their enemy was 'bourgeois revisionism' at home and abroad. Intellectuals, party leaders and state officials were attacked as 'capitalist roaders', who had betrayed the egalitarian principles of communism. Organised life in China effectively collapsed in the face of this upsurge in revolutionary fervour. One prominent feature of this process was described as 'putting politics in command', applying standards of ideological correctness to almost every aspect of human existence, economic, social, personal, professional and so on. Those whose behaviour did not conform to revolutionary principles were therefore guilty of 'political' crimes and were thus subjected to a process of 'political re-education', whose overt purpose was to root out old values and implant new ones.

Perhaps the most grotesque and ambitious programme of cultural engineering, however, occurred between 1975 and 1979 in Cambodia, renamed 'Democratic Kampuchea'. Under the leadership of Pol Pot and the Khmer Rouge, an attempt was made to eradicate literally every vestige of the old regime. History was said to have started again at the 'Year Zero'; money and all forms of commercial activity were abolished; towns and cities were emptied as populations were forceably resettled in the countryside; and anyone suspected of dissent or opposition was imprisoned or, more usually, summarily executed. Such policies resulted in the death of between one and three million people through famine, disease and open repression, in a country with a total population of just over seven million. Pol Pot and the Khmer Rouge were finally overthrown in 1979 by a full-scale Vietnamese invasion, which installed a 'puppet' government in their place.

Summary

1   Reaction refers to a desire to resist or perhaps reverse historical change. It can take one of three different forms: traditionalism or the desire for continuity with the past; reactionary radicalism, the wish to 'turn the clock back', reclaim a past Golden Age; or enlightened conservatism, the belief that a flexible attitude to change can help in the long run to preserve an institutional or social system.

2   Much of Western political thought is underpinned by the idea of progress, the belief in human advance and development, reflected in the spread of material affluence and the growth of personal freedom. Progressivism is based upon a faith in reason, the capacity of human beings to understand their world and solve the problems that confront them. Conservatives, however, have traditionally believed that this faith is misplaced.

3   Reform and revolution can be contrasted as means of bringing about change. Reform stands for a process of evolutionary or incremental change; it holds out the prospect of change through consent and respects the virtues of caution and pragmatism. Revolution, on the other hand, stands for an abrupt and typically violent break with the past; its virtue is that it has the capacity to bring about fundamental, root-and-branch change.

> **4** Political revolutions bring about the removal and replacement of a regime or system of government, not merely a change of government or within the ruling elite. Social revolution is usually understood to refer to the transformation of the system of ownership or mode of production, implying that political events reflect deeper social development. Cultural revolutions ultimately aim to recreate the human individual, rooting out values and beliefs that upheld the old order and fostering ones that will sustain the new order.

Further reading

Cohan, A. *Theories of Revolution.* London: Nelson, 1975.

Croce, B. *History as the Story of Liberty.* New York: Norton, 1941.

Fukuyama, F. *The End of History and the Last Man.* Glencoe, IL: Free Press and Harmondsworth: Penguin, 1992.

Goldstone, J.A. (ed.). *Revolutions: Theoretical, Comparative and Historical Studies.* New York: Harcourt Brace Jovanovich, 1993.

Kirk, R. *The Conservative Mind,* 7th edn. London: Faber, 1986.

Nisbet, R. *History of the Idea of Progress.* New York: Basic Books, 1980.

Oakeshott, M. *Rationalism in Politics and Other Essays,* rev. edn. London and New York: Methuen, 1991.

Tucker, R. *The Marxian Revolutionary Idea.* London: Allen & Unwin, 1970.

Bibliography

Adorno, T. W. (1950) *The Authoritarian Personality*. New York: Harper & Row.
Alter, P. (1989) *Nationalism*. London: Edward Arnold.
Althusser, L. (1969) *For Marx*. London: Allen Lane.
Anderson, B. (1991) *Imagined Communities*. London: Verso.
Anderson, P. (1974) *Lineages of the Absolutist State*. London: New Left Books.
Aquinas, T. (1963) *Summa Theologiae*, ed. T. Gilby. London: Blackfriars.
Arblaster, A. (1984) *The Rise and Decline of Western Liberalism*. Oxford: Basil Blackwell.
Arblaster, A. (1994) *Democracy*. Milton Keynes: Open University Press and Minneapolis: University of Minnesota Press.
Ardrey, R. (1967) *The Territorial Imperative: A Personal Inquiry into the Animal Origins of Property and Nations*. London: Collins.
Arendt, H. (1951) *The Origins of Totalitarianism*. New York: Harcourt Brace.
Arendt, H. (1958) *The Human Condition*. Chicago: University of Chicago Press.
Arendt, H. (1961) 'What is Authority?', in *Between Past and Future*. London: Faber.
Arendt, H. (1963) *Eichmann in Jerusalem*. New York: Viking.
Arendt, H. (1963) *On Revolution*. New York: Viking.
Aristotle (1958) *Politics*, trans. Sir Ernest Barker. Oxford: Oxford University Press.
Arrow, K. J. (1963) *Social Choice and Individual Values*. 2nd edn, New York: John Wiley.
Austin, J. (1954) *The Province of Jurisprudence Determined*, ed. H. L. A. Hart, London: Weidenfeld & Nicolson.
Avineri, S. (1968) *The Social and Political Thought of Karl Marx*. Cambridge: Cambridge University Press.
Avineri, S. and De Shalit, A. (eds) (1992) *Communitarianism and Individualism*. Oxford: Oxford University Press.
Bachrach, P. (1967) *The Theory of Democratic Elitism*. London: London University Press.
Bachrach, P. and Baratz, M. (1981) 'The Two Faces of Power', in F. G. Castles, D. J. Murray and D. C. Potter (eds), *Decisions, Organisations and Society*. Harmondsworth: Penguin.
Bakunin, M. (1973) *Selected Writings*, ed. A. Lehning. London: Cape.
Bakunin, M. (1973) *Bakunin on Anarchy*, ed. S. Dolgoff. London: George Allen & Unwin.
Barbalet, J. M. (1988) *Citizenship*. Milton Keynes: Open University Press and (1989) Minneapolis: University of Minnesota Press.
Barber, B. (1984) *Strong Democracy: Participatory Politics for a New Age*. Berkeley: University of California Press.
Barker, J. (1987) *Arguing for Equality*. London and New York: Verso.
Barnes, B. (1988) *The Nature of Power*. Cambridge: Polity Press.
Barry, B. (1989) *A Treatise on Social Justice, Vol. 1: Theories of Justice*. Hemel Hempstead: Harvester Wheatsheaf.
Barry, B. (1990) *Political Argument*. Hemel Hempstead: Harvester Wheatsheaf.
Barry, B. and Hardin, R. (eds) (1982) *Rational Man and Irrational Society?* Beverley Hills, CA: Sage.

Barry, N. *et al.* (1984) *Hayek's 'Serfdom' Revisited.* London: Institute of Economic Affairs.

Barry, N. (1989) *An Introduction to Modern Political Theory,* rev. edn. London: Macmillan.

Barry, N. (1998) *Welfare.* Milton Keynes: Open University Press and Minneapolis: University of Minnesota Press.

Bauman, Z. (1988) *Freedom.* Milton Keynes: Open University Press.

Beauvoir, S. de (1968) *The Second Sex,* trans. H. M. Parshley. New York: Bantam.

Bedau, H. A. (ed.) (1971) *Justice and Equality.* Englewood Cliffs, NJ: Prentice-Hall.

Beetham, D. (1991) *The Legitimation of Power.* London: Macmillan.

Bell, D. (1976) *The Cultural Contradictions of Capitalism.* New York: Basic Books.

Bellamy, R. (ed.) (1993) *Theories and Concepts of Politics: An Introduction.* Manchester and New York: Manchester University Press.

Benn, S. and Peters, R. (1959) *Social Principles and the Democratic State.* London: Allen & Unwin.

Benthal, J. (ed.) (1974) *Human Nature.* London: Allen Lane.

Bentham, J. (1948) *A Fragment on Government and an Introduction to the Principles of Morals and Legislation,* ed. W. Harrison. Oxford: Basil Blackwell.

Berger, P. and Luckmann, T. (1971) *The Social Construction of Reality.* London: Allen Lane.

Berlin, I. (1969) 'Two Concepts of Liberty', in *Four Essays on Liberty.* Oxford: Oxford University Press.

Bernstein, E. (1962) *Evolutionary Socialism.* New York: Schocken.

Berry, C. (1986) *Human Nature.* London: Macmillan and Atlantic Highlands, NJ: Humanities Press.

Béteille, A. (1983) *The Idea of Natural Inequality and Other Essays.* Oxford: Oxford University Press.

Birch, A. H. (1964) *Responsible and Representative Government: An Essay on the British Constitution.* London: Allen & Unwin.

Birch, A. H. (1972) *Representation.* London: Macmillan.

Birch, A. H. (1993) *The Concepts and Theories of Modern Democracy.* London and New York: Routledge.

Blowers, A. and Thompson, G. (1976) *Inequalities, Conflict and Change.* Milton Keynes: Open University Press.

Bobbio, N. (1987) *The Future of Democracy: A Defence of the Rules of the Game.* Minneapolis: Minnesota University Press.

Bodin, J. (1962) *The Six Books of the Commonweal,* trans. R. Knolles, ed. K. D. McRae. Cambridge, MA: Harvard University Press.

Bogdanor, V. and Butler, D. (1983) *Democracy and Elections: Electoral Systems and Their Consequences.* Cambridge: Cambridge University Press.

Bookchin, M. (1982) *The Ecology of Freedom: The Emergence and Dissolution of Hierarchy.* Palo Alto, California: Cheshire Books.

Bottomore, T. (1984) *The Frankfurt School.* London: Horwood.

Bottomore, T. (1985) *Theories of Modern Capitalism.* London: Allen & Unwin.

Bottomore, T. (1993) *Elites and Society,* 2nd edn. London: Routledge.

Bramwell, A. (1989) *Ecology in the 20th Century: A History.* New Haven and London: Yale University Press.

Brandt, R. B. (1992) *Morality, Utilitarianism and Rights.* Cambridge: Cambridge University Press.

Britton, S. (1977) *The Economic Consequences of Democracy.* London: Temple Smith.

Brown, M. B. (1995) *Models in Political Economy: A Guide to the Arguments*, 2nd edn. Harmondsworth: Penguin.
Brown, N. O. (1968) *Life Against Death: the Psychoanalytical Meaning of History*. London: Sphere.
Brownmiller, S. (1975) *Against Our Will: Men, Women and Rape*. New York: Simon and Schuster.
Bryson, V. (1992) *Feminist Political Theory: An Introudction*. London: Macmillan.
Buchanan, J. and Tulloch, G. (1962) *The Calculus of Consent*. Ann Arbor, MI: Michigan University Press.
Buck, P. W. (ed.) (1975) *How Conservatives Think*. Harmondsworth: Penguin.
Burgess, M. and Gagnon, A. G. (eds) (1993) *Comparative Federalism and Federation*. Hemel Hempstead: Harvester Wheatsheaf.
Burke, E. (1968) *Reflections on the Revolution in France*. Harmondsworth: Penguin.
Burke, E. (1975) *On Government, Politics and Society*, ed. B. W. Hill. London: Fontana.
Burnham, J. (1941) *The Managerial Revolution*. New York: Day.
Calvert, P. (1990) *Revolution and Counter Revolution*. Milton Keynes: Open University Press.
Campbell, T. (1981) *Seven Theories of Human Society*. Oxford: Oxford University Press.
Campbell, T. (1988) *Justice*. London: Macmillan and Atlantic Highlands, NJ: Humanities Press.
Canovan, M. (1996) *Nationhood and Political Theory*. Cheltenham: Edward Elgar.
Carmichael, S. (1968) 'Black Power', in *Dialectics of Liberation*. Harmondsworth: Penguin.
Chamberlain, H. S. (1913) *Foundations of the Nineteenth Century*. New York: John Lane.
Charvet, J. (1982) *Feminism*. London: Dent.
Clark, J. C. D. (ed.) (1990) *Ideas and Politics in Modern Britain*. London: Macmillan.
Clarke, P. (1978) *Liberals and Social Democrats*. Cambridge: Cambridge University Press.
Cohan, A. (1975) *Theories of Revolution*. London: Nelson.
Constant, B. (1988) *Political Writings*. Cambridge: Cambridge University Press.
Cooper, D. (1967) *Psychiatry and Anti-Psychiatry*. London: Tavistock.
Cooper, D. (ed.) (1968) *The Dialectic of Liberation*. Harmondsworth: Penguin.
Cranston, M. (1973) *What are Human Rights?* London: The Bodley Head.
Crick, B. (1983) *In Defence of Politics*. Harmondsworth and New York: Penguin.
Crick, B. (1987) *Socialism*. Milton Keynes: Open University Press.
Crick, B. (ed.) (1991) *National Identities: The Constitution of the United Kingdom*. Oxford: Basil Blackwell.
Croce, B. (1941) *History as the Story of Liberty*. New York: Norton.
Crosland, C. A. R. (1956) *The Future of Socialism*. London: Cape.
Crosland, C. A. R. (1974) *Socialism Now, and Other Essays*. London: Cape.
Dahl, R. A. (1956) *A Preface to Democratic Theory*. Chicago: University of Chicago Press.
Dahl, R. A. (1958) 'A Critique of the Ruling Elite Model', *American Political Science Review* (52).
Dahl, R. A. (1963) *Who Governs: Democracy and Power in an American City*. New Haven, CT: Yale University Press.

Dahl, R. (1982) *Dilemmas of Pluralist Democracy.* New Haven, CT.: Yale University Press.

Dahl, R. (1989) *Democracy and its Critics.* New Haven, CT: Yale University Press.

Darwin, C. (1986) *On the Origin of Species.* New York: New American Library.

Davies, J. (1971) *When Men Revolt and Why.* New York: Free Press.

Dawkins, R. (1989) *The Selfish Gene.* Oxford: Oxford University Press.

Devlin, P. (1968) *The Enforcement of Morals.* Oxford: Oxford University Press.

Dicey, A. V. (1939) *Introduction to the Study of the Law of the Constitution,* ed. E. C. S. Wade. London: Macmillan.

Dickinson, G. L. (1926) *The International Anarchy.* London: Allen & Unwin.

Djilas, M. (1957) *The New Class: An Analysis of the Communist System.* New York: Praeger.

Dobson, A. (1990) *Green Political Thought.* London: HarperCollins.

Downs, A. (1957) *An Economic Theory of Democracy.* New York: Harper & Row.

Doyal, L. and Gough, I. (1991) *A Theory of Human Need.* London: Macmillan.

Drewry, G. (1975) *Law, Justice and Politics.* Harlow: Longman.

Dunleavy, P. (1991) *Democracy, Bureaucracy and Public Choice: Economic Explanations in Political Science.* Hemel Hempstead: Harvester Wheatsheaf.

Dunleavy, P. and O'Leary, B. (1987) *Theories of the State: The Politics of Liberal Democracy.* London: Macmillan and New York: New Amsterdam.

Dunleavy, P. et al. (1993) *Developments in British Politics 4.* London: Macmillan and New York: St Martin's Press.

Dunn, J. (1979) *Western Political Theory in the Face of the Future.* Cambridge and New York: Cambridge University Press.

Dunn, J. (1989) *Modern Revolutions: An Introduction to the Analysis of a Political Phenomenon,* 2nd edn. Cambridge: Cambridge University Press.

Durkheim, E. (1951) *Suicide: a Study in Sociology,* trans. J. A. Spaulding and G. Simpson. Glencoe, IL: Free Press.

Durkheim, E. (1982) *The Rules of Sociological Method,* ed. S. Lukes, trans. W. D. Halls. London: Macmillan.

Durkheim, E. (1983) *The Division of Labour in Society* trans. W. D. Halls, intro. L. Coser. London: Macmillan.

Dworkin, R. (1990) *Taking Rights Seriously,* rev. edn. London: Duckworth.

Easton, D. (1979) *A Systems Analysis of Political Life,* 2nd edn. Chicago: University of Chicago Press.

Easton, D. (1981) *The Political System.* 3rd edn, Chicago: University of Chicago Press.

Eckersley, R. (1992) *Environmentalism and Political Theory: Towards an Ecocentric Approach.* London: UCL Press.

Esping-Andersen, G. (1990) *The Three Worlds of Welfare Capitalism.* Oxford: Polity.

Essien-Udom, E. V. (1972) *Black Nationalism: A Search for Identity in America.* Chicago: Chicago University Press.

Eysenck, H. J. (ed.) (1973) *The Measurement of Intelligence.* Lancaster: Medical and Technical Publishing.

Fanon, F. (1962) *The Wretched of the Earth.* Harmondsworth: Penguin.

Figes, E. (1987) *Patriarchal Attitudes.* New York: Persea.

Fine, B. (1984) *Democracy and the Rule of Law: Liberal Ideals and Marxist Critiques.* London: Pluto.

Finer, S. E. (1974) *Comparative Government.* Harmondsworth: Penguin.

Flathman, R. (1966) *The Public Interest.* New York: John Wiley.

Flathman, R. (1972) *Political Obligation.* New York: Atheneum.
Freedan, M. (1991) *Rights.* Milton Keynes: Open University Press and Minneapolis: University of Minnesota Press.
Freud, S. (1930) *Civilisation and its Discontents,* trans. J. Rivière. London: Hogarth.
Freud, S. (1962) *The Future of an Illusion,* trans. W. D. Robson-Scott. London: Hogarth.
Friedman, D. (1989) *The Machinery of Freedom,* 3rd edn. New York: Harper & Row.
Friedman, M. (1962) *Capitalism and Freedom.* Chicago: University of Chicago Press.
Friedman, M. and Friedman, R. (1980) *Free to Choose.* London: Penguin.
Fukuyama, F. (1992) *The End of History and the Last Man.* Glencoe, IL: Free Press and Harmondsworth: Penguin.
Galbraith, J. K. (1962) *The Affluent Society.* Harmondsworth: Penguin.
Galbraith, J. K. (1967) *The New Industrial State.* Harmondsworth: Penguin.
Galbraith, J. K. (1992) *The Culture of Contentment.* New York: Sinclair-Stevens.
Gallie, W. B. (1955/6) 'Essentially Contested Concepts', *Proceedings of the Aristotelian Society,* 56 pp. 167–97.
Gamble, A. *et al.* (1989) *Ideas, Interests and Consequences.* London: Institute of Economic Affairs.
Gandhi, M. K. (1961) *Non-violent Resistance.* New York: Schocken.
Garner, R. (1993) *Animals, Politics and Morality.* Manchester: Manchester University Press.
Gasset, O. Y. (1961) *The Revolt of the Masses.* London: Unwin.
Gellner, E. (1983) *Nations and Nationalism.* Oxford: Basil Blackwell and Ithaca, NY: Cornell University Press.
Gilder, G. (1982) *Wealth and Poverty.* London: Buchan and Enright.
Ginsberg, M. (1965) *On Justice in Society.* Harmondsworth: Penguin.
Gobineau, J. (1970) *Gobineau: Selected Political Writings,* ed. M. D. Biddiss. New York: Harper & Row.
Godwin, W. (1976) *An Enquiry Concerning Political Justice.* ed. I. Kramnick. Harmondsworth: Penguin.
Godwin, W. (1977) *Caleb Williams,* ed. D. McCracken. Oxford: Oxford University Press.
Goldstone, J.A. (ed.) (1993) *Revolutions: Theoretical, Comparative and Historical Studies.* New York: Harcourt Brace Jovanovich.
Goodin, R. (1988) *Reasons for Welfare: The Political Theory of the Welfare State* Princeton: Princeton University Press.
Goodin, R. (1995) *Utilitarianism as a Public Philosophy.* Cambridge: Cambridge University Press.
Goodin, R. E. and Pettit, P. (eds) (1995) *A Companion to Contemporary Political Philosophy.* Oxford: Basil Blackwell.
Goodwin, B. and Taylor, K. (1982) *The Politics of Utopia.* London: Hutchinson.
Gorz, A. (1982) *Farewell to the Working Class.* Boston, MA: South End Press.
Gould, B. (1985) *Socialism and Freedom.* London: Macmillan.
Graham, K. (ed.) (1982) *Contemporary Political Philosophy: Radical Studies* London: Cambridge University Press.
Gramsci, A. (1971) *Selections from the Prison Notebooks,* ed. Q. Hoare and G. Nowell-Smith. Chicago: International Publishing Corporation.
Gray, J. (1992) *The Moral Foundations of Market Institutions* London: Institute of Economic Affairs.

Gray, J. (1995) *Liberalism*, 2nd edn. Milton Keynes: Open University Press.

Gray, J. and Pelczynski, Z. (eds) (1984) *Conceptions of Liberty in Political Philosophy*. London: Athlone.

Gray, T. (1990) *Freedom*. London: Macmillan and Atlantic Highoands, NJ: Humanities Press.

Green, T. H. (1911) 'Lecture on Liberal Legislation and Freedom of Contract', in *Works*, vol. 3. London: Longmans Green.

Greer, G. (1985) *The Female Eunuch*. New York: Harper & Row.

Gurr, T. (1970) *Why Men Rebel*. Princeton: Princeton University Press.

Habermas, J. (1975) *Legitimation Crisis*. Boston: Beacon.

Hague, R., Harrop, M. and Breslin, S. (1998) *Comparative Government and Politics: an Introduction*. 4th edn, London: Macmillan; US edn: *Political Science: A Comparative Introduction*. New York: St Martin's Press.

Hailsham, Lord (1976) *Elective Dictatorship*. London: BBC Publications.

Harden, I. and Lewis, N. (1986) *The Noble Lie: The British Constitution and the Rule of Law*. London: Hutchinson.

Harris, N. (1990) *National Liberation*. Harmondsworth: Penguin.

Harrop, M. and Miller, W. (1987) *Elections and Voters: A Comparative Introduction*. London: Macmillan and New York: New Amsterdam.

Hart, H. L. A. (1961) *The Concept of Law*. Oxford: Oxford University Press.

Harvey, D. (1989) *The Condition of Postmodernity*. Oxford: Basil Blackwell.

Hattersley, R. (1985) *Choose Freedom*. Harmondsworth: Penguin.

Hayek, F. A. (1960) *The Constitution of Liberty*. Chicago: University of Chicago Press.

Hayek, F. A. (1976) *The Road to Serfdom*. Chicago: University of Chicago Press.

Hayek, F. A. (1982) *Law, Legislation and Liberty*. Chicago: University of Chicago Press.

Heater, D. (1990) *Citizenship: The Civil Ideal in World History, Politics and Education*. London and New York: Longman.

Hegel, G. W. F. (1942) *Philosophy of Right*, trans. T. M. Knox. Oxford: Oxford University Press.

Hegel, G. W. F. (1977) *Phenomenology of Spirit*, trans. A. V. Miller. Oxford: Clarendon.

Held, D. (1980) *Introduction to Critical Theory*. London: Hutchinson.

Held, D. (1990) *Political Theory and The Modern State*. Oxford: Polity Press and Stanford: Stanford University Press.

Held, D. (ed.) (1991) *Political Theory Today*. Oxford: Polity Press.

Held, D. (ed.) (1993) *Prospects for Democracy: North, South, East, West*. Cambridge: Polity Press.

Held, D. (1996) *Models of Democracy*. Oxford: Polity and Stanford: Stanford University Press.

Held, D. and Pollitt, C. (eds) (1996) *New Forms of Democracy*. London: Sage.

Held, D. and Thompson, J. B. (eds) (1989) *Social Theory of Modern Societies: Anthony Giddens and his Critics*. Cambridge and New York: Cambridge University Press.

Heywood, A. (1997) *Political Ideologies: An Introduction*, 2nd edn. London: Macmillan and New York: St Martin's Press.

Hindley, F. H. (1986) *Sovereignty*, 2nd edn. New York: Basic Books.

Hirsch, M. and Keller, E. F. (eds) (1990) *Conflicts in Feminism*. London: Routledge & Kegan Paul.

Hobbes, T. (1968) *Leviathan*, ed. C. B. Macpherson. Harmondsworth: Penguin.

Hobhouse, L. T. (1964) *Liberalism*. Oxford and New York: Oxford University Press.

Hodgson, G. (1984) *The Democratic Economy: A New Look at Planning, Market and Power*. Harmondsworth: Penguin.

Hohfield, W. (1923) *Fundamental Legal Conceptions*. New Haven, CT: Yale University Press.

Holden, B. (1974) *The Nature of Democracy*. London: Thomas Nelson.

Honderich, T. (1990a) *Punishment: The Supposed Justifications*. Harmondsworth: Penguin.

Honderich, T. (1990b) *Conservatism*. London: Hamish Hamilton.

Hunt, G. M. K. (ed.) (1990) *Philosophy and Politics*. Cambridge and New York: Cambridge University Press.

Hutcheon, L. (1989) *The Politics of Postmodernism*. New York: Routledge.

Huxley, A. (1977) *The Doors of Perception and Heaven and Hell*. London: Grafton.

Jay, M. (1973) *The Dialectical Imagination*. Boston: Little, Brown and London: Heinemann.

Jefferson, T. (1903) *The Writings of Thomas Jefferson*, ed. A. A. Lipscomb and A. E. Bergh, 20 vols. Washington, DC: Memorial edn.

Jensen, A. R. (1980) *Bias in Mental Testing*. New York: Free Press.

Johnson, C. (1966) *Revolutionary Change*. Boston, MA: Little, Brown.

Joseph, K. and Sumption, J. (1979) *Equality*. London: John Murray.

Jowel, J. and Oliver, D. (eds) (1989) *The Changing Constitution*. Oxford: Clarendon.

Judge, D. (1993) *The Parliamentary State*. London: Sage.

Kamenka, E. (ed.) (1982) *Community as a Social Ideal*. London: Edward Arnold.

Kamenka, E. and Erh-Soon Tay, A. (eds) (1980) *Law and Social Control*. London: Edward Arnold.

Kautsky, K. (1909) *The Road to Power*, trans. A. M. Simmonds. Chicago: Black.

Kellas, J. G. (1998) *The Politics of Nationalism and Ethnicity*, 2nd edn. London: Macmillan and New York: St Martin's Press.

Keynes, J. M. (1965) *The General Theory of Employment, Interest and Money*. San Diego: Harcourt Brace.

King, A. (1975) 'Overload: Problems of Governing in the 1970s', *Political Studies* 23, pp. 284–96.

King, D. S. (1987) *The New Right: Politics, Markets and Citizenship*. London: Macmillan.

King, P. (1982) *Federalism and Federation*. London: Croom Helm.

King, P. (1998) *Toleration*. London: Frank Cass.

Kingdom, J. (1992) *No Such Thing as Society? Individualism and Community*. Buckingham, UK and Bristol, USA: Open University Press.

Kirk, R. (ed.) (1982) *The Portable Conservative Reader*. Harmondsworth and London: Viking.

Kirk, R. (1986) *The Conservative Mind*, 7th edn. London: Faber.

Koedt, A. (1973) 'The Myth of the Vaginal Orgasm', in *Radical Feminism* (pp. 198–207) eds Anne Koedt, Ellen Levine and Anita Rapone. New York: Quadrangle/ New York Times.

Kolakowski, L. (1978) *Main Currents of Marxism*, 3 vols. Oxford: Oxford University Press.

Kristol, I. (1978) *Two Cheers for Capitalism*. New York: Basic Books.

Kropotkin, P. (1902) *Mutual Aid*. London: Heinemann.

Kropotkin, P. (1912) *Fields, Factories and Workshops*. London: Nelson.

Kropotkin, P. (1926) *The Conquest of Bread*. New York: Vanguard.

Kropotkin, P. (1977) 'Law and Authority' in *The Anarchist Reader*, ed. G. Woodcock, (pp. 111–7), London: Fontana.

Kropotkin, P. (1988) *Mutual Aid*. Cheektowaga, NY: Black Rose.

Kuhn, T. (1962) *The Structure of Scientific Revolutions*. Chicago: Chicago University Press.

Kumar, K. (1991) *Utopianism*. Milton Keynes: Open University Press and Minneapolis: University of Minneapolis Press.

Kuper, J. (ed.) (1987) *Key Thinkers, Past and Present*. London and New York: Routledge & Kegan Paul.

Kuper, J. (ed.) (1987) *Political Science and Political Theory*. London and New York: Routledge & Kegan Paul.

Kymlicka, W. (1989) *Liberalism, Community and Culture*. Oxford: Oxford University Press.

Kymlicka, W. (1990) *Contemporary Political Philosophy: An Introduction* Oxford and New York: Oxford University Press.

Laing, R. D. (1965) *The Divided Self: An Existential Study of Sanity and Madness* Harmondsworth: Penguin.

Laquer, W. and Rubin, B. (1987) *The Human Rights Reader*. New York: New American Library.

Laslett, P. (1956) 'Introduction', *Philosophy, Politics and Society*, series 1. Oxford: Basil Blackwell.

Lasswell, H. D. (1936) *Politics: Who Gets What, When, How?* New York: McGraw-Hill.

Laver, M. (1983) *Invitation to Politics*. Oxford and New York: Basil Blackwell.

Le Grand, J. (1982) *The Strategy of Equality*. London: Allen & Unwin.

Leary, T. (1970) *The Politics of Ecstasy*. London: Paladin.

Lee, S. (1986) *Law and Morals*. Oxford: Oxford University Press.

Leftwich, A. (ed.) (1984) *What is Politics? The Activity and its Study*. Oxford and New York: Basil Blackwell.

Lenin, V. I. (1968) *What is to be Done?* Harmondsworth and New York: Penguin.

Lenin, V. I. (1970) *Imperialism, the Highest Stage of Capitalism*. Moscow: Progress.

Lenin, V. I. (1973) *The State and Revolution*. Beijing: Foreign Languages Press.

Lerner, R. (1987) *The Thinking Revolutionary: Principle and Practice in the New Republic*. Ithaca, NY: Cornell University Press.

Lessnoff, M. (1986) *Social Contract*. London: Macmillan and Atlantic Highlands, NJ: Humanities Press.

Levitas, R. (1990) *The Concept of Utopia*. Hemel Hempstead: Philip Allan.

Lindblom, C. (1977) *Politics and Markets: The World's Political–Economic Systems* New York: Basic Books.

Lindley, R. (1986) *Autonomy*. London: Macmillan.

Lively, J. (1975) *Democracy*. Oxford: Basil Blackwell.

Lloyd, D. (1979) *The Idea of Law: A Repressive Evil or a Social Necessity* Harmondsworth: Penguin.

Locke, J. (1963) *A Letter Concerning Toleration*, ed. A. Montuori. The Hague: Martinus Nijhoff.

Locke, J. (1965) *Two Treatises on Civil Government* New York: New American Library.

Lorenz, K. (1966) *On Aggression*. London: Methuen.

Lukes, S. (1974) *Power: A Radical View*. London: Macmillan and Atlantic Highlands, NJ: Humanitites Press.

Lukes, S. (ed.) (1988) *Power*. Oxford: Basil Blackwell.

Luxemburg, R. (1937) *Social Reform or Revolution*. New York: Three Arrows.

Luxemburg, R. (1963) *The Accumulation of Capital*. London: Routledge & Kegan Paul.

Lyon, D. (1984) *Ethics and the Rule of Law*. Cambridge: Cambridge University Press.

Lyon, D. (1994) *Postmodernity*. Milton Keynes: Open University Press.

MacCallum, G. (1972) 'Negative and Positive Freedom', in*Philosophy, Politics and Society*, 4th Series. Oxford: Basil Blackwell.

Machiavelli, N. (1961) *The Prince*, trans. G. Bau. Harmondsworth: Penguin.

MacIntyre, A. (1981) *After Virtue*. Notre Dame, IL: University of Notre Dame Press.

Macpherson, C. B. (1973) *Democratic Theory: Essays in Retrieval*. Oxford: Clarendon.

Maistre, J. de (1971) *The Works of Joseph de Maistre*, selected and trans. J. Lively. New York: Schocken.

Malthus, T. (1971) *An Essay on the Principles of Population*, ed. A. Flew. Harmondsworth: Penguin.

Mandel, E. (1969) *An Introduction to Marxist Economic Theory*. New York: Pathfinder.

Mandeville, B. (1924) *The Fable of the Bees*, ed. F. B. Kaye. London: Oxford University Press.

Mannheim, K. (1960) *Ideology and Utopia*. London: Routledge & Kegan Paul.

Marcuse, H. (1941) *Reason and Revolution: Hegel and the Rise of Social Theory*. New York: Oxford University Press.

Marcuse, H. (1964) *One-Dimensional Man: Studies in the Ideology of Advanced Industrial Society*. Boston: Beacon.

Marcuse, H. (1969) *Eros and Civilisation: A Philosophical Enquiry into Freud*. London: Sphere.

Marcuse, H. (1972) *An Essay on Liberation*. Harmondsworth: Penguin.

Marshall, T. (1963) 'Citizenship and Social Class', in T. Marshall,*Sociology at the Crossroads*. London: Heinemann.

Marshall, T. H. (1963) *Class, Citizenship and Social Development*. London: Allen & Unwin.

Marwick, A. (1989) *The Nature of History*, 3rd edn. London: Macmillan.

Marx, K. (1967) 'On the Jewish Question', in Easton, L. D. and Guddat, K. H. (eds) *Writings of the Young Marx on Philosophy and Society*. New York: Anchor Books.

Marx K. (1968) 'The Theses on Feuerbach', in Marx K. and Engels, F. *Selected Works in One Volume*. London: Lawrence & Wishart.

Marx K. (1968) 'Critique of the Gotha Programme', in Marx K. and Engels, F. *Selected Works in One Volume*. London: Lawrence & Wishart.

Marx K. and Engels, F. (1970) *The German Ideology*, ed. C. J. Arthur. London: Lawrence & Wishart.

Marx K. and Engels, F. (1976) *The Communist Manifesto*. Harmondsworth: Penguin.

Matchlan, T. R. (ed.) (1982) *The Libertarian Reader*. Totowa, NJ: Rowan & Littlefield.

McLellan, D. (1980) *Marxism After Marx*. London: Macmillan.

McLennan, G., Held, D. and Hall, S. (eds) (1984) *The Idea of the Modern State*. Milton Keynes and Philadelphia: Open University Press.

Mead, L. (1982) 'Social Programmes and Social Obligations',*Public Interest*, No. 69.

Meinecke, F. (1970) *Cosmopolitanism and the Nation State*. Princeton: Princeton University Press.

Mendus, S. (1989) *Toleration and the Limits of Liberalism.* London: Macmillan and Atlantic Highlands, NJ: Humanities Press.

Michels, R. (1949) *Political Parties.* Glencoe, IL: Free Press.

Midgley, M. (1983) *Animals and Why They Matter.* New York: Penguin.

Milgram, S. (1974) *Obedience to Authority: An Experimental View.* New York: Harper & Row.

Miliband, R. (1978) *The State in Capitalist Society.* New York: Basic Books.

Miliband, R. (1982) *Capitalist Democracy in Britain.* Oxford: Oxford University Press.

Mill, J. S. (1972) *Utilitarianism, On Liberty and Considerations on Representation Government.* London: Dent.

Mill, J. S. (1976) *John Stuart Mill on Politics and Society,* ed. G. L. Williams. London: Fontana.

Miller, D. (1976) *Social Justice.* Oxford and New York: Oxford University Press.

Miller, D. (1989) *Market, State and Community: Theoretical Foundations of Market Socialism.* Oxford and New York: Oxford University Press.

Millett, K. (1990) *Sexual Politics.* Simon & Schuster.

Mills, C. Wright (1956) *The Power Elite.* New York: Oxford University Press.

More, T. (1965) *Utopia.* Harmondsworth: Penguin.

Morrow, J. (1998) *History of Political Thought: A Thematic Introduction.* London: Macmillan.

Mosca, G. (1939) *The Ruling Class,* trans. and ed. A. Livingstone. New York: McGraw-Hill.

Murray, C. (1984) *Losing Ground: American Social Policy, 1950–1980.* New York: Basic Books.

Muschamp, D. (1986) *Political Thinkers.* London: Macmillan.

Nash, P. (1968) *Models of Man: Explorations in the Western Educational Tradition* London and New York: John Wiley.

Newman, S. L. (1984) *Liberalism at Wits' End: The Libertarian Revolt against the Modern State.* Ithica: Cornell University Press.

Nisbet, R. (1966) *The Sociological Tradition.* New York: Basic Books.

Nisbet, R. (ed.) (1972) *Social Change.* Oxford: Basil Blackwell.

Nisbet, R. (1980) *History of the Idea of Progress.* New York: Basic Books.

Niskanen, W. (1971) *Bureaucracy and Representative Government.* Chicago, IL: Aldine.

Nove, A. (1983) *The Economics of Feasible Socialism.* London and New York: Allen & Unwin.

Nove, A. (1986) *Socialism, Economics and Development.* London: Allen & Unwin.

Nozick, R. (1974) *Anarchy, State and Utopia.* Oxford: Basil Blackwell.

O'Connor, J. (1973) *The Fiscal Crisis of the State.* New York: St Martin's Press.

O'Neill, J. (ed.) (1993) *Modes of Individualism and Collectivism.* London: Gregg Revivals.

Oakeshott, M. (1975) *On Human Conduct.* London and New York: Oxford University Press.

Oakeshott, M. (1991) *Rationalism in Politics and other Essays,* rev. edn. London and New York: Methuen.

Offe, C. (1984) *Contradictions of the Welfare State.* London: Hutchinson.

Oldfield, A. (1990) *Citizenship and Community, Civic Republicanism and the Modern World.* London and New York: Routledge & Kegan Paul.

Orwell, G. (1954) *Nineteen Eighty-Four.* Harmondsworth: Penguin.

Orwell, G. (1957) 'Politics and the English Language' in *Inside the Whale and Other Essays*. Harmondsworth: Penguin.

Owen, R. (1972) *A New View of Society, or Essays on the Formation of the Human Character*. London: Macmillan.

Packard, V. (1960) *The Hidden Persuaders*. Harmondsworth: Penguin.

Paine, T. (1987) *The Thomas Paine Reader*, ed. M. Foot. Harmondsworth: Penguin.

Pareto, V. (1935) *The Mind and Society*, trans. A. Livingstone and A. Bongiaro. 4 vols. New York: Harcourt Brace.

Parkin, F. (1982) *Max Weber*. London and New York: Tavistock Publications.

Parsons, T. (1951) *The Social System*. London: Routledge & Kegan Paul.

Pateman, C. (1979) *The Problem of Political Obligation*. New York: Wiley.

Pateman, C. and Gross, E. (eds) (1986) *Feminist Challenges: Social and Political Theory*. Boston: Northeastern University Press.

Paul, E. F., Muller, F. D. and Paul, J. (eds.) (1989) *Socialism*. Oxford: Basil Blackwell.

Pavlov, I. P. (1927) *Conditional Reflexes*. New York: Oxford University Press.

Perry, M. (1988) *Morality, Politics and Law*. Oxford and New York: Oxford Univerity Press.

Pettit, P. (1980) *Judging Justice: An Introduction to Contemporary Political Philosophy*. London and Boston, MA: Routledge & Kegan Paul.

Pettit, P. (1997) *Republicanism: A Theory of Freedom and Government*. Oxford: Oxford University Press.

Pickles, D. (1964) *Introduction to Politics*. London: Methuen.

Plant, R. (1991) *Modern Political Thought*. Oxford: Basil Blackwell.

Plato. (1970) *Laws*, trans. and annotated, T. J. Saunders. Harmondsworth: Penguin.

Plato (1955) *The Republic*, trans. H. D. Lee. Harmondsworth: Penguin.

Ponton, G. and Gill, P. (1982) *Introduction to Politics*. Oxford: Martin Robinson.

Poulantzas, N. (1973) *Political Power and Social Class*. London: New Left Books.

Proudhon, P. J. (1970) *What is Property?* New York: Dover.

Pulzer, P. G. J. (1967) *Political Representation and Elections in Britain*. London: Allen & Unwin.

Rae, D. (1981) *Equalities*. Cambridge, MA: Harvard University Press.

Randall, V. (1987) *Women and Politics: An International Perspective*, 2nd edn. London: Macmillan and rev. edn Chicago: University of Chicago Press.

Raphael, D. D. (1990) *Problems of Political Philosophy*, rev. edn. London: Macmillan.

Rawls, J. (1971) *A Theory of Justice*. Cambridge, MA: Harvard University Press.

Redhead, B. (1984) *Political Thought from Plato to N.A.T.O.* London: Ariel.

Reeve, A. (1986) *Property*. London: Macmillan and Atlantic Highlands, NJ: Humanities Press.

Regan, T. (1983) *The Case for Animal Rights*. London: Routledge & Kegan Paul.

Reich, W. (1973) *The Function of the Orgasm*, trans. V. R. Cartagno. New York: Simon & Schuster.

Reich, W. (1975) *The Mass Psychology of Fascism*, trans. V. R. Cartagno. Harmondsworth: Penguin.

Rosenblum, N. (ed.) (1990) *Liberalism and the Moral Life*. New York: Cambridge University Press.

Rousseau, J.-J. (1969) *The Social Contract and Discourses*. Glencoe, IL: Free Press.

Rousseau, J.-J. (1978) *Émile*, ed. A. Bloom. New York: Basic Books.

Rush, M. (1992) *Politics and Society; An Introduction to Political Sociology,* Hemel Hempstead: Harvester Wheatsheaf.

Ryan, A. (1984) *The Political Theory of Property.* Oxford: Basil Blackwell.

Sandel, M. (1982) *Liberalism and the Limits of Justice.* Cambridge: Cambridge University Press.

Sassoon, D. (1997) *One Hundred Years of Socialism.* London: Fontana.

Schattschneider, E. E. (1960) *The Semisovereign People.* New York: Holt, Rinehart & Winston.

Schotter, A. (1989) *Free Market Economics: A Critical Appraisal.* New York: St Martin's Press and London: Macmillan.

Schultze, C. (1977) *The Public Use of Private Interest.* Washington, DC: Brookings Institute.

Schumpeter, J. (1976) *Capitalism, Socialism and Democracy.* London: Allen & Unwin.

Scruton, R. (ed.) (1988) *Conservative Thoughts: Essays from the Salisbury Review.* London and Lexington: Claridge.

Scruton, R. (1984) *The Meaning of Conservatism,* 2nd edn. London: Macmillan.

Self, P. (1993) *Government by the Market.* London: Macmillan.

Sen, A. and Williams, B. (eds) (1982) *Utilitarianism and Beyond.* Cambridge: Cambridge University Press.

Shennan, J. H. (1986) *Liberty and Order in Early Modern Europe: The Subject and the State 1650–1800.* London: Longman.

Shils, E. (1981) *Tradition.* London: Faber.

Singer, P. (1975) *Animal Liberation: A New Ethic for our Treatment of Animals.* New York: Avon.

Skinner, B. F. (1971) *Beyond Freedom and Dignity.* New York: Knopf.

Skinner, Q. (1978) *The Foundations of Modern Political Thought,* 2 vols. Cambridge: Cambridge University Press.

Skocpol, T. (1979) *States and Social Revolutions: A Comparative Analysis of France, Russia and China.* Cambridge: Cambridge University Press.

Smiles, S. (1986) *Self-Help.* Harmondsworth: Penguin.

Smith, A. (1930) *The Wealth of Nations,* ed. E. Cannan. London: Methuen.

Smith, A. (1976) *The Theory of Moral Sentiments.* Oxford: Clarendon.

Smith, A. D. (1986) *The Ethnic Origins of Nations.* Oxford: Basil Blackwell.

Smith, A. D. (1991) *Theories of Nationalism.* London: Duckworth.

Spencer, H. (1940) *The Man versus the State.* London: Watts & Co.

Spencer, H. (1982) *The Principles of Ethics,* ed. T. Machan. Indianapolis: Liberty Classics.

Stevenson, L. (1974) *Seven Theories of Human Nature.* Oxford: Oxford University Press.

Talmon, J. L. (1952) *The Origins of Totalitarian Democracy.* London: Secker & Warburg.

Tam, H. (1998) *Communitarianism: A New Agenda for Politics and Citizenship.* London: Macmillan.

Tawney, R. H. (1969) *Equality.* London: Allen & Unwin.

Taylor, P. (1978) 'Elements of Supranationalism' in *International Organisations: a Conceptual Approach,* ed. P. Taylor and A.J.R. Groom. London: Pinter, pp. 216–35.

Thompson, D. (ed.) (1969) *Political Ideas.* Harmondsworth: Penguin.

Thoreau, H. D. (1971) *Walden.* Princeton, NJ: Princeton University Press.

Thouless, R.H. and Thouless, C.R. (1990) *Straight and Crooked Thinking*. London: Hodder & Stoughton.

Titmuss, R. (1970) *The Gift Relationship*. London: Allen & Unwin.

Tivey, L. (ed.) (1980) *The Nation-State*. Oxford: Martin Robertson.

Tocqueville, A. de (1947) *The Old Regime and the French Revolution*, trans. M.W. Patterson. Oxford: Basil Blackwell.

Tocqueville, A. de (1954) *Democracy in America*, ed. P. Bradley. New York: Random House.

Tolstoy, L. (1937) *Recollections and Essays*, trans. A. Maude. Oxford: Oxford University Press.

Townsend, P. (1974) 'Poverty as Relative Deprivation: Resources and Style of Living', in D. Wedderburn (ed.) *Poverty, Inequality and Class Structure*. Cambridge: Cambridge University Press.

Tucker, B.R. (1893) *Instead of a Book*. New York: B.R. Tucker.

Tucker, R. (1970) *The Marxian Revolutionary Idea*. London: Allen & Unwin.

Vincent, A. (1997) *Political Theory: Tradition and Diversity*. Cambridge: Cambridge University Press.

Waldron, J. (ed.) (1984) *Theories of Rights*. Oxford: Oxford University Press.

Walzer, M. (1983) *Spheres of Justice*. New York: Basic Books, and Oxford: Martin Robertson.

Watkins, K.W. (ed.) (1978) *In Defence of Freedom*. London: Cassell.

Watson, D. (1992) *Arendt*. London: Fontana.

Watson, L. (1973) *Supernature*. London: Hodder & Stoughton.

Watson, J.B. (1950) *Behaviourism*. New York: Norton.

Weber, M. (1930) *The Protestant Ethic and the Spirit of Capitalism*. London: Allen & Unwin.

Weber, M. (1948) 'Politics as a Vocation' in *From Max Weber: Essays in Sociology*, trans. and ed. H.H. Garth and C. Wright Mills. London: Routledge & Kegan Paul.

Weber, M. (1963) *The Sociology of Religion*. Boston: Beacon.

Weldon, T.D. (1953) *The Vocabulary of Politics*. Harmondsworth: Penguin.

Welsh, W.A. (1973) *Studying Politics: Basic Concepts in Political Science*. New York: Praeger.

Wheatcroft, A. (1983) *The World Atlas of Revolutions*. London: Hamish Hamilton.

Wicks, M. (1987) *A Future for All: Do We Need a Welfare State?* Harmondsworth: Penguin.

Williams, P. (ed.) (1994) *Colonial Discourse/Postcolonial Theory*. New York: Colombia University Press.

Wolff, R.P. (1970) *In Defence of Anarchism*. New York: Harper & Row.

Wolff, R.P., Marcuse, H. and Moore, B. (1969) *A Critique of Pure Tolerance*. London: Cape and Boston MA: Beacon.

Wollstonecraft, M. (1967) *A Vindication of the Rights of Women*, ed. C.W. Hagelman. New York: Norton.

Wright, P. (1987) *Spycatcher*. Victoria, Australia: Heinemann.

Young, M. (1961) *The Rise of the Meritocracy*. Harmondsworth: Penguin.

Zubaida Sami (1989) *Islam, the People and the State*. London: Routledge & Kegan Paul.

Index

Note: numbers in **bold** refer to boxed information on a thinker or a political tradition.

absolutism, 29, 93, **164–5**, 202, 367
Acton, Lord, 55
Adorno, T., 141, 280, **281**
affirmative action, 292
Afghanistan, 119
Algeria, 275, 276, 375
alienation, 82, 263, 264, 323, 368, 373
Althusser, L., 123
American Revolution, 206, 229, 367, 372, 375
anarchism, 26, 28, 41, 42, 65, 66–7, 162, 168, 170, 171, 182, 364
  and democracy, 229
  and duty, 205
  and freedom, 256, 263, 266
  and obligation, 205, 207
  and the state, 80, 84
  and utopianism, 168
anarcho-capitalism, 67, 80
Anderson, B., 104
animal rights, 195–9
anomie, 36
anticolonialism, 101, **102–4**, 275, 375
anti-Semitism, 105, 162
anti-Westernism, 102
Aquinas, T., 35, 66, 157, **158**
Ardrey, R., 19, 25
Arendt, H., 57, 140, 208, 367, **368**
Argentina, 39
Aristotle, 34, 35, 55, 57, 66, **68**, 142, 157, 220, 295, 321, 368
  and democracy, 221, 230
  and forms of government, 68–9
Arrow, K., 250–1
Asquith, H.H., 39, 308, 309, 363
atomism, 34, 36, 43
Attlee, C., 355, 363
Augustine, 26, 35, **91**, 158
Austin, J., 93, 158

Australia, 69, 70, 94, 114, 212, 217, 306, 365
Austria, 70, 111
authoritarianism, 42, 105, 131, 135, 140, 141, 278,
authority, 53, 55, 84, 91–2, 122, 130–41, 150, 163
  charismatic authority, 38, 134–5, 136, 141, 150
  de jure authority, 136
  de facto authority, 136
  legal-rational authority, 38, 134, 135–6, 143–4
  and the state, 75–6
  traditional authority, 38, 134, 136, 140

Bachrach, P., 126, 127, 229
Bahro, R., **196–7**
Bakunin, M., 41, 42, 80, 205, 323
Baratz, M., 126, 127
Barry, B., 242, 248
Beauvoir, S. de, 21, **61**
Beetham, D., 141, 144, 362
behaviouralism, 8, 10
behaviourism, 21
Belgium, 49, 70, 212
Bell, D., 166
Ben Bella, A., 275
Bentham, J., 25, 173, 191, 194, 244–5, 359, **361**, 365
Berger, P., 147
Berlin, I., **30**, 255, 259, 261
Bernstein, E., **313**, 362
Bill of Rights, 154, 155, 189–90, 227
Bismarck, O. von, 52, 308, 309
Black Muslims, 48, 276
black nationalism, 100, 103, 276, 103, 276

Black Power, 48, 100, 276
Blair, T., 37, 40, 64, 166, 225, 238, 314
Bodin, J., 90, 96, **165**
Bookchin, M., 84, **197**
Bosnia, 96
Bright, J., 105
Britain, 69, 70, 85, 100, 110, 111, 113, 116, 119, 132, 134, 166, 212, 217, 365
  and democracy, 225, 236–7, 238, 250
  and elections, 236–7, 238
  and equality, 291
  and legal justice, 177–8
  and nationalism, 99, 100
  and rights, 188, 189, 190
  and toleration, 273
  and welfare, 32–3, 85, 306, 307, 308–10, 315, 365
Brittan, S. 79
Brownmiller, S., 20
Buchanan, J., **247** 251
Buddhism, 26, 195, 197, 282
Burke, E., 23–4, **139** 166, 167, 234, 235, 303, 304, 323, 351, 354–5, 359
Burnham, J., 79
Bush, G., 32, 97, 166

Cambodia, 92, 377
Canada, 49, 70, 94, 99, 111, 114, 307, 364
capitalism, 24, 25, 28, 69, 78, 81, 86, 146, 147, 318, 328, 335–46
  and citizenship, 213, 214
  and democracy, 227, 228
  and freedom, 260, 262, 263, 278, 279, 321–2
  and imperialism, 275
  and welfare, 314–16
Carmichael, S., 276
Castro, F., 150
Chamberlain, H.S., 47
charisma, *see* authority, charismatic
Chesterton, G.K., 350
China, 110, 119, 150, 218, 295, 367, 371, 375, 376–7
Christian Democracy, 138, 355
Christianity, 25, 26, 68, 134, 163, 195, 272, 274
Cicero, 208

citizenship, 74, 187, 194, 200, 201, 207–18
  active citizenship, 215–18
  citizenship rights, 211–12
  social citizenship, 194, 213–15
  world citizenship, 120, 211
civil disobedience, 181–5
civil society, 40, 56, 58, 74, 84, 86
Clausewitz, C. von, 59
Clinton, B., 166, 238
Cobden, R., 105
collectivisation, 28, 86, 326, 328–9
collectivism, 41–3
Commonwealth of Nations, 113
communism, 26, 59, 81–2, 257, 264, 296, 326, 373, 374
  Eurocommunism, 229
  orthodox communism, 41–3, 149, 370
  see also Marxism;
    Marxism-Leninism;
    neo-Marxism
communitarianism, 11, 30, 32–7, **34–5**, 41, 208, 310, 312
community, 32–7, 41, 58, 66, 140, 231, 310
concepts, 3–8, 10, 12, 14
  essentially contested concept, 6–7
confederations, 112–13
Confucianism, 71
Confederation of Independent States (CIS), 112, 113
conservatism, 11, 33, 34, 36, 101, 123, 137, 138–40, 266
  and authority, 137,140
  and change, 349–56, 359, 362–3
  and community, 36
  and duty, 204–5
  and equality, 295
  and human nature, 23
  and nationalism, 101
  and oligation, 204–5
  and order, 166–7
  and politics, 56–7
  and property, 322, 323
  and rights, 204–5
  and society, 166–7
  and welfare, 307, 308, 309, 311, 314–15
  see also neo-liberalism;
    neo-conservatism; New Right
Constant, B., **209**, 254–5, 264

constitutionalism, 64, 67, 69, 76, 92,
    136, 143–4, 208, 209, 227
Cooper, D., 283
cosmopolitanism, 101–6, 117–18
Crick, B., 53, 54, 58, 226
critical theory, 81, 146, 279, **280–1**
Croatia, 96
Cromwell, O., 367
Crosland, C.A.R., 311, **313**, 362
Cuba, 119, 150, 367
Cultural Revolution, China, 294, 295,
    376–7
Czechoslovakia, 119, 185, 372

Dahl, R., 78, 124–5, **223–4**
Daly, M., 47
Darwin, C., 18–19, 25, 26, 169, 303, 359
Davies, J., 371
Dawkins, R., 19, 25, 104
deconstruction, 13–14
democracy, 68, 220–52, 345–6, 366
    Athenian/classical democracy, 222,
        224, 225
    capitalist democracy, 222, 228
    consociational democracy, 70
    developmental democracy, 222
    democratic elitism, 227–8
    direct democracy, 222, 224–6
    majoritarian democracy, 223, 232–3
    mandate democracy, 236–8
    participatory democracy, 223, 224–5
    pluralist democracy, 223–4, 227, 228
    protective democracy, 222
    radical democracy, 222, 230
    representative democracy, 222,
        225–6, 233–40
    totalitarian democracy, 233, 248–9
    see also liberal democracy; social
        democracy
Deng Xiaoping, 376
Denmark, 116
Derrida, J., **13–14**
Descartes, R., 22
Devlin, P., 161, 167, 179–80
Dicey, A.V., 90, 154–5
Dickinson, G.L., 118
Disraeli, B., 309
Djilas, M., 335
Downs, A., **247**, 249
Doyal, L., 297
Durkheim, E., 36

East Germany, 185, 372
Eastern European revolutions
    (1989–91), 6, 86, 149–50, 366,
    367–8, 372, 375
Easton, D., 8, 53, 72, 73
ecologism, 11, 108, 168, 195, **196–8**
    eco-anarchism, 196, 197
    ecofeminism, 196, 198
    ecosocialism, 196, 197
ecology, 109, 196
    deep ecology, 196
    shallow ecology, 196
    social ecology, 196, 197
elections, 228, 236–8, 249–51, 363
elitism, 44–5, 79, 227–8, 231
    classical elitism, 79, 231
    modern elitism, 79–80, 228
Engels, F., 22, **82**, 129, 153, 328, 373
English Revolution, 206, 229, 269, 354,
    367
equality, 285–95, 297–9, 310–11, 312–13
    equality of opportunity, 286, 290–2
    equality of outcome, 286, 293–5,
        297–9
    formal equality, 286, 287–90
    and freedom, 258–9, 292, 293, 298
    legal equality, 286, 288, 292
    social equality 293–5, 296–300
Esping-Anderson, G., 306
essentialism, 20
Estonia, 92
Etzioni, A., 34
European Union, 49, 63, 89, 95, 108,
    114, 115–16, 117
existentialism, 13, 17, 368
Eysenck, H.J., 291

Fabian Society, Britain, 362, 364–5, 366
Fanon, F., **103**, 276
fascism, 36–7, 111, 164, 233, 249, 264,
    352
federalism, 114–16, 208, 209, 232
feminism, 11, 19, 30, 34, **60–2**, 81, 211,
    239, 273, 276–9, 289–90
    liberal feminism, 47, 60, 61
    and politics, 59, 60
    radical feminism, 19, 47, 60, 62,
        277–9
    socialist feminism, 60
Figes, E., 277
Firestone, S., 62

Foucault, M., 13
foundationalism, 12, 14
Fourier, C., 38
France, 12, 99, 100, 111, 119, 329, 332, 352
France, A., 288
Frankfurt School, *see* critical theory
freedom, 29, 57, 140–1, 160–1, 208, 253–83, 340, 342
    freedom of choice, 260–1, 342
    negative freedom, 29, 208, 255, 259–61, 340
    positive freedom, 29, 208, 255, 261–5
    republican freedom, 208
French Revolution (1789), 6, 101, 138, 139, 145, 156, 206, 208, 229, 233, 354, 367, 370–1, 373
Freud, S., 24, 278
Friedman, M., 38, 256, 260, 314
Fukuyama, F., 70, 226, 366
functionalism, 44
fundamentalism, *see* religious fundamentalism

Gaia hypothesis, 197
Galbraith, J.K., 46, 78, 344, 366
Gallie, W.B., 6
Gandhi, Mahatma, 103, 182, 183
Garvey, M., 103, 276
Gasset, O.Y., 233
Gaulle, C. de, 115, 135
Gellner, E., 99
Gemeinschaft, 36
gender, 46–7, 60
general will, 203, 204, 243–4
Gentile, G., 58
Germany, 70, 100, 111, 112, 113, 114, 154, 196, 306, 308, 332, 352
Gesellschaft, 36
Gilder, G., 215, 311
globalisation, 366
Göbbels, J., 376
Gobineau, J., 47
Godwin, W., 66, 171, 341
Goodman, P., 170
Gorbachev, M., 112, 195, 333, 356, 372
Gough, I., 297
Gould, B., 262
government, 64–77 *passim*
Gramsci, A., 83, 146
Greece, 100

Green, T.H., 30, 31, 262, 309
Greer, G., 24, 278
Groz, A., 46
Guevara, C., 104
Gurr, T., 371

Habermas, J., 147, 148, 281
Haeckel, E., 196
Hailsham, Lord, 155
Hart, H.L.A., 159, 200
Hattersley, R., 262
Hayek, F.A., 31, 38, 43, 295, 296, 321, 333, 335, 341
Heater, D., 212
Hegel, G.W.F., 4, 30, 38, 56, 58, 280, 366, 373
hegemony, 146
Heidegger, M., 13, 368
Hinduism, 26, 182, 195, 282
historical materialism, 4–5
Hitler, A., 37, 39, 92, 106, 117, 133, 135, 144, 248, 271, 352, 371, 376
Hobbes, T., 23, 65, 75, 77, 90–1, 96, 124, 156, 158, 159, 162, 163, 165, 201, 202, 203, 246, 259
Hobhouse, L.T., 31, 309
Hobson, J.A., 309
Hohfeld, W., 188
Holmes, O.W., 159
Hong Kong, 71, 85, 330
Hoover, H., 32
Horkheimer, M., 280–1
human nature, 16, 17–49, 163, 168, 171, 242, 254
human rights, 157, 184, 190, 191–5, 211, 256, 257
Hume, D., 4, 300
Hungary, 333, 339, 372
Huxley, A., 282

ideal-types, 6
idealism, 4
ideology, 145–7
India, 48, 99, 114, 149, 182, 183, 236, 330
individualism, 27–32, 215, 341
    possessive individualism, 301–2
individuality, 27, 31, 258, 262
Indonesia, 98
intergovernmentalism, 110–13
internationalism, 106, 117–18, 119–20

Iran, 352, 367, 375
Iraq, 39, 97, 371
Islam, 25, 68, 71, 102, 103, 160, 173, 272–3, 352, 367
Israel, 42, 69, 75, 98, 143
Italy, 111, 112, 212

Japan, 71, 112, 116, 330, 331
Jaspers, K., 368
Jaurès, J., 31
Jefferson, T., 44, 157, 191, **192**
Jensen, A.R., 291
Johnson, C., 370
Johnson L.B., 39, 215, 310, 365
Joseph, K., 295
Judaism, 25
justice, 175–85
   legal justice, 176–85
   procedural justice, 176–8
   restorative justice, 174
   substantive justice, 178–81
   see also social justice

Kant, I., 30, **117**, 280
Kautsky, K., 229
Kennedy, J.F., 37, 217
Keynes, J.M., 38, 344–5
Keynesianism, 86
Khomeini, Ayatollah, 71, **103**, 273
Khrushchev, N., 333
King, A., 79, 147
King, M.L., 48, 182, 183
Koedt, A., 279
Kristol, I., 36, **139**, 166
Kropotkin, P., 26, 34, 66, **169**, 171, 205, 323
Kuhn, T., 10
Kuwait, 97

Laing, R.D., 283
laissez-faire, 28, 29, 192, 260, 309, 337, 340, 341, 343, 353, 361
   see also capitalism
Laslett, P., 10
Lasswell, H., 59
Latvia, 92
law, 152–62, 166–7, 176–85
   command theory of law, 158
   consensus/non-consensus law, 179–80

international law, 158–9, 211
legal realism, 159
   see also natural law; positive law; rule of law
Le Grand, J., 315
Leary, T., 282
Lebanon, 75
Leftwich, A., 58
legitimacy, 122, 130, 141–50
Lenin, V.I., 38, 39, 59, **82–3**, 129, 228, 235, 275, 328, 333, 354, 363, 374–5
liberal democracy, 69–71, 73, 77–84, 105, 143, 145, 147–9, 155, 221, 226–9, 268, 282
liberalism, 11, 12, **29–31**, 34, 60, 81, 117, 119, 124, 129, 166, 168, 170, 340
   and authority, 137
   and change, 357–8
   classical liberalism, 28, 29, 43, 215, 340, 360
   and freedom, 256–65
   modern liberalism, 29, 31, 86, 138, 167, 214, 262, 290, 295, 298–300,365
   and nationalism, 105–6
   and politics, 55, 57, 58
   and property, 320–1
   and social justice, 300–2
   and the state, 77–9
   and welfare, 309–10
liberation, 273–83
   liberation theology, 274
   see also national liberation; sexual liberation; women's liberation
libertarianism, 29, 42, 138, 139, 160, 215, 256, 257, 311, 338, **340–2**
liberty, *see* freedom
Lincoln, A., 224
Lindblom, C., 78
Lithuania, 92
Liu Shaoqi, 376
Locke, J., 4, 65, 77, 144, 154, 157, 191, 192, 201, 202–3, 206, 209, 230, 260, 268–9, **269**, 287, 300, 303, 320, 322, 324
Lorenz, K., 19, 25
Louis XIV, 371
Lovelock, J., 197
Luckmann, T., 147
Lukes, S., 123, 128, 129
Luther, M., 26

Luxemburg, R., **83**, 228, 363
Lyotard, J.-F., **13**

Macauley, T., 357
MacCallum, G.C., 255
Machiavelli, N., **54**, 55, **209**
MacIntyre, A., **35**
MacKinnon, C.A., **62**
Macpherson, C.B., 28, **223**, 301, 324
Macmillan, H., 323
Madison, J., **209, 232**
Maistre, J. de, 156, **165**, 352
Major, J., 32
Malaysia, 71
Malcolm X, 48, 100, 276
Malthus, T., 303, 304
Manderville, B., 336
Mannheim, K., 147
Mao Zedong, **83**, 135, 150, 374, 376
Marcuse, H., 24, 128, 278, 279, 280, **281**, 282
market, 335–46
  see also capitalism; *laissez-faire*
Marshall, T.H., 210–11, 213–14, 217
Marx, K., 4–5, 9, 11, 20, 22, 38, 39, 40, 46, 59, 80, 81, **82**, 129, 146, 153, 156, 167, 194, 229, 263–4, 288–9, 290, 293, 296–7, 322, 328, 335, 343, 348, 367, 372–5, **373**
  see also Marxism
Marxism, 11, 12, 30, 34, 37, 42, 60, **81–3**, 102, 167, 168, 169, 170, 196, 280, 312
  classical Marxism, 81
  and democracy, 222, 228–9, 231, 235
  and equality, 293–4, 296–7
  and freedom, 260, 263–4
  and history, 37–8, 362, 363, 364, 367, 372–5
  and human nature, 20
  and ideology, 81, 129, 145–6, 275, 375
  and law, 156
  and nationalism, 275–6
  and obligation, 207
  orthodox Marxism, 279, 280
  and politics, 59
  and property, 322–3, 324
  and revolution, 81
  and rights, 214–15
  and social class, 45–6
  and the state, 59, 80
  and welfare, 311, 315–16
  see also Marxism-Leninism; neo-Marxism
Marxism-Leninism, 145, 150, 271, 275, 374, 375
Maslow, A., 297
materialism, 4–5
Maurras, C., 105
McCarthy, J., 271
McCarthyism, 271
Mead, L., 217
Meinecke, F., 99
Merchant, C., 198
Mexico, 111
Michels, R., 79, 231
Milgram, S., 141
Miliband, R., 145
Mill, J., 258, **361**
Mill, J.S., 22–3, 30, 31, 58, 94, 160, 161, 171, 223, 229, 230, 232, 234, 235, 240, 257–8, **258**, 262, 269–70, 289, 351, 360
millenarianism, 274
Miller, D., 296
Millet, K., 47, **61**, 63, 277
Mills, C.W., 228
Milton, J., 268
Mitchell, J., **62**
Montesquieu, C. L., 209
More, T., 168, 324
Mosca, G., 79, 231
Murray, C., 215, 311, 314
Mussolini, B., 37, 135, 144, 248, 352

Napoleon, 135
nation, 97–109
  cultural nations, 98–101
  political nations, 98–101
nation-state, 106–9, 116, 275
national liberation, 274–6, 375
nationalism, 97–109, 116, 120, 274–6, 364
  see also national liberation
natural law, 90, 156–9
natural rights, 28, 29, 157, 191, 256, 287, 360, 361
Nazism, 36, 48, 86, 92, 111, 128, 140, 145, 218, 271, 368, 375–6
neo-conservatism, 138, 139, 149, 166, 217, 345
  see also New Right

neo-liberalism, 138, 148, 216
  see also New Right
neo-Marxism, 123, 145, 147, 215, 280
neo-pluralism, 78
Netherlands, 70, 134, 329, 332
New Left, 128, 170, 222, 279, 281, 282
New Right, 32, 42, 78–9, 85, 138–9,
    148–9, 161, 162, 218, 300, 338, 340,
    365
  and change, 352, 353
  and equality, 294–5
  and freedom, 260, 263
  amd property, 320–1
  and welfare, 32–3, 216, 217, 311–15
  see also free market; neo-
      conservatism; neo-liberalism
New Zealand, 70, 236, 250, 365
Nicaragua, 367
Nicholas II, 354
Nietzsche, F., **13**
nihilism, 13
Niskanen, W., 79
Nixon, R., 166
Northern Ireland, 48, 99, 184
Nove, A., 334
Nozick, R., 11, 256, 300–1, 303, 307,
    320, 320–1, **341**
nurture/nature debate, 17, 18–21

Oakeshott, M., 56–7, **139**, 349, 351, 359
obligation, 200–7
  political obligation, 200, 201–7
O'Connor, J., 315
Olson, M., **247**
organicism, 44
Orwell, G., 3
Osbourne, J., 158
Owen, R., 20, 34, **169**

Packard, V., 128
Paine, T., **209**, 236, 351
Pakistan, 71
Pareto, V., 79, 231, 338
Parsons, T., 72, 123
paternalism, 138, 309
patriarchy, 47, 60, 134, 196, 277, 278
Pavlov, I.V., 21
permissiveness, 265–7
Peron, J. 39
Pettit, P., 208

planning, 327–35
  central planning, 328–9, 330–5
  directive planning, 328–9
  indicative planning, 329–30, 332
Plato, 3, 9, 11, **22**, 68, 157, 168, 201, 231,
    290, 323
pluralism, 44, 78, 146, 162, 209, 232
Pol Pot, 92, 133, 377
polis, 53
political correctness, 2–3
political philosophy, 8, 9–10
political science, 8–9
political theory, 8–15 *passim*
politics, 52–63 *passim*
positive law, 156–9
positivism, 10
  logical positivism, 10
postcolonialism, **102–3**
postmodernism, **12–13**, 14, 60, 61
poststructuralism, 12, 13
Poulantzas, N., 80
Powell, E., 167
power, 122, 123–30, 131–3
property, 318–27
  common property, 323–5
  private property, 319–23
  state property, 325–7
Proudhon, P.-J., **169**, 205, 321, 322
public/private divide, 55–8, 59, 63, 168
public interest, 241–52
punishment, 171–5

racialism, 19, 47–8, 105, 273, 288
rational choice theory, 9, 25, 81, 245,
    246–7
  public choice theory, 9, 25, 245, 246,
      247
  social choice theory, 9
rationalism, 21–3, 164, 165, 341, 357–8,
    363
Rawls, J., 11, **30**, 176, 258, 298–300,
    299, 300–1, 312, 341
Reagan, R., 32, 33, 37, 38, 149, 166, 352,
    365
referendum, 225
Regan, T., 199
Reich, W., 24, 141, 278
religious fundamentalism, 48, 102, 103,
    272, 273
representation, 233–40

republicanism, 54, 207, **208–10**, 264
  civic republicanism, 35, 208
revolution, 356, 359–64, 366–78
Ricardo, D., 38, 359
rights, 187, 188–99, 340
  citizenship rights, 210–13
  and freedom, 256–7, 268–9
  legal rights, 188–91
  moral rights, 188–95
  negative rights, 194
  positive rights, 194, 214
  welfare/social rights, 194, 211,
    213–15, 216
  see also human rights; natural rights
Roosevelt, F.D., 37, 39, 135, 310, 345
Rorty, R., **14**
Rothbart, M., 67, 84, **342**
Rousseau, J.-J., 11, 57, 93, 142, 170,
    201, 203, 204, **222–3**, 229, 230, 231,
    236, **243**, 244, 245, 264, 289, 293,
    294, 321
rule of law, 136, 153–6, 288
Rushdie, S., 160
Russia, 100, 119, 372
Russian Revolution (1917), 367, 369,
    371, 373–4

Saddam Hussein, 39, 97, 133, 371
Saint-Simon, C.-H., 38
Sandel, M., **35**
Sartre, J.-P., 17
satyagraha, 182, 183
Schattschneider, E.E., 126
Schröder, G., 64
Schumacher, E.F., 197
Schumpeter, J., 79, **223**, 227, 247
Scotland, 99
Scruton, R., 36, 137
separation of powers, 208, 209, 232
Serbia, 96
sexual liberation, 24, 274, 276–9
Shils, E., 350
Singapore, 71, 330
Singer, P., 198, **361**
Skinner, B.F., 21
Skocpol, T., 371
Slovenia, 96
Smiles, S., 32, 216
Smith, A.D., 99
Smith, Adam, 38, 43, 139, 303, 336, 337,
    340–1, 359

Smith, J., 40
social contract theory, 65–6, 137, 144,
    156, 201–3, 243, 299–300
social Darwinism, 19, 32, 303
social democracy, 29, 66, 86, 138, 166,
    205, 214, 262, 259, 290, 295–6,
    298–9, **312–13**, 338, 362, 365
  and social justice, 298–9
  and welfare, 307, 310–11
social justice, 175–6, 295–304
socialism, 33, 102, 119, 168, 170, 196,
    205, 242, 245, 279, 338, 345–6
  and democracy, 228–9, 231
  and equality, 293–300
  and freedom, 256, 259, 262, 263
  market socialism, 333, 339
  parliamentary socialism, 362, 364–5
  and property, 324, 326
  scientific socialism, 23
  see also Marxism; neo-Marxism;
    social democracy
Socrates, 22, 201, 204
South Africa, 184, 267
South Korea, 71, 85, 330
sovereignty, 89, 90–7, 107, 114, 115, 117,
    164, 236
  external sovereignty, 95–7
  internal sovereignty, 92–5
  legal sovereignty, 90–2
  parliamentary sovereignty, 93, 94–5,
    155
  political sovereignty, 90–2
Soviet Union, 6, 86, 92, 96, 97, 98, 111,
    112, 144, 149–50, 190, 326, 327–35,
    356, 368, 370, 372, 375
Spain, 99, 134, 181
speciesism, 198
Spencer, H., 19, 32, 303
Spooner, L., 320
Sri Lanka, 48
Stalin, J., 86, 92, 135, 150, 328–9, 371
Stalinism, 140, 280, 329, 368
state, 74–87 *passim*
  see also nation-state
Stirner, M., **341**
Sudan, 71
supranationalism, 109–20
Sweden, 306
Switzerland, 49, 98, 113, 114, 224–5,
    227
Syria, 75

Taiwan, 71, 85, 330
Talmon, J.L., 93, 233
Taoism, 282
Tawney, R.H., 255–6, 294, **313**
Taylor, C., **35**
Taylor, F.W., 329
Taylor, H., 258
Taylorism, 329, 331
Thatcher, M., 32, 37, 38, 39, 43, 115,
    135, 148, 166, 217, 291, 352, 365
theocracy, 91, 102, 103, 367
Thoreau, H.D., 28, 182, 183
Tibet, 110
Timbergen, N., 19, 25
Titmuss, R.M., 310
Tito, J., 150, 335
Tocqueville, A. de, **223**, 232, 370–1
toleration, 265–73
Tolstoy, L., 66, 171
Tönnies, F., 36
totalitarianism, 36–7, 58, 86–7, 93, 128,
    140, 164, 212–13, 280, 341, 321,
    341, 368
Townsend, P., 307
Tracy, A. de, 145
tradition, 350–1, 354
    see also authority, traditional
Trotsky, L., **83**
Tucker, B., 28, 320
Tulloch, G., 251

United Kingdom, *see* Britain
United Nations, 63, 89, 108, 118–19,
    157, 213
United States of America, 9, 49, 70, 94,
    97, 103, 111, 112, 119, 143, 154,
    189, 190, 213, 330, 375
    and conservatism, 138, 139, 149
    and democracy, 224, 228, 232, 238
    and federalism, 94, 113, 114, 117
    and law and order, 166, 178, 180
    and legal rights, 288, 292
    and nationalism, 98
    and welfare, 32–3, 215, 217, 306–7,
        310, 311, 314, 363
    see also American Revolution
universalism, 19, 27, 119
utilitarianism, 25, 29, 194, 204, 244–5,
    246, 299, 359, **360–1**, 365
utopianism, 167, **168–70**, 281

Venezuela, 149
Vienna Circle, 10
Vietnam, 275, 367, 375, 377
Virginia School, 9
Volkesgemeinschaft, 36

Wales, 99
Walzer, M., **35**, 175
Watson, L., 199
Watson, J.B.,
Weber, M., 38, 46, 76, 130, 131, 133–6,
    142
welfare, 304–16, 343, 345, 364
    welfare individualism, 305, 311
Wilson, W., 112
Winstanley, G., 274
Wolff, R.P., 200
Wollstonecraft, M., **61**, **289**
women's liberation, 273–4, 277–9
    see also feminism

Young, M., 291
Yugoslavia, 75, 96, 98, 150, 333, 335,
    339

Zen Buddhism, 3, 282